Principles of Business for CSEC® Examinations

Davion Leslie and Kathleen Singh

CSEC® is a registered trademark of the **Caribbean Examinations Council** (CXC). *Principles of Business for CSEC® Examinations* is an independent publication and has not been authorised, sponsored or otherwise approved by CXC.

CAMBRIDGE
UNIVERSITY PRESS

CAMBRIDGE UNIVERSITY PRESS
Cambridge, New York, Melbourne, Madrid, Cape Town, Singapore,
São Paulo, Delhi, Dubai, Tokyo, Mexico City

Cambridge University Press
The Edinburgh Building, Cambridge CB2 8RU, UK

www.cambridge.org
Information on this title: www.cambridge.org/9780521189576

© Cambridge University Press 2011

This publication is in copyright. Subject to statutory exception
and to the provisions of relevant collective licensing agreements,
no reproduction of any part may take place without the written
permission of Cambridge University Press.

First published 2011

Printed in Dubai by Oriental Press

A catalogue record for this publication is available from the British Library

ISBN 978-0-521-18957-6 Paperback with CD-ROM for Windows and Mac

Cambridge University Press has no responsibility for the persistence or
accuracy of URLs for external or third-party internet websites referred to in
this publication, and does not guarantee that any content on such websites is,
or will remain, accurate or appropriate. Information regarding prices, travel
timetables and other factual information given in this work is correct at
the time of first printing but Cambridge University Press does not guarantee
the accuracy of such information thereafter.

Contents

Introduction

This book is designed for students preparing for the Caribbean Secondary Education Certificate (CSEC®) examination in Principles of Business (POB). Of the 11 chapters contained in the text, 10 are dedicated to covering the CSEC® syllabus while the other provides a comprehensive overview of the school-based assessment (SBA) component of the examination. All the chapters are written using accessible language and illustrated using clear examples drawn from across the Caribbean. Each chapter is divided into two or three sections that are designed to encourage reading and discussion whilst also being interesting and easy to read. Each section has its own summary and activities, which are of three different types:

- **Quick questions** – questions and items designed for the easy recall of basic facts introduced in the section.
- **Applying what you have learnt** – activities designed to make the student think more critically about the content.
- **Model examination questions** – questions similar to those that the student will encounter in the CSEC® examination.

Interspersed throughout the book are numerous opportunities for students to interact with the content in meaningful ways as they reflect on what they read. These opportunities are provided through *Think about it* and *Now it's your turn* boxes. These boxes supplement the numerous *end of section questions and activities*, which also encourage and facilitate reflection. In addition, the accompanying CD-ROM includes a bank of multiple-choice questions (with answers provided) that assess students' knowledge of the content they have met in the text. This CD-ROM is also an excellent source of practice for the CSEC® examination.

It is the authors' intention to present the concepts as simply as possible without losing their core meaning. Where possible or necessary, the order in which the topics appear in the Caribbean Examination Council (CXC®) syllabus has been followed in the book; however, deviations have been made in some instances to ensure that concepts develop coherently and that ideas connect logically.

Please note that prices quoted are in Jamaican dollars unless otherwise stated.

Davion Leslie and Kathleen Singh
January 2011

1 From then to now

The *love* of money is the root of all evil. – *King James Bible*

Lack of money is the root of all evil. – *George Bernard Shaw*

Venezuela, led by Hugo Chavez, is allowing Caribbean countries to pay for oil using bananas and sugar cane – a modern example of the barter system.

Barter – a thing of the past?

On 22 December 2007, the President of Venezuela, Hugo Chavez, indicated that his country was prepared to let Caribbean nations pay partly in kind, using food items and services, rather than in cash for the oil they get from his country. Currently, 17 countries, including Antigua and Barbuda, Granada, Guyana, Jamaica and Saint Lucia, are members of the PetroCaribe oil alliance with Venezuela. Under this arrangement, Venezuela supplies oil to the members of the alliance, which can be paid for over a period of up to 25 years, at an interest rate of 1 per cent. It is this debt that Chavez has suggested may be paid with items such as bananas and sugar cane. In effect, Caribbean countries are allowed to swap bananas and sugar cane for oil – essentially a cashless transaction. This is just one of many examples that bring into focus one of the issues to be discussed in this chapter – the barter system, a system for trading without money.

In this chapter you will:

- discuss early trading and systems of exchange
- explain why money is necessary
- discuss different types of economic systems
- classify and describe business organisations.

Life before trading

Can you imagine a society in which people did not **trade**? In such an economy, you and your family would have to produce everything that you wanted to consume. Your wants would be satisfied directly by your production and not through **exchange** or the purchasing of goods that others had produced. Earlier societies were structured in this way – there was no trading and wants were satisfied directly. This type of system came to be called **direct production** and was not without its faults. Could you imagine what would happen, for example, if a flood destroyed your rice crop? Without trading, you would not have any rice to eat. Alternatively, what if you had more rice than you could consume? What would you do with the surplus? Furthermore, it may not be possible to produce a little of everything that you wanted to consume. These problems quickly led members of early societies to trade with each other in what was called **indirect production**.

What was early trading like?

Trading requires that you produce more than you want to consume so that you can exchange the surplus. Early societies quickly realised that trading made it possible for them to produce one or two items in excess of their needs, rather than producing a small amount of everything. This came to be known as **specialisation**, since each member of these early societies was now concentrating on the production of one or two **goods** or **services**. Of course, having given up the production of some items, there needed to be a way to access these for consumption – in other words, the farmer with an entire field of corn and yams may want some chicken and rice. A system of exchange, therefore, became necessary so that this farmer could access what he did not produce himself. This system was the **barter** system.

☞ Now it's your turn

1 Explain two differences between direct and indirect production.

2 Why did trade become necessary in early societies?

The barter system

It is quite likely that your only experience with trading is using money to buy what you want. From an early age, you may have realised that money can be used as a **medium of exchange**; that is, you can use it in exchange for what you want. Early societies, however, operated without the concept of money and all trading activities were done without a medium of exchange. In these societies, goods and services were exchanged directly for other goods and services in a system that came to be known as the barter system – the oldest system of trading known to man. As our opening account with Chavez's offer to the Caribbean has shown, however, barter is still practised in modern economies.

A transaction in a barter system is possible when a **double coincidence of wants** occurs. Each party must have an item to exchange with the other party before trading can take place. This means that bartering between individuals was possible only in a simple economy. As the **economy** developed and more products, **producers** and **consumers** entered the market, the direct exchange of goods without the use of money was no longer possible. With the advent of the internet, and as communication across long distances becomes easier, bartering between individuals and businesses has become more popular.

↻ Making connections: history

Do you know about the triangular trade? If not, talk to a history teacher or read up on it. How was barter used in the triangular trade?

Problems with the barter system

As mentioned above, barter is not feasible in developed economies where there are many products, producers and consumers. Some of the reasons for this are discussed below.

A lack of double coincidence of wants

Each party in a barter transaction must have an interest in the other party's commodity. For example, if a butcher has meat and wants a hammer, he must find somebody who has a hammer and wants meat. When this fails to occur, we say that there is a lack of double coincidence of wants. This occurred very often in the barter system and, as a result, the time it took to make a transaction was very high.

 Think about it

Imagine that you want to trade in a market that uses a barter system. Although there are people in the market who have what you want, they do not want what you have. Discuss what you could do to create a double coincidence of wants.

Indivisibility of commodities

Some commodities, by their very nature, cannot be divided without a significant drop in their value. For example, a carpenter, having built a house, cannot give up a piece of the house in exchange for a meal. Nor can a farmer give up a piece of meat for a shirt, without killing the cow. It therefore became difficult to trade items that had a high value. How could the carpenter trade his house for a meal? How many meals should he get for his house? How many meals does he want anyway?

Absence of a store of value

It is difficult to store wealth in the form of commodity, since many commodities perish or lose value rapidly over time.

Absence of standard value

It is difficult to agree on a standard exchange rate between two items. For example, how many goats should the farmer give the carpenter for building him a house? The absence of a standard value means that one party often loses out in a barter transaction.

The money economy – an improvement in the barter system

The problems experienced by those trading in the barter system required the development of a better system of exchange that could more efficiently facilitate specialisation and trade. This resulted in the introduction of money as a medium of exchange – but money has not always been paper and coins as we have in the modern world.

Previously, various items, which had their own intrinsic values, were used as trading instruments. For example, shells, gold and silver have been used as money in various societies, as well as cattle and agricultural produce. When objects that have other uses are used as money, they are called **commodity money**. For example, cattle can be used as money but they can also be slaughtered for food; similarly, gold can be used as money or it can be fashioned into jewellery.

Many problems are associated with the use of commodity money – primarily because commodities are not always easily divided and the same items can often vary in quality and therefore value. Also, they are not always portable, which makes carrying out large transactions with them difficult. It makes sense, therefore, to use paper as money, since it has none of these problems. Of course, it should be obvious to you that the paper on which money is printed has little or no value, which means that it is not commodity money, but rather **fiat money**. In other words, the government is prepared to redeem a banknote for the value stated on its face. If the money loses the backing of the government then the paper it is printed on is only useful for starting a fire!

Think about it

The problem with commodity money is related to the innate value of the objects being used as money. Consider, for example, what would happen if you had $100 entirely in coins that you could melt down and create an item that is of a value greater than $100. Would you spend these coins or would you melt them down? Does this problem arise with fiat money? Why or why not?

The uses of money – what can money do?

- **Money is a medium of exchange**: money can be used in exchange for other goods and services. As shown in Figure 1.1, individuals exchange what they have for money and use the money to buy what they want.

- **Money is a store of value**: can you imagine what would happen to your savings if there was no money, and you were forced to save your wealth in commodities, such as perishable tomatoes? Money is used to store wealth for a later date, because its value remains reasonably fixed over time.

- **Money is a measure of value**: in the same way as length is measured in metres and weight in grams, money is the unit of value. Prices are quoted using money and this simplifies accounting.

- **Money is a standard for deferred payments**: because money does not lose value quickly, items can be bought on credit with an arrangement to pay for them with money at a later date.

Business in your world

Store of value and inflation

Money is supposed to be a store of value, but if there is inflation this may not be the case. Inflation is what happens when prices rise and you are unable to buy the same amount with your money as you once could – in other words, money loses value. For example, if the annual inflation rate in a country is 10 per cent then it would take 10 per cent more money this year than it did last year to buy the same commodity. It also means that for wealth that is stored as money in the form of savings, the value of these savings decreases as time passes. This is not such a big problem in the Caribbean, where the inflation rate is between 7 and 12 per cent in most years. But imagine if you lived in Zimbabwe where, in 2008, the inflation rate reached a whopping 400 000 per cent. Would you then want to store your wealth in the form of money? Things got so bad in Zimbabwe that it was reported that businesses allowed workers to go and spend their money immediately after they were paid as it would have no value by the following day.

1 What is the inflation rate in your country? Do you think it is too high?

2 How can you ensure that the money you save does not lose value over time?

3 Some people insist on saving money under their mattresses at home. This money is never banked and can be accessed when needed. Why might it be a bad idea to save in this manner?

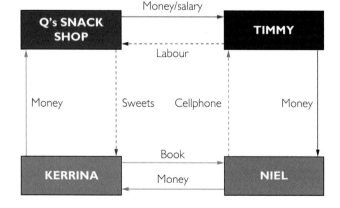

Figure 1.1 Money as a medium of exchange. Note that in all transactions, money is exchanged for a good or a service. No barter is necessary – people simply need to exchange what they have for money and use this money to buy what they want.

Modern forms of money

In addition to notes and coins, trading instruments may also take the following forms:

Credit cards

A bank may give a person a **credit card**, which they can use to buy things and then repay the money to the bank when they receive their monthly bill, or over a period of time. The credit card may be used to spend up to a set amount of money – when this amount has been reached, the card is said to have reached its limit. When this happens, no further spending can take place until the customer pays all or a part of the amount already spent. Usually, interest is charged only if the person does not pay the full amount owed at the end of the month.

Credit and debit cards allow users to avoid walking around with cash.

Debit cards

Debit cards are used by holders of bank accounts to buy goods or services without the need for cash. When used, a debit card (which looks like a credit card) transfers funds directly from your account to the merchant's account. Unlike credit cards, a debit card only allows you to spend your own money, which you have previously deposited in your account. These cards can be used to carry out regular transactions such as buying groceries and paying bills, and they are often used as a substitute for cash.

Electronic transfer

Electronic transfers, also called wire transfers, allow account holders to transfer funds from their bank to

☞ Now it's your turn

1 What is the fundamental difference between debit and credit cards?

2 Can you think of any advantages that credit or debit cards may have over money held in the form of cash? Talk to an adult who has a credit card, if this helps.

another bank and, therefore, avoid the use of cheques. Wire transfers are often used by businesses as opposed to individuals and often involve large amounts of money – often millions of dollars.

Tele-banking

Many banks allow customers to pay bills and arrange various payments over the telephone. With Tele-Scotia, for example, a service offered by the Bank of Nova Scotia (BNS), customers are able to pay utility bills, check account balances and transfer funds between accounts, all from the comfort of their home.

Bills of exchange

A bill of exchange is a written agreement in which one person (called the drawer) instructs another (called the drawee) to make a payment of a specified amount by a specified time to another party (called the payee). A cheque, therefore, is actually an example of a bill of exchange. Bills of exchange are popular when trading parties live in different countries or are separated by huge distances. A bill of exchange is a trading instrument since it can be endorsed by the payee to be paid over to a third party, who in turn may endorse it for a fourth party, and so on.

Summary – Section A

- In early societies, no trading took place and everyone provided for their own needs through their own production.

- With the advent of specialisation, barter was developed as a system of exchange in order to facilitate the swapping of excess goods.

- Money was developed in order to solve the problems associated with the barter system – including the lack of double coincidence of wants and indivisibility of commodities.

- Money has taken many forms over time including notes and coins and other commodities such as salt, cattle and shells.

End of section activities

Quick questions

Copy the following statements into your exercise book and complete them using the words from the word bank, which appears at the end of the activity.

1 When someone _____, they concentrate their productive efforts and resources on producing one or two goods in excess of their needs.

2 When someone produces all the items that they consume without specialising in any single item, they are involved in _____.

3 Indirect production required _____ since people had to be able to acquire what they did not produce.

4 The first system of trading known to man was the _____.

5 Money is a _____ because it addresses the problem of a lack of double coincidence of wants experienced in the barter system.

6 _____ cards allow a user to spend money that they have already deposited in a bank account.

7 Because money is a _____, comparing the value of two similar items can be done by simply examining their prices.

8 Businesses usually use _____ to move funds between their accounts and the accounts of their customers.

9 _____ may lower the value of money, if it is stored for a long time.

10 Money whose value is determined by the backing given to it by the government is called _____ money.

electronic transfers	barter system
specialises	direct production	fiat
inflation	debit	measure of value
medium of exchange	trading
commodity	credit

Applying what you have learnt

1 'Nobody wants money – rather individuals want the items that money can buy.'

   a Using your understanding of the idea of money as a 'medium of exchange', explain why people are willing to work for money.

   b Look up the meaning of the term 'derived demand'. Why is money considered to have a derived demand?

   c Have you ever done any work or a task for someone who agreed to pay you in kind? Perhaps you helped a sibling with some chores who in turn gave you a CD. Would this be considered barter? Why or why not?

2 It is often said that a barter system could not be maintained in a modern economy. Give three reasons why this is so.

3 People sometimes wish that money was like the leaves on the trees – freely available in abundance. Why would this not be feasible in a modern economy?

Model exam questions

Question 1

a Give two reasons why transactions were difficult to make in the barter system. (4 marks)

b Money solved many problems that the barter system had. Explain how money solved the following problems:

   i indivisibility (2 marks)

   ii lack of double coincidence of wants. (2 marks)

Question 2

a Trading became necessary only after indirect production started.

   i What is the difference between indirect and direct production? (2 marks)

   ii List two reasons why indirect production became necessary. (2 marks)

b Associated with indirect production is the phenomenon of specialisation. What does specialisation mean? (2 marks)

Question 3

a Describe the difference between indirect and direct production. (3 marks)

b Explain the role that specialisation played in developing the barter system. (3 marks)

c Discuss why the barter system could not work in the modern economy. (3 marks)

What is an economic system?

Your country owns many resources: its citizens have certain skills and abilities which they supply as labour; they also possess financial and material resources which they use to start and operate businesses. The country will also have natural resources, such as land, beaches or bauxite that can be exploited by businesses. Obviously, there must be a way for these resources to be organised. Who will own and control them? How will these resources be used to produce goods? Which goods will they be used to produce and how will these goods be allocated? The system that determines how these and other questions are answered is called an **economic system**. An economic system, then, is a mechanism which deals with the manner in which countries organise their means of production and which sees to the production, distribution and consumption of goods and services. Given that a country's resources are **scarce**, an economic system is designed to produce efficient solutions to some basic universal economic problems:

- What products should the country produce with its limited resources?

- How should they be produced so as to maximise output?

- For whom should they be produced?

☞ Now it's your turn

1 Why do countries need a system for allocating resources?

2 Why must an economic system produce 'efficient solutions' to the economic problems? What do you think is meant by 'efficient solutions'?

Types of economic system

It is customary to classify economic systems on the basis of the level of involvement of the state or private citizens in the economy. There are three popular economic systems: **free market**, **planned economies** and **mixed economies**. There are also a few countries that have **traditional economic systems**.

Traditional economies

Farming is an important activity in traditional economies.

In the previous section, we discussed the transition of economies from direct to indirect production through specialisation. Some economies, however, do not have this modern type of economic structure. Instead, people live in family groups or as tribes where they grow the food that they eat. These economies are described as being 'traditional', or 'subsistence' because long-standing systems of allocating resources are still in operation. Traditional economies are often found in countries that have not been modernised by technology or those that are steeped in customs, folklore and other traditional practices. Some parts of Asia, Africa and South America have traditional economies. In most traditional economies, farming and hunting are the main economic activities and these are carried out in roughly the same way as they were many generations before.

Free-market economy

Take a moment to think about this: how does a farmer decide that he will plant more tomatoes than carrots? If you were to start a business after the successful completion of your studies, how would you decide which industry to enter? Would you start a restaurant, a bookshop or an internet café? More than likely you would choose the business that you think would give you the best chance of making the most money. In the same way, the farmer may choose to dedicate more of his resources (land, labour and money) to tomatoes than to carrots because he feels that he can make more profit from selling tomatoes than he can from selling carrots.

This is the central principle of the free market system – there is little or no government interference or involvement in the market; rather individuals decide how to allocate resources on the basis of the market forces of demand and supply. In the free market, resources and the **factors of production** (such as land and factories) are owned primarily by private citizens who form and operate businesses in an effort to make as much profit as possible. These private businesses are not able to overcharge consumers, however, because if prices are too high then consumers will simply buy from another supplier. The presence of competition also ensures that firms are efficient in keeping costs down and producing high-quality goods, or they risk losing their customers to one of their many competitors.

Think about it

The main idea in a free market is that the government does not interfere in the operation of businesses. As a result, businesses respond to market forces and are free to set whatever price they think will make them maximum profit. To explore the idea of 'market forces', think about a butcher selling beef. What happens to the price of beef when:

1 it is Christmas?

2 a scientific study suggests that red meat such as beef is unhealthy?

3 eating chicken is linked to increased risk of heart attack?

4 people fear that they may catch mad cow disease from eating beef?

5 a drought affects the number of cattle?

6 people demand more burgers?

In each case, why does the price change? Is it because of actions of the government or changes in some factor in the market? How then would you define the term 'market forces'?

Advantages of the free-market economy

1 The presence of intense competition brings out creativity and innovativeness, and keeps prices down.

2 Individuals enjoy the freedom to put their labour, income and natural resources to the use that brings maximum profit.

3 Waste is minimised since production is driven by consumers' demand.

Disadvantages of the free-market economy

1 Wealth and income are often centralised in the hands of those who own the factors of production, resulting in huge income inequalities among citizens in the country.

2 Only those who have the means to purchase items are able to consume them. As a result, essential life-saving goods may be out of the reach of some consumers.

3 Firms often make profits at the expense of the environment, since they are reluctant to increase their costs by following safe, environmentally friendly practices.

4 Competition may be limited or completely absent in some industries as large firms either buy out smaller ones or prevent them from starting up.

5 Firms can use advertising to create artificial demand or they can restrict supply to create scarcity and ultimately cause prices to increase.

Now it's your turn

1 In a free market, prices are set and resources allocated by what some people call an 'invisible hand'. What is this 'invisible hand' and why do you think this term is used?

2 Why do large income inequalities exist in countries that have a free market?

Planned economic systems

Given the social problems that are usually associated with a free-market system, some countries have created planned economies in an effort to establish a more equal distribution of income. In this type of economy, a central authority (usually the government), rather than market forces, determines prices, output and production. The state owns all the resources and the government passes laws to determine what goods are to be produced and how much of each good is to be produced.

Advantages of planned economic systems

1 The wealth of a country is more equally distributed.

2 State provision of goods at low cost ensures that everyone is able to consume essential goods and not just those who can afford to buy them.

3 Sometimes it is better if there is no excessive competition in an industry. This wasteful competition is unlikely to exist in a planned economic system.

Disadvantages of planned economic systems

1 There is a large and often inefficient or even corrupt government agency responsible for decision making and policy implementation.

2 The government may not respond quickly enough to increased demand and this may result in shortages and rationing.

3 Competition is discouraged, leading to inefficiency and a lack of creativity.

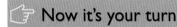 **Now it's your turn**

Some economic systems are described as 'hands-off' while others are described as 'hands-on'. Use the internet to determine meanings of these terms. Identify which economic system, either free market or planned, is hands-off and which is hands-on.

Mixed economic systems

Having reached this point, you may be thinking that neither the planned nor the free-market system adequately describes the economy in your country, and you are likely to be correct. Of course, as you have perhaps realised, no economy is entirely free or planned – both the government and private citizens are needed in the economy, even though most people agree that the government's role should be limited. An economy in which both private individuals and the government own productive resources is called a mixed economy. The part of the economy which consists of businesses controlled and operated by the government is called the **public sector**, while the part controlled and operated by private citizens is called the **private sector**.

Why do we need a public sector?

Traditionally, governments have shown that they are not very successful at owning and operating businesses. They are often inefficient, they lack accountability and are often wasteful and corrupt. These problems are all due to the fact that they lack a profit motive – the desire to make as much profit as possible. Even so, most Caribbean economies have an active public sector and the main reason for this is the fact that businesses in the private sector are driven by their need to make as much profit as possible while those in the public sector are driven by their desire to offer a service. The profit motive of private-sector businesses ensures that some of their products may be priced out of the reach of some citizens. If these are essential services such as the postal system or public hospitals, then the government may have to step in and take (or, in some cases, share) responsibility for offering these services.

Making connections: social studies

There are many political systems in the world – e.g. democracy, autocracy. What type of political system is usually associated with each type of economic system?

Summary – Section B

- An economic system is a mechanism which allocates scarce resources efficiently.

- There are four types of economic systems:

  - **Traditional**: economy with little or no specialisation; rather individuals live in family groups and tribes which are often self-sufficient.

  - **Free market**: economy with a marked absence of government intervention. Private citizens own majority of the factories and businesses.

  - **Planned economy**: an economy in which the government plays the dominant role in owning and operating businesses.

  - **Mixed economy**: perhaps the most common type of economic system, where both the government (the public sector) and private citizens (the private sector) own and operate businesses.

- While often inefficient, the public sector is necessary in order to ensure that essential goods and services are made available and affordable to those who otherwise would not be able to afford them.

End of section activities

Quick questions

Answer true or false to the statements below. If false, explain what is wrong with each statement.

1 It is the economic system of a country that determines how much money an individual earns as wages.

2 If resources were not scarce, a country would not need an economic system.

3 An economic system in which the government of the country is highly involved is called a planned economic system.

4 One expects that an economic system for a highly developed country will be mixed.

5 Members of a traditional economic system usually engage in indirect production and bartering.

6 In a free market, it is the consumers' decisions and actions that govern producers' decisions.

7 Even though consumers are sovereign, it is the profit motive that governs the free market.

8 In a planned economic system, producers are likely to switch production from pens to pencils if they think they can get more money from selling pens.

9 One expects that income will be fairly equally distributed among the population of a country with a planned economic system.

10 Advertising is an element of a free market that is likely to cause price movements that send the wrong signals.

11 Corruption of government officials is usually a concern that exists in most free markets.

12 Government's profit motive ensures that it often lacks accountability and becomes corrupt.

Applying what you have learnt

1 'Free and planned economies are extreme cases that do not exist in real life.'

   a Review the definitions of what free economies and planned economies are. Do you think any economy is totally free or totally planned?

b Are all economies mixed?

c Consider the following countries. Would you describe their economies as mixed, planned or free? (You may need to do a bit of research.) Justify your answers.

- Barbados
- China
- Cuba
- Trinidad
- Guyana

2 In a free market, governments make laws and regulations to protect consumers. Identify examples of different regulations that you think your government may need to make in the following industries:

a the restaurant and fast-food industry

b the advertising industry

c the banking industry

d the telecommunications industry (cellphone companies and so on)

e the entertainment industry (e.g. night clubs, street dances, stage shows.)

3 Is the public sector really needed? Compare the prices of the following services as offered by the public sector to the prices in the private sector:

a sending a parcel within your country by postal mail or by courier

b being treated at a public hospital or by a private doctor

c taking a public bus versus a private taxi

d attending public school or private school

Given what you have seen from your comparisons, why do people choose to use one sector over another?

Model exam questions
Question 1
a Give one advantage of:

  i a free market over a planned economic system

  ii a mixed economic system over a free market.

                                (4 marks)

b Outline two reasons why the public sector is needed in an economy.   (4 marks)

Question 2
a Give two reasons why a free market may be preferred over a planned economy.   (4 marks)

b Explain how resources are allocated in:

  i a free market

  ii a planned economy.   (4 marks)

c By giving a reason, state the type of economic system that each of the following groups would prefer:

  i producers

  ii consumers

  iii environmentalists

  iv the unemployed.   (6 marks)

Question 3
a Define what is meant by the term 'profit motive'.

                                (3 marks)

b How are prices kept within consumers' reach in a free market?   (2 marks)

c Explain why it is fair to say that most economies in the Caribbean are mixed.   (3 marks)

Public and private sectors – a quick reminder

In the last section we pointed out that most economies in the Caribbean are mixed – both the state and private citizens within the country own and operate businesses. We mentioned as well that the public sector, which consists of government-owned businesses, is often inefficient and unprofitable but is necessary because it offers essential services. The private sector, on the other hand, is made up of businesses operated by private interests who aim to maximise their profits. There are many types of profit-oriented businesses and many ways to categorise them. A useful system to use is to classify them on the basis of their status – whether or not they are incorporated.

Incorporation

Let us imagine that you leave high school armed with your ambition and your business education. You move on to university where you pursue a course in business administration, after which you feel compelled to start a business – perhaps you have always realised that the people in your community are in need of a restaurant, so you open one that sells the best local cuisine. Out of respect for the memory of your mother's cooking, you name it Homestyle Cooking, acquire the necessary permits and start operating your business. Here are a few things about your business to bear in mind:

1 Your business does not have any identity because it has not been **incorporated**. Incorporation is the process to go through if a business is to be able to trade under its own name, without its owner taking responsibility for the actions of the business. If a business is incorporated, it gets its own identity and, in the same way that parents cannot be punished for their children's crimes, the owner of an incorporated business cannot lose more than he has invested in the business if the business fails.

2 Because you are unincorporated, you have **unlimited liability**. This means that if the business goes **bankrupt**, your **creditors** may actually sell your personal assets to cover the debts of the business. In other words, what you stand to lose (your liabilities) if the business goes bankrupt is not limited to what you have invested in the business. Unlimited liability also means that if your restaurant is sued for, say, serving food that causes someone to get sick, you are the one responsible for paying any damages arising from this action.

Think about it

Beenie Man is a popular Jamaican reggae artiste whose real name is Moses Davies. However, is Beenie Man a separate identity from Moses Davies? Can Beenie Man do something for which Moses Davies is not responsible? Suppose Beenie Man is sued for saying something in one of his songs; can his personal assets be seized to settle the damages?

Sole proprietorship

To get a clear understanding of sole-proprietorship or sole-trader organisations, let us revisit the example of the restaurant that you will start after you leave university. If you remain the sole owner of Homestyle Cooking, then you are a **sole trader** and you are operating a **sole proprietorship**. A sole proprietorship is owned by a single individual who keeps all the profits and usually makes all the decisions. It is important to note that even if you employ other people who assist you with the decision-making aspects of the restaurant, then you still remain a sole trader because they are not entitled to a share of the profits.

A sole proprietorship is usually a small business whose future is tied up in the future of its owner. In addition, it is often unable to acquire capital to expand; it has a small market, minimum technology and can only produce on a small scale. It should be noted, however, that many sole-trader businesses eventually turn into large companies, so there is obvious scope for the growth of sole-trader organisations. Sole-trader businesses are popular in the Caribbean and, although many of them fail, they generate employment for many people and offer many services to customers that large companies do not provide.

☞ **Now it's your turn**

1 Sole-trader businesses are very popular in the Caribbean. Why do you think this is so?

2 Would you start a sole-proprietorship business after you leave school? Explain your decision.

3 Many young people want to be their own boss because of the freedom that this brings. Do you think this is a good attitude for someone who is thinking about starting a business? Explain your answer.

Many restaurants are run by sole traders.

Advantages of sole proprietorships

1 The owner makes all decisions, keeps all the profits and is usually highly involved in all aspects of the business. The result is that he or she develops a close relationship with the customers and knows first-hand how the business is doing.

2 Decisions are made more quickly because consultation time is minimal.

3 The business is easy to start – there are fewer legal requirements to start and operate a sole proprietorship.

4 Sole-trader businesses are usually small and, as a result, they need less capital to be established.

Disadvantages of sole proprietorships

1 The owner faces unlimited liabilities.

2 Although not a large amount, what little capital is needed to start the business may not be available from traditional sources such as banks. Banks are reluctant to lend to sole traders, because they:

- have unlimited liability
- lack **collateral** to secure loans
- are small and hence seen as a risk.

3 The business suffers from a lack of continuity – it usually dies with the owner.

4 The owner must endure long working periods, usually being the first to get to work and the last to leave. He is also unable to go away on holiday or for a long period of time.

5 The owner must depend on his or her own resources and ideas to keep the business running. Where these are limited, he or she may not be able to access any external help.

Partnerships

Continuing with the example of Homestyle Cooking discussed earlier, it is likely that given the problems you may face with the current arrangement as the sole owner of the business, you may contact one of your university friends and ask him to join you in running the business. Or, instead of starting the restaurant as a sole trader, you may have chosen to include him right from the start. Whether this friend joins the business at start-up or later on, the sole trader proprietorship has now become a **partnership**. A partnership is a business owned by between two and 20 people, who have a common aim of making a profit. You might also consider the following points about the partner whom you have brought into the business:

1 He is not an ordinary worker because he is entitled to a share of the profit. He would also usually bring some capital of his own to the business.

2 The amount of profit he gets would be determined by a document called a **partnership deed**, which also shows the salaries each partner will get (if any at all) and what interest partners will receive on the capital that they have invested in the business.

Your partnership obviously has certain advantages over the sole proprietorship that you had before. The main advantage is that, with two partners, the business can get a greater injection of capital than you alone would have been able to contribute. However, like sole traders, you and your partner are also exposed to unlimited liability and all the problems associated with this. In some partnerships, however, one partner may contribute capital but does not take part in the daily running of the business. This partner is called a **sleeping partner** and should not lose his personal assets if the business goes bankrupt – after all, he did not run it into the ground. Sleeping partners, therefore, normally have limited liability, but of course all partners cannot be sleeping partners.

Making connections: principles of accounts

A trading, profit and loss account is used to calculate the profit of a business over a stated period, usually a year. For a partnership, the trading, profit and loss account has a section called an appropriation account, while a sole proprietorship's accounts do not have this. Based on what you know about how profit is treated in each type of business, what do you think is the use of the appropriation account?

Advantages of partnerships

1 Having more owners means more ideas to be shared.

2 Each partner can contribute capital to the business; additionally, the business may have a better chance to raise extra capital from banks since partnerships are less risky than sole proprietorships.

3 The risk of continuity that exists for sole proprietorships is reduced for partnerships.

Disadvantages of partnerships

1 Owners still have unlimited liability.

2 Membership is limited to 20 people; this restricts the capital the business can raise and the growth potential of the business.

3 Partners may have disagreements that affect the continuity of the partnership.

Now it's your turn

Sheleka wants to start a business after leaving school. She is very good with computers and is thinking about opening up a graphic design business, where she will design and print programmes, advertisements, fliers and so on. She is trying to decide between starting up as a sole trader or as a partnership. What are some of the factors that she should consider when making this decision? Which one do you think she should choose? Give reasons for your answer.

Co-operatives

A co-operative is an incorporated business that has been established by a group of individuals to cater for their common needs. Members, who are also the owners, pool their resources for mutual gain and operate the co-operative on the following principles:

- voluntary and open membership
- democratic ownership – one member, one vote
- any **surplus** made by the co-operative is allocated to members.

Co-operatives are formed for many reasons. For example, a group of banana farmers may create a business to buy bananas from each farmer in order to sell them to large customers who want more bananas than an individual farmer can supply. This type of co-operative is called a **marketing co-operative**, and the main aim of these co-operatives is to find people who are willing to buy the products of the members. Other types of co-operatives are described below.

- **Retail co-operatives** are sometimes called consumer co-operatives and are organisations that buy in bulk and sell to their members at a reduced price.

- **Workers' co-operatives** are owned and operated by their workforce. For example, the craftspeople in a craft shop may actually own the shop. These workers, because they are also owners, are very motivated to work as hard as possible since they pay themselves by their own efforts.

- **Producer co-operatives** are created by people who are involved in production. The purpose of these co-operatives is to assist members to source machinery and equipment used in production; they may also share the workload.

15

Summary – Section C

- Businesses in the private sector are profit oriented and are usually incorporated or unincorporated.

- An unincorporated business does not have a separate identity from that of its owner and exposes its owner to unlimited liability.

- If the owner of a business has unlimited liability then he may lose more than he has invested in the business. If the business goes bankrupt he may lose his personal assets as well.

- Two examples of unincorporated businesses are sole proprietorships and partnerships. Sole proprietorships are owned by a single individual who keeps all the profit for himself or herself, while partnerships are owned by between two and 20 individuals who share the profit among themselves in a ratio determined by a partnership deed.

- Partnerships have many advantages over sole proprietorships: they allow partners to consult and share ideas and they allow for greater access to capital and bank loans.

- A co-operative is another example of a business in the private sector. Unlike sole traders and partners, however, the owners of co-operatives have limited liability because co-operatives are incorporated.

- Co-operatives are formed by people who are drawn together by their similar interests and needs. The aim of a co-operative is to address the needs of its members. Examples of co-operatives are marketing co-operatives and producer co-operatives.

End of section activities

Quick questions

Identify which of the following statements are true and which are false.

1 Some sole traders enjoy limited liability since they are incorporated.

2 Sole traders who employ others to run their business for them are now considered to be in partnerships.

3 Co-operatives are incorporated businesses whose owners have limited liability.

4 All unincorporated businesses have unlimited liability.

5 Sole traders do not need much capital to start their business. As a result, they have no problem acquiring loans from banks.

6 Some partnerships have limited liability.

7 Even if a partnership has unlimited liability, one or two partners may have limited liability.

8 Both partnerships and sole-trader organisations face the risk of lack of continuity.

9 The partnership deed shares profit equally among all partners.

10 Co-operatives are profit-oriented entities.

Applying what you have learnt

1 If you were starting a business, would you establish a sole-trader organisation or a partnership? What are some of the factors to consider as you think about choosing the form of business that you would start?

2 Why do you think a partnership deed is important? Make a list of some of the issues that you would want to put in your partnership deed if you and some of your classmates started a partnership.

3 Most lawyers and architects establish partnerships when they are starting their businesses. Why do you think this is so? Can you think of any other type of business activity for which a partnership arrangement is most suited?

Model exam questions

Question 1

Jan is about to start a business selling and repairing computers. She has been approached by Marie, one of her friends from college, who wants to join her as a partner in the business. However, Jan was thinking of starting the business by herself.

a Outline one benefit and one cost that Jan would encounter if she forms a partnership with Marie instead of operating as a sole trader. (4 marks)

b Explain why sole traders often need less capital than partnerships, but are often unable to raise it.

(3 marks)

c Outline two of the key issues that Jan and Marie should agree on before they start their partnership.

(4 marks)

Question 2

a What is meant by the term 'unlimited liability'?

(2 marks)

b Explain why some partners in a partnership may not be exposed to unlimited liability. (2 marks)

c Outline two problems that sole traders face as a result of the unincorporated status of their business.

(4 marks)

Question 3

a What is meant by a lack of continuity? (3 marks)

b Discuss two factors that may contribute to the continuity problem that small businesses face. (4 marks)

c Explain why sole proprietorships are more likely to experience a continuity problem than partnerships.

(3 marks)

2

> Corporation: an ingenious device for obtaining profit without individual responsibility. – *Ambrose Bierce*

Neal and Massy versus ANSA McAL: boardroom battle

In 2007, some of the largest players in the Caribbean corporate world became involved in one of the most exciting corporate battles of all times. Neal and Massy, a Trinidadian company, indicated that they were interested in buying a Barbadian company, Barbados Shipping and Trading Limited (BS&T). While we will discuss the ownership of companies in more depth later on in this chapter, some background information on company ownership may be helpful. When a company is formed, it raises money by selling shares to individuals or other companies who then become part owners of the company. Any shareholder who owns over 50 per cent of the company's shares becomes its owner since each share gives its owner one vote. Ownership of companies, therefore, often passes from one shareholder to another when boardroom deals are made in which shares are bought and sold.

To do this, Neal and Massy had to increase its share ownership of BS&T from its current level of 23 per cent to over 50 per cent and it offered existing shareholders of BS&T B$7.20 for each share. Shortly after it made this offer, another company, ANSA McAL, also

expressed its interest in becoming owners of BS&T and offered shareholders B$7.00 per share. Things really heated up when a third party, a consortium of individuals, got together and also started buying BS&T shares at B$7.50 per share. Thus the race to become the owner of BS&T began, with each party trying to get its hands on over 50 per cent of the company's shares. Neal and Massy was on target to seal the deal since the board of BS&T recommended it to the company's shareholders. In Barbados, many people opposed the sale of the locally owned BS&T to Neal and Massy, a foreign company, and some shareholders went as far as to file an injunction in court, blocking the sale. The impending takeover of the company was a major talking point in the Barbadian media with even the prime minister reportedly becoming involved in the issue. Eventually, ANSA McAL backed off and Neal and Massy called off the deal, citing the legal opposition that it was getting from the company's shareholders. This episode brings to the fore a few pressing issues about the subject of this chapter, limited liability companies.

In this chapter you will:

- identify the features of public and private limited companies
- discuss other forms of business organisations in the private sector – multinationals, franchises and conglomerates.

Why are some companies described as being 'limited'?

You will recall from Chapter 1 that some businesses are incorporated and expose their owners to limited liabilities; these businesses use the abbreviation 'Ltd' or 'Inc' to indicate their incorporated status. Generally speaking, most incorporated business (but not all – recall the case of co-operatives discussed in Chapter 1) are **companies** or **corporations**. A company is an incorporated entity with a legal identity separate from that of its owners, who have bought into the company. People who buy a part of a company are called **shareholders** and are said to have a share in the company.

Shareholders

A shareholder is an individual or another business that buys shares in a company and thus becomes a part owner of the company. As a part owner, a shareholder is entitled to receive a share of the company's profit at the end of the year. The amount of profit that a shareholder receives is related to the number of shares that he or she owns – with more shares resulting in a greater amount of profit.

The formation of limited liability companies

Once again, let us revisit the business we created in Chapter 1: the Homestyle Cooking restaurant. Homestyle Cooking started off as a sole proprietorship and then eventually became a partnership when one of your college friends joined you. The problem is that, whether the business is a sole proprietorship or a partnership, as the owner you are likely to face unlimited liability because the business is unincorporated. So now, after the business has grown a bit, you are thinking of incorporating the business and forming a limited liability company (LLC).

As a sole trader or a partnership you had very little administration to deal with; however, as an LLC this is not the case. There is a lengthy and sometimes expensive formation process to go through before you can become a limited liability company. The first step is the drafting and submission of two documents, the **articles of association** and the **memorandum of association**, to the appropriate authorities.

The articles of association

The articles of association lay down the rules that govern the internal running of the business. They contain information such as:

- the procedures for calling annual general meetings where shareholders meet to hear how the company is performing
- the rights and obligations of directors
- the election of directors.

The memorandum of association

The memorandum of association gives information about the company and governs its relationship with the outside world. It contains:

- the company's name, which must end with the word 'limited'
- the address of the company's registered office
- the objectives of the company and the scope of its activities so that prospective shareholders know what they are investing in
- the amount of money to be raised by selling shares.

These two documents are submitted to a body that has been set up by the government for this purpose. It has different names in different countries, but usually it is referred to as the Registrar of Companies or the Company Offices. This body inspects the documents and ensures that they are in order, and if this is the case then it will issue Homestyle Cooking with a certificate of incorporation. This certificate is proof that the company is duly registered and incorporated. Homestyle Cooking, a partnership, has now become Homestyle Cooking Ltd, a limited liability company.

👉 For you to research

Visit the website of the organisation responsible for registering companies in your country. If it does not have a website, visit one for another country (such as Trinidad and Tobago, Barbados or Jamaica). What are some of the services that this organisation offers?

Private limited companies

There is still one other important distinction to make regarding limited companies. When Homestyle Cooking Ltd is incorporated, it may be incorporated as a private limited company or as a public limited company. How are these two types of LLCs different? The distinction is simple, but first let us explore the basic characteristics of each type of company.

If you incorporate Homestyle Cooking as a **private limited company**, then it would have only a few owners, all of whom you would know. The company would have at least one shareholder but may have as many as 20. When drafting the articles of association, as a private limited company, you may also have imposed certain restrictions on shareholders regarding the transfer of shares. You would want to keep control over the business and, therefore, you may restrict shareholders from selling shares to outsiders without first getting permission from you and the other shareholders. You may even ask that they get this same permission before they can sell their shares to each other. As a private limited company, the shares of Homestyle Cooking cannot be sold or advertised for sale to members of the public. This means that new shareholders must be found through private consultation in what is called a private placement.

Advantages of private limited companies

1 Owners have limited liability since the company is incorporated.

2 More capital can be raised by private limited companies than by sole traders and partnerships.

3 Continuity is not a problem as it is for sole traders and, to a lesser extent, for partnerships.

4 Since existing shareholders must agree on the sale of shares to a new shareholder, the original owners of the company are unlikely to lose control of the company to outsiders.

Disadvantages of private limited companies

1 It is very expensive to satisfy the legal requirements to start the business.

2 The amount of capital the firm can raise is limited because it cannot sell shares to the public.

3 Since shares cannot be sold to the general public, it may be difficult to find a buyer if one of the shareholders wants to sell their shares.

Public limited companies

Public limited companies have their shares traded on the nation's stock exchange.

As a private limited company, Homestyle Cooking Ltd would be severely constrained when it came to raising capital: if it wants extra capital, it must be able to get existing shareholders to dig deeper into their pockets, or it has to find new shareholders of whom the existing shareholders approve. As the company grows larger, however, you will find that it needs more cash to buy machines, equipment and perhaps to open a new branch. To get this injection of capital, the company may decide to '**go public**', meaning it may have to change its status from that of a private limited company to a public limited company. As a **public limited company**, Homestyle Cooking Ltd would be able to sell shares to members of the public and therefore be able to raise more capital. Shares sold to members of the public by Homestyle Cooking Ltd may then be resold on the **stock exchange** – a market for selling second-hand shares. These shares are called 'second-hand', because they have already been sold by the company and are now being resold by existing shareholders.

☞ Now it's your turn

In Chapter I we looked at sole-trader organisations, while in this chapter we are examining companies. Look at the following features of both types of business ownership and say which form of ownership is best for this feature. Give a reason for each answer.

- ownership
- management
- funding
- risk
- continuity
- start-up.

 Now it's your turn

'On the stock market today, the volume traded was 24 500 units. A total of 12 shares advanced, 15 shares declined and 7 traded firm. The day's biggest loser was Quality Traders Ltd while the biggest winner was Tropical Foods Ltd.'

Have you ever watched your local news report and heard a report like this? If you haven't, then try watching your local business news, which gives a daily summary of the stock-market activities. Pay attention to words and phrases such as:

- shares advanced
- shares declined
- shares traded firm
- volume traded
- losers and winners.

Research the meaning of the phrases listed above.

As a public limited company, Homestyle Cooking Ltd does not have a limit on the number of shareholders it can have. The result is that there is likely to be a large number of shareholders, which is typically the case with public limited companies. For example, Neal and Massy, discussed at the start of this chapter, has issued almost 250 million shares and has hundreds (perhaps thousands) of companies, government agencies and individuals as shareholders. Public limited companies are normally very large and include some of the largest and most profitable companies in the world.

Share capital of public limited companies

As mentioned before, when Homestyle Cooking Ltd 'goes public', it sells shares to members of the public who become shareholders. These shareholders will fall into two broad categories.

Preference shareholders

The standard practice is that shareholders receive a share of the company's profit at the end of the year. Preference shareholders, on the other hand, would receive their dividend before other shareholders are paid – in this way, they can be more certain of their dividends at the end of the year. Additionally, their dividend does not depend on the level of profit the company makes – it will not increase when the company is more profitable and will not decrease if the company becomes less profitable. Instead, the dividend they receive will be a percentage of the amount they are investing in the company. Preference shareholders, therefore, do not

 Business in your world

Going public or going broke?

Take it from the experts – going public is expensive! Peter Clarke is one of the experts – he is the CEO of West Indies Stockbrokers Ltd – and he is on record as saying that private companies wishing to go public could spend as much as $TT2 million on the process. According to Clarke, this process could take up to two years and companies must be prepared to pay a small fortune for financial advice and a host of services related to legal, accounting, stockbroking, insuring, advertising and printing considerations. For small companies, the problem is even worse as the cost of

going public declines with the size of the company – as the size of the company increases, it actually costs *less* to go public. Clarke goes as far as to say that 'it wouldn't make sense for a company worth less than $TT40 million or $TT50 million to seriously consider listing'.

1 Going public is usually a source of pride and joy for the founders of companies. Why do you think this is?

2 If you had a business, would you want to go public? Why or why not?

face much risk and, as a result, they are not allowed to vote at the company's annual general meeting.

Making connections: mathematics

Homestyle Cooking Ltd has preference shares that cost $2.00 each. Each share pays a dividend of 12 per cent. If an investor has $30 000:

1   How many shares can he buy?

2   What will his dividend be at the end of the year if he invests all his money in preference shares?

Ordinary shareholders

These are the 'risk takers' of the company. They receive their dividends *after* preference shareholders have been paid and if the company does not make sufficient profit they may not receive any dividend at all! However, in years when the company makes high levels of profit, then ordinary shareholders will receive a higher dividend. The dividend that they will receive is therefore not stated up front and will vary from year to year depending on the profitability of the company.

Now it's your turn

If you were investing money in a company as a shareholder, which type of shares would you buy? If you were to buy both, which (if any) would you buy in greater quantity? Give reasons for your answers.

Think about it

Is it profitable to invest in shares? Some people 'play' the stock market – they buy and sell shares with the hope of making a profit. Share prices, however, do not change very quickly or by very much – for example, most share prices appreciate by only a few cents in a week. So, if a shareholder

buys a share for $1.20 it may eventually be sold for $1.35 – a profit of $0.15. Is this worth it? Well, if you had bought only one share, perhaps not. But what if you had bought two million or three million shares; is it worth it then? At two million shares, the profit is $300 000 and this could be made within a few hours or days. So, what do you think? Is it worth it?

Advantages of public limited companies

1   Public limited companies share some advantages with private limited companies: they are also incorporated and hence their owners are faced with limited liabilities and the business does not have any problem with continuity.

2   A huge amount of capital can be raised by selling shares to the public – more than a private limited company can raise.

3   Public limited companies are able to take advantage of their large size – for example, they may be able to buy in greater bulk and receive larger **discounts**.

4   They usually have a large share of the market and are able to dominate the market.

5   They do not have a problem raising additional funding as financial institutions are more willing to lend to public limited companies than to sole traders, partnerships or even to private limited companies.

Disadvantages of public limited companies

1   The costs to set up the business may be very high – many private companies cannot go public because the cost of going public is too high.

2   It is possible for an outsider – even a competitor – to buy enough shares to take over the company. If a person or entity controls more than 50 per cent of another company's shares, then that person or entity would have taken over the company.

3   Public limited companies must reveal more to the public about their yearly performances than private limited companies and must publish their accounts in the media. This opens up their business to public scrutiny.

4 They are tightly and rigidly controlled by the legal framework of the country in which they operate – even more so than private limited companies.

5 Owners are not managers and the commitment level of managers (directors) may not be as high as that of the owners (the shareholders). For the directors, it is merely a job while for the shareholders it may represent their life savings. This is referred to as the 'divorce of ownership and management' or as the 'agent problem'.

Summary – Section A

- Limited liability companies (LLCs) are large incorporated businesses that can be either privately or publicly owned.

- LLCs are owned by shareholders, who contribute money to start the business and have a yearly claim on the company's profit.

- Private limited companies have a few shareholders who are usually known to each other and they cannot sell shares to the general public.

- Public limited companies, on the other hand, are able to sell and advertise shares to members of the public.

End of section activities

Quick questions

Are the following statements true or false?

1 Some LLCs are unincorporated.

2 Shareholders are individuals who own and manage a company.

3 Private limited companies have a maximum number of owners.

4 Ordinary shareholders are not allowed to vote at company meetings.

5 The share of profit received by preference shareholders must be more than that received by ordinary shareholders.

6 The managers of a public limited company are usually the owners of the company.

7 One would expect to find the objectives of a company in its articles of association.

8 While public limited companies have to be registered with the appropriate authorities, private limited companies do not.

9 Only limited liability companies are allowed to sell shares in order to raise capital.

10 If one person owns all the shares in a company, the company is considered to be a sole trader organisation.

Applying what you have learnt

1 Buy your local newspaper – it should have a summary of the previous day's stock-market activity. Alternatively, you may log on to the website of your stock exchange to obtain this information. Assume that you have $50 000 to invest and choose some shares that interest you, making sure you have spent the entire sum of money. Make a record of all the shares that you have bought and the prices at which you bought them. Check the prices of these shares for the next two weeks and track the value of your investment on a daily basis. You may 'sell' on any given day or you may wait until the two weeks have passed to trade in.

a Did you make a profit?

b Why did you select the shares that you did?

c Why did you 'sell' when you did or wait for the two weeks to pass?

d Were there other stocks that you did not buy which performed better than the ones you bought?

2 What causes share prices to increase or decrease? If someone has shares in a company, explain whether they would buy more or sell their shares in the following situations. If people are anxious to sell or buy a share, what do you think will happen to its price?

   a the company has just announced that it is expecting a high profit

   b the company is about to release a revolutionary new product

   c other businesses in the industry are failing

   d the company has been bought by a larger foreign company

   e laws are about to be passed that will impose new regulations on the company if another business is about to introduce a product that will cause the company's sales to decline significantly.

Model exam questions

Question 1

   a Define the following terms:

      i incorporated   (2 marks)

      ii dividends.   (2 marks)

   b Outline the role played by any two of the following documents in the establishment of a business:

      i partnership deed

      ii articles of association

      iii memorandum of association.   (4 marks)

   c Give two reasons why the formation of a company is more difficult than the formation of a sole proprietorship.   (4 marks)

Question 2

   a Sole traders have what is called 'unlimited liability'. What does unlimited liability mean?   (3 marks)

   b Outline two effects of the unlimited status of sole traders on the formation and operation of sole proprietorships.   (4 marks)

   c How does the incorporated status of companies protect their owners?   (3 marks)

Question 3

   a Describe two advantages that large companies have over sole proprietorships.   (4 marks)

   b Why are there more likely to be more sole proprietorships than limited liability companies? (3 marks)

   c Give two reasons why an individual may prefer to operate a sole-trader organisation and **not** a company.   (3 marks)

The TCL Group – cementing its position in the Caribbean

The TCL Group is involved in cement manufacturing and is a good example of a multinational corporation.

The TCL Group is the leading producer and marketer of cement and ready-mix products in the Caribbean. It comprises of eight companies in Trinidad and Tobago, Barbados, Guyana, Jamaica and Anguilla, making it one of the Caribbean's multinational corporations. Some of the popular companies in the TCL Group are: Trinidad Cement Limited (TCL) and TCL Packaging Limited (TPL), both of which are based in Trinidad and Tobago; Arawak Cement Company Limited (ACCL), based in Barbados; and the Caribbean Cement Company Limited (CCCL), based in Jamaica. The TCL Group benefits from many advantages of having eight companies scattered across the Caribbean. The primary advantage is perhaps the manner in which the companies complement each other: the TCL Group's packaging company in Trinidad supplies the packages to its cement companies; and its cement companies supply its ready-mix company with cement to make pre-mix concrete. Another advantage is that the poor performance of any one company in a given year is usually cancelled out by another company that is performing well. For example, in 2007, Trinidad Cement Limited, facing severe local challenges, saw its export of cement fall by almost 13 per cent compared with 2006. In that same year, ACCL, its Barbados counterpart, managed to offset this decline by raising their export of cement by just over 24 per cent.

The TCL Group is one example of how large incorporated businesses in the private sector may use their size to their advantage. In this section you will be examining incorporated businesses in the private sector by discussing franchises and looking at large companies such as conglomerates and multinationals.

The private sector so far

We started our discussion about the private sector in Chapter 1 by looking at sole traders and partnerships – two forms of unincorporated businesses in the private sector. You were introduced to the example of Homestyle Cooking, a restaurant that started as a sole trader and then became a partnership in order to obtain more capital. Eventually, Homestyle Cooking was incorporated to become Homestyle Cooking Ltd, a private limited company and then, in order raise even more capital, it became a public limited company. We now move on to look at other ways in which the company may expand into other markets, industries and even into other countries.

Conglomerates

Over time, as Homestyle Cooking Ltd expands, it may invest in other companies and even find that it has come to own some of these companies. For example, Homestyle Cooking Ltd may buy shares in Islandwide Commercial Bank Limited, The Eagle Newspaper Company Ltd and Safe Travel Tours Ltd. Eventually, as it continues to buy shares in these companies, it may own more than 50 per cent of their shares and would effectively become the owner of these companies. Since these companies are in banking, media and transportation, respectively, while Homestyle Cooking Ltd is in the restaurant industry, Homestyle is now a **conglomerate**. There are a few important points to be made about conglomerates:

- Conglomerates are usually large companies and therefore, like public and private limited companies, they are often incorporated and their owners face limited liability.

- Conglomerates are organisations that have invested in other businesses called **subsidiaries**, which are involved in the production or marketing of unrelated products.

- Conglomerates must invest in unrelated businesses – for example, the TCL Group (discussed earlier in this section) is not a conglomerate because all the businesses that fall under the TCL umbrella are involved in the cement industry. For an example of a conglomerate see the case study of Barbados Shipping and Trading Company Ltd, below.

- The main advantage of a conglomerate is that the business spreads its risk over many unrelated industries through a process called **diversification**. Since it is unlikely that these different industries will all suffer at the same time, the business is assured that any losses made by a firm in one industry will be offset by profits from another firm in another industry.

 ## Business in your world

The Barbados Shipping and Trading Company Limited

The Barbados Shipping and Trading Company Ltd (BS&T) is considered to be Barbados's first true conglomerate and is still one of the largest companies in Barbados, employing 2500 people and owning 25 companies in various industries. The company has subsidiaries in the following industries: shipping, agriculture, pesticides, hardware, lumber, food, appliances, vehicles, insurance, shipping and aviation ground handling, animal feed, financial services, tourism, manufacturing and processing, paper products and real estate. BS&T is regarded as a strong and viable conglomerate because most of its subsidiaries and associates are leaders in their industries. Additionally, each firm brings complementary strengths and weaknesses to the group, resulting in the company making a profit of approximately US$24.9 million in 2008, with the potential to expand even further in the future.

1 Can you think of a few examples of conglomerates in your country?

2 Do you know how many different industries or lines of business each is in?

3 Why would a firm choose to operate in different industries?

Franchises

One of the most popular franchises in the Caribbean is KFC.

If Homestyle Cooking Ltd becomes really successful and becomes a household name, you may choose to open other branches elsewhere in the country or even overseas. One of the options you may pursue is a **franchise agreement**, which is an arrangement that allows you to sell the right to use the name of your business (and perhaps your unique recipes and ingredients) to another individual. This individual, who is called the **franchisee**, is said to operate a **franchise** and she does not have exclusive right to the products, recipes, ingredients and names that you (the **franchisor**) have developed. As the franchisee, she produces the recipes and products that you have developed and she is not able to deviate from the original method in any way, without permission from you, the franchisor.

Think about it

Why would you want to enter into a franchise agreement instead of starting your own business with its own brand?

The franchise must pay **royalties** to the franchisor, which is usually a percentage of money earned from sales and not from actual profit. Generally speaking, the franchisee faces the cost of setting up the franchise, though it is possible for her to get assistance from Homestyle Cooking Ltd. Furthermore, you may have some restrictions or guidelines regarding the construction, location and appearance of the franchise's building and its interior, and the franchisee will have to operate within these guidelines. You may also specify a particular uniform for the staff.

Think about it

Some popular examples of franchises in the Caribbean are Kentucky Fried Chicken, Burger King, TGI Friday's and McDonald's. From your experience with these franchises, do the following remain the same from one outlet to another?

- staff uniform
- building colours
- menu items
- prices
- opening hours
- any special offers

Types of franchise agreement

Broadly speaking, there are two types of franchise agreement:

1 A **dealer franchise** is one where the franchisee has been given the right to sell the franchisor's product but is also allowed to sell other products. This type of arrangement is most common with petrol companies; for example, a Texaco service station may sell car batteries and snacks not branded by Texaco.

2 A **brand franchise** is one where a new outlet is established to sell the franchisor's brand exclusively. For example, a Burger King outlet only sells

Burger King products and a KFC outlet only sells KFC products.

A franchising agreement is beneficial to both the franchisor and the franchisee. The benefits to the franchisor include:

- The company gets to take advantage of the specialised skills of the franchisee.
- The market is increased without expanding the firm.
- A guaranteed source of revenue, since royalties and fees are paid on turnover, not on actual profit.
- Risks and uncertainty are borne by the franchisee to a greater extent than by the franchisor.

The benefits to the franchisee include:

- The franchisor might advertise and promote the product nationally and as a result this is advertising for the franchisee as well.
- The franchisee is selling a recognised, established brand, so the chance of failure is reduced.
- Support services such as training and administration may be provided by the franchisor.

The franchisee may also face some disadvantages from entering into such an agreement:

- Most franchisors will demand a large fee just for the right to use their established name. This is a problem particularly because some franchisees operate as sole traders, who can have trouble acquiring capital to start up their business.
- Shared profits: in addition to the start-up fees, the franchisor often demands a share of the profit or a percentage commission on sales.
- The ripple effect: the failure of some franchises may impact negatively on other franchises that are doing well. This is sometimes referred to as the 'coat-tail effect'.
- Over-supervision: the franchisor may become too involved in the operation of the franchise.

Multinationals

Finally, it is possible that you will expand the business to such an extent that you may actually open another branch of Homestyle Cooking Ltd in another country. If this happens, the evolution of the business really has reached its peak as it is now a **multinational corporation** (MNC), since it owns or controls production facilities in more than one country. MNCs in the Caribbean are usually American- or European-based firms (such as Esso and Cable & Wireless), although there are some Caribbean firms which are also MNCs – the TCL Group and the Royal Bank of Trinidad and Tobago (RBTT) are just two examples. MNCs offer the following benefits to Caribbean countries:

- They reduce unemployment.
- They modernise the economy by introducing new technology.
- They offer world-class competition to local businesses and, by doing this, force local businesses to become more efficient in order to compete.
- They develop the human resources of the citizens of a country since they offer training and the scope for international experience.
- They require the output or products of local firms and thereby create opportunities for these firms to expand or stay in business.

Their presence in the economy, however, is often associated with the following concerns:

- Profits are repatriated (sent back) to their countries of origin.
- Their work practices and management styles may be incompatible with those of the Caribbean; this may displease local workers.

- Their workforce may be made up primarily of foreign workers.
- Multinational corporations (MNCs) usually operate outside their country of origin in an effort to reduce costs. This may mean that wages earned by workers in MNCs are very low.
- Most MNCs are so large and powerful that it is difficult for local governments to regulate them. For example, the government may be unable to address any substandard labour or environmental policies that may exist in these companies.
- MNCs notoriously have low levels of loyalty to the countries in which they operate – they are usually attracted to countries which offer tax incentives (such as tax holidays) and are likely to leave if labour costs increase or if incentives are withdrawn.

☞ Now it's your turn

1 Some companies expand into other countries through a franchise arrangement. Does it mean that these franchises are multinationals? Justify your answer.

2 What about conglomerates and multinationals – can a conglomerate also be a multinational?

Summary – Section B

- Large companies may eventually become conglomerates if they invest in other businesses in other industries.
- Conglomerates offer many benefits to owners; chief among them is the fact that they are able to diversify risk over many different and often unrelated industries.
- A large business may also become a multinational if it opens branches or comes to own businesses in other countries.
- MNCs are very important to Caribbean economies – they provide investment and employment for Caribbean economies.

- MNCs often face many challenges as they seek to set up their businesses in the Caribbean – their working conditions and practices are often a source of conflict as they are sometimes different from those which exist in the Caribbean.
- Another option that businesses use to expand their markets is to enter into franchise agreements, where the right to use their images, brands and products is leased to another person or business.

End of section activities

Quick questions

Say whether each of the following statements is true or false.

1 In a franchise agreement, the person who owns the rights to a product is called the franchisee.

2 LIME (a communication company in the Caribbean) offers cellular phone service. A number of stores sell phones that customers can use to access the LIME network. These stores are in franchise agreements with LIME.

3 In the franchise agreement that KFC has with local companies across the Caribbean, KFC owns the ingredient and the method of cooking, while the local companies own the restaurants and plant. This makes KFC an MNC.

4 Conglomerates are large businesses with many branches.

5 All multinationals are conglomerates.

6 A conglomerate must be a limited liability company.

7 Diversification is most notably a feature of franchise arrangements.

8 As a part of its franchise agreement with CELTA, Cairns Ltd is allowed to sell other products aside from CELTA's. This is an example of a brand franchise.

9 Royalties are usually paid as a percentage of profit.

10 Once a company sells its products in two or more countries, it is an MNC.

Applying what you have learnt

1 Indicate whether each of the following businesses is an MNC, a conglomerate or a franchise. Could some be more than just one type of business? Justify your responses.

   a JIT Inc started out making and selling blocks. Eventually, its owners built a hardware and a home centre store for do-it-yourself (DIY) repairmen. Finally, as business continued to boom, the company has gone into other areas such as pharmaceutical, canned goods and apparel.

   b PepsiCo is one of the largest soft drink companies in the world. An American company, it has expanded beyond its native shores by buying bottling plants and companies in other countries (such as Desnoes and Geddes in Jamaica). It has also expanded into other markets – such as the fast-food industry and the snack industry, having interests in Kentucky Fried Chicken, Taco Bell, Frito-Lay snacks and others. Recently, PepsiCo even announced that it has launched its own recording label.

   c Total was the tenth largest company in the world in 2007. A French company producing and providing oil and natural gas for domestic and commercial purposes, Total has expanded aggressively by entering into arrangements with Caribbean nationals and has also taken over the operations of traditional Caribbean giants such as Esso.

   d Ruby Tuesday is an American restaurant known for its casual dining experience. Like most American restaurants, however, it has found lucrative markets outside America by forming the right partnerships with local citizens. In these arrangements, it has been able to expand into other countries without actually owning premises in these countries.

   e Grace Kennedy is a Jamaican company that has a wide range of interests in many industries across the Caribbean. Originally the company focused on canned and other dry goods but has since expanded into many other industries, the most recent being the financial sector in the form of banks and investment houses.

Model exam question
Question 1

   a Explain what is meant by 'franchising'.   (3 marks)

   b Identify and describe an example of a franchise agreement in your country. Identify the **franchisee** and the **franchisor** in this arrangement.

   (3 marks)

   c Outline one advantage and one disadvantage for the franchisee in a franchise agreement.   (2 marks)

Comfortable public transportation – at what cost?

The Jamaica Urban Transit Company (JUTC), a public-sector entity, was established in 1998 at a cost of J$6 billion to provide public transportation within the Kingston metropolitan region, the capital city of Jamaica. Start-up capital was used to buy over 600 Mercedes-Benz and Volvo buses and to implement an electronic fare system. Between 1998 and 2006, however, the company made no profit and has cost the government a lot of money, racking up total losses of approximately J$7.4 billion.

The government of Jamaica (GoJ) remains committed to the operations of the JUTC and, between 1998 and 2006, the government absorbed approximately 78 per cent of the organisation's losses, amounting to a massive J$5.8 billion. In an effort to stem the losses, many cost-cutting measures have been introduced, including reducing the number of staff and introducing cashless transactions on buses, eliminating the need for conductors. For example, in 1999, shortly after the JUTC was established, there were approximately seven workers per bus; in 2006, after the implementation of efficiency measures, this number decreased to approximately four workers per bus.

The losses have continued, however, and the high accident rate that costs the organisation just over J$4 million monthly does not help. This problem is made worse by the poor work ethic and lack of commitment of the employees, shown for example by the fact that for the months of January and February, the JUTC lost a total of 3373 working days due to the high level of absenteeism of its workers. Notwithstanding the high level of losses, accidents and corruption, the JUTC is likely to continue to play a role in the transportation sector of Jamaica, since it is a large employer and provides vital transport services to its customers.

The inefficient and unprofitable operation of the JUTC brings into focus the topic for this section: public-sector entities.

Nationalisation

There is general agreement that, ideally, businesses should be owned by private individuals who are driven by the profit motive to be efficient and cost-conscious.

However, there are exceptional circumstances which may justify the government buying a private-sector business and essentially making it a public-sector operation. This process is known as **nationalisation**, and is justified under the following conditions:

- If there are important services which the private sector will not or cannot provide because it is unprofitable to do so – for example, providing electricity to rural areas, or the inland postal system. If these goods are left in the hands of private individuals, they will charge too high a price for them and, as a result, those who need them the most will not be able to afford them.
- If the government needs to gain control of the production of a good, such as energy or transport, that is too important to be left in the hands of private individuals.
- If closure is a risk and jobs may be lost.
- If increased accountability is desired. In such a case, it may be necessary to nationalise since the public does not have any control over or oversight of private companies.
- If the business sector is to be used as an instrument to further social goals for the benefit of the nation as a whole.

Disadvantages of nationalisation

1 Nationalised businesses are a drain on public finances as they often have to be supported by the nation's resources.
2 Nationalised industries are often inefficient and deliver substandard services.
3 Too much nationalisation may stifle the development of an effective, competitive private sector.
4 Nationalised businesses may be co-opted to support the political agenda of the government.
5 The government may not be able to invest sufficient capital to make nationalised businesses modern and competitive.

Nationalised industries

A nationalised industry is one that, like a private-sector company or partnership, offers a good or a service for sale to members of the public, but which is solely owned by and under the control of the government.

The most important point to understand about nationalised industries is that their products are offered for *sale* to members of the public, while other public-sector entities may offer their goods and services *free* of charge. One does not pay the judge or the stenographers to have one's case heard in court, nor does one pay the ministry of security in order to report a crime. This means that the court and justice system is not a nationalised industry. Utility providers, however, such as electricity or water companies usually charge for their services and, if they are owned by the government, they are nationalised industries.

Nationalised industries are incorporated businesses, and they therefore have a separate legal identity from that of their owner – the government. They are organised similarly to incorporated businesses in the private sector: they have a chairperson and a board, who are often appointed by the government minister whose department is responsible for that business. The board is accountable to the minister.

 ### Now it's your turn

In relation to public- or private-sector ownership of business, nationalisation has not been as popular as privatisation.

1 What is meant by 'privatisation'?

2 What are some of the reasons for privatisation in the Caribbean?

3 Can you think of some examples of firms in your country that have been privatised or nationalised?

4 Why do you think nationalisation is not as popular as privatisation?

Executive agencies

An executive agency is another type of business that exists in the public sector. Such an agency is usually linked to a department or ministry of government and is usually established to carry out specific duties and functions within that department. For example, the ministry responsible for transport within a country may decide to establish an executive agency to issue licences to new drivers.

The key point to note about executive agencies is that they are separate from the departments or ministries to which they are linked. As such, the management and funding of executive agencies are usually their own responsibility, with the government minister having very little control over their day-to-day operations. In regard to funding, it is likely that the government may allocate a small amount to these bodies but they have to make up the shortfall by charging the public for the services that they provide.

Now it's your turn

Why do you think executive agencies are created? Do you think all agencies of government can become executive agencies?

Local and municipal authorities

Have you ever wondered who is responsible for fixing your roads? The obvious answer is the government, but how does the government know that the road that runs from your school to your church needs to be fixed? What systems do they have in place to ensure that this piece of road is fixed? What about your public markets? Who repairs them or pays their bills? Once again, it is the government, but does the government sitting in parliament know about the needs of every single public market in every single community? Of course not. Instead, what exists is a system of **local government** that ensures that these services are provided. In other words, while the government in parliament is concerned about the economy as a whole, someone else needs to ensure that your community roads are repaired and your public market is adequately covered when it rains. This is the job of the local or municipal authorities.

A local or municipal authority is a government body which is responsible for addressing the welfare of people within a defined area. This body is usually elected (as opposed to appointed) and has responsibility for, among other things, public roads and highways; enforcing codes, regulations and standards that govern building and construction; maintaining order within towns and cities (such as arranging public parking and issuing permission for billboards); overseeing public

Think about it

You have heard people refer to a place as a 'town' and to other places as 'cities'. Do these words mean the same thing? If they are different, what makes them different? Furthermore, what is a municipality?

The terms are different and should not be used interchangeably. A **city** is usually defined as having administrative capacity – meaning it is an incorporated government entity that can provide government services to its citizens. A **town**, on the other hand, is just a collection of people in a central location. It has no administrative capacities and is unincorporated. A **municipality** is also defined in terms of its incorporated status and its ability to practise local self-governance. Cities (but not towns) are, therefore, municipalities.

facilities such as hospitals, markets and parks; and collecting taxes related to building, land and licensing. In short, a local or municipal authority is the visible manifestation of government that you encounter in your everyday life.

 Think about it

Before a person can build a commercial or residential complex (such as an office space, a plaza or a housing complex), they must seek and obtain permission from the local authority and submit copies of their architectural plans for the house. Why do you think this is so?

Local or municipal authorities have the following characteristics:

- **Continuity**: even though local government officials are usually voted into office and may eventually be voted out, the system of local authorities will continue even after the change of personnel.
- **The ability to enter into contracts**: as an arm of government, the local or municipal authorities are able to enter into contracts with private citizens to effect business deals. When these contracts are entered into, the authority acts on its own behalf and citizens within that authority's jurisdiction cannot be compelled to honour the contract the authority has made.
- **The right to sue and the possibility of being sued**: the authority can sue individuals or can be sued by individuals. Of course, as you would expect, when this happens the authority's identity is kept separate from that of the current holder of the office – hence a mayor cannot be sued for a city's errors.
- **The ability to collect taxes**: a local authority can collect taxes, fines and fees (such as land tax or licensing fees). These taxes will be used to fund its budget, which it also has a right to set.

 Making connections: social studies

Let us explore further the difference between central government and local government. Are the following tasks for local or central government?

1 managing the economy

2 ensuring that schools are repaired after a storm

3 preventing crime in the town centre

4 towing vehicles that are illegally parked in the town centre

5 providing an efficient public transportation system to and from school

6 destroying old, dilapidated buildings

7 inspecting new buildings for structural soundness

Government departments

Government departments are the different ministries of government responsible for creating policies and programmes for targeting specific areas (such as health, security, labour and transportation), which affect the quality of life of the people. Each department has a portfolio and is headed by a person who usually bears the title of minister. The minister is responsible for overseeing the ministry and for creating the broad policy framework that drives the ministry's operation. Government departments are not run to make profit; rather, their goal is to offer services that are essential for the nation's development. As a result, they rarely charge for these services or the charges may be minimal and, in some cases, may even be waived.

 Making connections: social studies

Who makes up the cabinet of a country? Find out about the members of the cabinet in your country. In light of what we have been talking about, what do you think is meant by 'minister without portfolio'?

Summary – Section C

- While, ideally, businesses are to be owned and operated by the private sector, it is sometimes necessary for the government to take over businesses that were once owned by the private sector. When this happens, it is called nationalisation.

- Nationalisation may be advisable if the government feels that a product is too important to be left in the profit-oriented hands of the private sector or if the imminent closure of a business would result in a major loss of jobs.

- Public-sector ownership may take many forms including nationalised corporation, executive agencies, municipal authorities and government departments.

End of section activities

Quick questions

Copy the sentences below into your exercise books, selecting the most appropriate word to complete each one.

1 If an important private-sector business is making little or no profit and is about to be closed, it is **more/less** likely to be nationalised.

2 Ideally, businesses are to be owned and operated by the **private/public** sector.

3 Nationalisation is less likely if a business supplies **luxury/essential** goods.

4 The nationalisation of a firm is likely to lead to an **increase/decrease** in the prices of the goods that this firm provides.

5 Nationalised industries offer goods **for sale / free of cost**.

6 Nationalised industries are **incorporated/unincorporated** businesses.

7 The board of directors of a nationalised industry reports to the **chairman/government**.

8 An executive agency is **independent of / dependent on** the government department to which it is attached.

9 The **local/central** government is also called a municipality.

10 Local authorities are usually **elected/appointed** by those whom they serve.

Applying what you have learnt

1 Among your classmates, organise a debate on the following statement: 'The government is too inefficient to own businesses.' Ensure that there are two teams – a proposition team and an opposition team. Make sure, as well, that each team has three speakers and agree on a time limit for each speaker.

2 Try to identify any nationalised business in your country. What products does it offer? Look back at the list of reasons why a firm may be nationalised. Are any of the factors on the list applicable to these nationalised industries?

Model exam questions

Question 1

a What is the main difference between companies in the public sector and those in the private sector?

(3 marks)

b Outline two reasons why a firm may be nationalised.

(4 marks)

c Discuss one major difference between a nationalised industry and a government department.

(3 marks)

Question 2

a What are executive agencies? (3 marks)

b Outline two reasons why executive agencies are formed.

(4 marks)

c Assess the likely impact that the formation of an executive agency may have on:

i the price of a government service

ii the quality of service offered by a government agency. (4 marks)

Question 3

a Identify any two forms of organisation in the public sector. (2 marks)

b List two characteristics of **each** type of organisation mentioned above. (4 marks)

c Discuss two characteristics of the type of products that are likely to be offered by the public sector.

(4 marks)

3 The business as a unit in a community

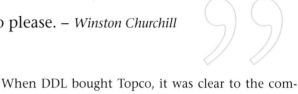

If you mean to profit, learn to please. – *Winston Churchill*

Demerara Distillers Ltd has created useful partnerships with its suppliers and is reaping the rewards.

DDL – making community involvement work

Demerara Distillers Ltd (DDL) is a Guyanese company, which has been in existence since 1952. DDL's core business is demerara rum and it is a leading supplier of rum to Europe and North America, but it has expanded and diversified into other areas over the years. For example, in 1993 DDL bought Topco, a producer of fruit juices, and has turned the company around from a simple producer of 75 000 litres of juice with annual revenues of G$10 million, to a large manufacturer of 1.5 million litres of juice with annual revenues of G$300 million. The way DDL approached this is a story in itself and a classic example of the importance of a company developing a relationship with its **stakeholders**.

When DDL bought Topco, it was clear to the company that the market for fruit juices was not being fully exploited by Topco and, as a result, it set about building a new packaging plant with the capacity to process five million pounds of fruit annually. This is where the company met its first obstacle: the farmers who supplied Topco with fruit could not, with their current resources and methods of production, meet the new plant's higher demand for fruit. In addition, each farmer was concentrating on the production of the same fruit, ensuring that Topco had an excess of one fruit but very little, or none, of the others. DDL therefore decided that the farmers needed financial support to make various changes in their methods of production and to grow other fruits as well.

To this end, the company formed a partnership with the Institute of Private Enterprise Development (IPED), a business specialising in granting small-business loans. Through this partnership, a win–win situation was created: loans were issued to farmers who were able to increase their revenues by increasing or switching production and Topco had a guaranteed supply of fruit. This idea worked so well that, within two years, the farmers had increased production from 750 000 pounds of fruit to 1.2 million pounds. In addition, their standard of living has improved, and the relationship between the farmers and DDL and Topco has been strengthened.

Following from the account above, there are many points that we could make relating to the importance to businesses of forming productive and beneficial relationships with people and entities that have an impact on the business. These will all be explored in this chapter as we talk about businesses interacting with their stakeholders.

In this chapter you will:

- discuss the functions of a business
- identify people or entities affected by business activities
- discuss what role is played by each stakeholder
- discuss expectations that the community may reasonably have of a business
- outline the functional areas that are usually found in a business
- discuss the functions and responsibilities of management
- discuss styles and types of leadership
- construct and interpret organisational charts
- discuss sources of conflict within an organisation
- discuss the options available to management and workers during a conflict
- discuss possible conflict resolution strategies
- identify principles that facilitate the development of a good relationship between management and workers.

SECTION A   The business as a unit

The functions of a business

Businesses exist to make a profit and to satisfy their stakeholders. In the process of doing this, however, there are other functions that they perform, some of which are:

- **To make and maximise profit**: businesses are created and remain in operation so that their owners can make as much profit as possible. Profit maximisation occurs when the difference between a firm's income (from selling goods) and its expenses is at its largest. Firms will adjust their prices and products until they are maximising profit.

☞ Now it's your turn

Do you think all businesses in the private sector try to maximise profit or are some businesses satisfied as long as they are making some level of profit? Why might businesses deliberately not try to maximise profit?

- **To create employment and income**: in order to produce goods and services to satisfy their customers, firms pay people to work for them. The business activities of firms, therefore, are responsible for the growth and development of the area they are located in, and for improving the lives of the local residents; as a result, firms are seen as an integral part of the local community.

- **To be a good corporate citizen**: firms are good corporate citizens when they act unselfishly and play a part in the social development of the country by donating to charity, assisting special-interest groups and granting scholarships.

- **To satisfy needs and wants**: all firms offer products (either a tangible good such as a chocolate bar or an intangible service such as car repair) that they hope consumers will buy in order to satisfy their needs and wants. Without being offered these products, the public would have no need for these companies and the companies would make no profit.

- **To take risks**: firms must be prepared to take risks in order to make profits. Some of the most successful firms are the ones that choose risky routes that gave high returns instead of less-risky options with lower returns.

Stakeholders

If you had a business, to whom would you pay attention? Well, certainly you would ensure that your consumers were satisfied and, if you had co-owners, you would also want to keep them happy. Who else? What about your employees and managers? Well, they are responsible for the day-to-day running of the business and so you would have to look out for their interests as well. Is there anyone else? What about your suppliers, or banks and other financial institutions, or even the government? Would you take any interest in them and, just as importantly, would they take any interest in you?

The people to whom you would pay attention and who would take an interest in your business are called stakeholders. Stakeholders are individuals or entities who have an interest in the affairs of the business, usually because they are affected by them.

Think about it

Are all your stakeholders equal? Are some stakeholders more important than others? Do all your stakeholders have the same interest in your business? Can you think of examples of stakeholders who may have conflicting interests in your business?

There are two types of stakeholders:

Primary stakeholders

Primary stakeholders are those stakeholders who have a direct interest in the organisation and its success. These are people or entities whose fortunes are directly linked to the organisation and, as a result, they take a keen interest in its affairs and ability to settle debts. Primary stakeholders normally have a legal relationship with the business, meaning the business is legally obliged to honour their claim on the organisation's resources. Primary stakeholders include:

- **Owners**: owners are interested in the return on their investment in the business. Owners are usually people who have invested money in the business. These people are either shareholders or partners and their primary concern is that the business makes a profit on their investment.

- **Management and employees**: this set of stakeholders would be interested in their job security, professional mobility and remuneration. Salary, in particular, is an issue with the potential to be contentious and, as a result, employees and the business are often at odds where this is concerned.

- **Suppliers**: suppliers are interested in the ability of the business to repay its debts, since most of them supply goods to the business on credit, and need to know that they will be paid.

- **Customers**: customers purchase the goods and services from the business. The customers are the price setters of the business – by altering their demand they can affect the price at which the product is sold.

- **Banks and other financial organisations** that lend money to the business: these stakeholders are concerned about the ability of the business to repay their loans with regular and timely interest payments. While shareholders are paid out of the profits and, therefore, may not be paid if the business does not make a profit, lenders such as banks are not paid based on profit and expect to be paid whether or not the business makes a profit.

- **Government**: tax-collection agencies, regulatory bodies and consumer-protection agencies may have some demands that they may reasonably make of the business. The business is often obliged to respond favourably to these demands.

Secondary stakeholders

Secondary stakeholders are those who have a public or special-interest stake in the business. Very often they do not have a legal relationship with the business and, as a result, the business is under no legal obligation to pay attention to their claim, though it may be good to do so in order to create goodwill with the public. Secondary stakeholders include:

- **Trade unions**: these are organisations that represent the interests of workers. They pressure the business to improve the salaries, benefits and working conditions of its employees. They analyse how the business is performing over a given period to determine what requests to make of the business on behalf of the workers.

- **Pressure groups**: these organisations are formed to represent special interests or issues about which society at large may be concerned. For example, as society has become more concerned about the environment, environmentalists have formed pressure groups in an effort to protect the environment against large businesses. Pressure groups try to get businesses to support whatever interest they represent.

Pressure groups often protest in front of businesses in an effort to call attention to their causes.

- **The community**: the business operates in a space occupied by other entities and groups, which together are called communities. The word community can also be stretched to include institutions such as the church, the family, the school, interest groups and so on. The community, then, is an external force with which the business comes in contact during its operations. Businesses show that they are good members of the community by being good corporate citizens. They sponsor sporting competitions, make donations to charities, have special-interest groups and offer scholarships.

The functional areas of a business

So far we have looked at the business by outlining some of the functions that it performs and the various stakeholders that are affected by these functions. Now let us go further and see how the business is organised to carry out these functions. The functional areas of a business describe the four main departments that are established to address the various functions of a business. These areas are:

- **Production**: this department is responsible for ensuring that the product is delivered on schedule and at an acceptable quality standard. Capacity planning (determining the quantity of resources required), product design and quality control are obvious roles that this department also plays. In most businesses, the production department is also responsible for ensuring that the stock is managed and that the machines are maintained in excellent condition.

- **Finance**: this department ensures that the financial resources of the business are properly managed and that a proper account is kept of the firm's resources, in line with the legal requirements of the country. This department is responsible for producing financial statements at the end of the year, keeping records of transactions during the year and ensuring that corporate and income taxes, and other employee deductions are turned over to the government.

- **Marketing**: this department ensures that the brand image is always seen in the best light. It is primarily responsible for making sure that the business offers the right mix of product at an ideal price using the best promotional strategies and through the right channels. Specifically, this department is involved in ensuring that the customer is satisfied with the product the business offers and that the business creates a good impression every time it interacts with the public.

- **Personnel**: this department is sometimes referred to as the human resources department and is responsible for creating and implementing the legal and social environment within which the human resources of the business – its employees – will feel comfortable. In addition, it ensures that the business has the right mix of employees to achieve its objectives.

Think about it

Small businesses (such as the sole proprietorships we discussed in Chapter 1) do not always have departments that are in charge of each functional area. Rather, the owner is usually in charge of each functional area and manages all the duties of that 'department'. What do you think are some of the advantages and disadvantages of this?

The functions of management

As we have seen in the discussion about the functional areas of the business, there are at least four departments, each of which would have its own manager. These department (or functional) managers will in turn have other managers to whom they report. This chain of management continues ever higher until it reaches the board of directors, who ultimately report to the shareholders. In short, a business has many managers who all play a role in the smooth operation of the business. But what exactly are the functions of management?

- **Planning**: this is the process of establishing objectives and setting operations in motion to achieve these objectives. Planning has been described as a bridge between where the business is now and where it wants to be in the future. As such, planning is essentially anticipating what is likely to happen and ensuring that contingencies are in place to deal with these eventualities. Management is usually involved in strategic planning, which is different from the type of operational planning in which non-management workers are involved. Strategic planning is focused on the business as a whole (not on individual departments) and is more long term than operational planning. A typical employee, for example, may be concerned about the actions to take to increase sales while management may be thinking about how to position the company and its image in the minds of the public.
- **Organising**: this function is concerned with ensuring that the business is structured in order to achieve its objectives. Organising makes certain that departments and work units are created to complete major tasks and that sufficient authority is allocated to each

department. Through this function, management establishes the organisational structure of the business, ensures the smooth flow of communication, allocates and delegates tasks and responsibilities, and ensures that the requisite resources to complete these tasks and execute these responsibilities are available.

- **Directing**: this is the function that calls on management to create an environment that encourages employees to work towards achieving the objectives of the business through effective communication and leadership. In directing, management ensures that a structure exists that supports workers and provides guidance as they perform their tasks.
- **Controlling**: this function is related to the need to ensure that the human and financial resources of the business are harnessed to achieve its objectives. In controlling, management establishes performance standards, comparing actual with expected performance to see what corrective actions need to be taken to improve the operations of the business.
- **Co-ordinating**: this is closely related to organising and is concerned with creating a single cohesive unit out of the many departments and work units in the business. Efficiency is key to the co-ordinating function, as its aim is to ensure that the business runs as smoothly as possible and that no duplication of duties or cross-purposes exist.
- **Delegating**: this is the process of authorising subordinates to make decisions. It is the downward transfer of authority and is used by management to develop the skills of subordinates. Even though management may be delegating the authority to make decisions, the responsibility for the task ultimately still rests with management as responsibility cannot be delegated.
- **Motivating**: this is the process of creating a work environment that encourages workers to increase their productivity and their overall commitment to the business. Motivating ranges from creating a more comfortable environment for workers to providing training and scope for promotion.

Responsibilities of management

In addition to carrying out the functions described above, management also has several responsibilities to a number of stakeholders including owners and shareholders, employees, society, customers and government.

Owners and shareholders: in large companies, the owners are rarely the managers; instead, owners appoint directors who employ managers to run the company with the primary aim of maximising profits for owners. Some of the responsibilities that management has to owners and shareholders are:

- To maximise profit and surplus, thereby providing returns on the owners' investment. Managers maximise profit by ensuring that they employ cost-cutting measures to create efficiency.
- To protect the image of the company in the eyes of the public by avoiding unfair business practices, respecting the laws and becoming good corporate citizens.
- To spend and invest the company's money wisely, giving careful consideration to profit.
- To provide reliable, timely and accurate information at annual general meetings and at the end of various accounting periods.
- To work towards achieving the objectives of the business.

☞ Now it's your turn

Companies have what is called the agent problem – managers are agents and hence they do not have as much incentive to work hard since the money that they may lose does not belong to them.

1 Why does the agent problem develop?

2 How do the responsibilities of managers to owners help to prevent the agent problem?

Employees: employees represent one of the most important groups for which management has responsibility. Employees are responsible for determining the quality of the product and, ultimately, they are the ones most likely to come in contact with the customers. Very often, employees' effort is tied to their perception of how well managers are honouring their responsibilities to them. Some of the responsibilities that managers have towards employees are:

- Providing adequate and safe working conditions.
- Facilitating the growth and development of workers by ensuring that provisions are made for their training, both on and off the job.
- Creating an environment where good communication can prevail between workers and management. This may mean providing opportunities for feedback on workers' effort, keeping an open line of communication, and ensuring a relatively short and unbroken line of communication.
- Rewarding workers with fair wages.
- Honouring the rights of workers by awarding the leave, promotions and other obligations to which workers may be entitled as stipulated by their contracts and the law.
- Eliminating discrimination against minorities and special groups, such as the disabled and those living with HIV/AIDS.

Society: the obligations the business has to its customers, employees and owners are accompanied by the obligations that it also has to the wider society. The society includes the community in which the business operates, institutions such as the family, the church and schools and special-interest groups, such as environmentalists. The responsibilities that management has to society are:

- To support special causes that affect society at large. These include reducing discrimination against and promoting the rights of people living with HIV/AIDS, and also anti-drugs campaigns.
- To contribute to the economy by providing employment and paying taxes.
- To act as good corporate citizens by becoming involved in community and special-interest events such as public-awareness campaigns.
- To ensure that the organisation employs environmentally friendly business practices in its production.
- To encourage the development of local businesses by forming links with them. Management can do this by ensuring that, where the opportunities exist, the business buys from and sells to other local businesses.

Customers: perhaps the most important stakeholder to which the management has responsibilities is the customers of the business. Customers, having bought the organisation's products, have a legal and contractual relationship with the business. Against this background, the management has the following responsibility to the organisation's customers:

- To ensure that whatever contract is entered into with customers is honoured – this means that service is to be provided to customers in an uninterrupted manner consistent with what is stipulated in the contract.
- To provide warning and proper notification about the likely side effects of using or consuming a product.
- To ensure that information about the product (such as its ingredients, its nutritional value and instructions for use) is available to the customer.
- To provide compensation for damage or injury associated with using the product.

- To provide after-sales service for the products that the business sells.
- To use accurate and clear advertisements to promote the organisation's products.

Government: the business operates within an economic environment that is regulated by laws; it therefore has a number of responsibilities to the government, which include:

1 Honouring the law (as well as the spirit of the law) as set out by the government.

2 Remaining committed to the goals and objectives of government policy. For example, in an environment where the government is trying to reduce interest rates, banks are expected to do all they can to ensure that they do not charge high interest rates.

3 Paying taxes in a timely fashion, including income tax and other taxes collected on behalf of employees or from customers.

Summary – Section A

- Businesses are set up to make maximum profit. In doing this they also provide employment, satisfy wants and needs and support the community by being good corporate citizens.
- In carrying out its functions, the business interacts with many stakeholders directly (such as owners, management and employees and customers) and indirectly (such as trade unions and the wider community).

- The business has four main functional areas – production, finance, marketing and personnel.
- The management of a business carries out vital functions such as planning, organising, directing and co-ordinating.
- Management is also responsible for ensuring that the business honours its responsibilities to stakeholders such as customers, employees and society at large.

End of section activities

Quick questions

1 Which functional area of the business would be responsible for carrying out the following tasks?

  a creating and managing the budget for the production of a sample of a new product

  b setting the price for a new product

  c designing the packaging for a new product

  d drawing up wage slips for the employees in the production department

  e keeping a record of the raw materials used in production

  f appraising workers' performance

  g assessing the profitability of the business

  h designing a new promotional strategy

i researching a new product idea

j writing a letter of dismissal to an employee

2 Which management function would be concerned with the following activities?

  a carrying out performance evaluation of workers

  b creating a budget for the business

  c creating a department to be in charge of research and development

  d creating a five-year plan

  e planning an after-work social for the last Friday in every month

  f developing a mentorship programme with more experienced managers

  g creating a committee to develop and implement a new lunch system

Applying what you have learnt

1 Select a major sporting or entertainment event in your country and imagine that you have a business (it could be any type you want). If your business is selected to be the main sponsor for this event, what would you insist on getting out of the deal? Think along the lines of the following areas or any other area that you can think of:

- media coverage and exposure
- competitors' exposure and coverage
- signs and posters at the event (e.g. parking lot, location).

2 Why do businesses try to become good corporate citizens? What benefits can they possibly get from giving away millions of dollars in the form of sponsorships and scholarships?

3 Do you think small and large businesses focus on different management functions? Which management functions do you think may not be as important in a small business even though they may be important in a large business? Justify your selections.

4 We have stated before that the main aim of a business is to make as much profit as possible and that its activities are aimed at achieving this objective. What does this mean, however, in light of the fact that the business has so many responsibilities to society, the government and its customers? For example, do you think the responsibilities that the business has to society or to its employees may cut into its profits? If so, why does the business still make an effort to honour its responsibilities to the various stakeholders?

Model exam questions
Question 1

  a What is meant by the term 'stakeholder'?

                                         (3 marks)

  b Give two examples of stakeholders and state the interest that they have in the affairs of the business.

                                         (6 marks)

  c Why might a business be more willing to respond to the demands of some stakeholders than others?

                                         (3 marks)

Question 2

  a List any three of the main functional areas of business.   (3 marks)

  b Outline two roles played by any functional area listed in (a).   (4 marks)

  c How may the functional areas for sole traders be different from those for companies?   (3 marks)

Question 3

a Explain what is meant by the planning function of management. (3 marks)

b Managers are considered to be 'organisers' and 'controllers'. Identify the similarities and the differences between these roles. (6 marks)

c How is management in a large business different from management in a small business? (3 marks)

Question 4

Norlette Yearde has recently been employed by Herbert's Biscuit Company to create and strengthen relationships with members of the company's community.

a Discuss the difference between primary and secondary stakeholders. (4 marks)

b Outline two members of the community with whom Norlette could seek to build relationships (4 marks)

c Discuss three approaches that Norlette could take to build relationships with members of the company's community. (6 marks)

d Discuss three benefits that Herbert's Biscuit Company might obtain from forming relationships with members of its community. (6 marks)

Question 5

a List two obligations that management has to **each** of the following groups:

i owners

ii employees

iii society. (6 marks)

b Discuss how management's responsibilities to owners may conflict with their responsibilities to employees. (4 marks)

c 'The most important responsibility of management is to maximise profit.'
Explain why you agree or disagree with this statement. (4 marks)

d How does profit maximisation affect management's obligation to:

i customers?

ii employees? (6 marks)

Formal organisational structures

All businesses must organise their human resources in such a way as to achieve maximum productivity. The way in which this is done is called the formal organisation of a business. Among other things, the formal organisation will determine:

- the relationship between co-workers
- seniority and rank (who answers to whom)
- who is authorised to make decisions
- who executes decisions when they are made
- communication channels and protocol.

All formal organisations have certain characteristics; some of these are discussed below.

Hierarchy

The **hierarchy** in a business is the order or levels of management, from the highest to the lowest. The hierarchy of a business shows who is in charge of each task, each speciality area, and the business as a whole. The hierarchy of a business is determined by the vertical relationships in the business and shows the chain of command.

Chain of command

The **chain of command** is the unbroken line of reporting relationships from the bottom to the top of the business. The chain of command defines the formal decision-making structure and provides for the orderly progression of information up and down the hierarchy. Information is passed up the chain of command and decisions are passed down. The number of levels in the chain of command will determine the effectiveness of decision making. Information and decisions will be communicated slowly if unnecessary links or levels exist in the organisational structure.

☞ Now it's your turn

Does your class have a class president? If not, imagine that there is one. Suppose two students in the class are involved in a fight; how would this news get to the principal? Identify the different people through whom the message will pass before it reaches the principal.

Span of control

This refers to the number of subordinates who are under the direction of a manager. A team leader, for example, who manages a department with eight people is said to have a **span of control** of eight. A span of control is described as being narrow or wide – the more people under the control of a single manager, the wider the span of control is said to be. Figures 3.1a and 3.1b, for example, show two different ways of organising the employees in a factory. In Figure 3.1a, the eight employees are under the supervision of the factory manager, leading to a wide span of control. Compared with Figure 3.1a, the arrangement in Figure 3.1b gives the manager a narrow span of control as he supervises only two team leaders. These two team leaders, in turn, supervise four employees each. As a rule, if subordinates' tasks are complex and require a high level of supervision then a single manager should only have a few subordinates under her control. Wide spans of control may result in the manager being stretched too thin and subordinates becoming frustrated by their inability to get immediate assistance from, or access to, their leader. If the span of control is too narrow, then the risk is that subordinates may be overworked or over-supervised, again leading to frustration.

👤 Think about it

The span of control in a business may be compared to the class size in a school. Do you prefer large or small classes? Why would you prefer either one? What challenges do you think teachers and students have in large classes that they may not have in small classes? Do you think teachers have it easier teaching small classes? Why or why not?

The internal structure of a business and organisational charts

The internal structure of a business refers to the lines of authority, communication and relationship that exist within the business. The structure gives the relationship between each department and their relationship to or with management. For example, in a business it is not uncommon to find departments organised according to

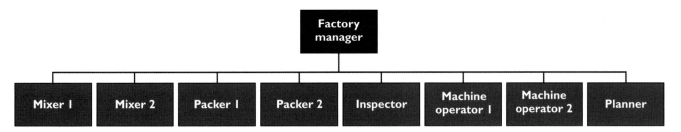

Figure 3.1a A wide span of control.

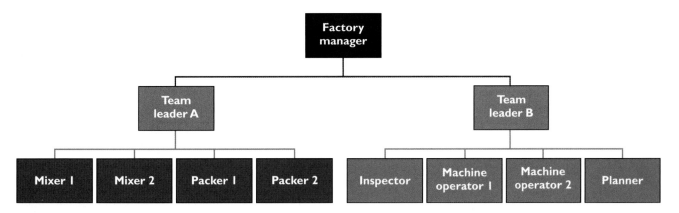

Figure 3.1b A narrow span of control.

their functions (e.g. sales, finance, human resources). Each department will have a relationship with the others and also a relationship with management.

Organisational structures are normally shown using an organisational chart – this is a diagrammatic representation of the working units within an organisation. An organisational chart uses lines to show how departments and individuals relate to each other and, therefore, it captures the nature of the working relationship of the individuals and departments in the organisation. An organisational chart will answer the following questions:

- What is the reporting relationship among individuals and departments in the organisation?
- What is the appropriate line of communication in the organisation?
- Which departments and individuals are responsible for each task?
- What is the span of control of each manager, team leader and head of department?
- How are resources allocated within and throughout the organisation?

There are many types of organisational chart, but the most popular are the hierarchical or T-Charts, and the matrix structure.

Hierarchical structures

The hierarchy in a business is its order or levels of management, from the highest to the lowest. The **hierarchical structure** is the traditional structure for most businesses – particularly medium-sized businesses. In this structure, the person in charge of each task, person, speciality area and the organisation as a whole is clearly shown. In this type of structure, decision making is shared throughout the business, employees are each given a role and procedures are laid down which determine their behaviour at work. A hierarchical structure uses horizontal and vertical lines laid out in a T-shape to show both span of control (horizontal lines) and chain of command (vertical lines). In this type of structure, there may be many levels of management – directors, senior management, middle-level management and lower-level management and then operational employees. As one moves down the organisation, the seniority

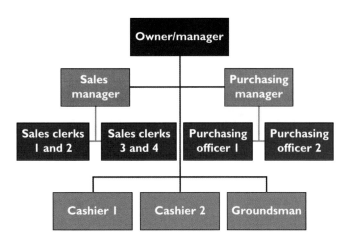

Figure 3.2 A simple organisational chart.

and responsibilities of managers decrease. A simple example of a hierarchical structure in a sole-trader organisation is shown in Figure 3.2.

There are three type of relationship among workers – horizontal, vertical and diagonal.

- **Horizontal relationships** exist at the same level and are shared by workers in the same or in a different department working at that level. For example, in Figure 3.2 the sales clerks and the purchasing officers are all working at the same level and hence they have a horizontal relationship. Horizontal relationships are equal.

- **Vertical relationships** exist from top to bottom or vice versa. Vertical relationships give an idea of the reporting relationship among workers – as a rule, workers at the bottom report to those at the top with whom they share a relationship. For example, in Figure 3.2, the sales clerks are all answerable to the sales manager and, hence, they have a vertical relationship.

- **Diagonal relationships** exist among workers at different levels in different departments. For example, in Figure 3.2, the purchasing manager and the sales clerks have a diagonal relationship. People in diagonal relationships have no reporting relationship with each other even though they are at different levels.

- The sales manager and purchasing manager are at equal levels in the hierarchy of the organisation – though the sales manager has a wider span of control (four employees) than the purchasing manager (only two employees).

- While the purchasing manager has more authority than a sales clerk or a cashier, the purchasing manager cannot exercise any authority over the clerks in the sales department or over any of the cashiers. This is due to the fact that they are in different departments.

- The business has two departments – purchasing and sales; the owner/manager is responsible for monitoring the work of the cashiers and the groundsman.

- The chain of command for, say, a sales clerk, is through the sales manager to the owner/manager.

- The sales clerks, purchasing officers, cashiers and the groundsman are all called operational workers – these are non-management workers who are simply responsible for implementing and executing the day to day tasks associated with allowing the business to meet its overall objectives.

- The organisational chart has three levels or tiers – from the lowest to the highest level in the organisation, there are only three tiers. This means that messages that originate at the highest level (owner/manager) pass through one tier before getting to the lowest level (operational workers). In other words, there is only one intermediary or middle level of management (sales and purchasing managers).

Larger organisations will have organisational charts that are 'taller' – more intermediary (or middle) levels of management will exist and the employee at the bottom of the chart will have to go through more tiers to get a message to the top of the organisation. Figure 3.3 shows such a multi-level organisation.

When you compare Figures 3.2 and 3.3, you will realise that Figure 3.3 shows an organisation with more tiers of management, resulting in a 'taller' organisational chart. In this organisation, more tiers separate workers at the lowest level from managers at the most senior level. A worker who reports to the production manager, for example, must go through the production manager, the chief operations officer and the vice president in charge of operations, before being able to get in touch with the chief executive officer/president.

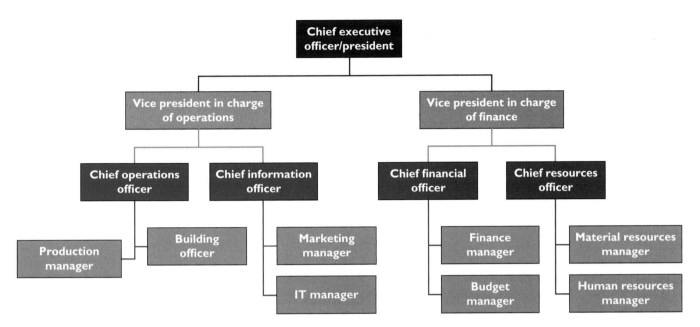

Figure 3.3 A multi-level ('tall') organisational chart.

☞ Now it's your turn

Some organisations are described as being 'tall'. What does this mean? What are the implications of this for lower-level workers and for senior management?

Matrix structures

This method of organising the workforce emphasises the coming together of people with specialised skills to form temporary teams. In the **matrix structure**, teams are formed as workers come together to work on projects or specialised tasks; as a result, in such an organisation structure, a person could be working on two different projects in different departments simultaneously, whereas in hierarchical structures this is not likely. This structure, therefore, is flexible in that it allows a worker to use his skill throughout the business without being limited to one department. When workers come together to form teams to work on a project, team members have their own responsibilities, which are reflective of their skills and talents. A matrix structure is shown in Figure 3.4.

From this matrix structure it is apparent that managers (as would be the case with workers as well) are not deployed to departments; rather they are assigned to teams working on projects. So, for example, Project A has two of the three managers (Managers 1 and 2), while Project B has all three managers.

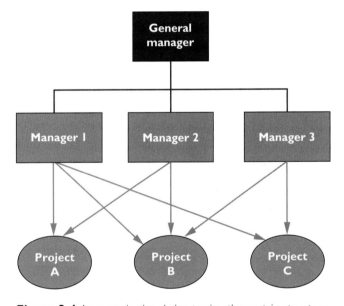

Figure 3.4 An organisational chart using the matrix structure.

For you to think about

Do you think it might be a challenge when lots of managers start working on the same project? Each project would include some operational (lower-level) workers, one of whom might actually be the team leader. What do you think might occur as a result of this apparent reversal of authority?

Summary – Section B

- A formal organisational structure describes how the human resources of a business are allocated. Among other things, it determines the hierarchy, chain of command and span of control within the business.

- A formal organisational structure is shown on organisational charts, which are usually of two types – either hierarchical or matrix.

- A hierarchical structure is one that shows the workers arranged in terms of authority and distinct work units or departments, while a matrix structure allows workers to be deployed temporarily to project teams.

End of section activities

Quick questions

Below is an incomplete organisational chart. Cells which require information are numbered from 1 to 10. Read the description of the business below and indicate in your exercise book who should be inserted in each numbered box.

Barlstow Academy is a small private school. The school is operated by a principal who is assisted closely by two vice-principals (VPs). The school has five grades (1–5) with a teacher in charge of each class. One teacher acts as grade co-ordinator for grades 1–3 and another teacher acts as a grade co-ordinator for grades 4 and 5. Both co-ordinators report to the same VP. The other VP is in charge of the canteen and the one physical education (PE) teacher/coach. The canteen is managed by a canteen manager and there are a chef and a cashier in the canteen.

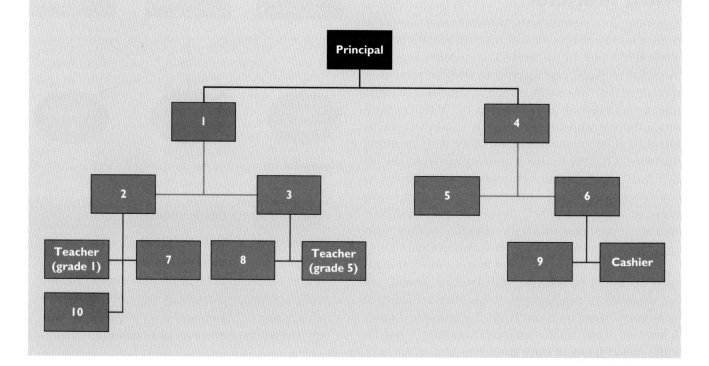

Applying what you have learnt

1 Draw an organisational chart of the staff in your school. Include the following if they exist in your school:
   - the principal and vice principals
   - the grade co-ordinators
   - the departments and their heads
   - the senior teachers
   - all other teachers
   - all other members of staff such as ancillary staff, canteen staff, administrative staff and security.

2 Does your school have a hierarchical or matrix structure? Why do you believe this is so? Which structure do you think is better for schools to have – a hierarchical or a matrix structure? Give reasons for your answer.

Model exam questions
Question 1
a Define the following terms:

   i organisational chart

   ii span of control. (6 marks)

b What is the main difference between a matrix structure and a hierarchical structure? (3 marks)

c Discuss two implications for management of using a matrix structure instead of a hierarchical one. (6 marks)

Question 2
a Differentiate between span of control and chain of command. (3 marks)

b What are two implications of a manager having a wide span of control? (4 marks)

c Organisations that are tall are likely to be inefficient. Give two reasons why this may be so. (6 marks)

Question 3
Kilkern Ltd is a small pottery company with one general manager. The company manufactures clay pots and jars that it sells to retailers and wholesalers. The company's production department consists of a manager and four workers, and its sales department has a manager, two cashiers and three sales clerks. Its finance department has a senior accountant and three bookkeepers. There are also two janitors who report to the senior accountant. Finally, the company has recently hired a product design specialist who reports directly to the general manager. All other managers also report directly to the general manager.

a Draw an organisational chart that captures the information above. (7 marks)

b What is the span of control of the sales manager? (1 marks)

c Outline the chain of command for one of the janitors. (2 marks)

Question 4
Miriam Hill Recreations is a large resort, spa and hotel. It has over 80 employees who are assigned to temporary teams as the need arises. The management of Miriam Hill, however, has recently questioned the effectiveness of the organisational structure of the business.

a Does Miriam Hill Recreations have a matrix or a hierarchical structure? Give reasons for your answer. (4 marks)

b Discuss two reasons why firms use a matrix structure. (6 marks)

c Outline two challenges that a matrix structure presents to an organisation. (6 marks)

d Discuss two problems that large organisations, such as Miriam Hill Recreations, are likely to experience with their organisational structure. (4 marks)

What is leadership?

We have said a lot about what we expect managers to do – to plan, to direct, to co-ordinate and to honour a number of responsibilities that they have to various stakeholders. But perhaps the most crucial aspect of managing is leading. Leadership is the process of influencing individuals and groups to set and achieve goals.

 What do you think?

Are managing and leading different processes? Are all managers leaders? Are all leaders managers? Which function of management is most closely related to leading?

Characteristics of a good leader

What do leaders do and what skills do they need to ensure that they are successful? These are important questions and, if you have ever been asked to lead others, you may have realised that they are not easily answered. The truth is that being a good leader is not easy. There are some key characteristics that leaders need if they are to be effective. These include the following:

- **Objectivity**: good leaders must be able to assess a situation without allowing their own personal views or opinions to lead them to a preconceived conclusion. When dealing with a situation, a good leader's decision should not be a foregone conclusion; they must be open to new ideas and courses of action.

- **Vision**: a leader must be able to create goals and devise a plan to achieve them.

- **Strategic thinking**: the leader must see and assess the big picture and should be proactive in creating a plan to address some of the issues identified from this assessment.

- **Emotional intelligence**: good leaders should be able to identify, understand and manage the emotions of those with whom they work. Good leaders should be alert to the emotions of the people they lead.

- **Confidence**: good leaders should inspire others with the confidence that they exude.

This confidence comes from being good at the job that they do and from understanding their limitations and being comfortable when they are corrected or are in need of assistance.

- **Empowering others**: good leaders provide for the growth and development of those they lead. They are able to delegate, motivate and promote growth in others.

 What do you think?

Do you think good leaders are born and not made? Can everyone develop the traits of a good leader or are they traits with which you are born?

Leadership styles

Leadership style refers to the approaches and behaviours – both real and perceived – that a manager uses to influence others. Leadership can be classified into one of the following three styles.

Democratic

Democratic leaders allow subordinates to participate in the decision-making process – they consult freely with subordinates and allow for contending views to exist until a decision is reached by consensus. For this reason, this leadership style is usually associated with consultative and participative leadership styles. In democratic leadership, consensus is usually reached after extensive discussion of all variables and options and after each person has been allowed a chance to give opinions and listen to others. In this type of environment, leaders are not seen as the ones who *make* decisions; rather they are merely responsible for *facilitating* (or 'refereeing') the decision-making process. The leadership skills emphasised in an environment where democratic leadership exists are related to the leader's ability to manage people so that decisions are arrived at in a consultative process. Democratic leadership has the following strengths:

- It motivates staff to become more committed to the results, since they were involved in the decision making and the planning process.

- It creates an opportunity for lower-level workers and managers to exercise and develop their decision-making skills.

- It is likely to improve the quality of the decisions made as more people were involved and more views were considered.

Democratic leadership has the following drawbacks:

- The decision-making process is likely to be lengthy as many views will have to be considered. This makes democratic leadership ineffective in some situations where decisions have to be made quickly.

- A democratic leader requires a greater level of skill than that required by other styles in managing workers and the decision-making process.

- Each time a decision is made democratically, it may adversely affect a minority view or group whose numbers do not allow them to have much sway over the final outcome.

Autocratic leadership

An **autocratic leader** is the opposite of a democratic leader. An autocratic leader does not involve others in the decision-making process; instead, he simply gives orders that are to be followed. Little or no consultation takes place; instead, the authority of the leader takes priority over the opinions of others and, for this reason, this leadership style is also known as authoritarian leadership. In an environment where decisions are made autocratically, the focus is on the tasks to be completed and not on the people involved in the task.

Autocratic leadership has the following strengths:

- It facilitates a quick decision-making process, which is useful in the event of an emergency or situations where speed in decision making is valued.

- Where decisions are complex or involve complicated information, followers may have little proficiency in decision making. The expertise of the leader may make autocratic leadership ideal.

- In environments where discipline is a problem, the heavy-handed approach of an autocratic leader may be needed to create order.

Some of the weaknesses of autocratic leadership are:

- It does not encourage workers to identify themselves with the ultimate success of a course of action.

- Workers are not likely to be committed to a course of action on which they were not consulted.

- It neither empowers workers nor develops their leadership or decision-making skills.

- It alienates leaders and workers, who are not likely to communicate openly and often.

Laissez-faire leadership

A **laissez-faire leadership** style is one in which workers have greater freedom to work on their own initiative, within certain parameters or boundaries. The leader sets the broad outline within which workers are expected to operate and then allows workers to determine the processes and steps to achieve given objectives and meet deadlines. Workers are required to be self-directed and highly responsible as they are not supervised or supported as closely as in a democratic or autocratic environment. They do not have complete freedom, however, as status or planning meetings may be held or guidelines and deadlines may be established without their involvement.

Some of the strengths of laissez-faire leadership are:

- It develops the leadership skills and competence of workers who are often called upon to use their own initiative, self-manage and create their own schedules.

- It also ensures that workers remain highly committed to the business as they were personally involved in the decisions and the actions that created the successful outcome.

Its weaknesses include:

- In the absence of direct and frequent communication, workers become susceptible to blunders and errors that may not be realised until it is too late.

- It requires a highly trained and responsible workforce which is capable of working on its own initiative.

☞ Now it's your turn

Is any one style of leadership better than the others? Is there a style that should be used at all times? Consider the situations below and state which leadership style is ideal for each. Give reasons to justify your answers.

1 when the organisation is meeting to discuss the budget for the next year

2 deciding which team member should take a free kick in a football match

3 during a fire in the office

4 in a group of nine students responsible for completing a project on leadership styles

5 when the teachers in the math department sit down to decide which topics should be on the next test

6 among a group of soldiers in a training exercise where they are rescuing hostages

7 when deciding what colour to paint the classroom

8 when a design team must come up with the design of a new product.

Conflict

A **conflict** is a disagreement between two or more organisational members or teams. Conflicts are inevitable in an organisation; traditionally they were viewed as unnecessary and harmful, and managers made an effort to eliminate all occurrences of conflict. A modern view is that if conflicts are managed properly many benefits can arise from them, even as their negative side effects are minimised.

Causes of conflict

Management style

A manager's style of managing and communicating with employees may be the stimulus that starts a conflict. Some managers are autocratic, leaving little or no room for discussion and interaction with employees. Such managers are likely to have conflicts, particularly if the workforce is highly trained and educated.

Competition for scarce resources

Conflicts often erupt as a result of scarce resources within a department or in an organisation. Most organisations, faced with limited resources, inevitably allocate more resources to one manager or department than to another. When this happens, the two competing managers/departments are likely to be in conflict. Another way in which conflicts may arise is within a department. If two workers, working on similar tasks, are allocated unequal amounts of resources, then there is likely to be not only a lack of co-operation but also conflict. Additionally, some organisations have incentive programmes that reward the most productive workers, and these programmes can foster conflict as opposed to co-operation.

Lack of communication

Imperfect communication is a feature of all organisations. When communication breaks down, the result is often misunderstanding and misperceptions. When there is miscommunication, there is normally a disagreement about goals, roles or intentions, which will result in conflict. Communication may break down inadvertently because the receiver is not listening actively or has simply misunderstood the sender (perhaps because of cultural, social or personal differences). However, sometimes the sender may deliberately withhold information so as to sabotage or embarrass a colleague.

Clash of personalities

Some people are quiet and reflective, do not speak very often and are always polite and considerate. They are quite anxious to keep the peace and are even prepared to accept the blame in order to do so. Others, however, are combative and prefer the argumentative approach, giving immediate responses with little thought, and often try to 'win' arguments by speaking loudly. If two argumentative people meet in an organisation then there is likely to be conflict.

Working conditions

If workers are displeased with the conditions under which they are asked to work, this may lead to conflict between management and workers. This conflict may also arise from salaries being inadequate, the physical environment of the workplace being unsuitable or working hours being too long. This kind of conflict may result in industrial action such as strikes, work-to-rule or go slow (these are discussed later in the chapter; see page 53).

Conflict resolution

So far we have said that conflicts are useful if they are managed properly – very often, a better organisational structure emerges from a conflict that would not have been developed had there not been a conflict. Conflicts should not be allowed to continue indefinitely – strategies must be employed to resolve conflicts within an acceptable time. Given the central role of trade unions in resolving conflicts, any discussion of conflict resolution must start with this important group.

Trade unions

A **trade union** is an organisation responsible for protecting the interest of workers who are its members.

Trade unions ensure that their members are fairly rewarded, that the working conditions are acceptable and that other aspects of their employment (such as promotions, holiday allowance and dismissal) are in keeping with what is required by their contracts and by the law. A trade union is instrumental in resolving conflicts as it holds great sway over workers – it is usually able to advise workers on when they should accept an offer from management as opposed to holding out for a better one. Additionally, they are usually responsible for mobilising workers to take industrial action. A trade union may perform the following functions:

- ensure that employees work under suitable conditions
- obtain fair wages for employees
- ensure that workers get the leave and holiday allowances due to them
- ensure that workers injured on the job obtain adequate compensation
- educate workers on their rights as an employee
- act as a negotiator on workers' behalf
- ensure that when dismissal of workers takes place, workers are treated fairly.

Employee strategies

When employers and employees are in conflict, employees may engage in industrial action in order to resolve the conflict. Industrial action can take the following forms:

- **Strike**: a strike occurs when workers refuse to work in order to put pressure on employers to address a grievance. A strike is a collective act, not a series of individual actions – a majority of workers must agree to stop working at the same time. When a strike takes place, the workers usually do not turn up for work or do so only to picket (which is the act of forming a line of protest – called a picket line – in front of the workplace). A strike is usually accompanied by a protest – workers may use placards and rallies to attract public support for their cause.
- **Sick-out**: a sick-out occurs when workers refuse to work, under the pretext of being ill – workers usually call in to inform the company that they are sick when in fact they are taking industrial action.
- **Work to rule**: workers may choose to turn up for work, but do only the minimum that is contractually required of them. They make no effort to engage in

overtime work, do not use their initiative to solve problems which are not explicitly defined as their jobs and ensure that they honour their contract to the letter and no more.

- **Go slow**: this happens when workers deliberately slow down the rate of production and output to put pressure on management to address their grievances. When go slow takes place, workers do not withdraw their labour; rather they simply do not exert the requisite level of effort. Go slow is closely related to work to rule, except that with go slow workers may do less than is contractually required of them.

Going on strike is a popular strategy used by workers to get the attention of management.

Employer strategies

Employers may take the following actions to resolve industrial conflicts:

- **Lockout**: in order to put pressure on workers, managers may initiate a lockout. This is a temporary work stoppage in which workers are prevented from accessing the organisation and, as a result, are unable to work. Lockouts may become necessary if the business feels that it is better to prevent everyone from working if key departments or individuals have taken strike action.
- **Scab labour**: a scab worker is one who is employed to temporarily replace a worker who is on strike. Scab labourers are sometimes called strike-breakers

(since they do not strike when unionised workers are on strike) or replacement workers.

Strategies to manage conflicts

Arbitration: this is the process of taking a conflict to an impartial third party for resolution. The arbitration process usually involves a hearing where the parties present their cases and the arbitrator makes a ruling. Generally, the result of the arbitration process is binding – meaning that each party in the conflict must accept the arbitrator's decision.

Mediation: this is similar to arbitration, except the impartial third party does not have the authority to make a settlement; instead, through communication, the third party tries to negotiate a mutually acceptable settlement. Mediation, then, is more of an *assisted* settlement while arbitration is an *imposed* settlement. In mediation, the mediator tries to explore areas of potential agreement between conflicting parties by talking to them separately. Separating parties, it is hoped, will cause them to reveal to the neutral mediator what they would not have revealed to each other. The mediator's job is to use this trust to achieve resolution.

Grievance procedure: this is the set of established steps to be taken if a grievance or conflict arises. The grievance procedure usually outlines what is expected of the trade unions, workers, management and owners. It also outlines at what point arbitrators and mediators would be approached and, if these fail, the minister of labour or relevant government officials. Usually, a strike is the last resort and is to be used only if all other options have failed. The trade union, therefore, has a responsibility to ensure that it pursues all other options before resorting to any form of industrial action.

Summary – Section C

- Providing objective, strategic leadership that empowers others is one of the fundamental duties of management.

- Democratic leaders allow followers to be involved in the decision-making process; autocratic leaders do not seek the opinions of followers when making decisions; laissez-faire leaders allow followers great freedom to complete tasks and use their initiative.

- Conflicts exist when workers or departments have disagreements for reasons such as management styles, allocation of resources, breakdown in communication, personality differences and inadequate working conditions.

- Trade unions play an important role in preventing and resolving conflicts by ensuring that workers are satisfied with their salaries and working conditions.

- Employees seek resolution to conflicts by taking industrial action such as going on strike, working to rule and going slow. Employers seek resolution by employing scab labour and using lockouts.

- Parties in a conflict may also seek arbitration and mediation as ways of resolving conflicts.

End of section activities

Quick questions

I State which of type of leadership is being demonstrated in each situation below (be prepared to justify your answer). If you cannot say which style is being employed, then explain why you are not sure.

  a A manager allows workers to work from home on a project, as long as they send a report of their activities at the end of each week.

  b The office manager places samples of paint on the notice board and asks workers to vote on the one they think should be used to paint the office.

  c Workers are allowed to submit different names for the company's newsletter so that the committee can select the best one.

  d Workers are placed in groups and given three weeks to complete a proposal for a new product design.

e At the start of each month, factory workers are told how many units of the product they should produce that month.

f The date for a class party is decided on after lengthy consultations with the members of the class, the class teacher and the principal.

Applying what you have learnt

1 Many people lead by inspiring fear in their followers. What do you think of this approach? Do you think it works? Is it effective at preventing disobedience and low effort in subordinates? Why would you support or discourage this approach?

2 In some countries, it is illegal for workers to strike. What do you think about this? Do you think every worker should have the right to strike? What about people such as doctors, police and firemen, who provide essential services? Should they have the right to strike as well?

3 Some people think that being a democratic leader is actually harder than being an autocratic leader. Why do you think this may be so? Democratic leaders practise what is called 'refereeing'; what is this and what impact does it have on how difficult a leader's job may be?

Model exam questions

Question 1

a List three qualities of a good leader. (3 marks)

b Give one advantage that autocratic leadership has over democratic leadership. (3 marks)

c State the type of leadership that would work best in a situation where followers are highly trained, educated and experienced. Give two reasons for your answer. (4 marks)

Question 2

a List three causes of organisational conflict. (3 marks)

b What roles do trade unions play in resolving conflicts? (3 marks)

c Discuss two strategies used by workers to resolve conflicts. (6 marks)

Question 3

a What is a trade union? (3 marks)

b List three functions of a trade union. (3 marks)

c How can trade unions help to manage conflict in an organisation? (3 marks)

Question 4

Carla works in an organisation that encourages workers to engage in open and frequent communication. Most decisions are fully discussed and Carla and her co-workers are allowed to contribute to the discussions.

a Name the style of leadership that exists in the organisation and give reasons for your answer. (4 marks)

b Under what conditions is this leadership style ideal? (4 marks)

c Discuss three ways in which Carla and her co-workers benefit from this leadership style. (6 marks)

d Outline two challenges that the organisation is likely to experience arising from the use of this leadership style. (6 marks)

Question 5

The workers at TDP Factory are upset about the dismissal of a worker, who they think was laid off unfairly. They are thinking of protesting but are waiting for the outcome of a meeting between their trade union and management.

a List three other potential sources of conflict between management and workers. (3 marks)

b Discuss two steps that the trade union can take in resolving the conflict between workers and management. (6 marks)

c Outline two actions that workers can take if they decide to protest. (6 marks)

d Discuss two reasons why protest actions should be a last resort. (5 marks)

4 Communication, information and the business plan

> You can have brilliant ideas, but if you can't get them across, your ideas won't get you anywhere. – *Lee Iacocca*

An environment that promotes effective and open communication is ideal in the workplace.

Talk is cheap – or is it?

Information is power – especially if it can be shared effectively and efficiently. The Government of Jamaica (GoJ) understands well the importance of sharing accurate information quickly and efficiently – after all, it has 14 ministries, over 50 agencies and thousands of employees who must all operate in synchronisation even as they pursue different goals and interests. One of the ideas recently suggested to the GoJ to develop efficient communication is that of using mobile phones on a closed user group (CUG). A CUG is an arrangement where a number of people are allowed to make calls to and receive calls from each other, usually for a fixed monthly rate. As more ministries experiment with CUGs to solve their communication problems, Digicel (one of the largest cellular service providers in the Caribbean) has partnered with Research in Motion (RIM), parent company for the BlackBerry line of products, and CISCO to show how mobile solutions can be used to create efficiency and reduce the government's communication-related expenditure. While Digicel has made great inroads in the consumer market for cellular phones and service, they have not been as successful in corporate communication. The hope is that some of the options that Digicel Business ICT Solutions have created will become the standard mode of communication within and between the ministries.

The attempts of the GoJ to solve its communication problem are relevant to all large businesses as, indeed, efficient communication is one of the most important concerns that businesses have. This is one of the issues that will be discussed in this chapter.

In this chapter you will:

- discuss considerations involved in business communication
- outline the role of a management information system (MIS)
- discuss the impact of an MIS on business operation
- discuss the nature and features of entrepreneurism
- describe the profile of a typical entrepreneur
- discuss why people may choose to establish their own businesses
- discuss the importance of primary and secondary sources of information
- discuss the options people have for sourcing capital to start their business
- discuss why collateral is important in the establishment of a business
- discuss the roles of business plans and feasibility studies in starting a business
- discuss ethical and legal considerations in operating a business.

SECTION A Communication and management information systems

The communication process

A nod of the head, a movement of the hand or an explicit 'yes' or 'no' – these are all examples of **communication**, each of which is relevant for specific occasions and situations. Communication is described as the sharing of information and understanding between or among agents. Communication is often seen as a process that takes place between the sender (creator) and receiver. The communication process involves a message being sent between these two agents and feedback being given. It means, therefore, that each agent – sender and receiver – is always alternating their roles when they give feedback. As receivers process messages from the sender, they will create messages of their own in the form of feedback – thus, feedback ensures that the receivers become the senders and vice versa. The communication process is shown in Figure 4.1.

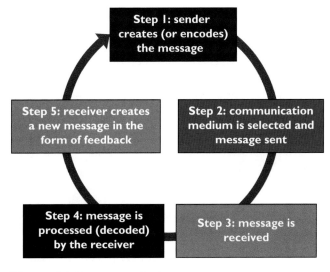

Figure 4.1 The communication process.

Communication media

How do you communicate with your friends, your family or your teacher? Do you use the same method for each – for example, while you may send your friend a text message or a message on Facebook, would you do the same with your teacher? Do you think the same method of communication is always suitable, regardless of the receiver? A communication medium is the manner in which you choose to transmit the message – for example, you may choose to write a letter, send an email, make a phone call or have a meeting. Each medium is discussed briefly below.

Face-to-face meeting

Meetings are ideal when an important, highly technical message is to be shared with a large group. The technical nature of the message ensures that repetition and explanation of the important points will become necessary and that a forum for questions and immediate feedback is presented. Face-to-face communication has the following major advantages:

- Feedback is immediate.
- Non-verbal communication (body language such as eye movement, posture and gestures) can also be used.

However, face-to-face communication also has its problems:

- Without guidance and leadership, meetings will not be productive.
- It is difficult to schedule meetings, especially those that involve many different people.

Face-to-face meetings are ideal for large group discussions and to facilitate immediate feedback.

- There is no opportunity to edit messages or feedback (and thereby correct errors) *before* they are sent.

Telephone

Telephone communication is a cost-effective way of sharing information and receiving feedback. As with meetings, it allows for immediate feedback but, unfortunately, it facilitates only limited non-verbal communication (tone of voice). Additionally, it solves the problems of scheduling that exist when meetings are to be held and allows distance and time to become insignificant. It is limited, however, in that only verbal information can be shared via the telephone.

Written communication

This is the most traditional form of communication and, hence, it is most frequently used for formalising or confirming communication that has already been made via email or the telephone. Written communication includes letters, memoranda (memos), reports and even flyers (for notice boards, etc.). The advantages of written communication include:

- The creation of a 'paper trail' – it acts as evidence of communication, since a copy of the message can be sent to many parties and one kept on file to act as corroborating evidence if the message is disputed at a later date.
- It allows for the message to be edited before it is sent and, as a result, ensures that there aren't as many mistakes, and therefore misunderstandings are less likely.

Its disadvantages include:

- The 'turn-around' time on messages sent using this medium is very long – a long time elapses from the sending of the message to the feedback being received.
- Little or no use of non-verbal methods to support communication – gestures, facial expressions, posture and tone are not included in this communication method.

Email and internet

Many new communication media have evolved with the introduction and widespread use of the internet and computers in businesses. Email, however, is the most popular of these forms of communication. An email is a message sent over the internet – it can be written or recorded and sent as a video or audio file. As the internet has evolved, messages can now be sent containing multimedia elements – sound, pictures, video and texts can be sent in the same message.

This ensures that an email can contain the main message as well as supporting visual aids. The uniqueness of emails is further enhanced by the fact that messages are sent and delivered instantly without regards to distance and time – an email can be *sent* and *delivered* even if the receiver is not immediately accessible (the receiver will simply *access* it at a convenient time). Emails also create the same paper trail that written communication does; indeed, given that emails are date and time stamped, they may perform this role better than traditional written communication. The major disadvantage of email communication is that senders and receivers may experience problems accessing the internet or operating a computer. Additionally, the cost of using this medium effectively and efficiently is very high and in some cases is prohibitive.

Think about it

Have you ever been cc'd in an email? To be cc'd, or copied in, is to receive a message which may be of interest to you but was originally created for someone else. In email etiquette, however, this is not always the case as the 'cc' option is often abused – most people simply use it to forward messages to everyone in their electronic address book. But exactly what does 'cc' mean? The abbreviation 'cc' is used to represent 'carbon copy' and is a reference to an era when computers and printers did not exist in offices. In order to make a copy of a written document, writers would use carbon paper to create a carbon copy. Carbon paper is a thin sheet of paper coated on one side with ink, which was placed between two sheets of paper – whatever is written on the top page would be traced out onto the bottom page, thus creating a copy. So, that explains 'cc' but what about 'bcc' – what does that mean? Both options are present when sending an email, but how are they different? Try sending a few messages to friends using each or both options and see how they receive the message with each option. How do these options help in creating a paper trail?

Choosing a communication medium

How does a sender determine the medium to be used in communication? What do you consider when you are sending a message? Do you share everything with your friends on Facebook? There are many factors to

be considered when selecting a medium of communication. Some of these factors are outlined below.

- **What is to be communicated?** Consideration must be given to the message being sent before choosing a method of communication – for example, if the message is confidential, then a face-to-face meeting may be best, while an official reprimand or warning may need to be a letter for record-keeping purposes. Additionally, if the message is to be heard or seen by many people, it may be best if it is written down so that each person can take a copy. Another consideration is the speed with which the message needs to be sent – verbal or electronic communication may be best if the message needs to be sent immediately. Finally, it is better to write down long messages than to burden the listener with many details they may soon forget.

- **Why is it to be communicated?** The purpose of the message is also important in deciding on the method to use. Messages that are official may need to be kept and are therefore best written down; messages for a large group of people should perhaps be written down and placed on a notice board. Messages that act as reminders may be announced at the time when the reminder is necessary.

- **Who needs to know?** If a message is to be disseminated among a large number of people, then it may be best to send it by email to everyone at the same time, as a memo to all receivers, or hold a face-to-face meeting.

Now it's your turn

Which medium of communication is best for each of the following situations? Justify your response, especially if you select two or more media for a situation.

1 reporting on the results of an advertisement campaign

2 explaining how the new telephone system in the office works

3 commending the members of a department on meeting the target for the month

4 warning a team member about his delinquent behaviour

5 deciding on the venue for the next staff retreat

6 sharing digital pictures from the last staff retreat

7 creating targets for each month.

Think about it

Facebook, Twitter and other internet-based methods of communication have become very popular recently. In addition, the popularity of more traditional forms of communication on the internet such as Yahoo!, Messenger and Hotmail Instant Messaging remains very strong. These have been joined by short messaging services (SMS) or text messages and BlackBerry Messenger using a BlackBerry PIN. Do you think it is ever advisable to use any of these forms of communication to communicate formal, official work-related information to a work colleague? Why or why not?

Barriers to effective communication

- **Overload**: if too much information is being processed by people and/or departments in an organisation, then overload is taking place. Overload results from people receiving irrelevant information, and it is a waste of their time to have to sort through it.

- **Inappropriate chain of command**: the more levels that information has to pass through before it gets to the receiver, the more likely it is to be changed. If the chain of command is too long, then information has to pass through many levels to get from management to workers. This may take time and delay the decision making. In 'flat' organisations, information is quickly shared between managers and workers with little or no risk that it may get corrupted.

- **Inappropriate span of control**: if the span of control is too wide, then a manager may not have enough time and energy to communicate properly with subordinates. In addition, subordinates may not be able to access supervisors because of the demand that exists for their time.

- **Change**: changes in managers may bring about changes in attitudes and communication styles that may negatively affect the communication process.

- **Rank or status in the company**: some people, as a result of their rank or status in the organisation, are unavailable for meetings and are generally inaccessible. Rank or status may also make lower-level workers timid and hesitant to share information. Additionally, highly ranked managers may be unwilling to listen to and accept suggestions from lower-level workers.

- **Electronic noise**: noise refers to any distraction that disrupts the communication process. Many people are unaccustomed to using technology in communication and may feel that technology is actually a barrier to communication. Some people also argue that technology has replaced much of the personal feelings and emotions that once existed in face-to-face communication. For example, many of the non-verbal elements of a face-to-face meeting cannot be replicated in a telephone conversation.

Management information systems (MIS)

When you think about it, a tremendous amount of information passes through an organisation on a daily basis – customers' demographic information, information on the nature of sales, inventory information and production details are just some of the examples of information a company receives in its day-to-day operations. The problem, however, is that this information is scattered throughout the organisation in different departments – for example, while the sales department may have information about the nature of sales, it may not be aware of inventory information. If the business really wants to harness the potential of the information that each department generates, then it must find a way to bring each piece of information together to create an overall picture of the firm. This is where the **management information system** becomes important. An MIS is used for capturing and sorting data and providing information for the efficient organisation and operation of the business. An MIS ensures that managers and other decision makers are armed with the requisite information for making decisions, capitalising on opportunities and carrying out day-to-day operations. In an organisation, the MIS plays the following roles:

- **Improves communication among employees**: since the MIS will create a greater level of interaction between departments, it is likely that communication among employees will improve as they work together to capitalise on the opportunities revealed by the MIS.

- **Delivers complex information throughout the organisation**: an MIS draws on information from different sources all over the organisation and, as a result, will reveal ideas and solutions that looking at the departments individually would not have done. In other words, the MIS sees the organisation as one system with many inter-related departments; however, without an MIS it is difficult to see the organisation as anything but a series of unrelated departments. Without a general overview, complex information cannot be provided, as information from one department is not likely to be weighed against information from another department.

- **Improves decision making in the organisation**: an MIS provides the information that can be used to make better decisions. It also assists the business in monitoring its activities and resources and, as a result, the business is better able to allocate resources throughout the organisation.

- **Provides a comprehensive and objective system for recording information**: once set up, the MIS will simply record all relevant information. If this were left up to individuals, then objectivity might be lost as employees choose to record information that appeals to them. Additionally, the MIS has the capability to record information captured by other information systems in other departments, and therefore it also combines relevant information.

- **Reduces labour-related expenses arising from manual activities**: an MIS is really a network of computers that capture information from other departments. It is more cost effective, more efficient and less prone to errors to have an MIS do this than individuals putting in many hours.

- **Supports the organisation's strategic goals and direction**: the MIS is able to deliver information that provides guidance for managers in achieving the goals and objectives of the organisation.

Challenges faced by the MIS

If an MIS presents so many benefits to the organisation, why do so many firms not have one? The truth is that, for many reasons, these systems are usually found in large businesses. An MIS works best when there are many departments from which it can draw information to create a comprehensive look at the organisation – small businesses may not have strict divisions of departments and hence may not benefit as much from an MIS. Additionally, and more importantly, an MIS is very expensive to set up, monitor and operate. This cost is often prohibitive for small businesses, which may have a problem investing in the requisite hardware and human resources to establish and operate an MIS.

Another challenge posed by the MIS – for both large and small businesses – is related to the risk that having an MIS poses. Information must be protected from outside breaches – such as computer hackers who may try to compromise the system by accessing the organisation's information. In addition, because the MIS provides information to guide decision makers, incorrect information will lead to flawed decisions. An MIS is only as effective as the information that it provides – if the system is poorly programmed or easily manipulated, then it is likely to generate incorrect information, which will in turn lead to poor planning.

🖉 End of section activities

Quick questions

1 The following are some advantages of various communication media. In each case, state which communication medium possesses that advantage (if there are many media with that advantage, list each one).

a allows sender to correct the message before it is sent

b allows quick sharing of messages

c is relatively inexpensive

d leaves a paper trail

e immediate feedback is possible

f facilitates non-verbal communication

g eliminates the need for scheduling

h allows visual aids to be used in communication

2 The following are some clues of some of the important ideas covered in business communication. What ideas are described by each clue?

a this occurs when too much information is processed by a person

b the person who creates the message in a communication process

c a distraction that disrupts the communication process

d a response to a message

e various ways of sending a message

f evidence that communication has taken place

g communication that takes place with body language

h oral communication without face-to-face contact

Applying what you have learnt

1 Form a line with 15 people. The person at the front of the line whispers something to the second person. Continue to pass the message from person to person down to the end of the line and compare what the person at the end of the line hears to what was originally said. Ensure that each person *whispers* to the next person and do not allow repetition of the original message. Is the final message the same as the original? What implications does this have for how businesses are organised?

2 An MIS captures information from each department and business unit in the organisation. Most businesses have at least the four basic functional areas listed below. What sort of information do you think an MIS should capture from **each** functional area?

a marketing

b human resources

c finance

d production

3 'Large businesses are better at communicating than small businesses because they are able to invest in expensive communication systems.' Do you think that this is true? Why or why not?

Model exam questions

Question 1

a List any three communication media. (3 marks)

b For each medium mentioned in (a), list one situation when it would be the best communication medium. (3 marks)

c Outline two factors that are to be considered when deciding on which communication medium to use. (6 marks)

Question 2

a With the use of examples, outline the communication process. (5 marks)

b Describe two factors that are likely to disrupt the communication process. (6 marks)

Question 3

a Define what is meant by a management information system (MIS). (3 marks)

b Outline two benefits that an MIS offers to a business. (6 marks)

c Discuss one factor that challenges the establishment of an MIS in an organisation. (3 marks)

Question 4

Cavell Francis is the general manager of Betta Life Ltd, a small company that employs eight workers. She is thinking of improving the communication system in the company. Currently, most communication takes place by face-to-face meetings or through letters, since no inter-office telephone system exists.

a Discuss two factors that Cavell should consider if she is to make the communication system in the organisation more effective. (6 marks)

b Discuss one advantage and one disadvantage of any other communication method that Cavell may choose to implement. (6 marks)

c Explain why face-to-face meetings may be ideal in a small organisation such as Betta Life Ltd. (4 marks)

d Discuss two reasons why communication is important for business. (4 marks)

Question 5

Carl Young and Associates Ltd is a large organisation, which has a traditional hierarchical organisational structure. Its communication system, however, is inefficient and often results in messages being delayed or corrupted. A consultant has told its managers that this may be due to the 'span of control' and the 'chain of command' of the organisation.

a Define what is meant by:

i span of control

ii chain of command. (6 marks)

b Explain how each concept in (a) may result in an inefficient communication system. (6 marks)

c Aside from those reasons offered by the consultant, discuss one reason why a large organisation may have an inefficient communication system. (4 marks)

d Outline how the breakdown in communication may affect workers in the organisation. (4 marks)

Who is an entrepreneur?

Claudia Pegus, a successful fashion designer from Trinidad and Tobago for over 20 years, is one of the Caribbean's leading entrepreneurs.

What do Gordon 'Butch' Stewart (from Jamaica), Claudia Pegus (from Trinidad and Tobago) and Sir Allan Fields (from Barbados) have in common? They are all considered to be **entrepreneurs** – people who organise a business venture and assume the majority of the risk of operating it. As entrepreneurs, these individuals started and operated businesses with profit as their motive. Entrepreneurs are known for their ability to see business opportunities where no one else has and exploit these opportunities to create profitable businesses. Given the unique nature of the products and services that new businesses created by entrepreneurs tend to offer, it is not unusual for them to fail. Indeed, many entrepreneurs are likely to have many failed attempts before they find a successful business opportunity. As a result, entrepreneurs must not only be smart with money, but must also be comfortable exposing their money and resources to risk. The following characteristics are important for entrepreneurs:

- They must accept all risks and responsibilities associated with operating the business. In addition, they must be tolerant of uncertainty and be willing to hedge their bets.
- They must be creative and innovative in the area, task or activity around which the business is built.

- Entrepreneurs must be flexible – they must be able to adjust their ideas, approaches or philosophy in a dynamic commercial environment.
- They must be excellent at management and executing all its functions.
- They must be self-driven and persistent – entrepreneurs must be able to remain motivated if and when the business is not doing well.
- Entrepreneurs must be self-directing – they must possess the ability to work on their own initiative and without direction from others.
- Entrepreneurs must be highly energetic and goal oriented – they must be willing to work hard to ensure that the business is very successful. For ordinary employees, it is likely that their loyalty to the business is tied to the salary that they receive. The entrepreneur, however, is aware of the fact that it is *his* or *her* money that is at risk and therefore he or she must be prepared to put in long hours to secure it.

Why do people establish their own business?

Would you start a business? Many people are afraid of taking the risk – even though they would like to make their own profit and stop working for others! Starting a business is often described as being similar to bungee-jumping – scary yet thrilling at the same time. Many people take the plunge of starting a business. Some of the reasons are:

- **Profit**: the chance of making a decent profit is very appealing and many people are willing to start their own business for this reason. Indeed, the richest people in the world are entrepreneurs – not movie stars, sport stars or any other celebrities.
- **Opportunity**: the opportunity to exploit an idea or to turn a skill into income has always appealed to many people who start their own business. For example, someone with a knack for designing clothes may choose to start a dressmaking company instead of working for someone else.
- **Financial independence**: the ability to be one's own boss is still a strong reason for starting a business. Many people do not like the stress associated with working for others; instead, they are happier when they can set their own hours

and make their own decisions. Additionally, many individuals prefer making their own money and being wholly in charge of their earning potential and job security.

- **Self-actualisation**: self-actualisation occurs when people realise their full potential. Many individuals feel that they are unable to self-actualise when they work for others as they are limited in what they are able to do. They may attempt to solve this problem by starting a business, which requires the full set of skills that they have.

Think about it

Carry out a survey of 5–10 classmates. How many of them would start businesses? What are the reasons that they give for wanting to start a business? For those with no interest in starting a business, what reason do they have for their decision?

Steps in starting a business

So you have decided you want to start a business when you leave school. Where do you go from here? We can see some of the steps you must take to go about establishing your business in Figure 4.2 below.

Financing a business venture

One of the most important issues on which you must decide if you are starting a new business is how you will finance it. This issue is important because if the capital is borrowed, it must eventually be repaid, with interest also being paid each year. Furthermore, if the decision is taken to organise the business as a limited liability company, then the selling of shares has implications for the ownership of the business. Finally, using personal sources of funding, such as savings, may limit the size of the business that can be established, since these personal sources of funding are limited. The sources from which an entrepreneur may raise capital include:

- **Loans**: borrowing to start a business is quite popular among entrepreneurs. Loans can be obtained from banks, credit unions, micro-finance institutions and small business associations. If loans are obtained to start the business, then interest will have to be taken out of the revenues the company makes on an annual basis. This is called servicing the loan. Entrepreneurs who start their business using loans often use collateral to secure the loans. A collateral is an asset owned by the borrower, which is offered as security for a loan, with the understanding that the collateral may be seized if the loan is not properly serviced (see pages 65–6 for more information about collateral).

Step 1: Conceptualisation

What kind of business will you start?
What products wll you sell?

Step 2: Research (market probe)

Who wants to buy your products? Is there a viable market for the product? What variations of the product will you have to offer? At what price will you be able to sell the product?

Step 3: Identification of resources

What human resources will you need? What raw material will the business employ? How much money will the business need?

Step 4: Creation of business plan

Where will you locate the business? Hou will you finance the business? How will the business be managed?

Step 5: Acquisition of funds

Where will you get funds? Will you use banks or credit unions? If bank, which bank will you use?

Step 6: Operation of the business

How will the business be managed? How will the workers and resources be distributed acorss the business's departments? What structure will be created for communication to flow?

Figure 4.2 Steps in starting a business.

- **Shares**: if the business is being established as a company, then it will sell shares to obtain the capital that it needs. Shareholders are entitled to receive dividends each year and this too is to be taken out of the profit. Dividends are paid, however, after interest and other expenses are paid.

 Now it's your turn

There is an ongoing debate over whether it is better to use loans or share capital (also called equity) to establish or expand a business. Do some research (on the internet, perhaps) and discuss the benefits and drawbacks of using each. How would you prefer to start or expand your business – through loans or shares?

- **Savings**: entrepreneurs often use their personal savings to start businesses. This can be amassed from years of diligent saving, from informal saving plans such as partners or sou-sou (see page 177) or from windfalls such as inheritance or winnings. Savings, however, are often insufficient to address all the needs of a new business and, for this reason, the entrepreneur may choose to start small and use the funds generated over time to expand the business. Using the profits to expand the business is described as ploughing back the profit into the business and is an important source of funds for expanding the business or for starting a new business.
- **Venture capital**: if you have a new business idea but lack the capital, then you may allow an individual to buy into the idea, by providing you with capital to start the venture in exchange for part ownership of the business. The money you obtain in this arrangement is called venture capital, but it comes at a high price. The venture capitalist will insist on a large share of the ownership of the business and, as a result, will also obtain a large portion of your annual profit. Many venture capitalists are also becoming less of a silent partner as they are insisting that they have more of a say in how and by whom the business is run, in order to secure their investments. A venture capital arrangement is different from a loan arrangement since a regular lender does not obtain ownership in the business, while a venture capitalist does.

The role of collateral

As mentioned before, collateral is an asset used to secure a loan. Collateral is used to offset whatever risk the lender feels he may not want to bear. For example, a borrower may promise to offer up his house as collateral if he is unable to pay back the interest and principal that he has borrowed from the bank. By offering his house as collateral, he reassures the lender by showing that he (the lender) has entered a win–win situation, where he will receive either a profit on his loan (in the form of interest) or a house. There are various types of collateral:

- **Property**: land and buildings (also called real estate) are popular forms of collateral since they are often very valuable and will remain that way for a long time. Long-term lenders do not like collateral such as motor cars, which may depreciate in value over the life of the loan – a motor car that is used to secure a 20-year loan may break down after only six years of the loan arrangement. Real estate is, therefore, ideal when the life of the loan is very long.
- **Plant and equipment**: the business plant is the business manufacturing facility with its expensive equipment and machines. These may not remain valuable for as long as real estate and, hence, may not be accepted for long-term loans; they are, however, ideal for medium-term loans.
- **Securities**: a security is a financial asset such as the shares held in a company. An individual may offer this as collateral in order to obtain and secure loans.
- **Stock**: the stock a business has may be used to secure short-term (30–90 days) loans. Many businesses borrow against their stock or take goods on credit with the promise to repay when stock has been sold.
- **Motor cars**: as mentioned before, these tend to depreciate (lose value) quickly and would not be used to secure long-term loans.

Now it's your turn

Items used as collateral are often expensive, have a stable value and are easy to sell – since lenders do not really want the collateral, they should be able to sell it easily without much cost to them. Against this background, which of the following are collaterals that you would accept if you had one million dollars to lend? In each case, justify your answer.

- jewellery
- a race horse
- a painting by a well-known artist
- a deed to a piece of land
- shares in a company
- a first-edition copy of the novel *Moby Dick*, signed by the author
- a guitar that belonged to Bob Marley
- one of Michael Jackson's famous white gloves.

A business plan is presented to potential investors as a way of obtaining capital.

The significance of collateral

Collateral plays an important role in accessing capital to establish or expand a business. Collateral creates a mutuality of interest and coincidence of desires in the financial market. There are many people offering loans and perhaps just as many (if not more) people attempting to access these loans. Very often, however, there is no coincidence of desires as lenders do not find the borrowers suitable – perhaps they are perceived as being risky borrowers who may default on their loans. Coincidence of desires between lenders and borrowers, however, is likely to be reached if borrowers are prepared to show their good faith by offering up something valuable as collateral.

Collateral also plays another subtle role – it compels the borrower to make an effort to repay. If the borrower knows that she stands to lose a valuable personal property – for example, her house – then it is very likely that she will make a greater effort to repay the loan than if there was no risk of losing anything. The collateral, then, is a way of anchoring the borrower's intentions with a real asset.

The business plan

One of the steps mentioned above when we discussed starting a business was the creation of the **business plan**. A business plan is a comprehensive written description of the nature and elements of a proposed business. The business plan will contain information on the marketing, financing and operation of the business. A business plan forces entrepreneurs to think about the logistics of starting and operating a business – after all, many business ideas exist, but are they all practical and profitable? The business plan is also essential if the entrepreneur will be seeking finance from banks or other lending institutions – these lenders insist on seeing how their money will be used, and the plan is perfect for this. A business plan has the following main sections:

- **Executive summary**: this section is a short description of the proposed venture and is important because it introduces the proposed business to the reader of the plan. It contains basic but important elements such as a description of the business, a discussion on the basic business model and the objectives or mission of the business.

- **Company background**: if the business has been in operation before the plan was written, then this is a useful section that shows information about the past performance of the business. Some businesses may have started out on a much smaller scale (perhaps from home) before the business plan was written – including information on the business from this early stage of operation may give some indication of your ability to operate a business profitably.

- **Operational plan**: this section outlines how the business will be managed and organised. Will there be departments and department heads? How many departments will there be in the business and what are they? How will an account be given of the resources of the business and what arrangements have been put in place to address critical issues for potential investors such as insurance and contracts?

- **Marketing plan**: this section addresses questions such as:

  - What competition exists in the market?

  - What makes the product unique when compared with others in the market?

  - How large is the market and what portion can the business hope to capture?

  - What are the current trends in the industry or market?

  - Is there a market leader which determines price or is the market more open?

  - What are the strengths and weaknesses of the products offered by the business?

  - How many units of goods are there and at what dollar value will you be able to sell them in a month or a year?

  - What plans are in place for advertising and promotion?

  - What are the strengths and weaknesses of the location of the business?

- **Financial plans**: in this section projections are made for the income the business is likely to generate over a five-year period. Expenses and funding for the same five-year period are also detailed. These estimates should be plausible and sufficient justification for them should be given. They should not be inflated or understated to gain an advantage – this is one of the most important sections for potential investors and it will be scrutinised; it should, therefore, be a fair representation of what the entrepreneur reasonably expects to happen.

- **Manufacturing analysis**: this section is essential only if the business is involved in production – businesses in retail or services may find this section unnecessary for their business plans. Details about the factory and its capacity, the machinery required, the stock to be used and the system of quality control to be employed are usually included in this section.

Information for planning

When you set out to write a business plan, you have to be very familiar with the market and industry into which you will be entering. This is because you need to include in the plan a great amount of detail on expected sales, the number of competitors, the target audience for your product, and the prices that you can reasonably charge for the product that you will offer. While you can easily obtain some of this information (such as who your competitors are) from the internet and other sources, obtaining other pieces of information may take more work on your part. To obtain the information you want, there are two main sources of information to which you may turn – primary and secondary sources.

Primary sources

Primary sources are useful when you require information that no one has gathered before. It is possible that other businesses may have wanted similar information in the past and would have spent some time gathering the information for their own purposes. You may now be able to use this information to suit your own purpose. If this information does not already exist, however, then you must turn to the market yourself to obtain the information. Since you are the first to collect the information, it is referred to as primary information. Primary information may be obtained through research, which may take the form of observations, surveys and interviews.

Secondary sources

These sources provide information that has already been collected by another company or individual but which you may also use for your own purpose. Secondary sources are usually in the public domain – meaning any member of the public is able to access and use these sources. The internet, for example, is a source of secondary information, since it contains information that anyone can access and use. A few secondary sources, however, are not as accessible by any member of the public. Consider, for example, a piece of research that another company has already done for its own internal use – it is unlikely that this piece of research would be available within the public domain, even though it becomes a secondary source of information when you use it for your own planning. Secondary sources of information include the internet, newspapers, advertisements, magazines, companies' publicly released financial records and information filed with the government if and when the business was incorporated.

Now it's your turn

You are about to start a business selling used cars. You have identified that you want to know the following information before you start the business. State whether you would use primary or secondary sources of information in each case. Justify your answer.

1 How many other used car dealers are in the area?

2 How many used cars are sold each year?

3 What laws govern the importation of used cars?

4 Do people prefer to buy used cars or new cars?

5 What factors determine the demand for used cars?

6 Which make and model of car is most popular in your country?

Taking the plunge – the last words

The research you do before you take the plunge of starting a business is not limited to providing information for the business plan only; you are also trying to discern from the research whether the business is feasible. Will you be able to make a profit or at least break even? To answer these questions, you may have to carry out a feasibility study. This is simply an assessment of the business idea, carried out to assess whether the idea is viable, practical and likely to return profit. The study is done before the business idea is implemented, as the results of the study will determine whether the idea will be implemented at all. In a feasibility study, the risks of the business and associated costs are weighed against the revenues that the business will generate. Non-monetary factors, such as the entrepreneur's belief in his ability, are not considered as a part of the feasibility study. Essentially, the business is feasible if it generates greater revenues than costs at an acceptable level of risk. The purposes of a feasibility study are discussed below.

- To determine if a business idea should be pursued by providing answers to important questions such as:
  - Is the business idea viable in its current form?
  - How much profit is the business idea expected to make over a given period?
  - For how long after its start-up is the business likely to make a loss?
- To evaluate alternative business ideas or models and to identify the ones which are most likely to be profitable.
- To identify the conditions under which a business idea is viable.
- To identify aspects of a business idea that are least profitable.

Role of planning

From the discussion on starting a business that we have had so far, you will be able to appreciate that planning is vital if you are going to be successful in launching your business and keeping it afloat. Earlier we had defined planning as the process of establishing objectives and setting operations in motion to achieve these objectives. However, we did not discuss the types of plan and the time frame over which various plans are made. Plans are divided into three broad categories based on the time frame that they cover – short term, medium term and long term.

- **Long-term planning** is also called strategic planning and involves the creation of the major goals of the organisation. It provides the overall structure within which the organisation operates on a day-to-day basis. These decisions will affect all other decisions made by all departments in the organisation. This kind of planning is important as it is what creates the focus of an organisation – without a broad vision or goal, the various departments of the organisation will not have a central idea around which to unite and the result would be a loss of momentum.
- **Medium-term planning** or tactical planning is the creation of goals that are tied into the organisation's strategic goals. These plans are more detailed and specific and usually have time spans of up to a few years. Creating an annual budget or a three-year plan are examples of medium-term planning. The importance of medium-term planning lies in the observation that, without these plans, strategic plans will not be achieved. In addition, without medium-term plans, each department would lose sight of the specific targets that they have for a given period – without these targets, it would be difficult to

assess whether the business is being effective or efficient.

- **Short-term planning** or operational planning is carried out by day-to-day management and focuses on individual employees or teams within departments. An operational plan may be the number of barrels that each worker should pack and store in a given week or the number of trips that each worker is to make in a day. These plans are used to determine the workload of departments and to create systems at the micro level within which employees operate – in short, these are the plans with which employees directly engage on a daily basis.

Ethical and legal issues to consider

Imagine that you have a company that sells cellphones, and you hear that the prices of cellphones will be increased on 1 March. Would you buy many cellphones in February (before the price increases) and sell them in March at the new price, thus ensuring that you obtain maximum profit? Would doing this be illegal? If it is not illegal, is it 'right'? This situation highlights the difference between illegal and unethical activities – illegal activities are prevented by law and hence are always wrong. Unethical business activities, however, are merely business practices that are not necessarily illegal but are frowned upon by society or other members of the industry. For example, some may argue that a supplier has the right to sell a product at any price at which consumers are willing to buy it. However, many may also argue that while it is not illegal it is unethical to sell products at new prices when they were bought under an old price regime.

It is always wrong for a company to engage in illegal activities – such as evading taxes, laundering money or selling cigarettes and alcoholic drinks to children. However, it is not illegal (simply unwise from a business perspective) to knowingly sell substandard goods or to sell products that lead to obesity in children. Businesses often gain short-term benefits from engaging in unethical business practices, but they usually suffer major loss of reputation in the long run as the market reacts against them. Some businesses engage in unethical practices because they are prepared to accept the fallout that is associated with doing so. Pepsi and Coca-Cola, for example, have often been accused of unethical business practices as they both target young susceptible teenagers who are anxious to develop the image that drinking Coke and Pepsi is supposed to offer. The following are examples of illegal and unethical business activities.

Illegal business activities

- **Evading taxes**: not paying taxes to the government that are due to them.
- **Money laundering**: knowingly accepting money from criminals. This is described as money laundering because criminals, such as drug dealers, use legitimate businesses to make 'dirty' money 'clean' by using it to carry out transactions such as investments. All returns on these investments now appear to be earned from a legitimate source of income and are considered 'clean'.
- **Insider trading**: employees of a business using their unique knowledge of the business and access to private information to buy and sell the shares of that business at huge profits.
- **Falsifying financial reports**: the final statements, which give an account of the performance of the business for the year, should reflect a true and fair view of the business.

Unethical business practices

- **Misleading advertisements**: the business should not claim that its products do more than they can actually do.
- **Unethical disposal of waste**: disposing of waste in a manner that is unfriendly to the environment is considered unethical in most countries and even illegal in a few.
- **Excessive executive compensation**: allowing senior management to earn excessively high salaries while the business may be making a loss or others in the business may be underpaid is considered unethical.
- **Kickbacks and bribes**: a kickback occurs when a business receives a contract by bribing the person or company responsible for giving out the contract; usually this bribe would take the form of cash.
- **Price fixing**: colluding with competitors to sell competing products for the same price. This eliminates competition among firms and is unfair to the consumers who are likely to be asked to pay high prices at some time in the future.

Summary – Section B

- An entrepreneur is a person who takes on a significant portion of the risk associated with starting and operating a business.

- In addition to being a risk taker, the entrepreneur should also be self-driven, self-directing and energetic.

- Entrepreneurship develops out of the individual's need to earn profits, become independent or self-actualise.

- In starting a business, entrepreneurs have many financing options, including loans (which must be secured by collateral), share capital, venture capital and their own personal savings.

- The business plan is an important aspect of starting a business. It is a detailed description of the proposed business, written before the business has been properly established and giving information on the financing, marketing and management of the proposed business.

- In writing a business plan, there are two broad sources from which information for the plan could be obtained – primary sources produce information that no one else has researched before, while secondary sources provide information previously researched for another purpose.

- Carrying out a feasibility study is also an important aspect of starting a business – this is an assessment of the viability of the business idea and ensures that money is not wasted.

- Businesses have to ensure that they avoid engaging in unethical and illegal activities since doing so may damage their reputation.

End of section activities

Quick questions

1 There are six steps in starting a business. At each step various decisions have to be made. Quinton is about to start a catering business offering fine-quality food and service for functions. Identify the step at which Quinton will make each of the following decisions:

- a what kitchen appliances he will need in order to produce high-quality finger foods

- b whether or not he should invite his mother to join him as a partner

- c what item should be included on his menu as his signature dish

- d determining the best products and services to offer

- e how many chefs and waitresses he will need on his full-time staff

- f how much of his savings he should invest in the business

- g who will be responsible for the chefs and waitresses when he is hosting a function.

2 You are a banker offering loans to various different people. Identify the collateral that you would accept in each of the following situations:

- a a long-term loan for a small amount of money

- b a short-term loan for a lot of money

- c a long-term loan for a lot of money

- d a short-term loan for a small amount of money.

3 a Define the term entrepreneur and list three characteristics that an entrepreneur has.

- b List three sources from which entrepreneurs may obtain funding for starting businesses.

Applying what you have learnt

1 You are about to start a business manufacturing cases for cellphones. You are now writing a business plan to take to the bank in order to obtain financing. Create an outline of what you would include in each of the following sections:

- a marketing
- b finance
- c operations
- d production.

2 Consider the following situation: the business club in your school wants to raise funds for its annual business expo. The president has suggested that the club hosts a movie evening, which would involve showing a good movie and selling popcorn, juice and cake. A member of the club revealed that he had a source that could get him the latest movie; the only problem is that it is bootlegged. Some members of the club have pointed out that buying bootlegged DVDs is illegal and unethical and they would not support the venture; others, however, have no problem doing this. They also feel that buying the original DVD is too expensive and would result in a major reduction of the profits they are likely to make.

a What should the club do?

b Bootlegging has been described as a 'victimless crime' – a crime in which the victim cannot be identified or does not exist. Do you think this is true? If not, who is the victim?

c Can an original DVD, bought for private home viewing, be shown publicly to make a profit? Look at the packaging of a few original DVDs and see what instructions for use are written there. Do some research on the internet and see if the club can show either an original or bootlegged DVD at their movie evening.

3 Find a few entrepreneurs – these may be small-business owners in your community or near to your school. Interview them to create a profile of an entrepreneur. You may want to ask some of the following questions:

a Why did you start your own business?

b Why do you think you have succeeded at running your own business?

c How did you finance the business?

d Did you write a business plan?

e What are some of the challenges that you now face as an entrepreneur?

f What special personal characteristics do you possess that help you in running your business?

4 Why may working for others prevent self-actualisation? How does starting your own business encourage self-actualisation? It is a fact that many entrepreneurs encounter repeated failures before they hit upon the right idea; why do you think this is so?

5 'It is easier to borrow than to lend' – what do you think this means and why may this be true? How does collateral help in addressing the differences in borrowers' eagerness and lenders' hesitance?

Model exam questions
Question 1
a What is an entrepreneur? (3 marks)

b Explain why entrepreneurs must be risk takers. (3 marks)

c Discuss the role collateral plays in the successful formation of a business. (4 marks)

Question 2
An entrepreneur is thinking of obtaining a loan – she must decide between a venture capitalist and a regular loan from the bank.

a Explain what is meant by the term 'venture capital'. (3 marks)

b What is the difference between venture capital and loan capital? (4 marks)

c Outline one factor that she must consider before accepting either type. (3 marks)

Question 3
a List any three areas of a business plan. (3 marks)

b Give two examples of information that one could expect to find in any section listed in (a). (4 marks)

c What role does a business plan play in establishing a business? (3 marks)

Question 4
Niel has decided to start a sole-trader business which would repair cameras and other high-tech devices. He is trying to identify how much capital he would need and how he could raise it.

a List two characteristics that you expect Niel to possess if he is to be a successful entrepreneur. (4 marks)

b Outline three steps that Niel must now take in getting the business up and running. (6 marks)

c As a sole trader, discuss two options that Niel has in obtaining finance. (6 marks)

d Discuss two reasons why Niel may have a problem raising capital. (6 marks)

5 Contracts, insurance and business documents

> "A long dispute means that both parties are wrong. – *Voltaire*"

The Windies cricket team celebrating a victory.

Windies cricket versus contracts

West Indies Cricket has been a part of the Caribbean culture for over a century. As a team, the West Indies (also known simply as 'the Windies') has taken on and beaten opponents such as the English, Australian and Indian cricket teams; but in recent times it has taken a serious battering from an unlikely source – contractual disputes. Between 2005 and 2009, the team had at least three disputes which have affected public perception of the team. The final dispute took place between 2008 and 2009 and was perhaps the worst one of all.

During this dispute, players expressed their dissatisfaction with a number of issues, but their main point of contention was the fact that they were playing without contracts. Senior players all made themselves unavailable for selection to the Windies squad until the West Indies Cricket Board (WICB) offered them contracts and addressed such matters as players' images and payments. As a result, the Windies had to travel to Bangladesh and South Africa with a second-string team to participate in a series in which they failed to register a single win. Given that they had sponsors who were counting on a first-rate team to attract viewers and showcase their brand, the dispute was very tense as there were many moments when the series appeared to be in doubt. If the team did not honour the contractual obligations that it had with the other teams in the series, then it would not only lose the income from the series but would also be fined for not turning up. As happened before, it took the intervention of various prime ministers in the Caribbean to address the problems that the players had with the board. The hope now is that the Windies has seen the last of its problems with contracts.

In this chapter you will:

- describe what is meant by a 'contract'
- describe features of simple and speciality contracts
- assess situations to determine whether or not contracts are valid
- differentiate between the discharge and termination of contracts
- discuss the role of documents and record keeping in business activities
- describe and prepare specified business documents for given business situations
- discuss the features of various payment instruments
- discuss the differences and similarities between insurance and assurance
- explore the principles of insurance
- discuss the need for insurance in various situations
- explain the role of insurance in trade.

SECTION A   Contracts

Oral and written contracts

Have you ever entered into a **contract**? Have you ever taken a taxi, bought a sandwich, ordered a pizza or sold an old textbook? Well, if you have done any of these or similar activities, then you have entered into a contract with others. A contract is simply a legally binding agreement in which one or more parties promises to undertake some obligation for another party or for other parties. By legally binding, we mean that if the promise, agreement or obligation contained in a contract is breached or disregarded, then the law can punish the party who is responsible for the breach.

In defining a contract, you would realise that we stayed away from using the word 'written', as a contract does not need to be written to be legally binding. If you board a taxi at your school gate, and there is a common understanding that the driver is to take you home, at which time you will pay him a fare, then an *oral* contract exists between you and the driver. If either one of you fails to do what is required – if you refuse to pay the fare or if the driver ends the ride halfway – then the guilty party is in breach of the contract. In short, an oral contract is just as binding as a written contract;

the difference is that parties in a written contract have material evidence (the contract itself) of the obligations that each party in the contract has.

☞ Now it's your turn

A contract is a *legally binding* agreement. This means that some agreements are not contracts. Look at the following list of agreements and distinguish between those that are contracts and those that are merely agreements:

- an agreement between friends to take a walk together
- an agreement between roommates to share the rent
- an agreement between a guy and his girlfriend to go on a date together
- an agreement on your part to become a member of a club
- an agreement between you and your friends to study together

- an agreement to allow your friend to call his mother on your cellphone
- an agreement to allow your friend to call his mother on your cellphone in exchange for his shiny new pen
- an agreement between friends to split the cost of a meal.

Having looked at the list above, how do you think an agreement becomes a contract?

Simple contracts and speciality contracts

Consider the following extract from a contract:

> In consideration of the mutual agreements herein contained, both parties agree that John Brown (hereafter called the Author or Creator) grants to XYZ Company Limited (hereafter called the Agent or the Distributor) the exclusive right to manufacture, advertise, promote, sell and distribute...

Now consider the following extract from a contract for the same arrangement:

> I, John Brown, agree that the XYZ Company Limited should become my agent and will be responsible for manufacturing, advertising, promoting, selling and distributing...

What is the difference between these two contracts? Which one is simpler to understand? The first extract is a sample of a **speciality contract**, while the second is an extract from a **simple contract**. The difference between the two lies in the fact that simple contracts are those created by and entered into by individuals on a daily basis – as a result, these contracts may be oral or written, using simple wording and language. Simple contracts usually involve matters that one may encounter in their daily, routine activities – such as taking a taxi, buying a movie ticket or accepting a small loan from a friend or family member. Speciality contracts, however, are those that require signing and special processes and procedures before they become valid. They are usually drawn up by a lawyer and involve extensive and complicated legal jargon. Examples of a speciality contract are a mortgage agreement, an agreement to sell a car, to buy an insurance policy or to employ a consultant to design a new marketing campaign.

Characteristics of a simple contract

Simple contracts have the following features:

- **Offer and acceptance**: for a contract to exist, an **offer** and **acceptance** must be made. An offer is a clear, unequivocal and direct approach or expression of interest of one party to another. A 'For sale' sign on a house, an advertisement in the papers, a display in a store window or a flyer on a post are *not* offers as no clear, binding conditions are present in these examples. Rather, all they do is invite members of the public to make an offer or to investigate what the offer is. For this reason, these examples are referred to as invitations to treat. An offer is often met with a revised offer, which is called a **counter-offer**. In a counter-offer, the original offer is rejected and a new offer made. If Ray makes an offer to Michelle, Michelle in rejecting Ray's offer may modify it somewhat and in its place make a counter-offer, which Ray may accept or again modify in some way to make another counter-offer.

Acceptance is the other half of an offer. Like the offer, the acceptance must be clear and unambiguous and should be made by the person to whom the offer was made. Acceptance is not merely agreeing with the conditions outlined in the offer, nor is it simply finding these conditions acceptable or satisfactory – the person accepting the offer must give a visible indication of his acceptance; this is usually found in their conduct. A handshake, for example, has traditionally been used to indicate acceptance – even though not all handshakes can be interpreted as acceptance. Conduct is important if acceptance is to be inferred. A shrug, a frown or a gesture may all be examples of conduct that suggest that acceptance has not been reached.

A handshake is a simple but effective way of indicating acceptance of the terms of a contract.

Oral acceptance, accompanied by gestures such as handshakes or other body language, is most popular, even though in some instances written acceptance is also required.

Think about it

It is often thought that silence indicates consent – but is this the case in contract law? Consider the following situation: vendors in street markets are notoriously pushy in getting potential customers to buy their products – they are very aggressive in turning a passer-by's interest into acceptance and this sometimes causes problems, as Shadiek discovered. Shadiek went to the market and was passing a cake stand where cheesecake was on sale. Taking an interest in the cheesecake, she asked about the price of a slice of the cake. The baker quoted a price to her and asked her if she wanted a slice. Shadiek response was that the price was unbelievably low, but she questioned whether the cake was freshly baked. The baker/seller, while explaining how and when the cake was baked, cut and parcelled a slice and gave it to Shadiek, insisting that she pay for it. Shadiek initially refused, saying she did not agree to buy a slice, all she had done was ask the price. The baker became upset, insisting that now that he has cut the cake she must buy it as others will not want the slice that he has already cut. Feeling sorry for the baker, Shadiek agreed to buy the slice but could not help feeling duped.

1 Shadiek did not say a clear 'no' when the seller asked her if she wanted a slice. Does that mean she accepted the offer?

2 Was Shadiek, in fact, duped?

Now it's your turn

Between offer and acceptance, parties entering into a contract often involve themselves in the 'battle of forms'. Imagine that Niel, in making an offer to C.J., sends C.J. a written statement of the offer, which he expects to be signed and returned if acceptance has been made. When he receives the acceptance, however, he realises that C.J. had indeed signed it

but not before making a few modifications to the original offer.

1 Has Niel's offer been accepted by C.J.?

2 Does C.J.'s action indicate that he is now making a new offer to Niel?

3 What needs to happen now for a contract to exist between the two parties?

- **Competence of parties**: this characteristic of a contract derives from the necessity of consent of each party before a contract can be made. For consent to occur, each party must be capable of understanding the obligations and terms of the contract and has the right to sign the contract, given its obligations. Competence of parties, then, refers to the ability and right of the parties to understand the terms of the contact, to give their consent and to sign the contract. Some people, for natural reasons or as a result of public policies, have been rendered incompetent and are not able to sign contracts. These people include:
  - a minor (a child under a prescribed age)
  - a person who is intoxicated
  - a person of unsound mind
  - a prisoner
  - a person who is losing his or her faculties on account of age.
- **Intention**: is every agreement a contract? Well, some of the examples we looked at earlier should already tell you that, no, some agreements are not contracts because the intention in forming the agreement was not in creating legal or commercial relations. Consider, as an example, a husband and wife agreeing that each will save 10 per cent of their respective income for 12 months in order to buy a new refrigerator. At the end of the 12 months the wife has not saved her 10 per cent and the husband sues the wife for breach of contract. However, it is difficult for the court to enforce the agreement as it did not constitute a legally binding contract. Indeed, in many countries, there is a presumption against husband and wife entering into contract, even though this presumption can be challenged. The point is that a contract must have built into it an intention to create a legally binding agreement that

usually involves commercial gain. The following agreements are, therefore, not examples of contracts:

- an agreement to help your neighbour cut his lawn
- an agreement to water your friend's plants while he is away on business
- an agreement to lend your brother your bicycle.

- **Consideration**: without consideration, a contract is invalid. Consideration is used by both parties to signal that they stand to gain from the contract and are prepared to give up something (regardless of how trivial it may be). Consideration is what both parties bring to the bargaining table and is used to show that whatever is received from the other party is not a gift. The following are some examples of consideration:
  - Yvonne asks Beverly to give her some private lessons and in turn Yvonne gives Beverly one of her CDs.
  - Sharon does the housework for Karen with agreement that Karen will drive Sharon to work.
  - Marlene gives Tamar money to go grocery shopping, with the agreement that Tamar can keep the change that is left.

Think about it

'Necessary, but not adequate'. This is an interesting idea when contracts and consideration are being discussed. A consideration is necessary for a contract to take effect, but it does not need to be adequate compensation for what is being exchanged. The presence of any consideration ensures that what is exchanged is not a gift; as a result, it is conceivable that a house may be sold for $1. Certainly, the house is worth more than just $1, but if both parties agree that this is sufficient in their case, then the courts will generally allow this to be accepted as consideration.

A manager may decide to work for an annual salary of $1; a private citizen may sell a piece of land to the government for $1 or a furniture supplier may sell some desks and chairs to your school for $1. These are all examples of the principle of consideration at work.

This practice of selling an item for far less than it is actually worth always puzzles some people. Why do you think it happens?

Validity of contracts

Let us now explore a few cases to see the factors that affect the validity of contracts.

Case 1

Janice, passing the movie theatre, buys a ticket for the early movie which starts at 5.30 p.m. Realising that she has some time on her hands, she decides to go home and take care of a few chores. She is late in returning, however, and decides she will watch the movie when it is shown in the evening at 8.15 p.m. The theatre refuses to let her in as the ticket is for an earlier showing. Janice argues that given that the ticket was not used before, is for the same movie at the same theatre and since the evening showing can still accommodate more individuals, then she is to be allowed inside.
Does she have a valid contract for the 8.15 p.m. showing?

Points to consider

- The movie ticket is a contract with a specific time, place, date and event.
- If the person does not turn up at the specified place, at the designated date and time, then the theatre has no obligation to honour any other claims using that ticket.
- The theatre may choose to allow her to watch the evening movie, but this is at the discretion of the theatre and it has no obligation to do so.

Case 2

Angela goes into a fast-food outlet and sees a combination meal advertised as the Fast Combo. The combo is advertised as containing a small Pepsi, two pieces of chicken and a serving of onion rings. She orders the meal, pays for it and when she receives it she realises that she has actually been given what she thinks is a cheaper, inferior brand of soft drink. She insists that she be refunded as this is not what she paid for. The managers, however, refuse, saying that she paid for a small soda and that any brand will do.
Is Angela entitled to be refunded?

Points to consider

- The company cannot be expected to advertise each brand of soft drink that it has – advertising one brand should not lead to the conclusion that no other brands are sold with the combo meal.

- The advertisement does not represent an offer – it is really an invitation to treat. The offer is made through communication between the cashier and Angela at the counter.

- The company is obligated to indicate to the customers at the point when the offer is being made – when the customer is at the cashier making the order – that no Pepsi is available and instead these are the brands/flavours from which the customer may choose.

- Failure to do so may mean that the customer should expect to be refunded.

Case 3

Jerome and Naudia are friends. Naudia is selling her new iPod and she recalls that Jerome had said a few weeks ago that he wanted to get an iPod for himself. Naudia approached Jerome, offering the iPod for $1200 and Jerome responded that he did not have any money and would not be getting any for another three months. Naudia decided that she would wait for three months, when Jerome would buy the iPod from her. She asked Jerome to secure the item by making a deposit of $200. At the end of the three months, however, Jerome refused to buy the item for $1200 as Naudia had been using it during the three-month period and this would have reduced its value. He insisted on getting back his deposit of $200. *Does Jerome have a valid case?*

Points to consider

- Jerome does not take possession of the item until he has fully paid for it.

- However, the agreement was that Jerome would pay $1200 for the iPod as it existed at that point in time.

- Further use would reduce the value of the item and it is reasonable to expect that the price of the iPod should be adjusted to reflect the additional three months of use.

- Though they may not have discussed whether Naudia should continue to use the item until Jerome pays for it, it is reasonable to expect that price agreements will not be valid if the item changes in value as a result of the seller's care after this agreement.

- If Naudia refuses to reduce the price, then one expects that she should return the deposit to Jerome.

Discharge of contract

A contract is said to have been discharged when the obligations outlined in the contract have been executed or terminated prematurely. In short, **discharge of contract** takes place when the parties in the contract perform the obligations they were contracted to do or when the contract is terminated before the terms have been honoured. Discharge occurs under the following situations:

- **Performance**: this happens when the agreement has run its course and all parties in the contract have performed their obligations. For example, if Cavel contracts Robert, a building contractor, to carry out repairs to her house; when the repairs have been satisfactorily completed and Robert has been paid according to the contract, then the contract has been discharged by performance. Usually, a contract gives a specific time period within which performance should be carried out – once performance takes place under this condition, the contract is said to have been discharged.

- **Breach**: if one party fails to honour the terms of the contract, then the other party may terminate the contract. A breach may be as a result of non-performance or poor performance: not honouring the terms in a timely fashion, doing less (or more) than is stipulated, incomplete or faulty work are all examples of breaches. Non-performance does not automatically result in a breach, but when it does the guilty party may be asked to pay damages – which is the monetary penalty imposed on the party who breaches a contract or, in more general terms, who wrongs another person.

- **Frustration**: this occurs when performance becomes impossible or even illegal given radical changes in events subsequent to the creation of the contract. Acts of God are common causes of frustration; changes in laws or in national policies are also likely to cause frustration. As an example, in 2007 the Government of Jamaica placed a temporary ban on the export of scrap metal – all Jamaicans who had contracts to supply foreigners with scrap metal may have experienced frustration. If performance is still possible – just more difficult – then frustration has not occurred and failure to perform may be interpreted as a breach.

Now it's your turn

Look at the following situations and decide which ones will justifiably lead to frustration in the context of discharge of contract. Justify each answer.

1 A traffic accident causes a traffic jam, resulting in you being too late to honour the terms of the contract.

2 You agree to supply a restaurant with six cakes every month at $800 each. This arrangement is set to run for a year. However, five months into the arrangement the government increases the tax on flour, one of your ingredients, and you can no longer supply a cake at a price of $800.

3 Floods cause extensive damage to roads and bridges, making travelling to honour your contract impossible.

4 Sickness causes you to work from home, where you do not have access to the internet and hence cannot email your work in time to meet a contractual deadline.

5 A four-hours' loss in electricity supply makes it impossible to use the computer and to honour a contract.

Summary – Section A

- A contract, which can be either written or oral, is a legally binding agreement between two or more parties. A contract outlines the terms, obligations and responsibilities that each party in a contract must honour.

- A simple contract is one that does not need to be written and is usually created in the regular day-to-day activities of individuals. Speciality contracts are usually written by lawyers using precise legal language and are used in special circumstances such as the buying of a house or insurance.

- A simple contract is created when offer and acceptance, supported by consideration, are made between competent parties intent on creating legal relations.

- A contract is discharged when all parties perform what they were obligated to do or when non-performance, breach or frustration result in the contract being terminated.

End of section activities

Quick questions

Read each statement below and say whether it is true or false.

1 A contract can exist without any word being said or written.

2 A contract exists whenever an agreement exists.

3 A simple contract is one that is not written.

4 A speciality contract must be drawn up by a lawyer.

5 Advertising a good with its price, quantity and conditions of sale constitutes an offer.

6 If a counter-offer is made, then the original offer is no longer valid.

7 John, who sells shirts, owes you $500 from a previous transaction. You then buy a shirt from him that also costs $500. Instead of paying him, you tell him to keep the money that he owes you. This is an example of consideration.

8 If a house has been destroyed by flood, then the contractor is no longer obligated to paint it as frustration has occurred.

9 A husband cannot have a contract with his wife.

10 With his parents' permission, a child can enter into any contracts.

Applying what you have learnt

1 Can you write a cast-iron contract? This is a contract that is so skilfully written, no party can find any loophole to escape performance.

This activity will need you to have a group of eight persons. Divide yourselves into two groups of four. The agreement that you have reached is that the members of one group will buy lunch for the members of the other group on day one, and then on day two the agreement will be reversed. Each group must write a contract to outline this. Exchange contracts and then try to ensure that the other group has no escape clause – it cannot escape buying the other group lunch. What are some of the factors that you must consider as you write the contract? For example, are you going to impose a limit on the cost of the lunch?

2 When the government leases a piece of land to a charitable organisation, they usually set the lease at $1 a year for a number of years – sometimes more than 50 years.

  a Why is the lease set this low?

  b Why a dollar? At a yearly lease that low, why not simply charge no lease at all?

  c How important is it to ensure that business arrangements are not seen as gifts?

3 Corie visits the supermarket and buys 12 items. At the cashier, he had to pack his bags himself as no member of the supermarket staff was available. When he reached home, not having stopped anywhere, he realised that one item for which he had paid (it was on his receipt) was not in his bag; nor was it in his car. He promptly returned to the supermarket and asked them to either refund his money or give him the item as he must have left it on the counter.

  a When does Corie take possession of (or 'own') the goods – is it after he has paid or after they have been packed?

  b Should the supermarket be held responsible for goods that Corie loses after he has paid for them – whether he loses them in the supermarket, on his way to the car, or on his way home?

  c What would you advise the manager of the supermarket to do about Corie's request?

  d Suppose a member of the supermarket staff had packed the bag instead of Corie. Would you advise the manager differently? If yes, how and why?

Model examination questions
Question 1

  a Define what is meant by each of the following terms:

   i invitation to treat

   ii consideration. (6 marks)

  b What role does consideration play in establishing a contract? (3 marks)

  c The value of consideration is often insignificant. Why is this so? (3 marks)

Question 2

Cartell had a deadline to meet at 4.30 p.m. and so he called a taxi company to pick him up at 4.00 p.m. at his office, reasoning that with a 15-minute drive he would get to his destination by 4.30 p.m. to honour the contractual deadline. The taxi company called him at 3.55 p.m. to say that the driver was experiencing car problems and would not get there in time. Furthermore, there was no other taxi close enough to pick him up and hence he would have to make other arrangements. Eventually, Cartell got to his meeting 10 minutes late and as a result his company lost a $100 000 contract and Cartell lost his job.

  a Define what is meant by discharge. (3 marks)

  b By giving a reason for your answer, say whether the taxi company experienced frustration or is guilty of a breach of contract. (3 marks)

  c Cartell is planning to sue the taxi company; advise him on the likely outcome of this action. (4 marks)

A business is usually involved in hundreds or even thousands of transactions and activities that need to be recorded. Much of the record keeping that takes place surrounds ordering, shipping and paying for goods. Hence many of the documents that you will be asked to discuss or prepare are generated when goods are to be bought and sold. Before we look at some of the documents used by businesses, we will briefly look at record keeping in general. The reasons why a business would want to keep a record of its transactions or actions include:

- Record keeping ensures that the business is able to satisfy its legal requirement to pay an accurate amount of taxes. Taxes are usually stated as a percentage of sales, profit or other sources of income; if the business wants to avoid errors in calculating and paying taxes, then keeping an accurate record of its transactions is important.

- Keeping records facilitates the auditing of the financial record, which is another legal requirement that the business has to honour. Proper record keeping creates a paper trail which justifies the spending that the business has to do.

- Record keeping helps to reduce security lapses that result in fraud, mistakes and misuse of resources on the part of workers. For example, an effective system of recording the purchase, use and sale of stock will ensure that stock is not being taken by workers for their own private use.

- Record keeping reduces wastage as a result of more detailed knowledge of which goods are available, in what portions and for what length of time. It is not uncommon, for example, for some businesses to order hundreds of new units of stock, not realising that they already have hundreds of units in stock. This leads to wastage, particularly if the stock is perishable.

- Record keeping feeds into the creation of systems that management implements to create efficiency. Record keeping ensures, for example, that the business knows how many debtors it has, the dollar value of their debts and when they are due to be paid. This helps in creating a cash-flow system, which helps the business to reduce the need to have idle cash in the business.

Indeed, any system that the business uses to monitor the flow of goods and resources into and out of the business must have record keeping as a central feature.

Business documents

Pro forma invoice

This is simply a document that indicates that one party is willing to sell goods to another party at a specified price or under certain conditions. The **pro forma invoice** is used to declare the value of the potential trade and hence is not evidence of a sale having taken place. It does not record how many units of the goods have in fact been sold but simply the willingness of one party to sell goods to another. For this reason, a pro forma invoice is not a true invoice and its details are not recorded by either of the two businesses named on the invoice as a sale or a purchase. A pro forma invoice will display the following information (see if you can identify these elements on the sample invoice in Figure 5.1):

- the supplier's details – name and address
- date
- pro forma invoice number – a unique number given to each invoice
- the customer's details – name and address
- terms of sale – whether the items are being offered on credit terms or immediate cash payment
- details about the goods – number of units, description (colour, shape, size, name and so on), unit price and total price
- discounts.

Purchase requisition

This document indicates the quantity and type of goods or services that a business will need within a given period. A **purchase requisition** can also be seen as authorisation for the person or department responsible for purchasing items to go ahead and place the order for the purchase. A purchase requisition form is useful if internal control is to be placed on the organisation's resources. In most organisations, purchasing is centralised – this means that no department is able to make purchases of stationery and other supplies that it may

Pro forma invoice			
Date: 12 December 2010		**Invoice number:** 09-3456	**Credit** [√] **Cash** [ ]
Supplier:		Lester's Office Supplies Ltd 68 Gordon Town Road Ginger Hall	
Customer:		Williams' Private Investigators 32 Williamsfield Ave Ginger Hall	
Units	**Description**	**Unit price ($)**	**Total price ($)**
30	Black ballpoint Hi Mark pens	35	1050
5 dozen	Assorted colour markers	420	2100
18 rolls	Clear Sure Stik masking tape	60	1080
65	Legal size Allways paper folders	23	1495
		Total	5725
		Discount (20%)	1145
		FINAL PRICE	**4580**

Figure 5.1 A sample pro forma invoice.

need; rather, a central purchasing department makes all purchases on behalf of each department. As a result, each department must communicate its needs to this purchasing department and the purchase requisition is used for this purpose. However, a member of a department cannot simply write up a requisition for more paper, send it to the purchasing department and expect that the department will honour the request. A part of the system of control that exists is that each department must have a person who approves all purchase requisitions; it is these approved requisition forms that will be sent to the purchasing department. Once the purchasing department receives the requisition form, it will go ahead and place an order for these items.

Making connections: principles of accounts

Purchasing goods with the intention to resell them is an important idea in accounting. However, many businesses also purchase goods (such as pens, papers, ink and staplers) that they do not resell. Do you think that these should be treated differently in accounts? Why or why not? How is each category of goods treated by accountants?

Statement of account

It may surprise you to know that many firms do business using credit transactions – they buy and sell items intending to pay or to be paid at a later date. When a business buys on credit, it has what is called an 'account' with the other firm from which it buys. From time to time (usually after a month or a quarter), the business would receive a printout of its account with the other firm. This statement of account is really a list of the transactions that the business has conducted, the amount of money it has already paid up and the amount that is still outstanding. When a business *receives* a **statement of account**, such a statement gives the balance that the business still owes its suppliers. From another perspective, if the business *gives out* a statement of account, then this statement shows the balance that another business owes it. A statement of account usually shows the following information (look at the sample in Figure 5.2 and identify each element):

- the name and address of the business
- the customer's name and address
- the period to which the statement applies
- the opening balance at the start of the period
- the transactions during the period

Statement of account		
Month: August/September	**Due date:** 21 September 2010	**Amount due:** $3685
Lester's Office Supplies Ltd 68 Gordon Town Road Ginger Hall	**Customer:** Williams' Private Investigators 32 Williamsfield Ave Ginger Hall	
Statement for: 12 August 2009 – 11 September 2009		

Date	Transactions	Amount ($)	Balance ($)
12 August	Balance from last period	3500	3500
19 August	Customer bought goods on credit	1600	5100
28 August	Customer paid cash	3815	1285
8 September	Customer bought goods on credit	2400	3685

Account summary		
Opening balance: $3500	**New charges (net):** $185	**Balance owed:** $3685

Figure 5.2 A sample statement of account.

- any payments made on the account during the period
- the closing balance at the end of the period.

Stock card

Businesses usually buy stock in bulk and store them in a warehouse in order to have a constant supply of items on hand. The business must also have some system of knowing which goods are available and in what quantity, and a **stock card** is ideal for this. Without a stock card, the business would find it challenging to determine the number of units of a particular stock available and it may find itself in the unfortunate position of not having enough to satisfy customers' demand or, in some cases, even having to temporarily halt production. For example, as simple as it appears, restaurants cannot do much business if they have no utensils to offer to their customers – regardless of how much food they have available to serve.

Transport documents

When businesses trade across international borders, documents are needed to support the efficient transfer of goods between buyers and sellers. These documents are called transport documents and are particularly useful when goods are to be sent as cargo on ships or on planes. As you can imagine, exporters and importers may be very anxious when they send goods – very often perishable and fragile in nature – by ship or plane across

many hundreds of kilometres. These goods pass through many ports and are transferred between many means of transportation (trucks, planes, trains and so on) and are exposed to being damaged, lost or even stolen. It is understandably very reassuring to exporters and importers to know that they have the necessary documents to act as evidence of the goods being sent. Some of these transport documents are discussed below.

Import licence

This document is used by governments to limit the quantity of certain items that can be brought into the country. An **import licence** is simply a permission granted (or sold) to an importer to bring a specified quantity of a good into a country within a given period. The government may be interested in ensuring that some goods are not imported as freely – for example, should the government place restrictions on the number of firearms that can be imported and sold? One of the ways to ensure such restrictions is to give only a few importers the right to bring these items into the country. Some of the reasons why an import licence may be needed are:

- The government may be attempting to reduce the outflow of foreign exchange, which is spent by local citizens when they import goods.
- To regulate the importation of hazardous and dangerous items such as unsafe chemicals, addictive drugs, explosives and firearms.

- To protect local industries, which may be threatened by large quantities of foreign substitutes on the local market.

Bill of lading

Imagine that you have valuable cargo to send by sea – would you be comfortable shipping it off and keeping your fingers crossed, hoping it gets to its destination safely? Perhaps not! This would be a very nerve-racking way of shipping items across long distances. One way to remove the uncertainty from the shipping process is to ensure that you receive a bill of lading from the carrier (the company responsible for transporting the goods). A **bill of lading** is evidence that one business (the shipper) has given another business (the carrier) cargo to transport to a specified place and usually to a specified individual (the consignee). A bill of lading is a contract between the carrier and the shipper; it obligates the carrier to deliver cargo in good condition to the consignee.

 For you to think about

A bill of lading is described as a negotiable item – its owners can endorse and sell it to a third party, who then takes possession of the good. This has implications for, among other things, who is responsible for the item in transit, who receives payment for the item from the consignee and who is to engage in contractual discussions with the carrier. The bill of lading, because it is negotiable, may also play the function of a 'medium of exchange'.

1 What is a medium of exchange and how can a bill of lading function in this way?

2 Is this an example of the barter system at work in the modern economy?

Airway bill

This document acts as further support to the agreement that exists between the carrier and the shipper. It is given to the shipper as a receipt of the good being received by the carrier and as evidence of the contract between them. The **airway bill**, unlike the bill of lading, is non-negotiable since it is not a document of title of ownership of the goods. In other words, possessing an airway bill does not necessarily mean that you possess the goods to which they refer. You cannot then sell the airway bill and by doing so sell the goods to which it pertains.

 Now it's your turn

If both the bill of lading and the airway bill act as evidence of the contract, why are both documents necessary?

Instruments of payment
Cheque

This is a very popular and convenient way of making payments – more than likely you have either seen or perhaps even received a **cheque** before and can perhaps remember standing in line in a bank to have the teller give you cash to the value of the amount written on the cheque. A cheque is really a written instruction in which an individual permits a bank, in which he or she has money, to make a payment of a specified amount to a specified person. The individual drawing up or writing the cheque needs to ensure that she has enough money in her account at the bank for the cheque to clear – otherwise, the bank may refuse to 'honour' the cheque and will not pay the amount. This dishonoured cheque is sometimes called a 'bounced cheque'. Cheques are negotiable – their ownership can be transferred from one person to another and, hence, they can act as a medium of exchange. To transfer ownership, the original owner of the cheque (the person whose name appears on the face of the cheque) needs to endorse the cheque by signing its back.

Think about it

Cheque or cash? Is any one payment method better than the other? Does it depend on the situation in which you find yourself? Look at each of the following situations and say which you think is the better way to pay – cash or cheque. Be prepared to explain your choice.

- buying a house for a large sum of money
- paying your fare on the bus
- shopping for groceries at the supermarket
- paying a gardener his salary at the end of the working day
- buying a battery for your watch

Now it's your turn

A cheque is likely to be dishonoured when insufficient funds are in the account to cover the amount written on the face of the cheque. What other reasons may cause a cheque to be dishonoured?

Debit and credit card

Debit and credit cards were covered in Chapter 1 (see pages 4–5), so we will not revisit them here. When a person talks about paying by plastic, however, they are referring to using a credit or a debit card. This is related to the fact that these cards are made from plastic and are swiped when payments are to be made. Revise these two ideas from Chapter 1 and see if you can identify the differences between the two cards.

Money order

As you have realised, having a chequebook from which you write cheques is one thing; having funds in the account to clear such cheques is another thing altogether! Some people, therefore, do not accept cheques, as receiving a cheque is no guarantee that there is money in the account to clear it. This is the major problem that **money orders** attempt to address. A money order is simply an arrangement in which one individual or organisation pays a sum of money to an institution – usually the post office or a bank – and asks this institution to make the payment to another individual or organisation. A money order is then sent to the person who can turn up to the post office or bank and claim the cash. The post office or bank usually charges a small fee for this service and may also have a minimum amount for which a money order can be sent. In addition to addressing concerns regarding dishonoured cheques, the money order also ensures that people without a bank account can still have access to a cashless system for making payments – particularly for large transactions.

Bank draft

A **bank draft** is another payment mechanism, which comes with the assurance that the bank will honour the payment. It is a type of cheque in which the bank guarantees that the funds to clear the cheque are available in the account. The person who receives a bank draft, therefore, has no reservations about the cheque and is, as a result, more likely to do business with the person who possesses the draft. Imagine, for example, how much more comfortable you will feel accepting a cheque for millions of dollars from a stranger if the bank issuing the cheque has guaranteed that it will clear.

Telegraphic money transfer

A **telegraphic money transfer** is often abbreviated to TT and is also known as a wire transfer. It is a method of transferring money from one account at a bank to another account at another bank. The accounts can be owned by the same person or a different person and, for this reason, a TT can be used as a method of payment. A TT eliminates the need to travel long distances across international borders with large sums of money; in addition, it is particularly useful when a business is involved in import–export trade and must make or receive payments across international borders. Try to imagine how impractical it would be to have to fly to China to pay a supplier for goods; furthermore, consider the implications for safety and speed if the payments were sent by mail.

Documentary credit

Would you sell one of your used *Principles of Business* textbooks to one of your classmates who is promising to pay for it in a month? To answer this question, not only would you think about the price that you would get, but also whether or not your friend is trustworthy enough to pay his debt. The fact that you know him and that you see him every day in class may make you think that you can enter into a deal with him – after all, it is unlikely that he will simply stop attending school to avoid paying the debt! In addition, more than likely the book will not fetch a high price and, hence, you may think he should not have a problem finding this sum.

Suppose that you are not selling a single used textbook but thousands of copies of books; suppose as well that your buyer was not a classmate whom you see every day, but a company in France. Would you still sell so many books on credit for millions of dollars to a business not known to you? Well, if you have doubts, you are not alone – many exporters have realised that this is a risky practice and they have sought reassurance by using **documentary credit**. This is a procedure in which a bank guarantees that it will pay for the goods being imported. By doing this, the creditworthiness of the importer is no longer an issue as the exporter knows that the bank's guarantee is solid and irreversible.

Documentary credit, which is sometimes called a letter of credit, requires that the importer deposits an amount to cover the transaction in an account at the bank undertaking to make the payment. In addition, the importer has to pay a fee for this service, which is usually a percentage of the value of the goods being imported. Usually, documentary credit involves two banks – one representing the seller and the other representing the buyer. The steps involved in the use of documentary credit are outlined below:

1 The buyer usually initiates the documentary credit process by going to his bank to request that a letter of credit be made payable to the importer.

2 The buyer's bank then sends a copy of the letter of credit to the seller's bank; the seller is then notified that the letter of credit has arrived.

3 This is an indication to the seller that if he goes ahead and ships the goods, then he will be paid as the buyer has already deposited money in an account to cover the transaction.

4 When he presents evidence that the goods have been shipped – these are usually a bill of lading and other documents that are required in the agreement – then his bank will ask the buyer's bank to transfer the money, which is then disbursed to the seller.

Think about it

A letter of credit costs the buyer, on average, between 1 and 8 per cent of the transaction cost. For example, if you are using a letter of credit to buy goods which cost $600 000, then the bank may ask you to pay as much as $48 000 in order to issue the letter of credit. Why would you agree to pay this? Why not simply buy on credit without going through the documentary credit process?

Insurance and assurance

Think of something valuable that you have – it may be a new cellphone, a Wii player or a laptop computer.

Suppose it is damaged. Would you want to have it replaced or fixed? Perhaps the more important question may be, would you be able to afford to replace it straightaway or would you have to save for a while? Instead of waiting until something happens, do you think it may be a good idea to start saving now in the event that a valuable item is damaged? Well, this is the underlying principle of **insurance** and **assurance** – making sure you are ready to deal with this eventuality.

Insurance is the pooling of risk. In return for a **premium**, an individual transfers his risk to an insurer. Insurance policies are taken out to guard against uncertainty. An insurance policy is taken out on an asset or possession and it allows a person to be reimbursed in the event of the loss of the insured property. The idea behind insurance is that the insurance company will restore an insured asset or item to the condition that it was in before the loss. Assurance, however, is a special type of insurance, and is taken out on a person's life. In this case, the insurance company gives the assurance that in the case of the death of the insured individual, the insurance company will stand the loss the family has suffered. As such the differences between insurance and assurance can be summarised as follows:

- Insurance is taken out on an asset or a possession, while assurance refers to a policy taken out on a life.

- While an insurance policy promises to restore the assets to the condition that it was in before the loss, a life assurance policy cannot promise that but can only promise a monetary payment to the family of the deceased.

Insurance policies are made possible with the payment of a regular premium. This is a regular (e.g. monthly, quarterly, annual) payment that the insured party or **beneficiary** pays to the insurance company. In the event of a loss, this money is then repaid to the beneficiary. It is often the case that a loss occurs before the beneficiary has paid enough to cover the loss. When this happens, the premiums of the other people in the insurance scheme are taken to pay this party. This can only work if there are other members in the insurance scheme, and they have not all suffered loss at the same time. Insurance, then, can be seen as a person putting money aside in the event of a loss by giving it to a company (called an insurance company) and taking it back if and when the loss occurs.

Think about it

Insurance is sometimes described as the transfer of risk, since insurance allows a person to transfer the risk of losing an insured property to the insurer. This transfer of risk sometimes creates what is called a moral hazard – because people know that they are protected by insurance, they take risks that they would not have taken otherwise. The problem with this is that these people have more accidents and this drives up the cost of insurance for everyone. If you had an insurance company, how would you discourage moral hazard?

Principles of insurance
The principle of insurable interest

Insurable interest refers to the legal right to insure, and is one of the most important principles of insurance as, without this principle, an insurance contract is not valid. This principle ensures that people who benefit from insurance in the event of a loss (of life or of property) are somehow connected to the loss. Imagine, for example, if it were possible to insure any building that you see, whether you own it, or were connected to it or not. Conceivably, in the event of a fire destroying the building, there may be many people who all have valid claims to a settlement from the insurance company. Three criteria for insurable interest must be met:

- **There must be something capable of being insured**: a property or an asset of some sort must be present.
- **The property must be the subject matter of the insured**: the insured must have a claim on the property or life.
- **The beneficiary must have a certain relationship with the insured**: the relationship the beneficiary shares with the insured object must be legally recognised and the beneficiary must desire the safety of the insured item and stands to lose in the event of damage or harm to the insured item.

The principle of utmost good faith

In applying for insurance, the applicant knows more about the item to be insured (the subject matter) than the insurer does, which is where the principle of **utmost good faith** comes in. The client has an obligation to ensure that he tells the insurer all the details that would affect the insurer's assessment of the risk that he is undertaking. These details are called material facts and are defined as facts that are known or ought to be known to the insured (client). A material fact is one that would influence the judgement of a prudent insurer in determining the premium or the feasibility of the policy. Even if a fact is not specifically asked for on the application form, the client must disclose this fact if it is material. If a fact only becomes known after the policy has been signed, it must be immediately communicated to the insurer. The contract may be declared void if all material facts are not declared and the company would have no obligation to meet the claims of the insured arising from the policy if important facts are withheld.

An example of a material fact is the health or medical history of an applicant for health insurance. Failing to indicate to (or taking steps to conceal from) the insurer that you have been diagnosed with a chronic medical condition may result in the policy being cancelled or not honoured in the event of your illness. In motor vehicle insurance as well, applicants must reveal their accident history in order to give the insurer a better picture of their driving skills and their overall risk.

The principle of legality

The principle of **legality** states that an individual cannot insure against an illegal act in order to avoid responsibility for it afterwards. Punishment for a crime or accountability or responsibility for an action cannot be transferred to someone else.

The principle of proximate cause

This principle holds that only those risks insured against can be compensated; it is crucial then that the cause of the loss be established. For example, a client cannot make a claim if fire started by arsonists (a deliberate act) destroys his house that he had insured against accidental fires. Also, some life insurance policies, for example, may not provide any settlement if the **proximate cause** of death is suicide. A proximate cause is an act to which one can attribute an event; it is an act that one can reasonably conclude set another event in motion or, if it were not done, would have prevented the event from occurring. For example, what is the proximate cause when expensive valuable paintings are stolen by looters during a hurricane? The insurance company may argue that the hurricane set the act in motion and is the proximate cause of the theft. By establishing a proximate cause of hurricane, the insurer may (but hopefully would not) refuse to pay for the paintings if they were not insured against hurricanes.

The principle of subrogation

Imagine that when you graduate from school, a driver runs a red light and slams into your car. Your car is badly damaged and you have lacerations and bruises on your hands and face. Since it was not your fault, your insurance company pays your medical expenses and ensures that your car is repaired. Later, however, the insurance company will seek reimbursement from the insurance company of the other party who was at fault. This is referred to as **subrogation** and is described as the insurer's right to pursue a claim from the party legally responsible for an accident. It is important to note that the insured gives up his right to pursue any claim or settlement with the third party once the insurance company has made a payment to the insured. This means that if, after an accident in which you were not at fault, subrogation results in a settlement that is significantly more than the insurer paid to you, you are not entitled to any of it. For example, if John is involved in a car accident with Paul, John cannot pursue any claim with Paul once John's insurance company has made a settlement. John's insurance company now has full rights to pursue the claim on John's behalf.

The principle of indemnity

The principle of **indemnity** ensures that the insured does not end up in a more advantageous position after an accident. The insurance policy is not to create a profit (or loss) for the insured but to ensure that the insured is returned to the position that existed before the loss. The insurer therefore has the right to make adjustments to a settlement to reflect the fall in value that an asset may have experienced over its life before the accident or loss. A car, therefore, will be replaced with money equal to the value of the car, not with a brand new car.

☞ Now it's your turn

Have you ever read *A House for Mr. Biswas*? It is a novel, written by Nobel prize winner V.S. Naipaul. The novel is set in Trinidad and Tobago and relates the many interesting experiences of the main character, Mr. Biswas, as he tries to find a house to call his own. One of the interesting incidents that the book highlights is the practice of 'insure and burn' (the characters in the book pronounced it as one word – '*insureandburn*'). This practice was popular at the time in the community in which Mr. Biswas lived, and consisted of insuring a property (usually one that has become problematic to maintain) just before you deliberately destroy it by setting it on fire. Of course, the insurance company must now pay for the property or provide a 'new' one.

1 Insure and burn is illegal – but should it be? If it is not wrong to destroy your own house, why is the practice illegal?

2 Which principle of insurance, if any, does this practice violate?

3 What do you understand by the term 'insurance fraud'?

The principle of contribution

If an individual has insured an object under many policies, he cannot collect the full amount from each policy. If he decides to collect the full amount from one policy, then that insurer has the right to ask for a **contribution** from the other insurance companies.

☞ Now it's your turn

The principle of contribution is said to enforce the principle of indemnity. Why do you think this is so?

Types of insurance policy

Insurance is necessary and advisable in any situation where risks and uncertainties exist. These risks and uncertainties become more pronounced and, hence, insurance becomes more important when the items are valuable or expensive – for example, while there is a high risk that you may leave your umbrella in the next taxi that you take, there is no need to insure the umbrella as it is relatively inexpensive. The same thinking, however, may not hold when we look at items such as your house or even your health – you would want to make sure that these are insured. Some of the types of insurance policy are listed below.

Auto insurance

This is perhaps the most popular form of insurance, particularly since all motor-vehicle owners are required by

Motor-vehicle insurance may seem burdensome – until you have an accident.

law to insure their vehicles. Once insured, a car owner enjoys three areas of projection:

- Property coverage to ensure that the car itself is repaired or replaced if damaged, stolen or destroyed.
- Medical coverage provides medical support to anyone injured by the operation of the insured vehicle.
- Liability coverage ensures that passengers or pedestrians who may be injured as a result of the operation of the car may receive any settlement that the court awards them.

There are three types of auto insurance:

- **Third party**: this policy does not cover the damage sustained by the insured vehicle; instead it covers only the damage to the other vehicle with which the insured vehicle was in an accident. Third-party insurance is the cheapest form of auto insurance and is suitable when the insured vehicle is of little or no value.
- **Third party, fire and theft insurance**: like basic third-party insurance, this policy does not cover the insured vehicle in the event of a collision. The policy is, however, extended to repair or replace the insured vehicle if it is stolen or destroyed by fire.
- **Comprehensive insurance**: comprehensive insurance is the most expensive form of auto

insurance and covers all damage sustained by the insured vehicle in a collision along with all the coverage offered by the other policies listed above.

Home insurance

This form of insurance protects houses from destruction by natural disasters and fire. The insurance contract for home insurance is likely to exclude some categories of risk and natural disasters. For example, for countries that are in the hurricane zone, it is standard practice to exclude damage sustained from hurricanes from the list of proximate cause. Home insurance also does not automatically include furniture or other inventory items in the house – the insured may have to spend more to get this built into the coverage plan.

Health insurance

This has become a high-profile issue in today's society as medical care has become a major concern of many countries. Health insurance involves making small monthly contributions to a scheme with the understanding that in the event of illness and/or disability, the insurer will pay all or most of the cost of medical care. Not all illnesses and disabilities will be allowed, but the contract should indicate which ones are.

Disability insurance

This provides coverage to people who are unable to work because of a disability. The coverage provided to such people is usually in the form of financial support – either a one-off lump-sum payment or a structured payment over a number of years.

Property insurance

This protects property (such as machines, jewellery, heirlooms and artwork) from destruction, theft or natural elements such as the weather. Property insurance can be tailored for specific risks such as earthquake, fire or flood insurance.

Marine insurance

Marine insurance ensures that the ship, as well as the cargo on the ship, is insured against eventualities that may occur at sea.

Liability insurance

In the event you are sued, then you may be covered by an insurer who promises to pay the damages for you. This is useful for businesses who are involved in activities that are highly risky or expose customers or workers to dangerous, potentially life-threatening situations. Care must be exercised, however, as the insurer cannot provide protection against carrying out illegal activities.

Insurance and trade

Insurance companies are regarded as an aid to trade since they compensate for losses to cargo and vessels. Insurance establishes a line of responsibility for losses among traders and therefore provides certainty where uncertainty exists. In providing this certainty, insurance makes people more willing to trade.

Traders whose vehicles or cargo are insured are more likely to obtain financing from investors and financial institutions. In addition, the presence of insurance ensures that traders are more likely to send goods across long distances since insurance provides some reassurance against losses or damage that may occur in transit.

Summary – Section B

- Record keeping is needed in a business to reduce the risks of fraud, errors on tax returns and to complement the management systems that the business uses.

- There are many business documents, including pro forma invoices, purchase requisitions, statements of account and stock cards.

- Businesses also use transport documents, such as bills of lading and airway bills, especially when they send goods across international borders by plane or by ship.

- A business has many payment options available to it. These range from traditional means such as cheques and debit or credit cards to more contemporary methods such as electronic transfers.

- Businesses also use documentary credit to make payments with traders in other countries. This method ensures that, before the transaction takes place, the seller is sure of being paid.

- Insurance is the pooling of risk and is used to protect individuals against uncertainties. Assurance, on the other hand, is a special case of insurance and is used to guard against financial losses associated with death.

- Insurance is built around seven main principles: utmost good faith, insurable interest, indemnity, legality, proximate cause, subrogation and contribution.

- There are various types of insurance policy, with each policy addressing a different type of risk or protecting a different type of asset. Some of the popular types of insurance policy are auto insurance, home insurance, health insurance and liability insurance.

- Insurance facilitates trade as it removes much of the uncertainty that exists in regular trading activities.

✏ End of section activities

Quick questions

1 Below are some characteristics of business documents and payment methods. Use the clues to determine which document or payment method is being described.

   a used to indicate the balance customers owe for goods they have bought on credit

   b a negotiable trade document given to the shipper by the carrier

   c instructions for a bank to pay a certain amount to an individual

   d a document used by the government to minimise the loss of foreign exchange

   e a non-negotiable trade document transferred between the shipper and the carrier

   f a short-term loan from a bank used to make payments

   g payment method in which a bank's guarantee replaces the trustworthiness of the buyer

   h what a department would need to complete in order to buy stationery

   i a cashless means of making payments which does not require a bank account

   j making a payment by moving money from one account to another

   k a description of the terms under which goods will be made available

   l a cheque that comes with the issuing bank's guarantee

   m shows the quantity of goods available for sale

2 Below are some situations and actions that are not allowed in insurance. Identify which principle of insurance prevents each action or situation.

   a You cannot expect to be paid by Timz if his insurance company has already paid you.

   b You cannot insure yourself against speeding tickets.

   c You cannot collect the full amount from all the companies that have insured the item that has been destroyed.

   d A wealthy man cannot insure a perfect stranger simply because he can afford to do so.

   e The insurance company may refuse to pay you money if fire destroys your house during an earthquake, unless you are insured against earthquakes.

   f You cannot profit from the loss of an insured item.

   g When applying for auto insurance, you cannot omit the fact that your motor vehicle will be used to transport paying passengers.

Applying what you have learnt

1 Have you ever sent a package abroad by FedEx or another courier service? Research the mechanisms that these courier services offer to ensure that the sender or recipient can follow or track the package as it moves from one country to the next. Do you think that you would feel reassured using a courier service to send an expensive painting by Michelangelo to America?

2 Look at the statement of account opposite and answer the questions which follow.

   a How much does the customer owe at the end of the month?

   b What are the new charges (net) during the month?

   c Describe the transactions that you think took place on 17 and 28 July.

   d Why did the balance not change after the transaction that took place on 17 July?

3 In most countries auto insurance is compulsory – it is a crime to drive a vehicle that is not insured. Why do you think this policy exists? Do you think that this is fair, particularly since some drivers have driven for over 50 years and never had an accident, yet they have to pay insurance every year?

4 If two people go to a car dealer on the same day and buy similar cars – same year, model and value – it is likely that they will each have insurance policies

Statement of account			
Month: July	**Due date:** 1 August 2011		**Amount due:** _____

Gordon's Repairs and Eelctronics 68 Davidson Ave Tamarind Dist	**Customer:** McGann's Farm and Garden Supplies 14 Summit Way

Statement for: 1 July 2011 – 31 July 2011			
Date	**Transactions**	**Amount ($)**	**Balance ($)**
July 1	Outstanding balance		1800
July 13	Television repairs and servicing	2100	3900
July 17	Stereo system and speakers (invoice # 687-423)	4100	3900
July 23	Cheque # 123-987-876	1600	2300
July 28	Extension cable (invoice # 687-430)	1200	3500
July 31	Balance		3500

Account summary		
Opening balance: $1800	**New charges (net):** _____	**Balance owed:** _____

that are very different in terms of value, even if they use the same insurer. This is related to the fact that the cost of an insurance policy is determined by factors related to the owner as well as to the car. Explain why each of the following factors will result in the insurance cost increasing:

a if the owner had many accidents before

b if the owner had never owned a motor vehicle before

c if the owner intends to use the vehicle to carry public passengers

d if the owner intends to have other people driving the vehicle

e if the owner got his driving licence only a few months ago

f if the vehicle is to be used as a part of the owner's work – such as delivering goods.

Model exam questions
Question 1

a List any three documents that businesses use in their day-to-day activities. (3 marks)

b Discuss the functions of any two of the documents you listed in part (a). (6 marks)

c Discuss why small businesses may have needs for documents that are different from the needs that large businesses have. (3 marks)

Question 2

a State two reasons why businesses need documents. (4 marks)

b Discuss two ways in which transport documents provide reassurance during trade. (6 marks)

c What is the major difference between a bill of lading and an airway bill? (4 marks)

Question 3

a List any three methods of payment suitable for paying a supplier overseas. (3 marks)

b Define any two of the payment methods listed in (a). (6 marks)

c Explain how payment methods facilitate trade. (3 marks)

Question 4

a Why do cheques 'bounce'? (3 marks)

b Discuss one other payment method that is ideal if you have doubts about a customer's cheques. (3 marks)

c Outline the process involved in setting up a documentary credit between a company and its customer. (6 marks)

Question 5

a What is the difference between insurance and assurance? (3 marks)

b Define each of the following principles of insurance:
  i subrogation
  ii contribution
  iii indemnity. (6 marks)

c Discuss two factors to consider before you decide to insure an item that you own. (6 marks)

Question 6

Hannah has just bought a house and has decided that she wants to have it insured. She went to the insurance company and took out a policy that promised to restore the house in the event of any natural disaster (flood, earthquake and so on). After a few years, Hannah eventually established a hairdressing salon in her living room. One day, an electrical overload caused a fire and destroyed the house. Hannah has made a claim to her insurance company and is waiting for them to arrive at a decision.

a Define what is meant by each of the following:
  i proximate cause
  ii utmost good faith. (6 marks)

b Discuss why each of the principles listed in (a) may cause the insurance company to refuse to pay Hannah any money. (4 marks)

c Suppose she had taken out a separate insurance policy on her hairdressing equipment; should she expect to receive a settlement from this policy? (3 marks)

6 Production

> Consumption is the sole end and purpose of all production. – *Adam Smith*

Given the islands' shared history, there is no shortage of bananas across the Caribbean.

From Jamaica to Windward Islands – what's the big difference?

The Caribbean is a group of islands with more than just the Caribbean Sea in common. Perhaps the most striking feature of the Caribbean islands is the impact that 200 years of transatlantic slavery had and continues to have on each country's economy. Slavery in the Caribbean left each nation clinging to an agriculture-based economy for a number of years. In the early parts of the 20th century, much of the production in the Caribbean was associated with crops that were a major part of the Caribbean's history – bananas and sugar. These products were exported in their raw, unprocessed form or were refined and processed further to develop products that were dependent on these crops. Eventually, the economies of the Caribbean diversified – tourism became a major source of income for most Caribbean countries and bauxite was discovered in Jamaica and petroleum in Trinidad and Tobago. This diversification, however, was limited as many countries were still overly dependent on agriculture and, where other industries had replaced agriculture, they were still dependent on natural resources. As Caribbean economies have learnt, developed countries have created synthetic substitutes for our natural products such as sugar and bauxite and therefore depending on these is risky. Furthermore, the kind of production that these natural products generate does not create a high level of value added. These ideas will be discussed further in this chapter as we examine the issue of production in the Caribbean.

In this chapter you will:

- identify the factors of production that are involved in the production process
- outline what is meant by productivity
- discuss the impact migration has on the production process
- discuss the importance of entrepreneurial ability as a factor of production
- classify production into levels and types
- discuss the characteristics of cottage industries
- discuss linkage industries in the Caribbean
- identify factors involved in location analysis
- discuss the differences between small and large businesses.

Introduction

You may never have thought about it before, but all businesses produce something that they offer for sale. From banks to your favourite bakery, a product is on sale that you or others are interested in buying. Sometimes it is not that easy to identify the products that businesses sell. For example, the bakery on the corner of the street sells cakes and pastries. What about the bank, however? What products does it sell? It takes people's money, keeps it safe and offers it back to them with some interest added on – but does it sell anything? Well, of course it does – banks are usually one of the most profitable types of business in any country and they cannot do this without offering some product for sale. If you want, you can think of the bank's product as the investment and saving options that it offers and the security that its customers get from banking with it.

This difference between a bank and a bakery is related to the difference between a good and a service – both of them are products, but goods are tangible and, as a result, they can be touched and stored. Services, on the other hand, cannot be touched – they can only be experienced or enjoyed. This distinction is crucial if you are to fully understand what production is.

Production

What then is **production**? We can start with the observation that at the end of the production process, a product – whether a good or a service – is produced. In other words, both the bank and the bakery are involved in production; they are simply producing different types of goods. We can add to this first observation by stating that, in order to produce, businesses need some resources that are used up and combined to create a final product. Essentially then, production is the process of using various resources to create a finished product.

Now it's your turn

Look at the list of business types below. Give examples of the products that they produce. Is each firm producing a good or a service? Could some businesses be producing both? Justify your answers.

1 utility companies such as electricity and gas companies

2 a private school for secondary students

3 a restaurant serving dinner in a romantic setting

4 a hospital specialising in heart surgery and transplant

5 an accounting firm that audits other firms' accounts

6 a private taxi providing a charter service.

Think about it

What exactly is a finished product? Well, think of work-in-progress as goods that are only part way through the production process. For example, the dough that the baker at Chelle's pastry shop has on the counter and is about to put in the oven to make a pizza is work-in-progress because the pizza is not finished yet. But suppose he had bought the dough from Jer's Bakery, which specialises in supplying pizza dough to other bakeries. Would this dough be a finished product to Jer? Do you agree that one firm's finished product is simply a work-in-progress for another firm? Why or why not?

The factors of production

As already discussed, resources are used or are combined to create a finished product. These resources are called **factors of production** and all production processes will have all or a combination of these factors. To identify the factors of production, let us take apart the production process of banana breads to examine what goes into making the finished product. Even without full knowledge of how banana breads are baked, we can identify the following important aspects of making a loaf:

- The manager of the bakery would obviously need ingredients – she has to think about the raw materials, both man-made and natural, that she may need. Eggs, bananas, flour, yeast and spices are ingredients that come to mind immediately. However, one that you may not think of or which you may take for granted is the land that is used to carry out the actual production. These resources are all lumped under the category **land/natural resources** as the first factor of production.

- In addition, the manager has to think about the labour that she will use. She has to employ a skilled baker, trained and experienced in baking and who is able to produce a banana bread of high quality. The factor of production that addresses these needs is referred to as **labour/human resources**.

- Of course, raw materials will have to be bought and bakers and other workers will have to be paid. Additionally, machines will be needed – industrial ovens and cake mixers will have to be bought and the business will also need state-of-the-art display shelves for the banana bread. In short, money is needed to finance the business and machines are needed to facilitate production. The money and machines needed are referred to as **capital/financial resources**, and this is the third factor of production.

- Finally, the bakery will not run itself – bakers will need instructions, schedules will have to be made up, resources have to be regulated and the business idea has to be kept alive. This is the work of the entrepreneur, who is a necessary element of the production process. This means that **entrepreneurial ability** is the fourth and final factor of production.

Land/natural resources

Land is not simply the surface of the earth; rather, it involves everything that is naturally produced in the environment – from sunlight, which is freely and abundantly available, to oil, which is scarce and expensive. Other examples of natural resources that would fall within this category are minerals from the earth's surface, fish from the sea and wood from the forest. Many businesses and industries are based on natural resources and these have been used by many Caribbean businesses. Some natural resources are renewable – they are replaced naturally at the same pace as they are being used up – while others are non-renewable. Non-renewable resources are those that take a long time to be replaced and therefore the rate at which they are being used up is much faster than the rate at which they are being replaced. This means that, at some point in the future, the world will not have enough of these resources to sustain current consumption levels. Popular examples of non-renewable resources are fossil fuels such as oil and coal. The availability of these resources now and in the future has implications for the operation of businesses which use these goods in their production process.

Natural resources in the Caribbean

The Caribbean, being a series of islands, is blessed with beaches and year-round sunshine. In addition, each island has industries built around the natural resources that are available. Some of the industries developed around the natural resources found in the Caribbean are discussed below.

Tourism

This is perhaps the industry that is most commonly associated with the Caribbean and is the greatest source of income for Caribbean countries. Tourism is most prevalent in Caribbean countries such as Jamaica, Barbados, the Cayman Islands, the Bahamas and Cuba. Tourism makes use of natural resources, such as beaches, vegetation, forests and food, found in the Caribbean. As an industry, tourism is linked to other industries such as agriculture (which grows food for tourists to eat) and construction, which builds the hotels that tourists stay in. It also provides foreign exchange for Caribbean states.

Banana industry

Bananas are one of the products that were very popular in the early years of the development of independent Caribbean territories. Bananas are grown in the Caribbean for export to European markets (particularly England) and also to American markets. In addition, the fruit is used to supply manufacturing and agro-processing industries in the Caribbean that use

Bananas, an important part of the history of Caribbean countries, are still grown widely throughout the Caribbean and exported to America and to countries in Europe.

the fruit to make juice, chips, nectar and concentrates. The economies of Windward and Eastern Caribbean Islands such as Saint Lucia, Saint Vincent and the Grenadines, and Grenada were built primarily around the exportation of bananas to a guaranteed European market, although other countries such as Jamaica, Trinidad and Tobago and Dominica also used it as a foreign-exchange earner.

Sugar industry

Like bananas, sugar was the mainstay of some Caribbean economies for a number of years. While there are now only six countries in the Caribbean producing sugar (Jamaica, Trinidad and Tobago, Barbados, Guyana, Belize, and Saint Kitts and Nevis), it has been described as the industry that is responsible for creating the Caribbean as a distinct group of people.

Bauxite industry

Bauxite is a cornerstone of the economies of Jamaica and Guyana. Bauxite is mined from the earth and is further refined to make aluminum, which is an important raw material in developed countries that produce machines and automobiles. Bauxite is mined in Jamaica and Guyana, but much of the refining that needs to be done to get it into a useable and saleable state is done elsewhere.

Oil and natural gas

Petroleum and its derivatives have been the major money-earner for the Trinidadian government for a number of years. Within the Caribbean, Trinidad and Tobago has the greatest reserves of oil and natural gas with Barbados and Cuba being the only other Caribbean countries with oil reserves, although they have considerably less than

Trinidad. Oil-producing countries in the Caribbean are able to refine oil to varying degrees; this allows them to reduce the number of barrels of oil that they import and, in Trinidad's case, even export oil to other countries.

Other industries

The Caribbean has also been able to develop industries around husbandry (animal rearing) and forestry, which is used to supply lumber used in housing and furniture. The availability of limestone has also led to the production of cement in countries such as Jamaica and Trinidad and Tobago. In many Caribbean countries, the natural resources available are used not just for exports but, increasingly, more industries are developing that process these raw materials right here in the Caribbean and then export the finished goods.

Labour/human resources

Labour is described as the effort made by the worker in order to ensure that production takes place. This labour is exerted under strict or implied contractual terms with clear instructions, conditions and objectives attached. Labour can be exerted in various ways and with varying degrees of physical exertion – the worker who spends many hours in the factory, lifting boxes and operating machines as well as the worker who spends hours in the office reading documents and writing reports have both contributed labour to the production process.

Labour and productivity

Do you remember when you started typing? More than likely, you were what is called a 'pick-typist' – you started typing with your left and right middle fingers. These fingers were poised over the keyboard as you searched for the right character. When you found it, instead of tapping that key alone, you would inevitably tap the key beside it as well, resulting in 'typos'. As you used the keyboard more frequently, you became more proficient at typing and you started using other fingers to type as well. Pretty soon, the thumb was designated for the space bar and the middle fingers were complemented by the introduction of the index fingers as well. In short, as you have no doubt discovered by now, the more often you typed, the fewer mistakes you made and the faster you were able to go.

This example describes the phenomenon of **productivity**. Productivity describes the relationship between inputs and outputs; it explores what happens to the output of a business as more units of each of the factors of production are included in the production process. Labour productivity is concerned with the extent to which an increase of one unit of labour (whether an extra hour or an extra worker or an extra dollar in wages) causes output to increase. For example, if labour hours are doubled and this results in output being tripled, then labour is said to be productive. In essence, if output increases at a faster rate than the increase in labour input, then labour is said to be productive. Of course, if labourers are able to produce more without increasing the number of hours they work, then this is also considered to be productive. Put simply, when workers become better at what they are doing so that they can produce more using the same quantity of or even fewer resources, then they are said to be productive.

The productivity of labour is an important concept to consider since entrepreneurs' decisions to remain in business are often related to the profits that increased labour productivity generates. Many foreign investors have relocated from the Caribbean to South American countries because of the productivity of workers in these countries relative to Caribbean territories. Indeed, many South American and Asian countries, such as Mexico and Taiwan, have created competitive industries built on the model of highly productive workers. As a result, many popular brands, who have their headquarters in rich developed countries such as the United States, have located their production facilities to these South American and Asian countries.

♻ Making connections: mathematics

Measuring productivity can be very tricky. In the first instance, you have to consider that productivity is measured over time – 'Are workers doing more this year with the same quantity of resources that they used last year?' Additionally, numbers can be very misleading when looking at change. For example, consider the table below, which shows the monthly output of a cheese factory with its associated labour costs over a three-month period.

	April	May	June
Labour costs ($)	20 000	25 000	22 000
Output (kg)	35 000	40 000	39 600

Now let us find out whether the factory workers were more productive in May than they were in June.

- The first point we note is that labour costs increased in May by $5000 and output increased by 5000 kg. It is tempting (but would be incorrect) to conclude that labour and cost increased by the same amount. Dollars and kilograms are different units and we cannot say whether 5000 kg is more than, less than or equal to $5000.

- To solve this problem of different units, we need to look at the output for each dollar

of labour for each month. This would give us a common unit for comparisons. For April and May, output per unit of labour costs is calculated as follows

$$\text{April:} \quad \text{Output per unit} = \frac{35\,000}{20\,000} = 1.75$$

$$\text{May:} \quad \text{Output per unit} = \frac{40\,000}{25\,000} = 1.60$$

- This means that each dollar paid to workers in April resulted in 1.75 kg of cheese being produced in that month; in May, however, each dollar of labour resulted in only 1.60 kg of cheese. It is obvious that the workers were less productive in May than they were in April.

- What about labour productivity in June compared to April and May? Calculate the productivity of labour in June in order to determine if the workers were more productive in June than they were in April or in May.

- Write down a formula using output and input for calculating the productivity of workers.

- Suppose output for each unit of labour is at the same level over a two-month period. What can we conclude about the productivity of workers?

Factors that determine labour productivity

How does labour become more productive over time? Perhaps if the question was personalised to become *'How do you become more efficient over time?'* you would immediately think of some strategies. The strategies that individuals use to increase their productivity are pretty similar to those that businesses employ to develop their labour productivity. Some of these strategies are:

- **Education and training**: this strategy ensures that workers are better equipped with the skills needed to perform the tasks to which they have been assigned. This strategy focuses on empowering individuals to make better decisions and to develop a deeper understanding of the tasks that they are performing. Education and training are likely to lead to a labour force that is better able to function in the workplace, will make fewer mistakes and will develop strategies to produce a greater level of output using the same quantity of resources. Education is slightly different from training – training usually involves an on-the-job component that education often lacks. Education is typically aimed at developing general knowledge about industry-wide practices, while training is focused on developing competence in working in a specific business situation.

- **Technology**: technology leads to efficiency as it greatly increases the capacity of the business to produce greater volumes of output. Some modern technological advances, such as the computer, have completely revolutionised how workers approach various tasks and have exponentially increased the capacity of the business. An important point to note, though, is that technology and labour must work together to create one seamless whole.

- **Human resource development and working conditions**: generally, a satisfied workforce is more likely to be productive. Human resource development, as a strategy, focuses on maintaining morale in the labour force by addressing the many needs of the workers. These needs may include health insurance, satisfactory working conditions and adequate and fair reward and recognition for work done. Indeed, working conditions can be singled out as one of the most important factors that determine productivity. The condition under which employees work is determined by many factors and range from the salaries they receive to whether or the air conditioner is working properly.

Think about it

Would you be *more* productive because you receive a salary or would it simply stop you from being demotivated? Many people think that since workers *expect* to receive salaries, then this will not motivate them; rather, motivating them requires that they get more than they expected. What do you think?

- **Operation design**: how the workforce and workspace are organised is likely to affect the productivity of workers. If machines that workers are to use are placed in awkward positions that reduce their accessibility, affect traffic flow through the workplace and make it difficult for multiple users to access the machines simultaneously, then this is likely to affect productivity. In addition, poor scheduling may lead to delays in the delivery of raw materials, leaving the workforce with nothing to do. If machines are sent out for maintenance during peak working hours, then workers become unproductive as they have nothing to do. Deploying workers without regard to their skills and competence may also lead to bottlenecking, particularly when production units are interdependent. Finally, workers are likely to be more productive if they work on the same task repeatedly. This method of deploying workers, which is called specialisation, ensures that they become experts at the task to which they have been assigned and which they perform repeatedly. Specialisation does have its drawbacks, however. It leads to monotony and boredom as it does not challenge workers and does not develop all their skills. Additionally, when workers work on only one part of the entire product, it is difficult for them to identify themselves with and take pride in the finished product.

For you to research

Use the internet to search for the term 'bottleneck'. Make sure you are able to say, in relation to production, what a 'bottleneck' is and how and when it is likely to occur.

Labour and migration

A country's labour force is affected by **migration** and, as a result, it is a useful concept to discuss. Migration occurs when citizens of a country or any geographically defined area permanently relocate to another country or area. Migration can be external or internal. External migration occurs when workers relocate to another country, while internal migration occurs when workers relocate within the country – usually from rural to urban areas.

Causes of migration

Migration tends to be discussed in terms of push and pull factors. There may be certain factors that a person experiences that make him want to move to a different country. These factors, which are usually unpleasant, are called push factors. At the same time, he may perceive that another country has better conditions and opportunities for living and working and, as a result, he may have an interest in living in that country. These factors that attract him to this country are called pull factors.

 Now it's your turn

The following are some factors that cause migration. Describe how each can be both a push factor as well as a pull factor.

1 crime

2 employment opportunities

3 living conditions

4 quality of healthcare

5 educational opportunities

6 religious persecution.

The effects of migration

Migration's effect on the labour force is twofold – on the one hand, the labour force is bolstered by the introduction of foreigners with their own expertise; on the other hand, the labour force is depleted by the migration of locals to other countries. To discuss migration, then, we must first establish a definition for net migration. Net migration is the difference between the number of people migrating to a country (immigrants) and those leaving the country (emigrants). In the Caribbean, there are more emigrants than immigrants and hence there is a negative net migration rate of emigrants over immigrants. Essentially, what this means is that the Caribbean loses more from migration than it gains. The following positive effects of migration on the labour force can be identified:

- Migration is likely to introduce to Caribbean economies experts and professionals trained in other countries.

- It has traditionally been difficult to find professionals to work in some areas because of the nature and emphasis of the Caribbean education system. If there is an inadequate number of trained locals to take up these positions, then they can be filled by immigrants. For example, it has been difficult for the University of the West Indies to find qualified people within the Caribbean to lecture in such departments as geography, mathematics and mathematics education. As a result, they have had to look to other countries.

- When highly trained professionals migrate to the Caribbean, they usually do so only when they are lured by a comparatively high salary. The high wages that immigrants to the Caribbean receive are likely to have a positive impact on the wages of the locals as well. This means that migration may actually cause the wages of all to increase – both locals and immigrants. This has a positive effect on the supply of labour among locals and may even stop the negative net migration rates.

The negative effects of migration on the labour force are centred around the idea of **brain drain** and its depletion of the local labour market. Some of these ideas are outlined below:

- When qualified Caribbean citizens, trained at the expense of Caribbean states, leave the territory, this is referred to as 'brain drain'. This problem is worsened by the fact that developed countries, such as the United States, England and Canada, which are the traditional destinations for Caribbean citizens, have tightened their migration policies. The result is that these countries are screening potential migrants more thoroughly and are mainly allowing only skilled and employable people to migrate. As a consequence, trained people are more likely than those who are not deemed fit for employment to leave the Caribbean. In recent years, Caribbean countries have also seen an increase in the number of advertisements placed by foreign companies and governments targeting local citizens. Caribbean nurses and teachers, in particular, have been leaving in droves to live and work abroad, further worsening the brain drain.

- Brain drain is also worsened by the fact that people who migrate are normally at their most productive age – they are young (usually between 25 and 35 years old) and would have contributed much to the economy had they stayed. They are also at the age when they are most likely to have children and this has implications for population growth and the size and quality of the future Caribbean labour force.

- An influx of low-skilled workers is likely to reduce the average wage rate for everyone – locals and immigrants alike. This is not a major problem for many Caribbean countries as

cross-border migration in the Caribbean is very low and most Caribbean countries have economies that are at about the same stage of development. However, in other countries such as the United States, the high rate of immigration of untrained, low-skilled foreigners (such as immigrants from Mexico and perhaps even the Caribbean) has led to a reduction in the wage that these workers are likely to get.

Other effects of migration

In addition to affecting the labour force, migration also has positive and negative effects on the wider economy. One positive effect, for example, is that migration creates remittances for Caribbean countries. Emigrants from the Caribbean are likely to send back to the Caribbean a portion of their earnings once they settle in another country. These remittances are an important source of funding for many Caribbean countries. A negative effect of migration, however, is that it is likely to put pressure on the resources of the destination country. Once again, this is not a major problem for Caribbean countries, but in many countries, immigrants are often unemployed and in some cases unemployable. The result is that they often have to be supported by the social welfare programmes of the destination countries. Overpopulation and its associated problems such as housing crises, strain on infrastructure and social resources and high crime rates, is also a potential problem of migration that the destination country faces.

🌐 Business in your world

Migration and the UWI

As we discuss the effects of migration, it is tempting to think that people migrate *from* the Caribbean *to* 'greener pastures' such as the United Kingdom, Canada or the United States and never the reverse. However, people also migrate from these countries to the Caribbean, though not as frequently. Ironically, even as people move away from the Caribbean because they cannot find employment, most people who migrate to the Caribbean do so in order to take up job offers.

The University of West Indies (UWI), for example, is one popular place of employment for migrants to the Caribbean. At the university, 37 per cent of its staff originated from countries and territories outside the Caribbean. These countries and territories include the United Kingdom, Ireland, Europe, Africa, the USA, South and Central America, India, Asia, Canada, Australia and New Zealand. Of course, the UWI has main campuses in three countries – Jamaica, Trinidad and Tobago and Barbados. As a result, these countries are expected to have a higher number of migrants than others in the Caribbean. Recent news has called into question the continued role of immigrants at the UWI. Professor E. Nigel Harris, Vice Chancellor at the UWI, made the revelations that given the high rate of crime in Trinidad and Tobago and also in Jamaica, foreigners are turning down offers to work at campuses in these countries. This is cause for concern since, without immigrants, the diversity that is so vital to the workforce of a university will not be possible at the UWI. This, it is feared, will significantly affect the quality of the graduates of the UWI and will have a ripple effect on the wider Caribbean economy.

Questions for discussion

1 Why would migrants leave developed countries such as the USA or the United Kingdom to live and work in a developing country such as Jamaica? What push/pull factors do you think would influence such a decision?

2 What can the UWI do to continue to attract foreigners to work there?

3 Is it likely to be more or less efficient to use labour from developed countries such as the USA? What benefits are there to this?

Capital as a factor of production

Capital is the money used to start a business. To see capital as money only and not as machinery and other goods and assets, however, is to misrepresent the idea of what capital is. Capital is really all man-made resources – financial and otherwise – used to start, operate and expand a business. It means then that capital includes money, the machines in the factory, the delivery car and vans used by the business and the building and premises on which it is located. In short, capital refers to all resources owned by the business.

Making connections: principles of accounts

Are you familiar with the basic accounting equation of asset = capital? If not, research what this means or ask a teacher or classmate to assist you. How does this equation reinforce what we have been saying about capital not just being money?

Forms of capital

Capital can be seen as serving different purposes and can be held in different forms. For example, a business is expected to have assets such as land, factory, machines and furniture that are not used up in the day-to-day running of the business. It is also expected to have some assets that have only a short life and which, as a result, are used up and replaced often to keep the

business operational. Each business, however, will more than likely have a portion of each form of capital in order to remain viable. Generally, there are three forms of capital, which are outlined below.

Fixed capital

Fixed capital is the capital that remains in the business for a long time as it is invested in fixed assets (such as land, buildings and machines). This type of capital is not fully used up in the production process and is different from, for example, raw materials and cash which, more than likely, have to be replenished frequently during (or at the end of) the production process. An asset such as a machine, for example, is bought once and used over many years – maybe as many as 20 years – before it needs to be replaced.

Working capital

Working capital is also called circulating capital and is used to keep the business going from one day to the next. Working capital is perhaps one of the most important types of capital as, without it, a business is not likely to remain viable regardless of how profitable it is. Working capital is a bit difficult to understand without some idea of accounting, but an example may help. Imagine that you have $2000 cash and that you are also trying to sell your new cellphone and expect that it will fetch about $3500. In addition, a friend had borrowed some money from you and he is to repay it tomorrow. The amount is $1000. You therefore have $2000 for certain but, if all goes according to plan, then very soon you should have another $4500 to bring your total up to $6500. This is money that you can spend either now or in the near future. This is your working capital – you can go out tomorrow and buy items valued at $2000 or you can even buy on credit items that are valued up to $4500 because you expect to get this amount soon.

Suppose you have a debt of $3000 that you will have to pay, do you still have $6500 as working capital? Well, in this case, you really only have $3500, because you must repay your debt. A business is faced with a similar situation – it must look at the money that it has now or will get soon (from selling its stock or collecting from its debtors) and then it must look at the debts that it must pay either now or soon. The difference between what it has or hopes to get and what it owes is its working capital. The amount of working capital that a business has determines the **liquidity** of a business – businesses that are very liquid have large amounts of working capital.

Venture capital

When a person starts a business, he or she will need money to purchase the fixed assets of the business and to finance its early expenses such as advertisements and utilities. This capital is called venture capital and it is perhaps now that the famous definition of 'money used to start a business' can be accurately used. For many businesses, the venture capital is obtained through a venture capitalist, as discussed in Chapter 4 (see page 65). These venture capitalists provide the seed money on the understanding that they share in the profit of the business or receive interest on their investments.

Entrepreneurial abilities as the fourth factor of production

In Chapter 4, we looked at entrepreneurs and their role in starting and operating businesses. They are the ones responsible for bringing together the other factors of production (land, labour and capital) discussed so far. Given the role that entrepreneurs play in organising production, they are considered to be the fourth factor of production. As a factor of production, entrepreneurs are expected to:

- Make decisions about the combination of the other factors in the production process. This is the key role of the entrepreneur as a factor of production. The entrepreneur, who sees the business as an entire unit, is expected to make decisions to optimise the use of each factor and to create a production process that minimises costs.

- Organise, schedule, co-ordinate and manage the other factors of production. This means creating systems for controlling the purchasing of raw materials and stock, developing systems for rewarding, controlling and developing workers and deciding which fixed assets to buy and how to use working capital.

- Anticipate eventualities affecting each of the factors of production and put in place effective plans to eliminate or minimise the occurrence of these eventualities.

Summary – Section A

- Products that are tangible and can be stored are called goods, while intangible products that can only be experienced are called services.

- Production is the process of using various resources to create a finished product – whether a good or a service.

- The resources that are used up in production are called factors of production and are classified under four major headings – land and natural resources; labour and human resources;

capital and financial resources; and entrepreneurial ability.

- The Caribbean has many industries – such as tourism, bauxite and agriculture – that have developed around natural resources.

- Labour productivity describes what happens to the output of a business when it increases the amount of labour that it employs.

- Labour is said to be productive when workers become better at what they are doing so that they can produce more using fewer or the same quantity of resources.

- Labour becomes more productive when workers are trained, educated and satisfied and when technology that they can use in production is available.

- Migration affects a country's labour force as it reduces the number of trained workers available for work even though it also has the potential to add qualified and skilled immigrant workers to the workforce.

- Resources owned by a business are called capital and this can be held in one of three forms: fixed capital, working capital and venture capital.

- Entrepreneurial ability is the factor of production responsible for bringing the other factors together by creating systems and processes that manage these factors optimally.

End of section activities

Quick questions

Write short answers in your exercise books to the following questions:

1 What are the four factors of production?

2 Under which factor of production would you classify machines and motor vehicles?

3 Give one example of an industry developed around a natural resource in your country.

4 Who are emigrants?

5 What is meant by the net migration rate?

6 List the three forms of capital.

7 How would you calculate the working capital of a business?

8 Give two examples of a non-renewable resource.

9 Give two ways in which workers may be made more productive.

Applying what you have learnt

1 There are four factors of production — land, labour, capital and entrepreneurial abilities. These factors were developed long ago when ownership of land was a major indication of wealth and was necessary for businesses to operate. Additionally, those who did not own land had no choice but to provide their labour in order to earn money.

a Can you think of any production process that does not use any of the factors of production?

b Do you think land and other natural resources have to be one of the factors of production? For example, think of internet-based companies, such as match.com, which arranges dates online. Does it use any/much land or natural resources? Should this factor be removed from the list?

c Are the factors all relevant when we look at producing services versus producing goods? Think of the following services and identify the four factors being combined in each:

i a taxi ride

ii a visit to the hairdresser/barber

iii watching a movie online

iv using a mobile network to make calls on your cellphone.

d Additionally, times have changed since the factors of production were first identified. In light of this, can you think of anything that should be *added* to the list as a factor of production?

2 Carry out a poll within your school (of between 20 and 30 students) to determine what percentage of your sample is likely to migrate after finishing school. For those who are thinking of migrating, determine their reasons for wanting to leave.

Which reasons are most popular? Classify them as push and pull factors and rank them in terms of popularity.

3 When looking at the working capital of a business, a useful principle to use is that of coverage – how many times does its money cover its debts? Take a business, for example, that has cash (whether in hand now or that it will receive soon) of $40 000 and debts of $16 000 has working capital of $24 000 and a coverage of 2.5 (calculated as 40 000 ÷ 16 000). This means that the company can pay off its debts twice and still have some money left. This is a good liquidity position to be in.

a Calculate the working capital and coverage for each of the following companies:

i JamTel Ltd: cash of $36 000; debts of $24 000

ii CariDeal Ltd: cash of $18 000; debts of $6 000

iii Windy's Ltd: cash of $27 000; debts of $18 000.

b Compare JamTel Ltd with Windy's Ltd; they both have the same coverage but different working capital. Which of them is in a better liquidity position? Explain why you think so.

c Compare JamTel Ltd to CariDeal Ltd; they both have the same working capital but different coverage. Which of them is in a better liquidity position? Justify your answer.

d Which company would you say is in the best liquidity position overall? Justify your selection.

Model exam questions
Question 1
a What is meant by the term labour productivity? (3 marks)

b Outline three factors that affect the productivity of labour. (3 marks)

c Herbert is a factory manager and wants to increase the productivity of the workers in the factory. He is thinking of making workers specialise in certain tasks. Advise him on the likely effect of this strategy on the workforce. (5 marks)

Question 2
a Define what is meant by the term migration. (3 marks)

b Outline two negative effects of migration on the labour force of your country. (6 marks)

c Discuss two positive effects of migration on the economy of your country. (6 marks)

Question 3
a What is meant by the term capital? (3 marks)

b Discuss three functions played by capital in a business. (6 marks)

c Outline any two sources of capital available to a business. (4 marks)

Levels of production

The part-time farmer with a patch of tomatoes growing in his backyard is involved in the production of tomatoes in the same way as the large farmer with hundreds of hectares of tomatoes. The difference, of course, is that the part-time farmer and the large farmer have different markets in mind when they planted their tomatoes. More than likely, the backyard farmer's thoughts have not gone beyond providing food for his family to consume, while the large farmer is thinking about exporting tomatoes to other countries. These two farmers are producing at different levels since they are producing on different scales and for different markets. In general, there are three levels of production and these are described below.

The subsistence level of production

This is production with personal consumption in mind. **Subsistence production** takes place when an individual produces enough of a product for his (or his family's) own consumption. Trading may take place if, after consumption, the producer finds himself with excess goods. If an economy is involved in subsistence production, then it means that it consumes all the goods that it produces and does not export to the rest of the world. Examples of subsistence production are:

- a do-it-yourself enthusiast who made the furniture for her house
- a gardener with a 'green thumb' who planted small crops in his garden
- a motorist who repaired his car by himself.

Subsistence production does not encourage growth in the economy as it is only through producing goods for sale that an economy can grow. Little or no technology is used in this type of production and the production process is usually manned by a single individual who works long hours to get a finished product. Usually, the producer has limited resources – small land space, no additional manpower or lack of capital – and therefore is not able to diversify into other products. As a result, all resources are usually tied up in one product or venture, which exposes such a producer to a high level of risk. For example, the available land that a farmer has may be tied up in one crop; if drought or rain destroys the crop or reduces its yield, then the farmer may lose all or most of what he has invested.

The domestic level of production

This level of production is concerned with satisfying the needs of the nation. At this level of production, each producer employs all the resources available to him to produce more than he will consume. The surplus is traded locally among producers of other goods. In this economy, the goal is to create self-sufficiency so that there is no need to import products to complement what is available locally. Traditionally, **domestic production** is usually seen as involving no export as well; the absence of import and export from the economy means that this level of production results in a closed economy – no trade with the outside world. To achieve surplus output, individuals in an economy producing at the domestic level usually specialise and use machinery and technology to increase their output.

Export level of production

Export production is the highest level of production and, ultimately, should be the aim of all economies. At this level, more than enough goods are produced to satisfy domestic consumption and the excess is exported. Since goods are being produced for another market, production needs to be of a high quality and should be produced in quantities that greatly exceed local consumption levels. This is achieved by employing heavy-duty machines and fixed capital in the production process. Additionally, whatever linkages among

Large-scale production for export is facilitated through the use of machines and technology.

industries that can be formed within the economy are exploited as the economy positions itself to maximise its output potential. We will study more about linkages later in the chapter (see pages 107–8), but think of the potential for increasing the export of banana-related products if farmers in banana-exporting countries were to be linked with manufacturers in these countries.

Types of production

There are three different types of production, which come together to form a process; each is therefore linked to and dependent on another as the output of one type becomes the input for another. This process starts with primary production and ends with tertiary production; secondary production connects these two types by making the output more useable.

Primary production

This is the first stage of production, which involves extracting raw materials from their natural environment – usually the land or sea. For this reason, **primary production** is also referred to as extractive production. This stage is described as 'primary' because it is the first stage of production and all the other stages depend on it – no production takes place which does not involve a product that can be traced back to the natural environment. Examples of primary production include farmers, miners and fishermen. The outputs of primary production – referred to as primary products – usually have not been processed and are often of little value until they have been further developed; this is done in secondary production. As an example, a piece of lumber (a primary product) is of little value to most people in its primary form. However, people are prepared to pay a lot of money for a piece of furniture constructed using this piece of lumber.

Secondary production

Goods produced by primary production are important because they form the basis of all subsequent production; however, they are usually not in a form that consumers can immediately exploit. **Secondary production** is the process of making banana bread from bananas, orange juice from oranges and furniture from trees. In secondary production, therefore, a primary product is further processed to change its form and increase its utility to the consumer. Alternatively, secondary production involves combining different primary products or even primary and secondary products to create one finished good. Secondary production, therefore, can be further subdivided into manufacturing and construction. Manufacturing usually involves the mere processing of raw materials to create another product. For example, making aluminum from bauxite, making sugar from sugar cane and making concentrate from fruit. Construction, on the other hand, usually describes what happens when manufactured goods (such as sugar, nectars and spices) are combined to give another product (such as a cake or juice). Secondary production is said to add value to a product – for example, orange juice has more economic value than the oranges as the manufacturer has made them more attractive to the consumer. As a result, orange juice is expected to be more expensive than oranges.

Tertiary production

'Why are snacks at the theatre more expensive than they would be elsewhere?' The answer is related to value added – a concept that was introduced when we looked at secondary production. **Tertiary production** refers to the production of services. In tertiary production, primary and secondary products are combined with labour to offer a service. An example of tertiary production is what takes place in a restaurant – primary products (such as fresh vegetables and fruits) and secondary products (such as chairs, plates and forks) are combined with labour (in the form of the chef, the waiters and whatever entertainment may be present) to offer a service. As with earlier stages of production, tertiary production uses the output of stages that occurred before it as its input. Value is again added to these outputs, however, making services more expensive than primary and secondary products. It is for this reason that snacks in a movie theatre are more expensive than they would be elsewhere. When you buy a snack in a movie theatre, you are not just paying for the snack but also for the opportunity to eat it while watching a movie in comfortable surroundings.

 Now it's your turn

Classify the following activities as primary, secondary (specify whether construction or manufacturing) or tertiary:

1 making concrete blocks
2 offering a tour of a historic museum site
3 making a television set
4 planting flowers for sale
5 selling pets

6 making pizza

7 making sugar from sugar cane

8 using cheese, butter, flour and eggs to make a cake

9 offering food for sale in a restaurant

Tertiary production – a fried fish served in a restaurant is the result of primary and secondary products being combined with labour to offer a service.

Cottage industry

Production in the Caribbean takes place in settings that are sometimes different from what we described in earlier sections of this chapter. One striking feature about production in the Caribbean is that much of it takes place in the home or in settings that were not intended for production. When production takes place in such settings, then it is described as a cottage industry. The term is derived from the fact that the home is the most popular non-industrial premises where production takes place. However, if the home economics department of

a school starts baking cakes that are distributed through nearby supermarkets, then this also falls under the label of **cottage industry**.

Production that takes place in a cottage industry is obviously likely to be very different from production that takes place in a factory. In the first place, one does not expect that a cottage industry will have large machines and advanced technology to aid in the production process. Rather, production is typically carried out using manual labour and hence the scale of production is very small. Usually, the products that are produced in a cottage industry are simple to produce, require very little capital and are made from raw materials available in the local environment. Labour used in a cottage industry is usually low-skilled and is often drawn from family members. As such, they may have no special training in the production of the particular product. Craft is therefore a popular product of cottage industry as this product is simple to produce, requires little or no capital and is usually made from items that are easily available in the natural environment.

Cottage industries face many challenges, including:

- Inadequate capital to expand the business.

- Little or no market research or marketing activity to promote the product or the business.

- Lack of technical knowledge about the product and about how to manage a business.

- Homogeneity of products – producers in cottage industry usually have products that are very similar, offering no real variety to consumers and hence reducing the chance that any one producer will have any distinct advantage.

Linkage industries

Two industries are said to be linked if the output of one industry becomes the input of the other industry. For example, the goods produced in the agricultural industry are used by the tourism industry to produce local cuisine for tourists. Many other industries are linked and some linkages are more subtle than others. For example, if a new factory is built in a previously secluded area, then a taxi service is usually required to ferry employees to and from work in the factory. Here the factory is linked to the taxi service. The taxi service is also linked to mechanics, car dealers and petrol stations and these are, in turn, linked to other industries. The ripple effect that occurs when industries are linked is one of the main benefits of the **linkage industries** and we will discuss this in more detail below (see 'Benefits of linkages').

Types of linkages – forward and backward

Generally, every linkage creates two relationships – which form the type of linkages (forward and backward). Let us revisit the idea of the tourism industry being linked to the agricultural industry. In this linkage, the output of the agricultural industry becomes the input of the tourism industry. This one linkage provides both a forward and a backward linkage. From the perspective of producers in the agricultural industry, this is a **forward linkage**, since their output is used by producers in the tourism industry. A forward linkage occurs in an industry when its output is used by another industry. Using the same example of linkage between the tourism and agricultural industries, also gives us the idea of **backward linkage**. The tourism industry is experiencing a backward linkage because it must depend on the output of producers in the agricultural industry. A backward linkage, therefore, exists when an industry has to depend on another industry for its input.

 Now it's your turn

Describe the following linkage that exists in each of the following relationships between industries/firms. In each case, identify the firm/industry involved in the forward and backward linkage.

1 the airport and car rental companies

2 the hospital and private ambulances

3 furniture makers and hotels

4 bauxite mining companies and car makers

5 bakers, flour mills and bakeries

Benefits of linkages

- **Increased economic performance**: linkages create relationships among firms that allow the economy to take advantage of the opportunities that exist for growth and development. For example, the building of a hotel creates many linkages throughout the economy as primary producers of lumber and cement get a chance to increase their production, service producers such as contractors, carpenters and masons also become economically active, and related support industries such as restaurants and taxi services also benefit.

- **Increased employment**: when an industry is linked to another, the growth of one industry directly stimulates the other industry as well. So, for example, the growth of the tourism industry leads to increased demand for agricultural products and hence increased employment in the agricultural sector. In other words, when industries are linked, the growth of one industry is distributed across other industries in the economy. This creates employment as more people are needed to supply the products that a growing economy needs.

- **Increased investment**: linkages ensure that more of the nation's output is used at source. So, for example, linking the banana industry and the food processing industry may result in the development of products such as ready-made banana porridge, banana cake, banana-flavoured sweets and ice cream. Using the products at their source, meaning where they were first produced, increases investment since producers will have to inject capital into the processing of these products.

- **Reduced demand for foreign currency**: this results from the reduced dependence on imported goods that linkages bring. Imported goods are bought with the currencies of other countries and hence if importation is replaced with production at source, then demand for foreign currency is also reduced.

- **Diversification of the economy**: the Caribbean has a long history of primary products dominating the economy. Linking these primary industries to secondary and tertiary industries will create other vibrant industries, resulting in a more diversified economy.

Location analysis

One of the most important decisions that a firm will ever have to make is where to locate its production facilities. This decision is important as building a production plant is very expensive and is usually an investment that shows commitment to a location for a number of years. Some of the factors to consider before a location decision is made are:

- **Availability of raw materials and supplies**: when deciding on a location, it is ideal to be close to suppliers so as to minimise transportation and delivery costs. If raw materials are perishable and fragile, then they are likely to be damaged during delivery if they have to be transported over long distances. The aim, therefore, is to reduce the distance between the production facility and the suppliers.

- **Proximity to market**: firms want to know that they are close to the major target markets for their products. Customers should be able to easily access the firm's distribution outlet so as to purchase its products. One of the challenges that producers may experience is that there is a trade-off between locating close to suppliers and raw materials while also being accessible to customers. Closeness to suppliers or raw materials may mean being far away from residential or central areas. Firms try to address this problem by having distribution points that are accessible by the general public.

- **Infrastructure**: the availability of good road networks and support services such as hospitals, police stations and schools is also a factor to consider. If these are non-existent or in poor condition, then it may affect the ability of the business to attract labour, customers and suppliers. Poor road networks also affect the cost structure of the business as it may have to use circuitous routes over poor-quality roads to transport goods to and from its production facilities.

- **Utilities**: the reliable, consistent supply of water and electricity is important for the operation of the business. The costs of these utilities should not be prohibitively high so that it becomes unprofitable to do business.

- **Transportation**: it should not be difficult for customers, employees and suppliers to access the business. Reliable transportation is therefore important if the production facility is to be kept operational.

- **Labour supply**: a business can gain a competitive advantage from having a good-quality, committed workforce. Locating the business in an area where there is always an available supply of highly trained workers is, therefore, key. In many Caribbean countries, for example, the tendency is for university graduates to settle in urban centres and, hence, production facilities located in rural areas may have a challenge finding qualified workers.

- **Governmental regulations and incentives**: the government may give tax breaks and other incentives for locating in a certain area. Additionally, zoning laws may also prevent firms from locating in some areas. These laws may be enacted to preserve an area or to protect housing developments taking place in the area.

- **Clustering**: firms operating in the same line of business are usually located close to each other. This **clustering** takes advantage of **economies of scale**, a concept that we will discuss in the next section.

Small firms

This era has rightly been described as 'the age of the entrepreneur'. Many people are opting to start their own businesses instead of joining the corporate ranks. Experts suspect that this is related to the fact that increased access to computer technology and the information that it provides has created new opportunities for starting businesses or has simplified the process of starting and managing a business. In this section, we will look at the functions of small businesses and how they differ from large businesses.

Functions of small businesses

It is important to note that small businesses and large businesses have pretty much the same basic functions – to create employment, provide goods and services and provide positive return on their investors' capital. However, the size of small businesses allows them to perform some functions that large businesses would not be able to. Some of these are:

- **Personalised service**: the size of small businesses allows them to offer services that appeal to customers in a very personal way. The owners of small businesses usually know their customers by name and habits. As a result, a small business may stock the brand that its customers are most likely to buy and may modify products to suit the needs of its customers. A small corner shop, for example, may sell flour with some cornmeal already mixed in; in a large supermarket chain, however, a customer would have to buy both cornmeal and flour separately. Small businesses may also offer services that large businesses would find unprofitable – for example in some small shops, for a few dollars more, a customer may actually have his bun cut open and butter or cheese placed in the middle.

- **Breaking bulk**: small businesses offer goods in small quantities. Customers are able to buy less than what was meant to be one unit – as an example, some small corner shops in Jamaica will actually cut a loaf of bread in half or even into quarters and sell each piece individually. Cheese, cooking oil, butter and margarine and ketchup are other products that small shops will sell in small quantities as well. This process of selling small quantities of a product is known as breaking bulk; when small businesses break bulk, they ensure that customers are not forced to buy a huge portion of a product in order to enjoy just a small amount. Breaking bulk is also very useful when consumers are not able to afford all that was meant to be sold as one unit.

- **Unmet demand**: if you think of the economy as a bucket, then large businesses can be likened to large rocks that are placed in the bucket until the bucket cannot take any more. But even when the bucket is full of rocks, there is still space between the rocks into which you can pour sand. The sand finding space in a 'full' bucket is similar to small businesses finding space to satisfy demand in the economy. Even when large businesses appear to be meeting all the demand for goods and services in the economy, there is still a portion of the market that has needs that can be met only by small businesses.

- **Responsiveness to opportunities**: small businesses are also more flexible and responsive. A change in consumer taste can be reflected on the shelves of small businesses within a day. This is related to the fact that the management of small businesses is less complicated and cumbersome and hence consultation takes less time. In large businesses, on the other hand, there is usually a delay of several months before changes can be effected.

- **A source of information**: small firms are very close to customers and are therefore acutely aware of what customers want. Large producers, who sell to these small businesses, can use the demand of the small businesses as an indication of what customers want.

Growth and small businesses

Small businesses do not stay small forever; they eventually grow into large businesses that command the industry's attention – or, at least, that is the hope of the owners of most small businesses. Change in the size of a business is likely to affect the business in a number of ways – not all of them positive. From its structure to its ability to export goods, a business is likely to find that things are not easy when its size increases. In this section, we look briefly at the effect that growth has on various aspects of the operations of a business.

Growth and organisational structure

In Chapter 4, we looked at the structure of a business and we indicated that most businesses will have either a matrix or a hierarchical structure. Growth is likely to cause one of two things to happen – either a widening of the span of control or a lengthening of the chain of command for the following reasons:

- As growth occurs, the number of subordinates who report to a single supervisor is likely to increase as more workers are taken on in each department.

- Additionally, more departments may be created and this too may widen the span of control for the managers to whom these department heads report.

- Another likely possibility is that more middle-level positions may be created and this will result in more levels existing between senior managers and low-level workers (in other words, the chain of command may be lengthened).

If a matrix structure is used, the growth of the firm is likely to mean that this structure has to be replaced as it becomes too difficult to manage it given the number of workers in the business.

Growth and capital

As the business grows, it is likely that more capital will have to be pumped into the business. Fixed capital will have to be increased as more heavy-duty machines and equipment will be needed. Working capital will also have to be increased as the day-to-day expenses of the business increase. As the business increases in size, however, it becomes far easier for its owners to access capital and it should not be difficult to attract interested investors to the business.

Growth and labour

Growth's effect on labour is often unclear. It is logical to think that a large business would need more workers than a small one and to a certain extent this is true. However, the increase in demand for labour is not proportionate to increase in size – as some of the demand for additional labour will be satisfied by investment in technology.

Growth and scale of production

This is an interesting idea that should be explored in detail. Economy of scale is the chief advantage that large businesses have over small businesses. As the size of a business increases, then it will find that it is possible to increase its output with a less than equivalent increase in costs. For example, it may be possible to increase output by 12 per cent while the related increase in cost is less than 12 per cent. Economies of scale can be classified in two ways – internal and external. These two ideas are discussed in more detail in the following sections.

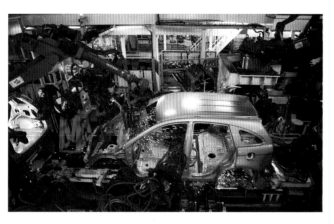

Mechanisation and automation create economies of scale.

 Making connections: mathematics

A firm's output is tripled. Under which of the following conditions is it experiencing economy of scale?

1 if its cost of production is doubled

2 if its cost is more than tripled

3 if its cost of production remains unchanged

4 if its cost of production is halved

Internal economies of scale

Internal economies of scale are the benefits to a firm arising out of its own increase in size or scale of operations. These economies affect or benefit only one business and are a direct result of the activities of that business. There are four types of economies of scale:

- **Technical economies of scale:** technical economies of scale occur when the business invests in machines and technology that allow it to increase its output faster than its costs. Machines and technology allow the workers to become more productive when they are used intensely and effectively. Since these machines represent a one-time investment, and whose use contributes very little to the overall cost structure of the business, they create economies of scale when they are used repeatedly and intensely.

- **Financial economies of scale:** large firms are able to borrow money more cheaply (at lower interest rates) than small firms. The cost of their capital is therefore low relative to small businesses. It should come as no surprise that the size of a firm will determine the rate at which it can borrow money. Small firms are perceived as being risky and unstable; as a result, banks and other financial houses are unwilling to lend to them. The situation is worsened by the fact that they usually do not have any collateral. Small firms, therefore, usually have to raise money from other sources of finance, which are normally more expensive. Large firms, on the other hand, are able to borrow money from banks that are willing to lend to them since they are perceived as being stable and risk free.

- **Bulk-output economies of scale:** large firms produce in bulk and, as a result, they also buy in bulk. This usually results in them receiving sizeable trade discounts that small businesses are unable to access.

- **Labour-related economies of scale:** as the scale of operation increases, the business is likely to employ more workers, trained in specialised areas and with highly developed skills. Workers are likely to be organised to perform specialised tasks; this is likely to make them more productive.

External economies of scale

External economies of scale occur outside a firm, within an industry. They are the reductions in cost which any business in an industry might enjoy as the industry grows. With external economies of scale, all firms within the industry will benefit. External economies of scale are more likely if the firms in the industry are located (concentrated) in one geographical location or in close proximity to each other. External economies of scale may arise for various reasons:

- **Clustering**: firms in the same line of operation locating close to each other. For example, many restaurants locate themselves close to their competitors. This creates external economies of scale as it allows them to share support services such as security, cleaning and maintenance. Additionally, a single supplier can be found who uses one delivery schedule to service all firms within a geographical location, resulting in reductions in transportation costs.

- **Labour**: when firms in the same line of business cluster around each other, then a pool of labour, particularly trained for firms in that industry, generally makes itself available for the industry. Often labour may move from one firm in the industry to another, resulting in savings for the second firm since the labour has already been trained. Schools and colleges sometimes offer courses tailored specifically for these industries.
- **Collusion**: co-operation and collusion are more likely if firms are in close proximity. Advertisement and research and development costs may be shared if firms co-operate.
- **Dis-integration**: this refers to the practice of breaking up a production process into distinguishable parts/tasks and allocating each part/task to firms in the industry. Dis-integration is the ultimate in collusion and co-operation and will lead to specialisation and eventually economies of scale for the industry.

Diseconomies of scale

There is a point beyond which any further increase in size will lead to a more than proportionate *increase* in cost. When increases in size lead to larger increases in costs, this is referred to as **diseconomies of scale**. As with economies of scale, there are two types of diseconomies of scale: internal and external. Internal diseconomies of scale affect an individual firm in the industry while external diseconomies of scale affect the entire industry. Internal diseconomies of scale result from the difficulties of managing large businesses. Some of these are:

- **Communication**: large firms will find that communication costs and problems will rise proportionately to size. As size increases, word-of-mouth communication will have to be replaced with high-tech, expensive formal communication systems. Not only do these communication systems add to overhead costs, they are usually less effective and motivating than face-to-face communication. Additionally, co-ordination of activities between

various departments in a large business is not a problem that small businesses have to cope with.
- **Disparities between departments**: the optimum quantity of output may be different for two departments. For example, in a factory making shirts, the dyeing department may be most efficient, processing 700 shirts per day, while the sewing department is most efficient at 1000 shirts per day. Since the two departments are interdependent, this bottleneck will result in an inefficient overall system.

Growth and use of technology

As the business grows, there will be a greater need to invest in technology in order to effectively manage the many different operations of the business. Given the growth of the business, the firm should be in a better position to make financial investments in the technology required. Large businesses are, therefore, more likely to have high levels of technology use. Production that is heavily dependent on fixed capital (such as machines and equipment) is said to be **capital intensive**. A production process that depends more on the pool of labour available to it, however, is said to be **labour intensive**. Large businesses are more likely than small businesses to be capital intensive.

Growth and potential for export

Large businesses have a greater potential than small businesses to export products. This is related to the fact that they are able to produce the quantities required to satisfy an export market. Additionally, the quality of their products is more in keeping with what is expected of exported goods. Finally, exported products usually have a standardised appearance and features – all products must be consistent. This is possible in a large business because of the introduction of technology, which has unvarying results.

Technology in production in the Caribbean

The Caribbean has traditionally been involved in primary production, which has always been very labour intensive – a large pool of unskilled workers is needed to plant and harvest crops. Machines that are used in primary production are often inefficient, unreliable and outdated. In Jamaica, for example, it is popular to jokingly describe the boilers in the sugar factories as items to be donated to the museums. The challenge that Caribbean countries face relative to technology in production is that, as developing countries, they find the cost of these machines and technology to be restrictive. For that reason, most production processes continue to be labour intensive, even though machines now exist that could make the process more efficient.

In many developed countries, production has been automated and mechanised. Production takes place using a conveyor-belt model – inputs move along a production line and machines perform various tasks and processes on the raw material at each stage of the process. Checks and balances are pre-set and occur automatically, and hence the production process requires fewer workers. In the Caribbean, due to the high costs involved, this model is often not possible. Rather, workers often work by hand to complete tasks that otherwise could have been done using machines. The lack of automation and mechanisation may result in:

- **Lack of standardised output**: each batch or product may be slightly different in taste and appearance from its predecessor.
- **Reduced quantity of output**: fewer units are produced if machines are not employed in the production process.
- **High production costs**: machines reduce the cost of producing each unit of a good.

Computer-aided design (CAD) and computer-aided instruction (CAI)

Computers can be used to help in design by creating simulations of hypothetical situations as determined by the computer operators. A CAD programme, for example, can simulate what would happen if three workers were employed and not two; or what would happen if the positions of machines in the factory were changed. This reduces the need to actually make the changes and then decide whether they were effective or not. Computer technology in the form of CAD is, therefore, an aid to factory layout and production design. CAI is another application of technology that, like CAD, has the potential to benefit business. CAI involves the use of computer and related technology to deliver instruction and training. Using CDs, the internet and other software and programmes, businesses can use CAI to:

- Address the educational development needs of the workforce: learning modules can be designed by managers to ensure that workers are exposed to best practices associated with the workplace. These modules can be placed on a CD or on the internet, so that workers can access them at their own pace and convenience.

- Complement the on-the-job training that workers receive: as employees go about performing the tasks assigned to them, new machines, technology, ideas and processes will be developed and introduced into the workplace. Workers will develop expertise in these innovations over time as they work with them. This kind of expertise is developed through on-the-job training that takes place as a natural result of the work routine. This training, however, may be insufficient, may take too long and may not address specific needs; as a result, managers may develop modules of information to be passed on to workers through CAI.

Summary – Section B

- In a country, production can take place at different levels, namely the subsistence, domestic and export levels of production. Each level of production is associated with different levels of output and employment of technology.

- Traditionally, productive activities take place in one of three sectors – primary, secondary (which includes both manufacturing and construction) and tertiary. The sectors are interdependent as one sector's output is the input for another sector.

- Small businesses operating from homes, schools or from other non-industrial premises are referred to as cottage industries. The production that takes place in these businesses is usually carried out with manual labour and these businesses therefore require very little capital.

- Linkages exist when businesses depend on each other – either for a market or for supply. Linkages create many benefits for the Caribbean, including increased employment, investments and the creation of a more diversified economy.

- When deciding where to locate their operations, businesses consider factors related to transportation, labour, raw material and market. They may also choose to locate close to firms offering similar products in order to take advantage of economies of scales.

- Economies of scale are one of the benefits that large businesses enjoy. They occur when a firm is able to increase its scale of production without a proportionate increase in cost. Economies of scale may result from the firm's own activities or from the activities of the industry within which the firm operates.

- Small businesses offer many benefits to society. Not only do they create employment opportunities, they also offer a highly personalised service, smaller or fewer units of a good to suit the customer's pocket and act as intermediary between large suppliers and customers.

- As businesses grow larger, they will face many challenges and experience many benefits. Firms will find that they have greater access to capital, greater potential to experience economies of scale and to target a larger export market. On the other hand, an increase in size is also likely to cause greater challenges in management and communication and the potential to experience diseconomies of scale.

- Caribbean businesses have not been able to embrace automation and mechanisation as they should, given the level of capital investment associated with these processes. Many Caribbean businesses are, as a result, still fairly labour intensive.

End of section activities

Quick questions

Say whether each of the following statements is true or false. For those that are false, what is wrong with them?

1 Farming does not require technology and, hence, it is an example of the subsistence level of production.

2 Secondary production produces goods with a lower value added than those produced in primary production.

3 The production of clothing items such as shirts and pants from locally made fabric is considered to be a manufacturing activity.

4 Cottage industries suffer from homogeneity. This means each batch of goods that they produce is same as a previous batch.

5 June's Block Factory supplies blocks to Pete's Construction Company; June's, therefore, has a forward linkage with Pete's.

6 Labour-intensive production is more efficient than capital-intensive production.

7 A large soft drink manufacturing company is more likely to locate closer to its suppliers than to its consumers since consumers may not buy directly from them.

8 Firms cluster in order to keep a closer eye on their competitors.

9 For economies of scale to occur, cost of production must decrease when output increases.

10 When all firms in the industry benefit from the action of a single firm, this is known as external economies of scale.

Applying what you have learnt

1 Look at the following products (some are goods and others are services) and rank them in terms of how well you think they will do in a cottage industry. Put the product that you think is most feasible for production in cottage industry first and the one that is least feasible last. Be prepared to justify your list.

   a cabinetry (furniture manufacturing)

   b recording studio

   c television repairs

   d pastry making

   e interior decorating

   f private math classes

2 Think of a raw material from the natural environment and trace its movement through the different types of productive activity. For example, what good is it used to produce in primary production? How is it used in secondary production – in both manufacturing and construction? What about tertiary production – what services is it used to deliver? How many ways can it be used in each sector?

a Based on the raw material that you have chosen, discuss the different linkages that are possible.

b At what stage is it the most expensive? Why?

3 Take a walk on a plaza or shopping centre in a busy business district. What stores do you see? What are the common characteristics of these stores? Look at the following list of stores and say which ones you would expect to find on a plaza. In each case, say why you would or would not expect them to be there.

a a restaurant

b a bottling plant for soft drinks

c a nightclub

d a movie theatre

e a block factory

f a flower farm and shop where potted plants are grown for sale

g a mechanic shop

Model exam questions

Question 1

a Explain what is meant by the term 'primary production'. (3 marks)

b Give two reasons why primary production is so popular in the Caribbean. (4 marks)

c Discuss two benefits that may result from Caribbean nations developing industries in secondary and tertiary production. (6 marks)

Question 2

a In deciding where to locate a business, why is proximity to raw materials important? (3 marks)

b For what kind of business would proximity to consumers be important? (2 marks)

c Jan is thinking about starting a business in primary production and Timz is thinking about starting one that offers a service. Discuss two differences in the way they may make their location decisions. (6 marks)

Question 3

a Explain what is meant by the term 'cottage industry'. (3 marks)

b List three challenges that cottage industries face. (3 marks)

c Discuss two initiatives that the government could implement to help cottage industries in your country. (6 marks)

Question 4

a Using an example, explain what is meant by the terms 'forward linkages' and 'backward linkages'. (4 marks)

b State any three benefits of increasing linkages among industries in your country. (3 marks)

c Explain how linkages may help a country move from the domestic to the export levels of production. (4 marks)

Question 5

a What is meant by the term 'economies of scale'? (3 marks)

b Explain two reasons why a firm may experience internal economies of scale. (4 marks)

c Give two reasons why small firms continue to be of importance to the economy. (4 marks)

d Explain one benefit and one challenge that a business may experience as it increases in size. (4 marks)

Question 6

Susan has a small home-based business which sells prepackaged lunches to offices in her neighbourhood. She is thinking of expanding the business to accommodate dine-in customers as well as to service more offices.

a State two benefits that small businesses, such as Susan's, offer to the economy. (2 marks)

b List **two** changes that Susan will experience in **each** of the following areas if she expands her business:

i organisational structure

ii capital

iii scale of production. (6 marks)

c By giving examples, discuss two ways in which Susan can use the idea of linkages to help her expand the size of her business. (6 marks)

d Discuss two problems that Susan would face if she operates a large business instead of a small one. (6 marks)

115

7 Marketing

> It used to be that people needed products to survive.
>
> Now products need people to survive. – *Nicholas Johnson*

Avis Car Rental – still second best after a successful marketing campaign?

Million-dollar lines

Some advertising lines are permanently etched in our minds – Nike gave us 'Just do it' in 1998; De Beers created 'Diamonds are forever' in 1948; M&Ms left us with the timeless line 'Melts in your mouth, not in your hand' and Geico gave new meaning and life to the insult 'It's so simple, a caveman can do it.' These lines were all part of successful ad campaigns that bought tremendous popularity for the products they were advertising. Perhaps the most successful and memorable advertising

campaign was created by Avis, the car-rental company. Avis used a brazen and risky approach of embracing the fact that they were second-best to launch a campaign that won the hearts and, more importantly, the pockets of consumers. In 1963, Avis was the obvious second choice for people who wanted to rent a car and Hertz was the unmistakable leader of this industry. Avis not only accepted their position as number two, they flaunted it. Avis gained a lot of attention when their campaign made the bold claim 'We are second best – we try harder.' One ad proclaimed that when renting a car, Avis 'just can't afford dirty ashtrays. Or half-empty gas tanks. Or worn wipers. Or unwashed cars. Or low tires. Or anything less than seat adjusters that adjust. Heaters that heat. Defrosters that defrost'. Avis went as far as to advise customers to 'go with us next time. The line at our counter is shorter'. Of course, as you can imagine, an ad campaign this bold almost did not run as the market research that the company carried out suggested that it would fail. The ad campaign, however, was a tremendous success – prior to the campaign Avis was a small unprofitable company with an 11 per cent share of the market and revenues of $34 million. Within a year of the ad campaign revenues rose to over $38 million and for the first time in 13 years the company recorded a profit, of $1.2 million. Within four years, the company's market share increased to 35 per cent. Of course, all of this hinged on one line 'We are second best – we try harder': truly a million-dollar line.

The story of Avis and its successful advertising campaign provides an excellent backdrop for the issue we will be exploring in this chapter – that of markets and marketing.

In this chapter you will:

- develop an understanding of the term 'markets' and 'marketing'
- identify elements of the 'marketing mix'
- identify activities associated with marketing
- discuss the importance of market research
- discuss packaging as a marketing activity
- discuss marketing-related legal issues such as patent, copyright and trademark
- discuss the elements involved in the promotional mix of a firm

- discuss the process involved in setting the price of goods
- outline the process involved in moving a product from the producer to the consumer
- discuss the type and role of transportation in marketing
- explore solutions to various problems that are likely to be encountered in the distribution process.

SECTION A   The marketing mix

Marketing and markets

What do you think **marketing** is all about? You know that when you watch television your favourite programme is interrupted every ten minutes or so by advertisements; you may also have seen ads elsewhere – on billboards, in the newspapers and on flyers in the street. As a result, when you think of marketing, your first thought may be of 'advertisements'. However, this is not the only activity involved in marketing – it is a much broader field of interest to management and involves a number of activities that we will explore in this chapter. Before we dive into a discussion on marketing let us first think about markets.

A **market** is not a difficult idea to understand if you remove from your mind the notion that a market is *necessarily* a place where goods and services are sold. One talks of the market for used cars, or for cellphones or for textbooks. In these instances, the word 'market' does not refer to a place where used cars, cellphones or textbooks are sold. Rather, the term, as used in this context, refers to the total number of buyers and sellers and potential buyers and sellers of used cars, cellphones or textbooks.

To a seller, then, a market is not necessarily a place – rather it is a situation in which a sale is possible. Put simply, a market is a collection of selling opportunities. So, as a student in school, you may be in the market for textbooks and would perhaps want a new set every year. For that same reason, however, you are not likely to be in the market for used cars – you are too young, have no money to buy one and perhaps do not have a licence.

Of course, this definition of a market differs from the type of market you will be used to. When you go to the market to buy provisions you go to a place where provisions are for sale; you do not go to a 'collection of selling opportunities'. Can a market be a physical place, as well? Well, of course, a market can be a place where goods are bought and sold. Do not forget that it does not *necessarily* have to be a place – it can be a situation or a context that allows transactions to occur. As long as communication exists between the parties involved in the transaction, then a market can exist. Taken from this perspective, then, a market may also be seen as a situation that is created by buyers and sellers who through communication seek to effect mutual exchange.

☞ **Now it's your turn**

Each of the following sentences uses the word 'market'. Comment on the meaning of the word in each context and describe the market which is being referred to in each case. Is it a physical marketplace?

1 Farmers are aware of the fact that the market has been flooded with pears over the past year.

2 Everybody wants to own a cellphone these days resulting in a seller's market for cellphones.

3 Most families visit the market on Saturday to buy farm produce.

4 The Browns are putting their house on the market because they are migrating.

5 The company has had to turn to the stock market for further capital.

6 The government has gone to the loans market to secure financing for hurricane repairs.

What is marketing?

Now that you have a clear understanding of markets, let us revisit the idea of marketing. So far, we have said that marketing is not synonymous with advertising as it is not limited to this one activity. Marketing is a management process that involves profitably satisfying consumers' wants and needs by anticipating and addressing their concerns. These concerns usually involve looking at

- **The product**: How is it designed? What needs does it satisfy? How can it be improved?
- **The price**: Can it be lowered? Does it create the right image of the product? Does it reflect not just the cost but also the value of the product?
- **Promotion**: How can we get customers' attention and keep it? How can we effectively inform customers about the product?
- **Place**: What is the most effective way to distribute the product to the consumers?

Taken together, these are called the four Ps of marketing and make up the **marketing mix**. Much of marketing is concerned with finding the right marketing mix for the firm. In addition to the marketing mix, firms are also concerned with various marketing activities such as market research, packaging and branding.

Marketing mix

The marketing mix refers to the decisions that a firm makes about its products, their prices, how they are promoted and distributed. Each element of the marketing mix (the four Ps of marketing) can be adjusted to more effectively address the customers' needs. For example, the firm may decide to make its product available in smaller portions at lower prices so that low-income families may be able to afford it. If it does this, then it may need to change the way its product is promoted and distributed. As you can see, the four Ps are all inter-related – changing one usually has a ripple effect and results in a change in all the others. In this section, we will spend some time on each element of the marketing mix.

The first P – product

Rightfully, the product is the first element of the marketing mix that we discuss as it is the element that most broadly affects the other elements. The product can be a good (a loaf of bread), a service (a visit to the hairdresser), an event (the Barbados Crop Over Festival), an idea (how to make crispy fried chicken the way KFC does), a person (a footballer playing for Manchester United) or a place (Kaiteur Falls in Guyana). Generally, products that consumers buy with the intention to use up or consume can be divided into different categories:

- **Convenience products**: these are frequently bought products that require a minimum amount of thought and consideration. These products are usually low priced and easily available. Examples include household items such as toothpaste, soap and detergent.

- **Shopping products**: products that are bought only after a great deal of consideration and comparison of their price and quality. Examples include appliances, furniture and clothing.

- **Speciality products**: products with special and unique characteristics or brand identification and appeal for which consumers are willing to make a special effort. Examples include luxury items such as jewellery.

- **Unsought products**: these products do not sell themselves – rather the marketer has to make the public aware of them through advertising. The consumer either doesn't know about these products or is not interested in buying them because they are not essential. Examples include life insurance.

The second P – price

A **price** is the value of an item in monetary terms. A price is the sum of money charged for a good or a service. It is a reflection of the value of the item, since how much money consumers are prepared to pay for an item is indicative of how badly they want the item or how much value they place on the item. Although the standard practice is to quote the price of a product in money (remember that in Chapter 1, we said that money is the unit of account), it is also possible to quote the price in terms of other values. For example, your sister may lend you her new CD if you agree to do her chores for a week. The price for borrowing the CD in this case is a week of chores. In general, then, the price of an item is the sum of values that consumers are prepared to give up for benefiting from the consumption of the product.

⟳ Making connections: economics

In economics much is made of the concept of opportunity cost. What does this term mean and how does it relate to pricing?

Pricing is an important task since it has implications for the image of the product, the profitability of the business and the quantity of goods that can be sold. Pricing has the following functions:

- **Profit maximisation**: it is the price that the firm sets that determines the extent to which it can recover its cost. Low prices may maximise sales but not profits as each unit sold adds very little to actual profit. High prices, on the other hand, may discourage sales and may also not lead to profit maximisation. The right price will maximise profit because it maximises the number of units sold and will eventually lead to economies of scale.

- **Quality leadership**: consumers associate high price with high quality and vice versa. Price can be used to position the product in the market.

- **Cost recovery**: a price is used to either completely or partially recover cost. If an organisation has other sources of revenues, then it may decide to use its price to simply recover a portion of its cost.

- **Survival**: the price a firm chooses may be one that allows it to simply break even. This price may be maintained until the situation improves and the business feels that it can charge a higher price.

Pricing strategies

Businesses do not randomly pick selling prices for their products. As you will find out, the price of a product has a major influence on how many units consumers will demand. Prices are, therefore, well thought out and carefully analysed, with broad objectives providing a guiding philosophy of pricing. Some of the most popular pricing strategies are:

- **Mark-up pricing**: mark-up pricing is the most basic method of pricing and involves simply adding an amount to cost in order to obtain a profit. The amount added to cost is known as a mark-up and is usually expressed as a percentage of cost. If it costs $12 to produce a unit of a product, for example, the producer may choose to mark it up by 25 per cent and sell it for $15. One of the advantages of this pricing strategy is that it allows the firm to cover its price floor. The price floor is the price below which the product cannot be sold, since below this level a loss will be made. The price floor for any product is the cost of producing the product.

- **Price skimming**: price skimming is a pricing strategy usually employed with new products, which involves charging a high price for people who are anxious to be among the first to own the product. These 'early adopters', as they are called, are likely to buy the product even if the price is very high at first since they want to be among the first exclusive group of owners. As early adopters fall off, the price of the product is reduced to attract other users.

- **Penetration pricing**: instead of introducing a new product with a high price, a business may choose the opposite approach of introducing it at a low price, which is then increased as the product gains a foothold in the market. This strategy is known as penetration pricing. An initial low price is likely to secure new customers who were previously loyal to other brands, thus leading to market penetration.

- **Loss-leader pricing**: a loss leader is a product that is sold at a loss in order to tempt customers to buy other products from which the business can make substantial levels of profit. A loss-leader pricing model, therefore, is used for products which complement each other (products that are consumed together). It is put into practice by selling one product at a low price and then charging a high price for the other. Alternatively, a more popular role of the loss leader is to lock the customer into a brand and from there make them a part of a captured market. For example, entry-level printers are sold at very low prices. Printer manufacturers, however, make up the losses they make on the printers themselves by selling the replacement ink cartridges at very high prices.

- **Going-rate pricing**: going-rate pricing involves businesses in the same market charging similar prices, which all hover around a perceived 'going rate'.

☞ For you to research

There are many other pricing strategies. Use a search engine on the internet (or check a marketing text-book) to find out about some of these strategies. You can use the keywords 'pricing strategies' in your search. Some of the pricing strategies you may want to look at are listed below.

1 perceived-value pricing

2 predatory pricing

3 price discrimination

4 psychological pricing

5 prestige pricing

The third P – promotion

It is not enough for a business to have good products sold at attractive prices. To generate sales and profits, the benefits of the products have to be communicated to customers. In marketing, this is commonly known as 'promotion'. A business will have a 'promotion mix' that is made up of a blend of **advertising**, **personal selling**, **sales promotion** and **public relations** tools. While advertising is the most popular form of promotion – perhaps because that is the most visible aspect of the promotion mix – the marketing campaign of a product depends largely on all four elements.

Advertising

This method of promotion uses print or electronic media to deliver a persuasive and/or informative message. The two basic elements of an advertisement are the message

(what is being communicated) and the medium (how you choose to get the message across). Advertisements are of different types, ranging from the basic ads that inform the public about a change of opening hours to the aggressive ads that discredit a competitor's products. The types of advertisements include:

- **Informative advertisements**: these ads seek to provide basic fact-based information about a product or event. It may be an ad that lists the name and other details of a new product or one that indicates that a business has changed its office phone number. These ads are usually unexciting in their delivery since they seek to deliver information in a clear, precise fashion.
- **Persuasive advertisements**: these ads are used to make a product appear more appealing to consumers. The strengths of the products are usually emphasised in these ads as producers try to get the attention of uninterested consumers. Since persuasive ads are usually used for products that have been on the market for a while, the ads can afford to be more exciting in their delivery and medium. These ads frequently use celebrities and sport stars to endorse the products in an effort to bolster the product's appeal to the public.
- **Comparative advertisements**: these ads use direct comparisons with competitors' products to establish which product is superior. The names of competitors and their products are likely to be mentioned in these ads if they contain assertions that are based on facts such as surveys.
- **Reminder-oriented advertisements**: when a product has been on the market for a long time and has established itself as reliable, its demand may fade as new products are introduced to the market. At this stage, reminder-oriented ads are used to reinforce previously held notions about the product and keep the product in the forefront of the public's mind.

Why do firms advertise?

As outlined in the list above, the reasons why a firm advertises include:

- to create public awareness and provide the general public with information about developments such as the introduction of a new product, a change in price, a change in design and so on
- to persuade the public to consider purchasing the product or to change their brand loyalty

- to create a brand image for the firm or its brands
- to assert the superiority of its products relative to the products of competitors
- to reassure customers in the face of new developments
- to position the product in the minds of the public – for example, to change the public's perception that the product is an expensive luxury item that only the wealthy can afford.

Advertising media

When advertising, should a business use the print media or the electronic media? And if it chooses print, should it use newspapers or magazines? These are important questions to answer as there are various advantages and disadvantages of each medium. In general, print media ensure that members of the public will have multiple exposures to the ad, since they can go back to the ad again and again. Some popular print media in which ads are placed are:

- **Newspapers**: newspapers offer a quick turnaround time as ads can be printed the day after they are placed.
- **Magazines**: magazines attract dedicated readers drawn from a focused background, who are more likely to respond to the ads.

Electronic media allow for more creativity through the use of multimedia such as music, voice and videos. The most popular electronic media are:

- **Radio**: radio is a medium that usually has a particular theme (e.g. sports, music, news) and is ideal for targeting people drawn to these themes.
- **Television**: television is a medium that incorporates pictures and videos along with audio to get the message across.

 For you to research

Use the internet to search for advertising media. In addition to the ones discussed above – newspapers, magazines, radio and television – which other media exist? What are some of the advantages of these media?

Public relations (PR)

PR is a sustained effort to create a positive image of the firm and its products by controlling its communications with the public. PR is not the same as advertising, as the information given in PR is not always as rehearsed or scripted with the customer in mind.

PR is usually effected in the following ways:

- **Scholarships**: setting up funds that cover tuition and perhaps other related fees for qualified members of the public who are studying (usually at the tertiary level). Some firms may limit access to the scholarship to students who are pursuing an area of interest related to the firm. A partnership made up of lawyers, for example, may sponsor students who are pursuing degrees in law.

- **Sponsorships**: a firm may sponsor an event that it believes the public will support. Sponsoring the event may involve putting up cash for the event or providing material resources such as a venue or lunches for participants. The firm, as a sponsor, may insist that its name be tied to the event's title so that whenever the event is mentioned in the media, the name of the firm will also be mentioned. This is to further ensure that the firm gets publicity and recognition from sponsoring the event.

- **Donations**: making donations to support various organisations and responding to any national disasters that may occur is a major part of creating a good positive image. A firm may, for example, adopt a local school, donate money to charity organisations such as Food for the Poor, or set up foundations focused on special interests, such as discrimination against people living with HIV/AIDS.

- **Special awards**: the firm may create a programme to recognise and award individuals or businesses making valuable contributions to national development or to the development of the industry in which the firm operates. Awards may be given, for example, to people for their contribution to sports, law enforcement, music or the arts. Generally, as a result of these awards the firm is seen as having an interest in the development of these areas and this may translate into greater sales.

Sales promotion

A sales promotion occurs when a temporary promotional measure is put in place to increase market demand or sales. This promotional measure usually includes an incentive system that tries to 'tempt' consumers into making a purchase. The firm may run a competition, for example, which can be entered by post, if the entrant includes proof of purchase of the product, e.g. a receipt from a store or

BOGOF is perhaps the most popular sales promotion technique.

the product's packaging. Sales promotion is usually introduced for a limited time, with a high level of advertising so that consumers feel a sense of urgency to participate. Usually, entering the competition is not a challenge (the question is not difficult to answer or the process is not hard to follow), as the firm wants as many people as possible to enter the competition, since doing so usually requires buying the firm's products. Examples of sales promotion are:

- **Price promotions**: these include offering discounts to customers either in the purchase price or in the form of rebates. A rebate is a chance for the buyer to recover a portion of the purchase price of the item if he or she mails back to the seller a form included in the product. Price promotions encourage customers to buy more of the product but generally do not create loyal customers.

- **Vouchers and coupons**: a coupon or voucher is a card or note that allows holders to access special offers or discounts when they visit participating stores to make the purchase. Coupons and vouchers are usually distributed through newspapers and hence are usually available to any member of the public. Alternatively, the coupons or vouchers may be distributed when a customer buys a product, in which case the coupon becomes valid the next time the customer makes a purchase at the store or buys the product. A coupon or voucher may be valid on a particular day or for a set period (usually up to a month) and may be limited to a single product or to a line of products. Coupons and vouchers are usually effective at market promotion, even though the business offering the coupon may find that customers use the coupons to buy what they would have bought anyway. The result is that no new purchase may result from issuing coupons or vouchers.

- **Gift with purchase**: a firm may offer gifts to customers who make purchases at or above a certain value. Alternatively, the business may offer a tiered approach to giving gifts – customers qualify for gifts of different values depending on how much money they spend. Usually the gifts offered are relatively inexpensive when compared with the item being purchased. It is sometimes difficult to find gifts that appeal to a wide cross-section of people – the young and the old, men and women, and so on.

- **Competitions and sweepstakes**: firms usually entice customers to submit answers to competitions once they have proof of purchase of the firms' products. Usually participating in the competition or sweepstake is not based on skill or knowledge but on chance (winners are drawn from a drum or selected by a computer programme). The prizes for these competitions vary but are usually very appealing and may include cash, vacations or even a supply of the sponsoring firm's products.

- **Loyalty or frequent user rewards**: repeat customers may get discounts or even free products as the number of times that they buy the product increases. Airlines, for example, give free trips or reduced-cost trips to customers who fly a certain number of times or a certain distance with them.

- **Buy one get, one free (BOGOF)**: these offers encourage a customer to buy a product in order to get a second product at no charge. Usually, the free product is either exactly like the one the customer buys (which is not always ideal) or the free product is of equal or lower value. Another variation of the BOGOF offer is to get a second product at a reduced price – perhaps half price.

Personal selling

Personal selling is one of the oldest forms of promotion. This strategy uses a sales force to make face-to-face or telephone (or, more recently, internet) presentations to push sales and build relationships. In these presentations, the product is usually displayed, its use is demonstrated and potential customers get a chance to interact with the product. As a strategy, this process is very effective as the potential customer gets a highly personalised treatment, and has the chance to ask questions that experts in the products are on hand to answer. If the product is technical and requires lengthy explanations about its use, then personal selling is ideal. Some products such as photocopiers, network servers and heavy-duty printers are usually sold in this way as buyers need to be shown how to set up, use and service these machines.

The fourth P – place

So far, we have looked at three of the four Ps of the marketing mix – product, price and promotion. This section will explore the last P – placing the product. Place refers to how the business distributes its products to its customers. The place is where the business can expect to find people interested in its products and, as a result, where the sale is realised. Placing the product usually involves a **distribution chain**, which is the system set up for moving the product from the factory floor to the consumers. This system, which is outlined in Figure 7.1, usually takes into consideration many companies, called intermediaries, who are all partly responsible for how quickly and at what price the product reaches the consumers. It should be pointed out, however, that some businesses use what is called **direct selling** – the business sells directly to the consumers without going through any intermediaries or agents. When intermediaries are used, they take the form of wholesalers or retailers who join the manufacturer and the consumers as the other parties in the distribution chain.

Figure 7.1 The distribution process.

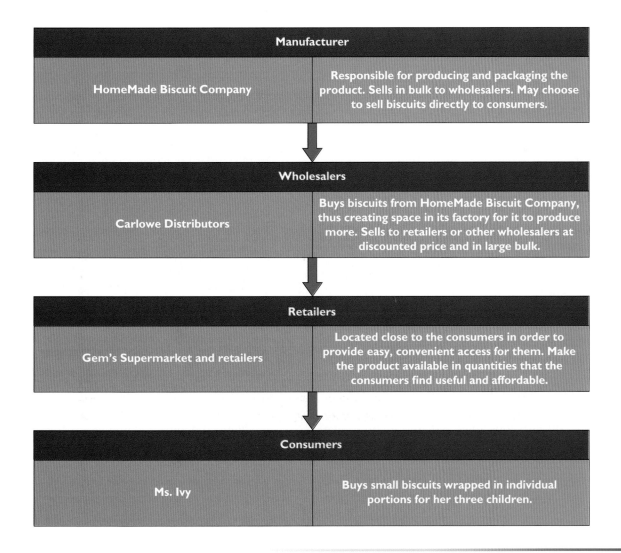

Manufacturer

The manufacturer, having produced the product, must now think about making it accessible to the consumers. The manufacturer would have produced many units of the product and usually does not have the facilities to sell individual units to the consumer. In other words, each consumer does not usually go directly to the manufacturer to buy the small number of units of the item that he or she will need for personal consumption. The manufacturer usually designs his operations to sell many units of the item and so sales made by the manufacturer are usually made to middlemen who buy in bulk and sell in smaller quantities. Indeed, if you think about it, you probably don't know where many of the producers of the products that you consume are located; you may not even know their names, particularly if these products are imported. In short, the manufacturer usually does not interact with the consumers.

Wholesalers

Wholesalers are businesses that buy products in bulk from the manufacturer and then sell them in smaller quantities to retailers. Wholesalers usually sell quantities that are too large for the needs of the consumers and, hence, consumers usually do not buy from wholesalers. A new tendency, however, is for consumers to buy directly from wholesalers, thus cutting out the retailers. Wholesalers play many functions in the distribution chain. Primarily, they offer goods in large quantity at discount prices to retailers so that retailers can sell smaller quantities to consumers at a profit. Additionally, they take the finished products from the manufacturer as soon as they are ready, clearing space and making it possible for the manufacturer to produce more units even before the consumers have bought a single unit of the product.

Retailers

A **retailer** is a business that buys products in large quantities, either from wholesalers or directly from the manufacturer, with the intention to sell these products to consumers. Retailers are at the end of the supply chain, the last link in the distribution process; as a result, they interact directly with consumers and are a useful source of marketing information about the consumers. Retailers also break bulk, making it possible for the consumers to access the product in quantities that are more suited to their needs. In addition, retailers may even transform the product slightly so that consumers are more likely to purchase it. For example, many computer producers distribute computers with limited software already installed. Some retailers, however, may choose to modify the product before selling it by installing software that the customer may need. There are various methods of retailing employed in the Caribbean; some of these are discussed below.

- **Shops**: these are most prevalent since they are often established as small sole-trader enterprises in communities. Shops usually sell items needed on a daily basis or which can be easily parcelled out into smaller units. These items include dry goods such as rice, flour and sugar along with meat, condiments and baked goods such as bread. Shops are usually very small and are operated in a very informal manner, often as cottage industries.

- **Department stores**: a department store is really a shop with a greater degree of variety, organisation and sophistication. As a result, some of the practices that exist in a shop may not exist in a department store. Work is divided and, as a result, labour is also divided – it is unlikely, therefore, that the owner will be serving customers. This affects the chance of credit being extended to customers or of any deviation from standard practices (such as discounts being offered). In addition, portions are not always as small as those in shops. Examples of popular department stores around the world include Walmart, Burlington Coat Factory, Marks & Spencer and Bloomingdale's.

- **Mail order**: some stores allow customers to order goods over the telephone, which are then delivered through the postal system to a pre-arranged address. This is known as mail ordering. Payment is usually made before the goods are shipped and usually the buyer who uses mail order has to pay for shipping and handling.

- **E-commerce**: with the pervasive nature of the internet, buying and selling online were an inevitable outcome. E-commerce is the purchase of a product or service using the internet as the medium for placing the order. Usually the order is placed by going to the website of the seller offering the product and sometimes the product is one that can be delivered across the internet (such as virus-protection programmes and other software which are sold online). If this is the case, then there is no need to physically transport the product to a mailing address for the buyer. Many e-commerce transactions, however, involve goods actually being shipped to an address. Amazon, the largest retailer of books online, offers a wide selection of books that potential customers can browse, read samples from and reviews about before making an order online and paying with a credit card. The books are then delivered to a pre-arranged address within a few days. E-commerce has made it necessary for most businesses to create websites to go along with their traditional retailing as they seek to tap into the online market.

- **Tele-marketing**: this is another traditional method of retailing products. In this method, the sales force uses telephone conversations to meet new customers and make sales. Tele-marketing is regarded as an annoyance by many people and its popularity has declined in recent years.

- **Vending machines**: a vending machine is an automated system for dispensing packaged goods and collecting payment. Most vending machines are placed in areas – such as airports, lobbies and waiting areas – where people congregate or pass from time to time, often at odd hours. Vending machines are convenient for these areas since they are cheap to operate and can be accessed by the customers 24 hours a day with minimum delay. The machine usually has a closed, transparent glass door that allows buyers to see the items on sale; there are also buttons to the side that allow the buyers to choose the item they are interested in and, after the correct amount of money is inserted, the item is released to be retrieved by the buyer.

Consumers

In the distribution chain, the consumers are distinct from the customers. *Customers* are people and businesses who buy a product (usually in bulk) with the intention to resell it. *Consumers*, on the other hand, are people or businesses who buy a product intending to consume or use it up in some way. The consumers are the end users of the product, since after they have bought it, it is usually not resold or redistributed. Wholesalers and retailers are therefore customers, whereas an individual buying an item from a shop would be a consumer: in other words; the end user. Since wholesalers and retailers ensure that the product is moved from the manufacturer to the end users, they are referred to as intermediaries.

Summary – Section A

- Markets are not necessarily places where goods are bought and sold; rather, any situation in which trade is possible can be described as a market.

- The central role of marketing is anticipating and satisfying customers' wishes. This usually involves creating a marketing mix using the four Ps of marketing – product, price, promotion and place.

- There are many types of products, which differ from each other in how often they are bought and the level of thinking that goes into the buying decisions.

- The price of a product is its value to the consumers. When businesses set a price for their products, they often choose between skimming or penetrating the market. Additionally, businesses may choose to adopt a loss-leader or going-rate pricing approach.

- The promotion mix is made up of four strategies, each of which is combined in different proportions to create the promotion strategy of the business. The four elements of the promotion mix are advertising, public relations, sales promotion and personal selling.

- When deciding on how to distribute its product, the business sets up a distribution chain that includes intermediaries whose job it is move the goods from the manufacturer to the consumer or end user.

✐ End of section activities

Quick questions

Say whether each of the following statements is true or false. If the statement is false, explain why this is and suggest the right answer.

1 A market exists only if people who want to trade are able to communicate.

2 All markets require face-to-face meeting of parties who want to trade.

3 Shopping products are usually more expensive than convenience products.

4 Price skimming results in the product being accepted quickly by most people in the market.

5 A business which finds that it cannot take advantage of economies of scale should use penetration pricing.

6 Loss-leader pricing can be effectively practised when a store sells any two products that are usually consumed together.

7 When products are very different in form, functions and features, then going-rate pricing is not advisable.

8 Informative ads are usually very exciting and use many celebrities to endorse the product.

9 If a manufacturer of beauty products wants to advertise its products, then it is best to advertise in newspapers.

10 Sales promotion is usually employed to achieve temporary and immediate increases in sales.

11 Intermediaries are people who buy products directly from the manufacturer.

12 Retailing a product is most often done through shops.

13 Anyone who buys a product is referred to as a consumer.

14 Vending machines are ideal when there is a high and steady demand for a product.

Applying what you have learnt

1 A marketing mix is really a combination of four factors – product, price, promotion and place. Products that target different users will each have a distinct marketing mix. Describe the marketing mix (the four Ps) for each of the following products (How will the product look? What pricing strategy will you use? How will you promote it? How will you distribute it?):

a a phone for users with a low level of income

b a new, expensive laptop with many features.

2 Find a popular high-quality magazine and an ordinary daily newspaper. Take any two ads (if you can find two ads for the same product, that would be ideal). Compare the ads to see what similarities and differences exist between them. What do you think account for these differences or similarities? Which ad do you think is more effective? Why?

3 When setting a price for a product, some people think the cost of producing the good is the most important factor to consider. A product that is cheap to produce, therefore, should not be sold for a high price. Other people, however, think that the price of a product should reflect its value. As a result, a product that is cheaply produced can be sold at a high price if consumers value it and are prepared to pay a high price for it. Which do you think should be more important in setting price – cost or value? Do you think that setting price based on value is unfair? Why or why not? Which pricing strategy is most closely related to value and which to cost?

4 Distribution chains consist of a manufacturer, intermediaries and end users. Chains with no intermediaries are called zero-level chains; those with only one intermediary are called single-level chains; and those with more than one intermediary are referred to as multi-level chains.

a As a product is bought by one intermediary and resold to another, what do you expect to happen to its price each time it is resold?

b Do you expect the final price charged to the end users in chains with many intermediaries to be high or low? Why?

c Why are wholesalers less expensive than retailers? At what point in the distribution chain do you expect the product to be cheapest?

5 Many firms use competitions to promote sales. To enter these competitions, the firm may ask consumers to write its slogan on a piece of paper in order to qualify for the prize. In other instances, the firm may even write out the slogan with a few letters left out for consumers to fill in. As an example, Nike, whose slogan is 'just do it', may ask that entrants complete the slogan 'J_ _T DO _ T' in order to enter.

a Why do firms make it so easy for people to enter these competitions?

b Do you think these competitions work in increasing sales? Why or why not?

c How does the firm ensure that the money that it used to buy prizes and so on is recovered?

Model exam questions
Question 1

a Explain what is meant by:

i markets

ii marketing. (5 marks)

b List the four elements of the marketing mix. (2 marks)

c Carl Yung Associates sells two brands of MP3 player – one for the lower end of the market and the other for more wealthy buyers. Discuss two ways in which the marketing mix for each product may differ. (6 marks)

Question 2

a Identify the four broad strategies that a firm has when it seeks to promote its product. (4 marks)

b Identify, with reasons, the promotion mix that is ideal for a new product that is:

i hard to use

ii has many side effects. (6 marks)

c A firm must choose between using a magazine or a newspaper ad. Discuss any two factors that its marketing manager must consider before making a decision. (4 marks)

Question 3

a What is meant by the term 'distribution chain'? (3 marks)

b Why may a firm choose to avoid using intermediaries in distributing its products? (3 marks)

c Discuss two roles of intermediaries in the distribution process. (6 marks)

Question 4

a Give two reasons why it is important to sell a product at its right price. (4 marks)

b What is the main difference between a price-skimming strategy and a penetration-pricing strategy? (3 marks)

c List three conditions under which it is suitable to use a price-skimming strategy. (3 marks)

Question 5

Bridget realised that her fashion store attracts many people but that very few of them actually buy anything. Her pricing strategy has always been to charge prices similar to her competitors but now she is thinking of changing her approach to pricing.

a What is the name of the pricing strategy that Bridget now uses? (1 mark)

b By giving a reason, state another pricing strategy that Bridget can use. (3 marks)

c Discuss two sales promotion techniques that Bridget can use to increase her sales. (6 marks)

d Outline one advantage and one disadvantage of using sales promotion to increase sales. (6 marks)

e Suggest two reasons to Bridget why many people who visit the store do not buy. (4 marks)

Introduction

While creating the marketing mix is of paramount concern to the business, there are other activities that are also involved in marketing. For example, the business has to determine what portion of the market is likely to buy its products and the characteristics of the typical consumers of its products. This requires market research, which is one of the key activities of marketing that falls outside the marketing mix. Various other activities, such as packaging and branding, also have to be considered when looking at marketing. In this section, we will spend a considerable length of time looking at these activities. We will also examine in more detail the idea of selling, which is closely related to marketing. Finally we will widen our scope and look beyond the business to issues such as transportation and consumerism.

Market research

Information is very valuable to the marketing department of a business. The more a business knows about its consumers and the market in which its products are sold, the more effectively it can design its marketing campaign to reach these consumers. The information that a business uses to design its marketing strategy is obtained through carrying out **market research**. Market research is a systematic study of the market, carried out by a business to gather information about its customers and the market in which its products are sold. Market research plays the following roles:

- It identifies the consumers' taste and thus provides answers to questions such as:
  - What to produce?
  - What quantity to produce?
  - What design, appearance, aesthetics and features should the product have?
  - For whom to produce; that is, who is the firm's target market?

  When deciding on the market for which to produce, a firm usually looks at its target market. The target market is the set of people in the total market who are most likely to consume the firm's products. For example, the market for motor vehicle insurance includes all people who own a motor vehicle. An insurance-service provider,

however, may identify and target the truck drivers in that market by offering discounts and special offers for owners of large vehicles.

- It identifies the products that are likely to compete with the firm's. People taking part in the market research will indicate which product they are most likely to buy in the future or have bought most frequently in the past. This allows the firm to see which other products satisfy the same demand as the firm's. It is sometimes difficult to identify the competitor for a firm's product. For example, what competes with a Burger King Whopper? Certainly, another burger made by McDonald's or KFC would. But what about chicken and other meals produced by these fast-food outlets? What about Chinese takeout or pizza? In short, does anything that can be eaten compete with a Burger King Whopper?

- It gives a profile of typical consumer behaviour. A firm would be very interested in finding out what goes through a consumer's mind as he tries to decide what products to buy. Furthermore, it may also want to answer questions such as:
  - When do consumers buy the product?
  - With what other products do they usually consume the product?
  - How is the product used after it is bought?

- It helps the business decide on a marketing budget and on how to allocate funding. Market research, for example, indicates what level of investment will be needed for advertising, promotion and other marketing campaigns.

- It will help the firm in its strategic management. Market research will indicate new business and product opportunities in which the business can invest. It will also indicate trends and patterns that the business can anticipate and for which it can be prepared.

- It keeps the business in touch with the feelings, preferences, likes, dislikes, emotions, views, traditions, culture and beliefs of the market. Market research allows the business to keep up to date. It ensures that the business is not offering unfashionable, culturally irrelevant or politically incorrect goods. For example, the release of the movie *Collateral Damage*, in which terrorists attack an American city, was postponed because producers thought it would be inappropriate coming so soon after the 9/11 terrorist attacks.

- It reveals options and courses of action that the firm might otherwise not know about. Many firms, for example, ask consumers to submit ideas for new uses for the product that the firm can look into.
- It leaves important decisions in the hands of the market (the users of the product). The business has a greater chance of offering the right good to the market, since the market decides what is to be produced and how it will perform, appear and operate.

- It saves money for the business. If the business knows what goods to produce and in what quantity, then it will not waste money producing a good that will not be demanded by the public or producing too many units of a good.

🌐 Business in your world

Market research at work – the case of WD-40

You know that blue and yellow can with the red top? The one with the red straw in it and the lubricant that can be used for just about anything? WD-40, that's the one – the lubricant created by rocket scientists! WD-40 is certainly one of the 'must haves' around any home. The product is 60 years old and has done well to remain popular even though a number of other products now purport to offer the same or even improved benefits. The product was created by rocket scientists in the 1950s

for use in the aerospace industry. After 40 attempts, they managed to work out the water-displacing formula that made the product work and hence it became known as WD-40 (a shortened version of what would have been a clumsy name: 'water-displacing formula number 40'). To maintain its position as the product of choice, the manufacturers have had to use market research extensively. Its market research, however, has always been consumer-based. For example, in 1998, the company asked customers to tell them how they use WD-40. It received 400 000 responses and the company decided to feature the top 2000 uses on

its website. Some of the uses that consumers suggested include:

- removes graffiti from latex fences
- removes paint from jeans
- cleans DVDs – after using WD-40, clean them with soap and water
- removes dried cement from hair
- cleans food stuck in refrigerator.

The company also turned to its consumers after that for inspiration as to how the product could be improved. This led to a number of small innovations – for example, when customers kept complaining that they were always losing the straw through which the lubricant is sprayed, the manufacturer started making cans with the straw attached. Additionally, in response to complaints that the straw only allowed for spraying in one direction, the manufacturers made sure that the straw was flexible and could spray at different angles. WD-40, at 60 years old and going strong, certainly owes its long life to its effective use of market research.

Discussion

1 Visit the WD-40 website (www.wd40.com) and look through the list of uses that others have come up with for the product. Looking at this list, who would be your target market for the product?

2 Do you think the approach that the manufacturers of WD-40 have taken to market research is an effective one? Why or why not?

Types of market research

Observational research forces the observer to make conclusions that may be too hasty.

Observational research: in this type of research, trained people observe and record the actions of potential buyers. Observational research is popular in supermarkets and department stores where shoppers' behaviour can be observed as they choose between the many options available. The major problem with observational research is that observers may be forced to make assumptions about the actions of potential buyers since no or only limited communication takes place with them. Sometimes observational research may be combined with customer interviews (a process called ethnographic research) to minimise this problem. The advantages of observational research are the fact that it is inexpensive to conduct and can be easily organised in a short time.

Survey research: this approach to gathering information uses questions and answers to collect data. In survey research, people are asked questions about their knowledge, likes and dislikes, consumption pattern and buying behaviour. The questions are usually administered to a sample of the population using a questionnaire. The sample may be chosen randomly, in which case each person in the population has an equal chance of being in the sample, or purposively. If the members of the sample are purposively selected then a deliberate effort is made to select some people and reject others. Survey research is more thorough than observational research and, as a result, it is likely to produce results that are more accurate. On the other hand, it is very expensive, time consuming and difficult to administer. Indeed, many businesses have to identify outside experts, who are trained in the area of survey research, to carry out survey research on their behalf.

Experimental research: in the experimental-research method of collecting primary data, two groups of subjects are chosen, with one group being exposed to a controlled situation to see how their behaviour and reactions would differ from those of the other group. For example, a business selling a pharmaceutical product may be interested in seeing the effects of the product on women's weight. To determine this, the firm may compare the weight changes in a group of women who used the product with those of a control group who did not. Experiments are often impractical and many legal issues can be involved which make experiments difficult to carry out. For example, it is difficult and likely to be illegal to get pregnant women to take a new drug in order to observe its effects on the unborn children. Experiments, however, usually provide useful and factual information, which sometimes is the only type of information that matters. For example, a survey in which people's opinions are sought cannot be used to determine if cellphone use causes brain damage.

Focus-group interview: a focus group is a small group of people who meet under the direction of a discussion leader to communicate their opinions about an organisation, its products, or other issues. Participants are allowed to talk freely about their experiences related to the product or to competitors' products so that the business may have a better idea as to how to design and market its own products. The discussion leader tries to focus the discussion on important issues and ensures that it does not become too unstructured. Focus-group interviews may also include samples of the product or competitors' products so that actual interactions with the product may spur some of the discussion. A firm designing a new hair product for men may invite 12 men to discuss their experiences in taking care of their hair. The firm organising the focus group may choose to keep its identity a secret and, indeed, the focus-group discussion may never mention this firm's name or its products. However, the discussion should generate information the business finds useful. The free-form nature of the focus group setting encourages honesty in the responses and thus focus groups provide high-quality marketing information. They run the risk, however, of becoming unstructured and hence the discussion leader needs to be very skilled at directing the discussion.

 Now it's your turn

A firm is thinking of developing a line of microwaveable ready meals and has conducted a focus-group interview. Below is an extract from one participant's reflections on her experience with ready meals produced by other companies.

> I don't like to cook and I only have a few meals that I have mastered. I have tried other ready meals and to tell you the truth I just can't be bothered with them. The ingredients are not always the best ones. When you put vegetables and chicken in the same container, either the vegetables are overcooked by the microwave or the chicken is still icy. That makes no sense. Plus the container gets so hot that it is difficult to open it after you take it out of the microwave. You have to leave it on the counter and then it gets cold again. Also, why do they have to have the cover sealed onto them so that you cannot take them off before you microwave the meal? Microwaving the meals with the covers on traps the moisture in the container and causes it to get soggy. I can't be bothered with ready meals any more and so I usually buy fast food or just eat out when I don't want to cook.

I Who do you expect to have been the participants in such a focus-group discussion? Why?

2 Even though the participant above was not talking about the firm specifically, why would this information still be useful?

3 Discuss three pieces of information that the firm conducting the focus-group session can use to design and develop their ready meals.

In-depth interview: an in-depth interview is more structured than a focus-group session. Usually, an interviewer will meet with participants one at a time to ask them specific questions about the product or the firm. The discussion is usually centred around the questions that the interviewer asks. Since each interview session has only one respondent, the interviewer has a chance to probe the participant to get lengthy and detailed follow-up responses. On the other hand, interviews are time consuming and hence if the business uses this method of market research, it cannot expect to hear from a large percentage of the total market.

Branding

Every business hopes that its products will become the leader in whatever market it competes. One can hardly think of a phone and not think of brands such as BlackBerry and Nokia; or think of computers and not think of Dell and HP. These brands are market leaders and they are widely recognised by most consumers. A **brand** is a name, sign, symbol or combination of all three that is used to identify a particular product. Once a brand has been created, a producer usually sells many products under the same brand.

Branding is the set of activities that a business performs that ensure that consumers associate its products with high quality and solid performance. Branding involves activities such as consistently delivering on promises and claims made in ads and articulating a clear, consistent message through ads and how the product is 'positioned' in the market.

The ultimate aim of branding is to create brand image and ultimately **brand equity** – consumers should identify with the brand each time they decide to buy a product distributed under the brand name. Some brands have created strong brand equity within a specific aspect of the market – Volvo, the Swedish car company, for example, has created brand equity as a safe family vehicle, while Ferrari, the Italian car manufacturer, has created strong brand equity as a sporty, fast car.

Packaging

A product's **packaging** has been called the 'silent salesman' because of its ability to grab and hold consumers' attention and then persuade them to buy the product. A product's package also plays a practical role in securing and protecting the product. When we speak of packaging, we are referring to the set of activities involved in enclosing the goods for protection, distribution and use. In a much wider sense, however, the term packaging describes not just the act of putting goods in packages, but also the act of taking goods produced by another firm and creating a system of labelling, warehousing and distribution for these goods. As an example, Grace Kennedy Foods (GKF), the Jamaican retail giant, buys canned food from other producers which it then packages for distribution and sale. When GKF 'packages' a product, then, this involves more than just putting the product in a container with the company's name on it; rather, this process includes identifying retailers, warehousing and preparing the goods for transportation.

Packaging takes place at different levels and with different parties in mind. The manufacturer packages the product with the wholesalers, retailers and end users in mind. To this end, the manufacturer of canned vegetables will create packages that are of individual-serving size – one can of vegetables may serve a family of four. Alternatively, the manufacturer may expect that consumers will buy up to four cans and will therefore create an easy-carry four-pack combo. The four-pack combo would be attractively packaged since it is what the consumers will see on the shelves.

Of course, wholesalers and retailers buy in bulk and the manufacturer must take them into consideration when it packages the product. The result of this is that a number of four-pack combos are placed in large boxes for wholesalers and retailers to buy. These large boxes that wholesalers and retailers buy need not be attractively packaged since the consumers are not likely to see them. Furthermore, wholesalers and retailers do not decide what products to stock based on how attractively they are packaged; instead, they stock goods based on what end users want. The packaging of goods for intermediaries, then, is based on practical reasons such as storage and **agglomeration** (bulking together smaller units for ease of handling).

Roles of packaging

- Packaging distinguishes the product from those of competitors. One can easily identify a product based on the name and colour scheme used on the packaging. Many brands are easily identified regardless of the product that is being marketed because they remain consistent in their colour and design. Grace Kennedy Foods, for example, uses a red background overlaid with text of a neutral colour regardless of the canned food that it is packaging.

- Packaging advertises the product at the point of sale. Consumers who have no brand loyalty or who are first-time buyers are likely to choose any brand when they buy a product. If one package is more attractive than another, then they may make a decision based on this factor.

- Packaging protects the product. Products must be protected from damage due to transportation, handling and stocking. In addition, packaging ensures that the product is not contaminated by outside agents such as dust, water and – in some cases – air. Packaging may be designed with tamper-proof features (such as bottle caps that pop the first time they are opened), which ensure that consumers can tell if they are buying a product that has been opened before.

- Agglomeration: this refers to the practice of bulking together items for the purpose of handling. When selling sweets, for example, the manufacturer may bulk together 500 sweets in a bag because it is easier to transport the bag than the individual sweets.

- Packaging provides information: a package lets consumers know the producer's name and address, ingredients used in the product, instructions for use and nutritional information. It also provides additional information such as expiry date, warning of side effects and the amount or quantity in the package. Packaging also contains symbols that the manufacturer needs consumers to know. Such symbols may indicate that the product is poisonous, flammable or fragile.

Now it's your turn

A product's packaging usually has symbols that act as warnings to consumers and intermediaries about how the product should be consumed, handled and stored. Some of the popular symbols used are shown below. For each symbol, see if you can give a few examples of products on whose packages you will expect to find the symbol.

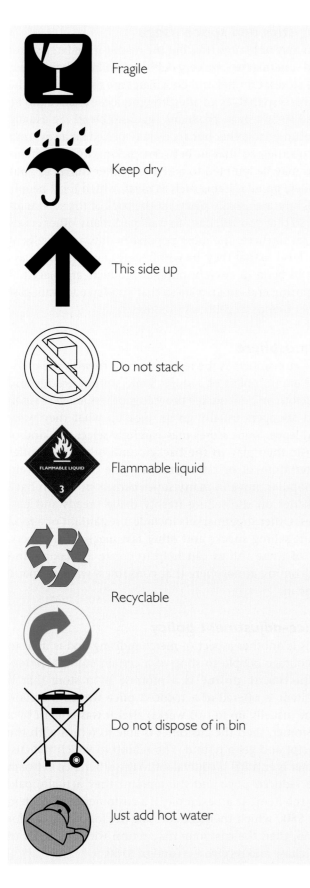

Fragile

Keep dry

This side up

Do not stack

Flammable liquid

Recyclable

Do not dispose of in bin

Just add hot water

Copyright and patent

Copyright protection

Copyrights, **patents** and **trademarks** give the owners of property the exclusive right to use, distribute and modify their property for a specified number of years. Usually, the word 'copyright' is associated with intellectual property (ideas and the products created with these ideas such as books, videos, music, photos and computer software), while patents cover inventions of new products. A copyright holder is protected from duplication and unrestricted use of their content. This protections lasts for up to 50 years after the death of the author, at which time the product enters the public domain. Patent holders, on the other hand, usually have fewer years (usually a maximum of 20) to enjoy the exclusive rights to the product before it can be copied by someone else. Creating an imitation of a product is usually considered illegal, particularly if the imitation carries the same brand name and logo as the original. Handbags made by companies such as Coach, Gucci, Fendi and Prada are exclusive and expensive and have been imitated widely. These imitations are usually available at unbelievably low prices in many stores.

Copyright infringement

Copyright and patent laws have become very important as globalisation spreads and borders are opened up. The internet, along with technologies that quickly duplicate other people's properties and ideas, have become a major challenge as products such as songs, movies, videos, books and software are easily stolen and distributed using modern technology. A trademark is a brand name that is registered to be used exclusively by one entity. Most trademarks were registered years ago, long before internet trading started. A company may, therefore, find that its trademark has already been registered as a domain name by someone else. When KFC wanted to build its website, for example, it found that the domain name was already in use. KFC therefore had to pay thousands of dollars to buy this domain name.

Patents and copyrights ensure that when consumers buy a product they can use it under stipulated conditions. The laws also ensure that these products cannot be reproduced for commercial purposes without direct permission from the producers. A good example of this law regards the purchase and use of movies, videos and recordings on DVDs and audio CDs, which unfortunately are usually copied and sold to support a thriving yet illegal bootleg industry. If you take an original DVD, for example, you are likely to see the warning that the product is 'licensed for private home viewing only. Any other use is prohibited'. This means that, among other things, the DVD is not to be shown to a paying audience, nor should excerpts of it be shown in another movie or broadcast without permission from the owners of the rights.

Selling on copyrights and patents

Patents and copyrights can be sold or leased, in which case the right to use the product is transferred to or shared with another party. One instance of this happening, which we have already discussed (see pages 26–9), occurs when a franchise agreement is created. Under such an agreement, one business (the franchisor) allows another business (the franchisee) the right to create and distribute its ideas and products in exchange for royalties or licensing fees. Usually, the franchisee is required to identify the product as the franchisor's and, therefore, use its name, logo and so on. The franchise contract is very specific as to how the product or idea can be distributed and used. For example, the franchisee may be prevented from selling any other products (as with KFC franchises) and is not allowed to modify the product beyond the ways allowed by the franchisor. Failure to honour these conditions may result in the franchise being taken away.

Merchandising

Of course, all the marketing activities of the business are done with one thing in mind – selling more units of the product. This is where merchandising becomes important. **Merchandising** is essentially what happens at the point where the purchase decision is made. When businesses attempt to sell a product, they use various strategies to ensure that their showroom is strategically arranged to maximise visibility and encourage browsing. Alternatively, if its products are being sold through another agent, then it may make recommendations and provide guidelines to the intermediary on how to display the products. Merchandising, then, is concerned with how to effect purchase at the point where the consumers encounters not just the goods of one business but also many other options from competitors. As an activity it is concerned with logistics, space management and creating an atmosphere that encourages browsing and ultimately purchase.

Logistics and space usage

You may not know this, but the managers of large stores and supermarkets are very deliberate in how they lay out the stores. Candies and chocolates are right next to the cashiers so that, as an afterthought, loose change can be used to buy these products; eggs and bread are usually consumed together but are usually placed far away from each other, so that in between picking up both items you may be tempted to add a few other things to your trolley; popular items such as meat, which most people will buy, are usually placed at the back of the supermarket so that you will have to walk past many other goods to get to them; the most popular brands are usually at eye level so that they are within easy grasp without having to bend or stretch; popular products are placed at opposing ends of an aisle so that you have to walk past other brands to get both products.

Atmosphere

The atmosphere is the feeling associated with the physical environment of a store. Some stores are large and spacious and encourage browsing; others are very small and shoppers usually go in, pick up what they want and leave. Some stores may carefully select the kind of music they play in the background; others may offer entertainment or refreshments while customers wait. A popular move in many supermarkets now is to have bakeries on site selling freshly made breads and pastries. Other supermarkets include a restaurant or a food court selling snacks and other fast meals to shoppers. All of these things can help to create a relaxing and welcoming atmosphere that consumers want to spend time in.

Price-adjustment policy

This is another aspect of merchandising and is used to encourage people to shop at a certain store. A **price-adjustment policy** is a promise by a store that if an item is offered at a reduced price within a certain time (usually up to two weeks) after it was bought by a customer, then the customer is able to return with the receipt and get a refund. The refund to which the customer is entitled is equivalent to the difference between the reduced price and the amount they actually paid for the item. As an example, if a customer buys an item for $500 which then goes on sale the following day for $350, then the customer may return with the proof of purchase and receive a refund of $150.

Selling

Most wholesalers and manufacturers have a sales department or team that is responsible for selling the product. These salespeople will use various techniques to approach a potential customer and to convert their interest into sales. Some of these techniques are listed below.

- **Cold calling**: cold calling refers to the practice of approaching people (whether over the telephone or face-to-face) who have not asked for any information about the product, and who are not expecting a visit or telephone call.
- **Profiling**: identifying the people who are most likely to buy a product and focusing on them.
- **Demonstrations**: salespeople may use the product in real contexts to convince potential customers that it is easy to use, effective and so on.

Cold calling is one technique used to approach potential customers.

- **Sell core benefits**: salespeople usually associate their products with the general benefits that the product offers. A salesperson selling books, for example, may advertise that he is selling knowledge.

Maintaining customer relationships

Firms, regardless of the quality of their products, are not likely to sell many units if they are not perceived as having their customers' best interests at heart. As a result, firms must ensure that they maintain good relationships with their customers if they hope to become market leaders. Much of the business that a firm does is actually by word-of-mouth referrals. People are likely to recommend the firm to their friends if they had a good experience with its products. The onus is on the firm, then, to ensure that it creates a memorable experience for its customers. There are various strategies that the firm can use to build customer relationship, some of which are:

- **After-sales service**: this may include free delivery of the product, setting up the product (particularly electronics) and servicing and repairing the product periodically.
- **Honouring warranties**: a warranty is a promise to the customer to repair or replace the product if it malfunctions due to manufacturing flaws. Maintaining a good customer–firm relationship requires that the firm honours warranty obligations in the event the product does not perform as promised.
- **Selling quality products that reflect their price**: quality and price usually have a unique relationship – expensive products are expected to be of high quality. As a result, consumers expect that the items they purchase will follow this tradition – the more expensive the product, the more likely it is to be of high quality. If this does not happen, then the relationship between the customers and the firm is likely to be poor.

Terms of sale

The phrase **terms of sale** refers to the arrangements that a business has with its customers as to how payment for goods will be made. While the most traditional arrangement of paying immediately upon receiving the goods remains fairly popular, other payment arrangements have developed over time, which offer greater flexibility to consumers. In general, when deciding the most appropriate terms of sale, the consumer is faced with choosing between finding the money immediately or paying over a longer period of time. Some of the terms of sale used by businesses are discussed below.

Cash sale

If the customer pays at the time the sale occurs, then a cash sale has taken place. A cash sales transaction does not have to involve cash as the method of payment – whether the customer pays with cash, credit or debit cards or a cheque, this is still cash payment. A cash payment is simple to carry out, as usually no identification, paperwork or approval process is required.

Credit sale

Buying an item that is paid for at a later date is known as a credit sale. With credit sales, the buyer takes possession of the item before making the payment and usually without even having to make a deposit. Most retailers (who sell to consumers) do not offer credit sales, as the consumers may not be buying in a large enough quantity to justify credit sales. Additionally, the issue of trustworthiness is important in credit sales and this is difficult to establish with end users with whom no close relationship exists. Manufacturers and wholesalers, however, usually have credit arrangements with their customers. Credit sales usually have a specific time frame within which payment is to be made – usually from one to three months (30–90 days). Credit sales are not automatic – all buyers may not qualify and approval has to be sought from a sales officer or even a manager. This means that the paperwork and record keeping necessary with credit sales may actually be a huge expense for the business. Additionally, some of the debtors will never pay and this is a loss that the business will have to absorb.

Layaway plan

In this arrangement, the customer is given a time frame within which to pay for the item. The item is placed on 'layaway' for the customer – meaning the firm promises to hold the item until the customer has finished paying for it. At the end of paying for the product, the buyer takes possession and ownership of the item. If the time elapses or the customer stops paying, then it is likely that the firm will not refund any money paid down on the item placed on layaway. **Layaway plans** also create record-keeping issues for the firm; in addition, they may not result in a sale even though the seller might have turned away other potential customers while the item

was on hold. On the plus side, they provide more protection for the firm against bad debts since the customer does not take possession of the item before paying for it.

Hire purchase

Hire purchase is similar to layaway plans, except that a hire-purchase agreement allows the customer to take possession of the product before paying for it completely. In a hire-purchase agreement, the seller asks the buyer to pay for the item by making a deposit and then equal and timely (usually monthly) instalments thereafter. The final price that the consumer pays is usually higher than the cash price as the buyer must pay for the convenience of using the item before having fully paid for it. Hire-purchase agreements are usually made on furniture and appliances or on items that are quite durable. This is because in hire-purchase agreements, the item acts as collateral for the agreement – in the event the customer defaults on the payments, the item has to be returned. Hire-purchase agreements usually run for a long time; as a result, the risk of the customer defaulting on the agreement is very high.

Cash discount and trade discount

A discount is an opportunity to pay less than the full cost that the seller offers to the buyer. There are two types of discounts – cash discount and trade discount. A **cash discount** is offered to a customer when he or she either pays immediately or within a certain time, if the items were bought on credit. A **trade discount**, on the other hand, is used to encourage bulk buying. It is offered when customers buy in bulk, whether they pay immediately or use another payment arrangement. In theory then, customers may get trade discounts when they buy a large number of units of a good on credit and then get cash discounts when they make the payments.

Consumer protection

Some companies are so large that their annual income is more than some countries earn from selling their goods. These large companies are expected to deal fairly with consumers, who are small individual units with little or no power. Usually these companies treat consumers fairly, since it is in their best interests to do so. However, if they abuse their power in the market and treat a single customer unfairly, then that customer may choose to withdraw his patronage from that firm. He may also choose to tell all his friends about the unfair treatment and they may also take their custom elsewhere.

All things considered, the business will probably only lose a few customers as a result of this, which would have little impact on a large business. For this reason, the consumer may need protection from large businesses that seek to abuse their power.

In Caribbean territories, the government protects consumers through laws that create minimum standards which companies must meet. Laws in the Caribbean that protect consumers address issues such as:

- protection against defective products or unsatisfactory services
- the promotion and presentation of goods in such a way that the public is misled
- accuracy and language use in labelling and packaging
- the pricing and display of items offered for sale
- the extent to which one firm can control a market and determine price
- firms colluding against consumers
- contracts of sale that are unfair to consumers – harsh conditions of credit, demands for payment for unsolicited goods and so on
- honouring contractual obligations to repair, service, install or rebuild a product that has been sold
- the accuracy of measuring instruments such as those used at gas pumps and in stores.

Usually, in an effort to enforce the laws and protect consumers, the government creates agencies that report to a minister or are associated with a ministry. These agencies usually have specific aspects of consumer protection that they oversee. In Barbados, for example, which has a fairly well developed system for consumer protection, the Ministry of Trade, Industry and Commerce is responsible for enforcing the proposed Consumer Protection Act. This is done through various agencies that all operate under the auspices of the ministry. These agencies include:

- the Fair Trading Commission, which prevents unfair trading practices and unfair terms in contracts
- the Barbados National Standards Institute, which prepares and implements national standards relating to structures, commodities, materials and practices
- the Department of Commerce and Consumer Affairs, which enforces trading standards and protects consumers by ensuring that goods and services are safe and legal

- the Office of Public Counsel, which protects consumers against utility companies such as the electricity and gas companies
- the Office of the Supervisory of Insolvency, which protects consumers who go bankrupt with outstanding debts.

The agencies mentioned above are also present in most Caribbean countries, even though they may have different names. Jamaica, for example, has a Consumer Affairs Commission, a Fair Trading Commission, an Office of Utility Regulation and a Bureau of Standards which seek to protect consumers. In Trinidad and Tobago, the Consumer Affairs Division, the Trinidad and Tobago Bureau of Standards and the Anti-Dumping Authority all work under the umbrella of the Ministry of Trade and Industry to protect the interests of consumers. Finally, in Guyana, the Consumer Protection Act of 2004 established a Consumer Affairs Commission to investigate cases of abuse of power on the part of businesses.

Bureau of standards

A standard is a condition, limit or rule that producers are asked to meet in the goods that they produce or services that they offer. For example, when a motorist goes to a service station and buys 50 litres of petrol, the pump may display '50 litres' but in fact the consumer may have received 0.05 litres less (or more) than the quantity indicated. Errors like these are expected in instruments that seek to measure out exact values – but the error needs to have a limit. A standard may, therefore, be established that sets the maximum variance between what the consumer pays for and how much he actually gets. Standards are usually developed and administered by a standards body that ensures that consumers are aware of the standards and that producers comply. This body is called a **bureau of standards** and most countries have one. These national-standards bodies usually work within standards that are established at an international level by international standards organisations.

Standards work in another practical way that benefits consumers. Standards may refer to the agreed dimensions, features, qualities or behaviour of different products, regardless of the brand or country of origin. From this perspective, a standard may be a consistent feature that is present in all products. For example, all bank cards are the same shape and size regardless of the country of origin or the issuing bank; the dimensions of wheelchairs and doorways are also standardised and, as a result, disabled people never have to worry about accessing a ramp.

Making connections: industrial arts

Do dining tables and dining chairs have standard dimensions? If I take a dining chair made for one table and put it by another table, would I be able to sit on the chair and just as comfortably reach and use the table? What about the following aspects of house design: are they standardised? Ask a teacher from your industrial arts department or investigate for yourself.

1 placement of light switches and sockets (location in house and height above the ground)

2 size of kitchen sinks and drainage

3 size of windows

4 size and design of electrical outlets

5 size of doors

The bureau of standards in a country has the following functions:

- It ensures interchangeability of products by guaranteeing that design, features and dimensions are standardised.

- It removes much of the danger from using, consuming or operating products by ensuring that all products behave in a predictable way and that minimum standards are met.

- It facilitates trade between the country in which it operates and other countries by ensuring that products created in its home country can be used in other countries.

- It disseminates innovation – when computer parts and accessories are made to meet a standard design, then all owners of computers are now able to buy these accessories and add them on to their computers. For example, the proliferation of thumb drives was made easy by the fact that all thumb drives were made to fit into a Universal Serial Bus (USB) port that was already of a standardised design on all computers.

The ombudsman

The **ombudsman** is a person appointed by the government to regulate its activities and to investigate cases of abuse of power of state agencies. An ombudsman, for example, may be asked to investigate whether the government agency responsible for issuing licences to operate restaurants acted improperly by refusing to issue a licence to a person who is visually impaired. The ombudsman may investigate and force the agency to answer questions but they cannot overturn the decision or change the laws governing the issuing of licences. They may make recommendations that the laws be changed, however, or that the decision be reversed. Usually, however, the effectiveness of the ombudsman is dependent on the co-operation of the agency and, for this reason, the ombudsman may not be very effective. Nevertheless, the ombudsman is there because of the need to have an independent party carrying out investigations, passing judgement and making recommendations in the event of a conflict. If it is left up to the state agencies to police themselves then it is likely that a conflict of interest will occur.

It is also possible that a business may appoint an ombudsman to police the business. If this happens, the business sets up an office that investigates complaints made by its customers. In the same way as a government ombudsman cannot reverse decisions, a business ombudsman also cannot do much more than make recommendations and suggestions for improvements. Usually, however, the recommendations of the ombudsman carry a great deal of weight as his or her reports may be publicised and may bring national attention to the business and its operations.

Transportation

One of the major logistic issues for managers is that of transportation. Traditionally, land transport using roads has been most popular in the Caribbean; however, transportation by sea and air offers an alternative and becomes necessary when trade among the islands occurs.

Land transport in the Caribbean
Road transport

Transportation by land usually occurs either through road or rail, with road transportation being used more frequently. Road transportation takes advantage of the fairly well developed road networks that criss-cross each territory in the Caribbean. These road networks link main cities and towns to rural and outskirt areas and hence are used for transportation within each country.

Road transportation has the following advantages:

1 The main advantage of road transportation is that it is fairly easily accessible by all businesses and individuals – roads are free to be used by all without the extensive paperwork and administrative procedures associated with using planes or ships.

2 The fact that companies often have their own fleet of vehicles means that they have greater control over the goods during transportation, as they were not contracted out to a third party for transportation.

It also has the following disadvantages:

1 The main disadvantage of road transportation is that it cannot be used for transportation among the islands.

2 Additionally, land transport has to be supported by roads that have to be frequently serviced and repaired. This comes at great cost to the government of each country.

Rail transport

Rail is fairly unpopular in the Caribbean, with passenger trains all but dying out. Countries such as Guyana, Trinidad and Jamaica have limited cargo trains for transporting bauxite and sugar cane. These railways do not cover the entire country in each case, however, as they only link areas that are involved in the farming or mining of these products with areas involved in their processing. Railways offer the potential for great cost savings in the Caribbean since the infrastructure that supports rail transport does not require servicing as frequently once it has been constructed. One of the disadvantages of railways is that they do not usually follow a network structure as roads tend to do – they usually have one fixed route across a country and hence they do not offer the same accessibility as roads do.

Sea transportation

Transportation by sea usually takes the form of huge ships that carry containers filled with goods. Containers are made so that once they reach port, they can be attached to huge and powerful trucks and transported over land to their final destination further inland. The chief advantage of sea transportation in the Caribbean is that it allows for huge, bulky items to be transported easily between ports. As a result, it supports the growth of businesses as it encourages economies of scale. Unfortunately, however, the producer or marketer loses control over the cargo while it is at sea as it has been entrusted to the care of shippers.

Transportation by sea is popular within the Caribbean as most countries have easy access to deep-water ports.

Air transport

The use of air transport is fairly well established in the Caribbean. In addition to the Caribbean's own airlines (such as Caribbean Airlines and Air Jamaica), other airlines associated with other countries also fly to the Caribbean. These airlines facilitate transportation of cargo and are the most popular form of transportation for tourists and other passengers to and within the Caribbean. Air transportation is also used to facilitate trade within a country, since some countries have more than one airport. In Jamaica, for example, some businesses use small planes to transport goods from Norman Manley International Airport in Kingston to Donald Sangster International Airport in Montego Bay.

Air transportation has the following advantages:

1 Air transport offers fast and fairly reliable transportation to and within the Caribbean.

2 The presence of airports in all Caribbean countries makes all countries accessible by air.

It also has the following disadvantages:

1 Its cost is prohibitive, particularly when being used for transportation within a country.

2 In addition, it requires a great deal of logistical and infrastructure support that is expensive for Caribbean governments – even those who do not own airlines.

3 Finally, the goods are once again turned over to a third party (in this case, the airline) who assumes responsibility for them during transit – very often, however, luggage and cargo can be lost for weeks at a time as they are sent to the wrong destination.

Other types of transportation in the Caribbean

In countries such as Guyana, where there are many large rivers, transporting goods by barge is very popular.

In Trinidad, where oil production is an important industry, pipelines are popular. These pipelines are used to transport oil from oil fields to processing plants. In addition, Barbados extracts oil but sends it to Trinidad where it is processed and then sent back to Barbados. The two countries, therefore, have a pipeline transportation system to facilitate this trade. River transportation is also popular in countries such as Belize and Guyana. River transportation is often facilitated using barges. A barge is a boat built with a flat bottom and is usually used on rivers and canals. Some barges are motorised and can move on their own; others must be pulled by motorised ships. Barges are used in Belize to transport timber within the country and to other destinations within the region. In Guyana, river transport is necessary given the number of large rivers that run through inhabited areas in the country.

Transportation and trade

Transport is essential for trade at all levels – among firms within a country, among firms in different countries within the Caribbean and especially between a firm in the Caribbean and its trading partners in other regions (whether the United States, Europe, Asia or even Africa). Transportation becomes important when raw materials or finished goods are being moved between traders.

It also becomes an important consideration when the human element of production that facilitates trade is to be moved efficiently. While much trading can take place over the phone and internet, some items are best bought only after actually inspecting them. This often requires transportation of labour at a domestic, regional or even international level. Domestic transportation occurs when traders are located in the same country and is usually facilitated by the road network in each Caribbean country. At the regional level, which occurs when traders are in different Caribbean countries, trade is usually facilitated by sea (for cargo) or air transport for passengers. The same is also true of international trade – trade between countries located in different regions of the world.

Transportation is an aid to trade as the efficiency of transportation contributes to the price buyers are asked to pay for goods. If transportation costs are high, then this may be passed on to the consumers in the form of higher prices. Transportation is also related to the market share that a producer can command. Firms that have access to markets in other countries through efficient transportation systems are more able to increase their sales, taking advantage of economies of scale and capturing a greater share of this market. At the same time, countries with large, modern and secure harbours, airports and docking facilities are likely to have more efficient transportation systems and are equally likely to generate more trade.

Challenges to effective transportation

Transportation systems in the Caribbean – be they air, land or sea – are subject to a number of challenges that may undermine the effectiveness of the distribution system of a business. The most obvious of these challenges is delayed shipment, which may occur for a number of reasons including labour unrest and inefficiency at ports. In addition, spoilage of goods during transportation is a risk that producers and marketers face. This risk is associated with delays in transportation and misdirection of goods. Misdirection of goods occurs when goods are mistakenly sent to the wrong destination. This is usually as a result of an error on the part of the shipper in the labelling and sorting of goods to be shipped.

Producers also face the problem of warehouse facilities being inadequate and lacking security. As a result, goods left overnight to be shipped or goods that have been shipped and are waiting in a warehouse to be collected may be damaged or they may even be stolen. Ports in the Caribbean have also come under greater scrutiny as governments view them as a point of weakness in the fight against guns and drugs. Industrial unrest also affects the efficient transportation of goods as workers at ports, airports and even private shipping companies may walk off the job temporarily in an effort to obtain better working conditions. When this happens, then the goods that were to be transported are held 'ransom' until the workers return to work.

Some of the problems identified above may be addressed by taking the following steps:

- Proper scheduling should be implemented whenever goods are to be transported. The schedule should allow for unexpected delays in the shipping process by adding what is called 'slack time' to the period required for goods to be transported.

- Insuring cargo to be transported provides reassurance in the event of damage, spoilage or theft.

- Having a clear policy regarding delivery and transportation should help the business to associate the activity of transportation to a particular department, thereby making it someone's responsibility.

- Using shippers that allow virtual tracking is a little more expensive but helps in preventing cargo being misdirected. FedEx, for example, gives each customer a unique personal tracking code that allows the sender (or even the receiver, if the code is shared with this person) to log on to a website and track the package from the point of departure to its destination. The site allows the sender/receiver to see how much time is left for the cargo to be delivered and what city or country the cargo is in at the time of logging on.

Summary – Section B

- Market research is used to collect and analyse information in the market and can be conducted using observation, survey, experiment or interview.

- A business tries to develop a positive image of its brand in the public through a process known as branding. The aim of branding is to develop brand equity.

- Packaging, the 'silent salesman', is used to protect the product and to help in selling it at the point of sale. A product's packaging also provides useful information to the public about, for example, the nutritional value of the product or the name and address of its distributor or producer.

- Many products are protected by copyrights and patents, which ensure that their original creators are the only ones to profit from the sale of these goods.

- Businesses engage in merchandising in an effort to sell their products – merchandising occurs when a business takes practical and strategic steps in organising or setting up its business to take advantage of the browsing and shopping time of customers.

- When customers buy from a business, they may be asked to pay cash or may be allowed to settle their account in a number of ways. These are called terms of sale and each has implications for when ownership of the goods occurs and the amount of paperwork involved in the transaction.

- Customers must be protected from large businesses that may abuse their power. Generally, the government protects consumers by ensuring that laws are enacted and organisations created to prevent unfair business practices that harm consumers.

- Transportation in the Caribbean usually takes the form of road, air or sea. In addition, for special goods such as oil and timber, other methods of transportation such as pipelines and barges may be necessary.

✎ End of section activities

Quick questions

Write short answers to the following questions in your exercise book.

1 How is a focus-group interview different from an in-depth interview?

2 Why is packaging called the 'silent salesman'?

3 Packaging is said to perform the function of agglomeration; what does this mean?

4 How are goods packaged differently for intermediaries from how they are packaged for end users?

5 How are patents and copyrights different? How are they similar?

6 When a salesman makes a cold call, what is he doing?

7 How are layaway plans different from hire purchase?

8 How are cash discounts and trade discounts different?

9 What does a bureau of standards do?

10 List four areas of consumer activity in which the government usually protects consumers.

11 Which countries in the Caribbean use pipelines to transport goods? What types of goods are transported using this method?

Applying what you have learnt

1 You are about to launch a new laptop onto the market and you want to find out some of the features that you should include on the product. Organise a focus-group session with five of your classmates and spend 15 minutes discussing laptops: how they use them, what problems they have with them, what they like about them and how they could be improved. From this make a list of the ways in which your laptop would be different from others already on the market.

2 Get a few brochures from furniture stores that offer hire-purchase arrangements as a means of paying for an item.

   a What is the cash price of the item?

   b What are the hire-purchase terms?

   c Work out how much a consumer would actually pay if the item is paid for using a hire-purchase arrangement.

   d Some stores offer a 'no-deposit policy'. Why might this cost more than a regular hire-purchase agreement?

3 Make a list of the organisations in your country that are responsible for protecting consumers. Visit the websites of a few of these organisations and make a list of some of the areas in which they protect consumers. Can you think of other areas in which consumers need protection?

4 A popular size of bottle for soft drinks usually advertises that it contains 590 ml of soda. If you measure the amount of soft drink in the bottle, however, you may find that it may be as much as 592 ml or as little as 588 ml.

   a Why do you think this is so?

   b Why does the bureau of standards allow excess or shortage in each bottle?

   c How much excess or shortage do you think is acceptable?

Model exam questions

Question 1

A producer of chocolate bars is about to launch his product in a new market. He is also aware of the fact that he needs to do some market research.

   a List two pieces of primary information and two pieces of secondary information that he may want to find out from the market research that he does.
   (4 marks)

   b He is thinking of using an observational research method. What does this method entail and why might it not be the best method for him to use?
   (4 marks)

   c Suggest one alternative method that might be more effective. Give a reason why the method might be more successful.
   (3 marks)

   d By giving a reason, suggest and justify a pricing strategy that he might use in the new market. (4 marks)

   e The market research reveals that consumers are unwilling to pay high prices for chocolate bars. Explain how the distribution chain can be used to reduce prices.
   (5 marks)

Question 2

a What is meant by branding? (3 marks)

b Outline two ways a business can build its brand image. (4 marks)

c Explain why copyrights and patents are an important consideration in marketing. (4 marks)

Question 3

a What does the term 'merchandising' mean? (3 marks)

b Outline how the following considerations may be used by a firm to merchandise its products:

   i store layout

   ii atmosphere. (6 marks)

c What role does a sales team of a business play in merchandising its product? (4 marks)

Question 4

a Outline one advantage and one disadvantage that road transportation has compared with air transportation. (4 marks)

b Discuss how transportation is an aid to trade. (4 marks)

c A business in your country is distributing the following goods. Which method of transportation should the business use for each good and why?

   i fragile, perishable flowers from the flower farm to a shop all the way across the country

   ii large bulky pieces of furniture to a country in Europe

   iii an urgent order of pens to another Caribbean island (6 marks)

d Discuss two ways in which a firm might use transportation as a part of its marketing plan to gain an edge over its competitors. (6 marks)

8 Price determination

> Teach a parrot the term 'supply and demand' and you've got an economist. – *Thomas Carlyle*

Hurricane Ivan washed away hundreds of acres of crops – and quite a few houses – in 2004.

Hurricane Ivan and tomato prices

In September 2004, Hurricane Ivan passed over Jamaica. It was a Category 5 hurricane, which means that it had sustained winds of up to 240 km/h. The hurricane carried with it rainfall of up to 35 inches and caused severe land slippage and damage to property. The island's agricultural sector was most severely affected with many crops that were in season being washed or blown away. Total damage as a result of Hurricane Ivan stood at US$360 million and an estimated 35 per cent of this was to be found in the agricultural sector. In the aftermath of the hurricane, prices went through the roof. The shortage of fresh fruit and vegetables caused severe price appreciation, in some cases as high as 500 per cent, and

nowhere was this more evident than in the price of produce such as vegetables and starch. The price of tomatoes, for example, climbed from a pre-Ivan price of $50 per pound to a high of $200 per pound after Ivan – a price increase of 300 per cent! These price increases sent a signal to farmers to increase their production of tomatoes and, as a result, many farmers dedicated their land and resources to planting tomatoes after Hurricane Ivan. Unfortunately, tomatoes did not turn out to be the money earners that the farmers thought they would be. The farmers came to realise that since they all planted their crops at the same time, they were all ready for the market simultaneously. The market was therefore flooded with tomatoes and this caused the price to decrease from $200 to as low as $5 per pound. Producers were not amused; however, consumers were delighted!

In this chapter we will be examining how prices are determined in a market. As you have realised from the case study above, price is a reliable and significant predictor of what consumers and suppliers will do.

In this chapter you will:

- develop an understanding of the terms 'demand' and 'supply'
- discuss how market forces interact to set prices
- discuss the different market structures within which businesses operate.

Demand and quantity demanded

How are prices determined? Prices are determined by two forces – **demand** and supply. Demand and supply are two of the most important concepts in economics, a subject that tells us how scarce resources are to be utilised most efficiently. But what exactly do we mean by demand? What goods do you demand? Would you want a new cellphone with the latest gadgets and features? How about a modern digital camera? You may well want these items, but do you demand them? Well, in technical terms, you cannot demand items you cannot afford to buy. So, if you have an interest in or a desire for a new laptop, a new digital camera or some new designer clothes without the means of paying for them, then you do not demand these items. Of course, it stands to reason that if you *can* afford to buy these items but have no interest in them, you are still not demanding them. Demand exists, then, when two conditions are met – first, you want an item and would be willing to buy it and, second, you have the means (money or other resources) to buy the item. Demand, then, is the willingness and ability to buy a product at a particular price.

There is a difference between demand and **quantity demanded**. Quantity demanded refers to the number of units of a product that consumers are willing to buy at a certain price. When price changes, the quantity demanded is expected to change; but demand does not. In other words, consumers' demand for the product may not change when price changes – consumers still desire the product and want it just as much as before the price increased, even though they cannot afford to buy as many units of the product. The reduced quantity that consumers now buy is not related to a change in demand but to a change in price. This is the essential difference between demand and quantity demanded, and we will explore this in much more detail as we go through the chapter.

The nature of demand

The nature of demand is a fairly easy concept to grasp because it is one with which you interact often, without being aware of it. What happens when there is an increase in the price of a product that you consume? Given that you have limited resources, the natural reaction to this price increase is to buy fewer units of the product. This is perhaps not a choice you make out of a decreased desire for the product but simply one of economics – you will buy what you are able to afford. This observation is formalised as the *law of demand*. The law of demand describes the relationship between price and quantity demanded. The law tells us that at high prices, the quantity of a product that consumers demand will be low; conversely, at low prices, consumers demand a greater quantity of the product. In other words, the law of demand describes the *inverse* relationship between price and quantity demanded. The law should also be seen as describing what happens when the price of a product changes. Generally, one expects that as the price of a product increases, consumers will buy fewer units of the product. Additionally, and somewhat expectedly, when the price of a product decreases, the expectation is that quantity demanded will increase.

The demand curve

It is clear that there is a relationship between quantity demanded and price. This relationship is said to be an inverse one as a change in price in one direction (whether an increase or a decrease) results in a change in quantity demanded in the opposite direction. This relationship can be plotted on a graph to produce a demand curve. The demand curve, then, is a diagrammatic representation of the law of demand; it shows the number of units of a product that consumers are willing to buy at each price. For this reason, the demand curve is frequently referred to as the demand schedule. The curve is plotted with price on the vertical axis and quantity demanded on the horizontal axis. Each price is then mapped on to a corresponding quantity of the good to reflect the number of units associated with it. Table 8.1 shows, for example, the number of packets of biscuits that consumers are willing to buy at various prices.

The table shows that quantity demanded falls as the price of biscuits increases. If this relationship is plotted, a curve which slopes downwards is obtained. The curve's downward slope is indicative of the fact that at high prices (take, for example, a price of $10) the quantity demanded is very low (only five packets of biscuits are being demanded) but at low prices (for example, at a price of $3) the number of packets of biscuits being demanded is very high, at 33.

Price ($)	Number of packets of biscuits
3	33
4	29
5	26
6	23
7	20
8	16
9	10
10	5

Table 8.1 Number of packets of biscuits demanded by consumers at various prices.

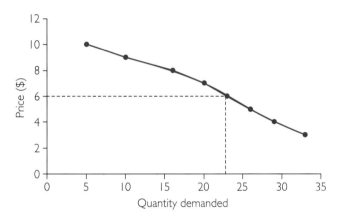

Figure 8.1 The demand curve.

You can use the demand curve to determine the quantity demanded at any price. For example, in Figure 8.1, a straight line has been drawn horizontally from a price of $6 until it reaches the demand curve and then vertically until it reaches the horizontal axis. The point at which the line crosses the horizontal axis is the corresponding quantity being demanded at a price of $6. A quick check of Table 8.1 confirms what is shown graphically – at $6 consumers demand 23 units of the product. Even though the demand curve is really just that – a curve – it is often drawn as a straight line. Traditionally, however, it is still referred to as a curve.

Factors affecting consumer behaviour

How do consumers decide how many units of a product to consume? So far, we have been paying a lot of attention to price and how this factor affects the quantity demanded. However, price is just one of the many factors that impact the demand curve, even though it is perhaps the most important one. Below, we discuss some of the factors that affect the demand curve. It is important that you are able to map these changes on a graph, so pay keen attention to any supporting diagram for each factor.

Price

The law of demand is very clear – when the price (P) of a product changes, then its quantity demanded (Q) will also change. The law goes on to explain the direction of the changes – as P changes in one direction, then it brings about changes in Q in the opposite direction. Now, continuing with the example of biscuits and revisiting and simplifying the graph shown in Figure 8.1, let us look at what happens when the price of biscuits increases. This is shown in Figure 8.2.

> ### ☞ Now it's your turn
>
> Can you work out what will happen if price decreases? Make up an example and draw a graph to show the effect of a reduction in price on the quantity demanded.

An increase in price leads to a reduction in demand for two reasons. Aside from the fact that your experience has confirmed that this relationship between P and Q is true, we can use basic economic analysis to reach

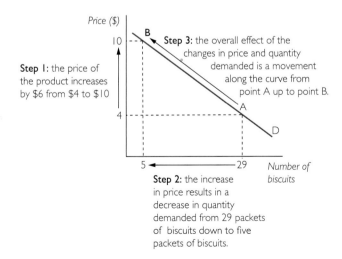

Figure 8.2 An increase in price and its effect on quantity demanded.

this same conclusion. The first reason for this relationship is called the substitution effect. An increase in the price of biscuits causes some consumers to buy cheaper substitutes for biscuits. This leads to a reduction in the number of packets of biscuits that consumers desire, as their demand is being satisfied by another product. Another reason for the relationship between P and Q lies in what is called the income effect. When the price of biscuits increases, the consumer suffers what is similar to a reduction in income, since his income cannot buy as many units of the good as before. Price increases, therefore, result in a loss in the buying power of consumers' income and, ultimately, in a reduction in quantity demanded.

Making connections: mathematics

1 How are dependent variables different from independent variables?

2 When these variables are graphed, on which axis is each placed?

3 In the relationship between quantity demanded and price, which variable is independent and which dependent?

4 Does the graphing of the demand curve follow the tradition, observed in part (2) above, regarding the axis on which independent and dependent variables are placed?

Think about it

Does an increase in price always result in a decrease in quantity demanded? The following products may not always follow the law of demand. Why do you think this is so?

1 table salt

2 cigarettes

3 alcoholic drinks

Can you suggest other goods that may not follow the law of demand? Give reasons for your suggestions.

Income

Income has a peculiar but expected effect on demand. To properly understand this effect, look at Table 8.2. In the table, we show what happens to the demand for biscuits as a consumer's income increases.

With an increase in income, the consumer can buy more biscuits – not just at current prices but at *all* prices. This means that even at high prices, the consumer can buy more biscuits than she used to be able to afford. The result is that the old demand curve is no longer valid, since that demand curve shows how many packets of biscuits the consumer could afford to buy given her previous income level. As the graph in Figure 8.3 shows, at each price level the consumer's increased income allows her to buy more packets of biscuits and hence there is a new demand curve, which is a rightward shift of the old demand curve.

An increase in income, therefore, allows consumers to buy more units of a good at all prices. This is shown as a rightward (outward) shift of the demand curve, from D1 to D2, in Figure 8.3. A decrease in income, on the other hand, results in the consumers being able to buy less and this is shown as a leftward (inward) shift of the demand curve. You should also be aware of the fact that there are subtle and indirect ways for income to change, without workers actually being paid more or less. If the government increases taxation (either by introducing new taxes or increasing the level of existing taxes) then consumers have less disposable income to spend and this is effectively a reduction in income. The reverse is also possible – consumers may be asked to pay less of their income in taxes and this would mean that they have more money to spend.

Price ($)	Quantity demanded *before* income increased	Quantity demanded *after* income increased
3	33	42
4	29	39
5	26	35
6	23	32
7	20	28
8	16	23
9	10	18
10	5	12

Table 8.2 Number of packets of biscuits demanded by consumers before and after income increases.

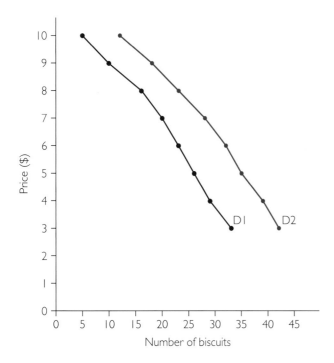

Figure 8.3 An increase in income and its effect on quantity demanded.

The demand for some goods, however, does not follow the observation that we have made so far regarding income's relationship with demand. For these goods, demand may actually decrease when income increases. In other words, these goods are not attractive to consumers when their incomes increase. The reason for this is tied up in how these goods are perceived. Consumers associate some goods with a particular lifestyle – taking the bus may be indicative of a low income and, when income increases, consumers take more taxis or buy their own vehicles. Demand for bus travel, therefore, is likely to decrease when income increases. Such goods, whose demand decreases when consumers have higher income, are called **inferior goods**.

 Now it's your turn

Can you name some other examples of inferior goods – products whose demand is likely to decrease when consumers have higher income?

The price and availability of substitutes and complements

A product has a **substitute** if there is another good that satisfies the same demand as the product does. So, for example, any product that provides information on

Some products complement each other naturally – fries with fried chicken have always been a favourite.

business and its operation – whether the internet, another textbook or a CD – competes with and is a substitute for this textbook. If there is an increase in the price of a good that has a close substitute, then consumers are likely to switch their demand to the substitute, particularly if its price has remained unchanged. The extent to which consumers will switch their demand between substitutes is determined by the degree of substitutability of the products. If the products are close in functions and features, then a change in the price of one will have a large impact on the demand for its substitute. For example, chicken and fish are close substitutes – consumers can easily switch from one product to the other – hence, a change in the price of fish is likely to have a large impact on the demand for chicken. On the other hand, while the internet can indeed be used as a substitute for textbooks, they are not close substitutes, and an increase in the price of *Principles of Business* textbooks is not likely to send *Principles of Business* students flocking to the internet. Some goods actually have no substitute at all – no other product satisfies the respective demand that they do. The best example of such a good is perhaps table salt – a product which is highly insensitive to changes in price and income given its lack of substitutes.

Complements, on the other hand, are products that are consumed together. People will often buy bread along with cheese, for example, or wafer cones along with ice cream. Other examples include buying a computer and signing up to an internet service provider at the same time. These are all complements, and this is an important consideration when one thinks about demand, since if products are bought together the price of one affects the demand for the other. If the price of a product increases, then consumers are likely to buy less of the product and any other product that it complements or that complements it.

 Now it's your turn

Below is a list of some popular products. For each one find a substitute and a complement. Compare your substitutes to your classmates' – which are closer? In each case, do you think changes in the price of substitutes affect the product's demand more than changes in the price of complements? Why or why not?

1 digital camera

2 ice cream

3 cheese

4 a ticket to see a movie

5 fried chicken

Taste, preference and culture

Complements, substitutes and other important economic ideas may be the last thing on your mind when you are hungry for some of your favourite fast food. You will also have some favourite products or brands that you will continue to buy regardless of their price or even the prices of their substitutes and complements. In other words, when we are looking at the factors that affect demand, we also have to look at basic factors such as brand loyalty, preferences, taste, culture and season. Coke and Pepsi, for example, have remained the favourite brands of soft drink among high school, college and tertiary students even though they are invariably sold for a few dollars more than other soft drinks. One expects that during the rainy season, the demand for umbrellas (and their prices as well) will sky-rocket and that in Jamaica, saltfish (which is a part of the national dish), will experience year-round demand. Other products, such as buns, cheese and fish, are consumed during Easter, and some foods (such as pork and seafood) are forbidden by some denominations and religious groups (such as Seventh-Day Adventists and Rastafarians). These are all examples of how non-monetary factors affect demand.

Movement of the curve versus movement along the curve

At the start of this chapter, we spent some time making a distinction between demand and quantity demanded. The essential point we made is that price causes quantity demanded to change but does not change demand. A change in quantity demanded will result in a movement *along* the curve – demand will simply move to a new point on the same curve if price changes. This is a crucial point and is worth repeating for emphasis: if price changes, the curve does not shift inward or outward; rather, there is a movement along the curve reflecting the fact that the higher or lower price has induced a decrease or an increase in quantity demanded.

But what about other factors such as income, price of substitutes and so on? A change in these factors will result in a movement of the entire curve – either inward (leftward) or outward (rightward). Figure 8.4 shows the difference between a movement along the curve and a movement of the curve. When any non-price factor changes, the consumers' demand at all prices will change and hence a new curve needs to be drawn. The old curve will shift outward if the change results in an *increase* in demand at all prices. In other words, the curve will shift outward if:

• income increases

• the price of complements decreases

• the price of substitutes increases.

Of course, an inward shift of the old demand curve will occur when the change in non-price factors results in demand decreasing. This occurs when:

• income decreases

• complements become expensive

• substitutes become cheaper.

Demand and elasticity

The law of demand is very helpful – it tells us that a change in price will result in an opposite change in quantity demanded. As such, it tells producers and marketers

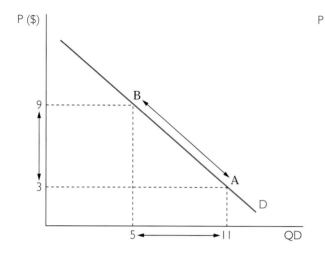
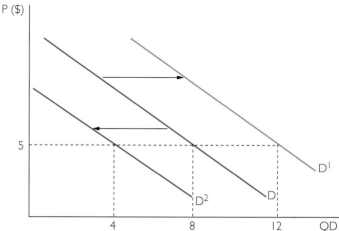

a A change in price causes movement **along** the curve between points A and B and results in a change in quantity demanded.

b A change in demand causes a movement **of** the demand curve. If demand increases, the curve shifts outward from D to D1, while a decrease in demand causes the curve to shift inward to D2.

Figure 8.4 Movement of the curve versus movement along the curve.

that if they increase the price of their product they should expect some decrease in demand as consumers switch to cheaper substitutes. The law does not tell us, though, by how much quantity demanded will change. In other words, knowing that demand will decrease if price increases is useful, but it may also be useful for the producers to know whether a small increase in price will result in a large or small decrease in quantity demanded. This is where the concept of elasticity becomes important. **Elasticity** refers to the responsiveness of demand to changes in underlying variables that affect demand. There are many types of elasticity – one for each variable that affects the demand curve (price, income, substitutes and complements). We will only be focusing on price elasticity of demand, however.

Price elasticity of demand (PED)

Some products have a very sensitive demand curve – a small change in price results in a large change in quantity demanded. Others, however, are very insensitive – changes in quantity demanded are minimal even when there are large changes in price. This observation is explained by the concept of **price elasticity of demand**. PED refers to the responsiveness of quantity demanded to a change in price. PED builds on the law of demand by indicating not just the direction of the change in quantity demanded (whether it will increase or decrease) but also the extent of the change

(whether quantity demanded will change by just a few units or by many units). PED is either elastic, inelastic or unitary.

Elastic demand: demand is said to be elastic if the rate of change in price is smaller than the rate of change in quantity demanded. Products that exhibit elastic demand are very sensitive to changes in price – a small increase in price results in most consumers switching to cheaper substitutes and, as a consequence, there is a large reduction in quantity demanded. Products that have elastic demand usually have many close substitutes to which consumers can turn in the event of a price increase. A good example of elastic demand is what happens at a taxi stand. Usually all taxis working the same route are parked at the same stand. Each car offers essentially the same service and, hence, each is a close substitute for the other. If one taxi driver charges a price that is only slightly higher than that charged by all the other taxi drivers, then he can expect to see demand for his service slashed dramatically as consumers simply stop taking his taxis and use one of the many available substitutes. In addition, if one driver decides to undersell his competitors and charges a price that is slightly lower than theirs, then he can expect to see potential passengers flocking to his car in droves.

Inelastic demand: demand is inelastic if changes in price result in only a small change in quantity demanded.

These goods have demand curves that are very insensitive and unresponsive to changes in price. Inelastic demand occurs when a product has no close substitutes and therefore consumers must continue to buy the product even when its price increases. Sellers of products with inelastic demand are assured of continued revenues even if they increase their prices. Cooking salt is a good example of a product with inelastic demand – regardless of the price increase, consumers will continue to buy roughly the same quantity of salt; in addition, consumers do not rush to buy more salt if the price of salt decreases.

👉 Now it's your turn

Look at the following list of products. Sort them into two groups – those that are elastic and those that are inelastic.

1 cellphones	**6** food
2 ice cream	**7** thumbtacks
3 pullovers	**8** petrol
4 sugar	**9** flour
5 clothes	**10** visit to the movies

Based on the list you have made and your knowledge of elasticity, explain how the following factors are likely to affect the elasticity of a product:

1 necessity of a good (ice cream versus sugar)

2 percentage of income spent on good (motor cars versus sweets and candies)

3 width of the good being referred to. Width refers to how the good is defined. When a good is being described it can be defined in a very general or wide way, such as 'food', or in a very specific or narrow way, such as 'ice cream'. Do you expect goods with wide definitions to have elastic or inelastic demand?

Unitary demand: it is possible that the change in price will result in an equal change in quantity demanded. If this happens, then demand is said to be unitary.

🧍 Think about it

Is $1 ever a lot? Can $1 be more than $100? Well, in absolute terms, $1 is not usually considered to be a lot and is never more than $100. In relative terms, however, $1 can be a lot and can be more than $100. Consider the situation where the price of an expensive cellphone with a price tag of $10 000 is increased by $100. Alternatively, consider the situation where a sweet that was being sold for $1 is now being sold for $2. Which set of consumers do you think have more right to be upset about the price increase? Well, cellphone users have to pay over $100 more, but this is actually only 1 per cent increase – a very small amount. Consumers of sweets, on the other hand, only have to pay one extra dollar, but this represents a doubling of the original price – an increase of 100 per cent. In theory, then, consumers of sweets have more reason to be upset since the rate of increase that they face is more than that faced by cellphone users.

Discuss

1 Goods, such as sweets, that are cheap are likely to be very inelastic. Why is this so?

2 Suppose a good that cost millions of dollars experiences a price increase of only a few per cent – say 5 per cent, how do you expect quantity demanded to change?

3 Why are rates of increase often more important than actual increases?

Elasticity and the demand curve

The three curves in Figure 8.5 show price elasticity of demand – in each case, price is cut in half and demand changes from A to B (a movement along the curve).

In Figure 8.5(a), a halving of price has quadrupled quantity demanded. Price decreases from $1000 to $500 (a decrease of 50 per cent) and quantity demanded has increased from one unit to four units (an increase of 300 per cent). This case shows elastic demand, since the change in quantity demanded (300 per cent) is more than the change in price (50 per cent). In Figure 8.5(b), a halving of price (a reduction of 50 per cent) has

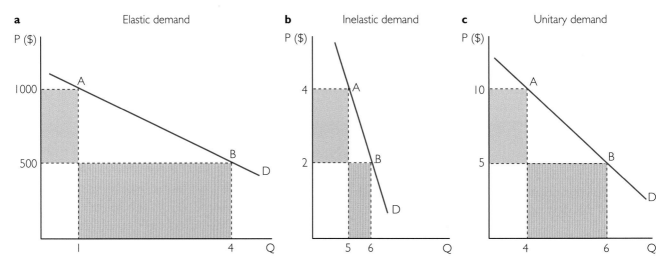

Figure 8.5 Price elasticity of demand.

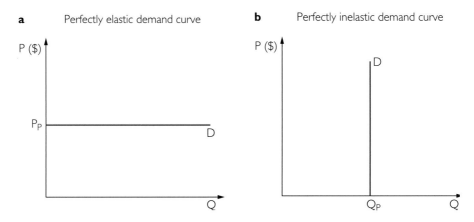

Figure 8.6 Extremes in elasticity of demand – perfectly elastic and perfectly inelastic demand.

resulted in quantity demanded increasing by one unit (an increase of 20 per cent). This graph shows inelastic demand since the change in quantity demanded is far less than the change in price. In Figure 8.5(c), a halving of price (a reduction of 50 per cent) has resulted in quantity demanded increasing by two units (an increase of 50 per cent). Since the change in price of 50 per cent is equal to the change in quantity demanded, this case shows unitary elastic demand.

If you look at each of the graphs in Figure 8.5, you will realise that the graph with an elastic demand, Figure 8.5(a), is relatively flat while the graph in Figure 8.5(b), which shows an inelastic demand, is relatively steep. It is important that you do not think that the flatter the demand curve, the more elastic demand is. Indeed, along a straight line, the elasticity of demand will vary between any two points. A curve that is perfectly flat, however, has what is called perfectly elastic

demand. Such a curve is shown in Figure 8.6(a). Products that exhibit perfectly elastic demand will see quantity demand equal to zero at any price above (or below) P_P. This may only be possible in theory, however, with markets such as the taxi-stand situation described earlier being a close example.

At the other end is a curve that is vertical, which has perfectly inelastic demand – a change in price brings no change in quantity demand since the product is a necessity with no substitute. Such a curve is shown in Figure 8.6(b) and it shows that products that have perfectly inelastic demand have one quantity that is demanded at all prices – high or low. This type of unresponsiveness to price is once again perhaps limited to textbook examples with no real example of perfect inelasticity in any market. Salt is perhaps the example of a product that comes closest to being perfectly inelastic.

Supply

When discussing price determination, **supply** is the other half of the model that must be discussed. Supply acts as a counter-balance to consumers' demand in price determination: while consumers are anxious to pay as little as possible for a product, suppliers are intent on collecting as much as possible. Supply is defined as a producer's willingness and ability to produce and/or sell a good. **Quantity supplied**, much like quantity demanded, is related to how many units of a good sellers are willing to supply at a given price over a specified period of time. To understand the nature of supply, you have to change perspective and start thinking like a seller, not a buyer. As a buyer, you are anxious to spend as little as possible in order to get the good that you want to buy. As a seller, your intention is to make as much money as possible and, therefore, you want to sell at the highest price possible. This means that the relationship between price and quantity supplied will be different from the relationship between price and quantity demanded.

The law of supply and the supply curve

The law of supply tells us what happens to the quantity of a product being supplied when its price increases. The law has the following essential elements:

1 At high prices, suppliers are willing to supply more units of the product, while at low prices they will cut back on their supply. This happens because suppliers are seeking to maximise profits, which they can do better when the price of the product increases.

2 This means, therefore, that there is a positive relationship between the price of a product and the number of units of the product that suppliers are willing to put on the market and, thus, a change in price in one direction (whether up or down) will cause quantity supplied to change in the same direction.

3 This means that the supply curve will have a different slope when compared with the demand curve. You will recall that the demand curve started in the top left-hand corner and decreased to the bottom right-hand corner, showing that when price is high, quantity demanded will be low and that when price is low, quantity supplied will be high.

4 The supply curve, however, starts in the bottom left-hand corner and increases to the top right-hand corner – showing a positive relationship between price and quantity supplied.

Let us go back to the biscuit example we used when we looked at the demand curve. In this case, however, we are looking at the example from the perspective of the seller. Table 8.3 shows the number of packets of biscuits that suppliers are willing to sell at various prices. As you can see, suppliers are willing to sell more units as the price of biscuits increases.

When these points are graphed with price on the vertical axis and quantity supplied on the horizontal axis, the result is a curve as shown in Figure 8.7.

The supply curve starts at the origin (where both price and quantity supplied are equal to 0) since at a price of $0, suppliers will not supply any biscuits at all. The curve continues to increase as price does, up to a price of $10 where the firm is willing to supply 37 packets of biscuits. Each price on the vertical axis corresponds to a given quantity supplied on the horizontal axis. In Figure 8.7 the corresponding quantity being supplied at a price of $6 is 16 units, which you can confirm by looking at Table 8.3.

Price ($)	Quantity supplied
3	4
4	7
5	12
6	16
7	20
8	25
9	29
10	37

Table 8.3 Number of packets of biscuits supplied by producers at various prices.

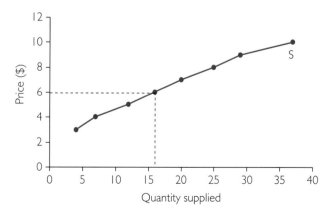

Figure 8.7 The supply curve.

153

Factors affecting suppliers' decisions

As with demand, the supply curve will respond in two different ways as underlying factors are changed. Movements will take place along the curve as price changes and the curve itself will move either inward or outward as other factors, such as costs and technology, change.

Price: as the price of the product increases, one expects that suppliers will be more likely to supply more units of the product as they seek to take advantage of increased revenues. Using the same reasoning, producers cut back on the quantity they supply when the price of a product decreases. These changes are reflected as movements along the supply curve, as shown in Figure 8.8.

Cost: this factor causes a shift of the supply curve as a producer's ability and willingness to produce a good are related not only to the price of the good but also to the cost of producing it. Cost refers to the amount that has to be spent on the inputs – such as raw material, labour, capital. As the price of inputs increases then the cost of production also increases; this usually results in some producers losing interest in producing the item. This is shown as an inward (or leftward) shift of the supply curve. If the cost of production decreases, then supply is likely to increase and this is shown as an outward (rightward) shift of the supply curve. Figure 8.9(a) and (b) show the movements of the supply curve associated with an increase and a decrease in supply.

Technology: technology allows for an increase in production as it usually causes economies of scale, synergy and efficiency to occur. If technology is introduced to the production process and is properly harnessed by producers, then this results in an increase in supply at all prices, and thus an outward shift of the curve occurs.

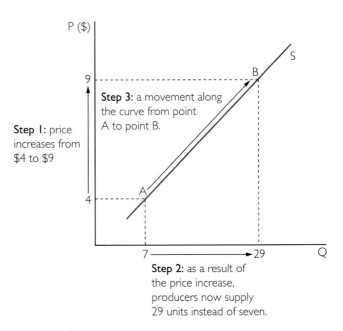

Figure 8.8 An increase in price and its effect on quantity supplied.

a

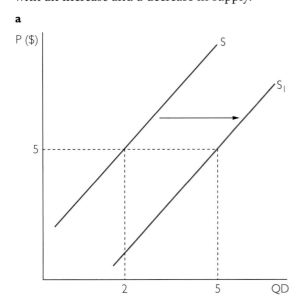

An increase in supply, caused by a reduction in the cost of production or an increase in technology being employed, causes the supply curve to shift from S to S1. This results in five units, instead of two, being supplied at a price of $5.

Figure 8.9 Movements of the supply curve.

b

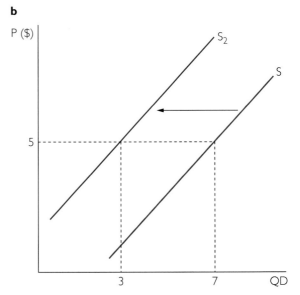

A reduction in supply, caused by an increase in the cost of production or a reduction in the level of technology employed, causes the supply curve to shift from S to S2. This results in three units, instead of seven, being supplied at a price of $5.

Prices of related outputs: producers must always decide how to use scarce resources to maximise profits. A baker, for example, must consider how best to use scarce raw materials, labour and factory space to produce a combination of goods such as biscuits, bread and buns. If biscuits are being sold for high prices, most of the producer's resources will go toward the production of biscuits. If, however, biscuit prices fall and the price of bread increases, then one can expect that resources will be directed towards the production of bread and hence fewer biscuits will be supplied. The price of bread, buns and other pastries is likely to affect supply of biscuits since producers must produce fewer units of one good if they want to produce more of another.

Price determination – equilibrium analysis

Now we can revisit the important question that we asked at the start of the chapter: how are prices determined? We have looked at how consumers behave given limited resources and faced with competing choices. We have also looked at the behaviour of suppliers, who are seeking to maximise profit. If you have been reading between the lines, you may have deduced that the interests of consumers and producers appear to be at odds – consumers want to buy items at low prices and suppliers want to sell these items at high prices. This is indeed true; however, a point can be found that is common to both parties. Let us take the case of the biscuit market we looked at earlier. In this market, consumers' demand ranged from five biscuits at $10 each to 33 biscuits at $3 each. On the other hand, suppliers were interested in selling between four biscuits at $3 each and 37 biscuits at $10 each. Between these two extremes is a middle ground that will appeal to both parties.

Table 8.4 shows both the demand schedule and the supply schedule on the same table so we can make some comparisons.

Table 8.4 shows what we already know – quantity supplied is increasing with price while quantity demanded is decreasing. But since we have put both supply and demand on the same table, we can deduce something else from it – we are now able to say the price at which the good will be sold.

Let us start by considering what is happening at a price of $3 – the lowest price on the schedule. At this price, consumers are willing to buy many packets of biscuits (33 in total) while suppliers are not anxious to sell as many (they only want to sell four packets of biscuits).

Price ($)	Quantity demanded	Quantity supplied
3	33	4
4	29	7
5	26	12
6	23	16
7	20	20
8	16	25
9	10	29
10	5	37

Table 8.4 Supply and demand schedules for biscuits.

At $3, therefore, there is a scarcity or a shortage of 29 units – 29 packets of biscuits are wanted by consumers that suppliers are not willing to sell. At $4, this shortage continues, but it is now smaller for two reasons. First, the higher price makes consumers want fewer packets of biscuits (only 29) and for the same reason (the higher price) suppliers are willing to sell more than they would at $3. The result is that at $4 there is a scarcity of 22 packets of biscuits on the market. At $5 there is a scarcity of 14 packets of biscuits, and at $6 there is a scarcity of seven packets of biscuits. Obviously, as the price increases, more packets of biscuits are available, and scarcity decreases.

At $7, consumers are willing to buy 20 packets of biscuits and suppliers are willing to sell 20 packets of biscuits. There is no scarcity as all the goods that are being supplied are being demanded. This is the middle ground between what consumers want and what suppliers are wiling to offer and it is called **equilibrium**. Since consumers are getting the number of biscuits that they want and suppliers are willing to sell this amount at the stated price, there is no inclination for either consumers or suppliers to change and this is the essential idea behind equilibrium. Equilibrium is a state of rest in which both parties are satisfied and are both benefiting. The fundamental theory of the free market is that all markets approach and settle at equilibrium. A market is in equilibrium when suppliers are willing to supply all the goods that consumers want at the price that consumers are willing to pay. Similarly, equilibrium occurs when consumers are willing to buy all the goods that suppliers are selling at the price that suppliers are asking. In short, at equilibrium quantity supplied is equal to quantity demanded – this is shown graphically in Figure 8.10.

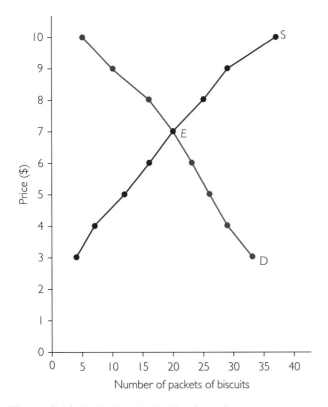

Figure 8.10 Equilibrium in the biscuit market.

We could continue the analysis using the information in Table 8.4. At $8, which is a price above the equilibrium price of $7, quantity demanded is now equal to 16 units and quantity supplied is now equal to 25 units. At this price, quantity supplied is more than quantity demanded and this is called a surplus. In other words, suppliers are selling more goods than consumers are demanding. This situation continues and worsens (the surplus gets larger) up to a price of $10, which has a surplus of 32 units. The essential points we have made in this section regarding equilibrium are perhaps best summarised as follows:

1 Equilibrium exists when both suppliers and consumers are in agreement on the number of units of a good to be sold and the price at which they are to be sold. This occurs when the quantity supplied is equal to the quantity demanded.

2 The price at which the quantity supplied is equal to the quantity demanded is called the equilibrium price.

3 At prices below the equilibrium price, quantity demanded is more than quantity supplied and this results in a shortage or scarcity on the market.

At prices above the equilibrium price, the quantity supplied is more than the quantity demanded and this results in a surplus on the market.

Think about it

'All markets approach and eventually settle at equilibrium.' Is this statement always true?

'A firm may sell at a price below its equilibrium price. This price will be very low and allows the firm to produce and sell many units and take advantage of economies of scale.' How likely is this to be true?

Excess goods lead to 'sale' signs being mounted in store windows as prices are slashed and equilibrium is maintained.

Graphing equilibrium

If we plot the supply curve and the demand curve on the same graph we produce two curves that intersect at the equilibrium point. This is shown in Figure 8.11.

We can also use graphs to help us understand better what happens when prices are set above or below the equilibrium price and why we can conclude that all markets return to and settle at equilibrium.

Case 1 – prices set below the equilibrium price

Figure 8.11 shows a simplified version of the graph drawn in Figure 8.10. On this graph we have drawn a horizontal line at p = $4. This line shows that at $4, quantity demanded is 29 packets of biscuits while quantity supplied is seven packets of biscuits.

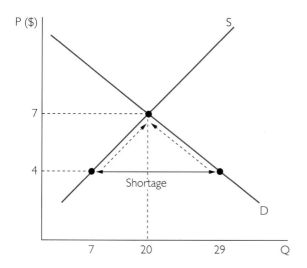

Figure 8.11 Prices set below the equilibrium price.

The scarcity is therefore 22 units. This scarcity is unsustainable, however, as it will cause prices to increase. This increased price will result in an increase in quantity supplied and a decrease in quantity demanded. This causes movement along the respective curves until the market returns to its equilibrium price of $7.

Case 2 – prices set above the equilibrium price

A price above the equilibrium results in a surplus as quantity being supplied is more than the quantity being demanded. Figure 8.12 shows the biscuit market in equilibrium with 20 units being supplied and demanded at a price of $7 each.

At a price of $9, however, there is a surplus of 19 units and the market will take steps to correct itself. Seeing

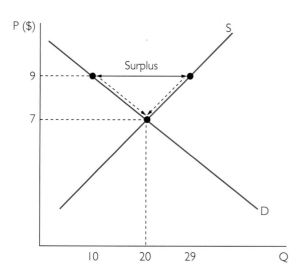

Figure 8.12 Prices set above the equilibrium price.

this surplus, suppliers will employ creative ways to clear stock – they will offer sales and discounts which all lead to reduced prices and ultimately to a reduction in quantity being supplied and increased quantity being demanded. Invariably, therefore, the market for biscuits will end up settling at a price of $7 and a quantity of 20 units.

Changes in equilibrium

The equilibrium point will change when either the supply or demand change. A shift of either curve results in a new equilibrium point with fewer or more units being sold at higher or lower prices. There are four possible basic cases of changes in equilibrium, all of which have been shown in Figure 8.13. In each case, the original equilibrium point is at E, with a price of P and quantity of Q. A shift in the supply or demand curve moves the equilibrium point to E_1 with a price of P_1 and quantity of Q_1.

Think about it

The equilibrium price is often called the 'market-clearing price'. Why do you think this is so?

Scarcity causes long lines as demand increases and prices go up.

Case 1 – an increase in demand: Figure 8.13(a)

If demand increases without a corresponding increase in supply, then this is similar to a scarcity and the result is an increase in price. This increase in price causes the quantity supplied to increase and the new equilibrium point to move to E_1, a higher point on the supply curve.

Case 2 – a decrease in demand: Figure 8.13(b)

A reduction in demand causes price to decrease as suppliers try to get rid of excess stock. Observing that the price is now lower, producers will reduce their supply by shifting resources into the production of other items. The result is that there is a movement along the supply curve to the new equilibrium point of E_1.

Case 3 – a decrease in supply: Figure 8.13(c)

When supply decreases, then fewer units are available for sale and scarcity is the inevitable result. This causes price to increase and, as a result, quantity demanded falls. This is shown as a movement along the demand curve to a new equilibrium point of E_1.

Case 4 – an increase in supply: Figure 8.13(d)

An increase in supply creates a surplus on the market and leads to a reduction of prices as suppliers try to clear stock. Seeing this reduced price, consumers now demand more units of the good, leading to a new equilibrium point of E_1.

Table 8.5 summarises the important points regarding changes in equilibrium and the effect of such changes on price and quantity.

Source of the change	Effect on price	Effect on quantity
Increase in demand	Rises	Rises
Decrease in demand	Falls	Falls
Increase in supply	Falls	Rises
Decrease in supply	Rises	Falls

Table 8.5 Changes in equilibrium as a result of shifts in the demand or supply curve.

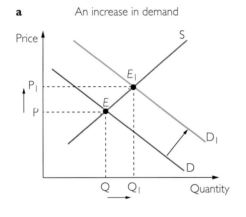

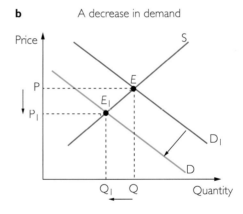

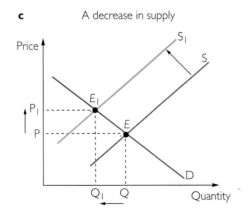

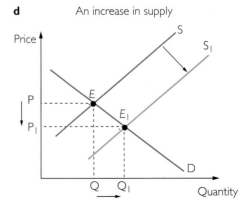

Figure 8.13 Changes in equilibrium.

Summary – Section A

- Prices are set by the interaction of demand and supply – market forces that represent, respectively, the interests of consumers and producers.

- The cheaper the price of a good, the more consumers demand; suppliers, on the other hand, will supply more units of a good if its price increases. These are called, respectively, the law of demand and the law of supply.

- Demand is also affected by factors such as consumers' incomes, their tastes and preferences and the price of related goods such as complements and substitutes.

- A change in price affects quantity demanded and causes a movement along the demand curve; a change in any other factor causes a shift of the curve.

- In addition to price, supply is affected by factors such as the cost of production, technology and the cost of related goods.

- A change in the price of a product also causes a movement along the supply curve, while a change in any other factor that affects supply causes the entire curve to shift.

- When the quantity of a good demanded by consumers at a particular price is equal to the quantity of a good supplied by producers at this price, then a market is said to be in equilibrium. All markets will approach and settle at equilibrium.

- If price is set above the equilibrium price, supply will exceed demand and the market experiences surplus. At prices below the equilibrium price, the market experiences scarcity as demand exceeds supply.

End of section activities

Quick questions

State whether the following statements are true or false. If a statement is false, explain what is wrong with it.

1 Demand for a product increases when its price decreases.

2 The demand curve shifts outward when income increases.

3 If the price of a product falls, then demand for its substitutes increases.

4 A good with no substitute is expected to have a very elastic demand.

5 Inferior goods have no substitutes and, hence, their demand will decrease when income increases.

6 When a market is in equilibrium, it is making maximum profit.

7 A rightward shift of the supply curve may result from an increase in technology.

8 If the producers of beds face an increase in the price of lumber used to make beds, then the supply curve for beds shifts to the right.

9 If the supply curve shifts to the left, then the equilibrium price will decrease and quantity will increase.

Applying what you have learnt

1 Economists have always wondered about what they see as a paradox – water, which is essential for life, is very inexpensive; diamonds, on the other hand, are not a necessity but are very expensive. Why do you think this is so? Is there any instance where you would pay more for a glass of water than for a diamond? If so, when? How does this help you to understand the paradox?

2 What do you and your friends think about each day when you buy lunch? From questioning your friends and from reflecting on your own experiences, identify

Price per kg ($)	100	140	180	220	260	300	340	380
Quantity supplied	220	260	320	400	500	640	740	800
Quantity demanded	770	680	610	550	500	460	400	320

how each factor that affects demand (e.g. price, income) is important in your decisions regarding lunch. Which factor appears to be most important?

3 The demand and supply for premium beef are shown in the table above.

 a Draw the demand and supply curves for premium beef, showing the equilibrium price and quantity. (Use a scale of 2 cm = 100 kgs on the horizontal axis and 2 cm = $20 on the vertical axis.)

 b What would be the shortage/surplus at a price of:

   i $180?

   ii $340?

 c Now assume that demand for premium beef increases by 180 kgs per week at all prices. Draw the new demand curve.

 d What is the new equilibrium price?

 e What may have caused the demand curve to shift outward by 180 kgs at all prices as it did in (c)?

4 Quantity demanded and supplied are usually functions of price. A supply function may be given as $Q_S = 3p + 5$ and a demand function may be given as $Q_D = -2p + 25$ (where p represents price in dollars).

 a Copy the table below into your exercise book and complete it to show quantity supplied and demanded at prices ranging from $1 to $10.

P ($)	1	2	3	4	5	6	7	8	9	10
Q_D	25					13			9	
Q_S			14				26			35

 b Plot these points on a graph paper and identify the equilibrium price and quantity. (Use a scale of 2 cm = $1 on the vertical axis and 2 cm = 5 units on the horizontal axis.)

 c Suppose you equated Q_S and Q_D (that is, let $Q_S = Q_D$) and solve this equation for P, what value do you get?

 d Substitute this value into both equations to determine Q_s and Q_D.

 e Why did you get these values for P, Q_s and Q_D?

5 Explain what effects each of the following changes is likely to have on the demand for bread:

 a the price of eggs falls

 b the consumption of bacon has been linked to heart disease

 c the government imposes a new tax on baked products

 d studies show that cereals such as cornflakes reduce the risk of a heart attack

 e fewer people consume breakfast as a result of their busy lifestyle

 f flour used to make bread becomes scarce.

6 Some governments implement price controls as a mean of controlling the economy. Price control may be one of two types: **a price ceiling**, which is a limit on how high a price suppliers can charge for an item or service. A price ceiling is placed below the equilibrium price and one example may be rent control. A **price floor**, on the other hand, is placed above the equilibrium price and is a minimum that buyers are allowed to pay for a service or a good. One example of a price floor is the minimum wage. Using your knowledge of demand and supply and equilibrium, say why price controls may be inefficient.

Model exam questions

Question 1

 a Using an example of a product of your choice, outline the law of demand. (3 marks)

 b Explain how each of the following factors affects the demand for a product:

   i the price of substitute products

   ii the imposition of a new tax on the product

   iii an increase in consumers' incomes. (6 marks)

 c Give one reason why some demand curves are perfectly flat. (3 marks)

Question 2

a Explain what is meant by the term 'equilibrium'. (3 marks)

b With the aid of a diagram, show what happens when a price is set below the equilibrium price.

c Suppliers often advertise their products extensively. Why do they do this, even when the market is in equilibrium?

Question 3

John Canoe sells Caribbean-style T-shirts for tourists. His business has been experiencing weak demand over the past two quarters.

a Outline how each of the following factors may have impacted the demand for John's T-shirts:

i a decrease in the number of tourists visiting the island

ii large all-inclusive hotels offering their own line of T-shirts. (6 marks)

b Discuss two factors that affect John's supply of T-shirts. (6 marks)

c By using an example, explain how John can use the idea of complements to increase demand for his T-shirts. (4 marks)

Question 4

The diagram below shows a market in equilibrium at point E_1, after its supply curve shifted outwards from S to S_1. Initial equilibrium point was at E.

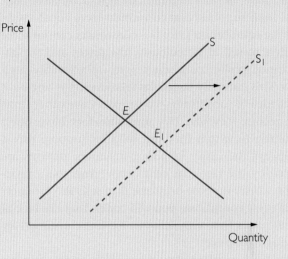

a Explain why the price has decreased after the supply curve shifted. (3 marks)

b Discuss one factor that could have caused the supply curve to shift as it did. (4 marks)

c Which equilibrium point is better for consumers? Give a reason for your answer. (3 marks)

Market structures

In our model of price determination that we have built so far, both suppliers and consumers have equal say in what the equilibrium price is – consumers cannot force suppliers to sell at ridiculously low prices and suppliers cannot exploit consumers with unbelievably high prices. This mutually beneficial relationship is one built on the idea of substitutes – consumers have other firms from whom they can buy and suppliers have other consumers to whom they can sell. But suppose this is not always the case? Suppose consumers' options are reduced by the fact that only a few firms sell a product, or, worse, suppose only one firm sells the product? Under these conditions, you will realise that the lack of choice means that suppliers can exploit consumers by charging high prices.

The term **market structure** refers to the number of buyers and sellers that exist in a market. Generally, a market structure ranges from one that has many sellers – each selling the same product – to one that has only one seller, who therefore has complete control over the supply of the product to the market. Traditionally four market structures are identified, and in this section we discuss each of them.

 For you to research

From the foregoing definition of 'market structure' we have identified that a market may have only one seller. Is it possible that a market may have only one buyer? Research the term 'monopsony' and give examples of the existence of this in real life.

Perfect competition

Perfect competition is a market structure in which there are many buyers and sellers, each buying or selling only a small portion of the total amount traded in the market. A perfectly competitive market is built on many assumptions, which may not exist in real life. The result is that a perfectly competitive market is unreal or impractical. The assumptions of a perfectly competitive market – and their implications – are discussed below.

- **Many buyers and sellers**: a perfectly competitive market has hundreds or even thousands of buyers and sellers. The presence of many buyers and sellers results in each firm or consumer accepting the price dictated by the market as opposed to making a price for itself. Each firm or consumer in a perfectly competitive market is said to be a price taker and not a price maker. The firm must accept the price set by the market as, if it sells above that price, it will lose all its demand. Each seller supplies only a small portion of the total amount traded in a market and, hence, its actions will not affect the overall market supply – a firm can exit the market or reduce its supply without creating scarcity or even without any consumer taking notice, since there are many other suppliers. In the same way, no one consumer buys a large enough portion such that he can become a price maker. Each consumer buys such a small portion of the total market supply that if he exits the market, suppliers are not overly affected by this. In short, no one consumer can hold the market to ransom with his demands, insisting on lower prices, since his importance to the overall market is offset by the fact that there are hundreds or even thousands of other consumers.

- **Homogeneous products**: the first assumption outlined above led to the inevitable conclusion that no one supplier or consumer is a price maker. How is this possible? How can we conclude that a firm cannot ask consumers to pay more for a good than other firms are asking them to pay for similar goods? Certainly, you may be prepared to pay more for a Pepsi than you would pay for a locally made soda; or you may perceive that one cellphone is more luxurious and of a higher quality than others and, as a result, you are prepared to pay a few more dollars. In short, if a product is different in features, quality, form and functions from others with which it competes, then its seller or producers can become price makers. To prevent this from occurring, the assumption made under perfect competition is that firms in the same market sell homogeneous products; that is, the products sold by firms operating in the same market are similar in functions, forms, features and quality. The assumption of homogeneity does not mean that firms must sell the same brand; rather, the assumption is that even where different brands exist, the products remain fairly similar in form and functions. For example, even though there are many brands of soft drink – Pepsi, Coca-Cola, Sprite, 7Up, Mountain Dew, Busta, D&G and Bigga – each soft drink is sufficiently similar that large price differences become impossible.

Think about it

Can different brands ever be homogeneous? Are two products different simply because their brands are different? Can you think of two products that are homogeneous even though they are different brands? What do you think makes them homogeneous? Alternatively, think of two brands that offer similar products but which are heterogeneous. What makes them so?

- **Perfect information**: this assumption becomes necessary to ensure that no one consumer or supplier is a price maker. This assumption states that buyers and sellers are aware of existing prices and the availability of products. As a result, buyers know when a supplier is charging a price that is too high in the hope of becoming a price maker. Similarly, each seller knows the price at which all other consumers are buying and, hence, knows when a buyer is making an offer that is too low. If perfect information exists, then consumers can act as a check and balance on suppliers and suppliers can do the same for consumers.

- **Freedom of entry and exit**: under perfect competition, new firms can easily enter the market to share in the profits that exist in the industry. Additionally, firms can easily exit the market if they find that more profits can be made elsewhere.

- **No transport or advertising cost**: if prices are to remain common across all firms in the industry, then transportation and advertising costs must be assumed to be non-existent.

- **Free mobility of factors of production**: there are no restrictions on where or how the

factors of production can be employed within a perfectly competitive market. This makes freedom of entry and exit possible.

Taxi service is remarkably homogeneous from one cab to another.

Perfect competition in practice

Of course, from reading the assumptions stated above, you would have concluded that perfect competition is absurd! After all, firms *are* price makers, products are *not* homogeneous, you *have* overpaid (and underpaid) for items before and enough barriers exist that prevent a new firm from just entering a market. In other words, perfect competition does not exist because it operates on assumptions that are flawed and impractical. We do not deny this. There are examples that come very close to perfect competition – for example, the taxi stand is almost perfect in many ways. At a taxi stand, a number of the assumptions of perfect competition are met, as we attempt to show below.

- **Assumption 1: the existence of many buyers and sellers leads to price taking**. This is indeed true, barring late-night taxi services or special circumstances such as charters and emergency. There are usually many taxis parked on the stand and each of them must accept the price charged by all the others as, otherwise, commuters simply choose another taxi.

- **Assumption 2: homogeneity of products**. This is also true of a taxi stand to a great extent.

Even though each taxi offers a service that uses a different car or model, the service is essentially the same. Additionally, while you perceive one taxi as offering a more reliable or sophisticated service, the differences are not likely to compel you to pay a higher fare.

- **Assumption 3: perfect information**. Passengers and taxi drivers alike usually know the fares charged for various legs of the journey. If taxis are asked to go off route, however, then usually no standardised schedule of rates exists and this may lead to imperfect information.

- **Assumption 4: freedom of entry and exit**. It is perhaps at this point that the assumptions of perfect competition break down most drastically. There are many barriers to entry for potential taxi operators. The cost of buying a vehicle may be too much and may keep some people out of the market. Additionally, people interested in becoming taxi operators have to seek licences and permits from the government and these may not be granted. Additionally, some insurance providers may not insure vehicles that are to be used to transport passengers. It is clear then that, as a result of the assumption of freedom of entry and exit, the market at the taxi stand is not perfectly competitive.

Why then do we study perfectly competitive markets? Well, the answer is very simple. It is under perfect competition that the market performs best at allocating scarce resources among sellers and buyers. If we study this market structure, therefore, it provides a benchmark against which we can judge other markets that are not as efficient at allocating scarce resources. Perfect competition is therefore an ideal that we hold up as a standard for other market structures to meet. When we study other market structures, which are far more practical than perfect competition, we look at the extent to which they deviate from or conform to the principles under which a perfect market would operate.

Monopoly

A market structure is said to be operating under a **monopoly** if there is only one supplier of a product for which there are no close substitutes. The only supplier of a particular brand of soft drink is not a true or pure monopoly since there are soft drinks that are close substitutes. In practice though, since people interested in this brand of soft drink have no option but to go to this supplier, we refer to this supplier as a monopoly. Monopolies are developed and sustained because of the presence of barriers to entry. A barrier to entry is a legal, financial or structural factor that prevents other firms from entering a market. Some of the barriers to entry that create and sustain monopolies are discussed below.

- **Legal restrictions**: in some instances, the government may actually establish monopolies by passing laws that give one firm the right to operate a business and prevent others from competing with it. This may happen with firms in the public-sector (such as the postal system) or with private-sector firms such as licensing only one cable-service provider to offer their service in a certain area. The government creates monopolies for a number of reasons – in the Caribbean, for example, the government has used this as an incentive to attract foreign multinational companies, offering them a guaranteed, captive market.

- **Patents**: if one firm uses a patented product to offer a good or service, then it may be impossible for other firms to also offer the good or service. Patents, therefore, provide protection for monopolies as, without the right to use the patented products, other competitors cannot enter the market. Microsoft Corporation, for example, has patented protection for the use of Windows and hence has a virtual monopoly on the software industry. Patent protection is usually short-lived as competitors often develop close copies of original ideas that satisfy the same demand.

- **Control of a scarce resource**: if a supplier has control of a scarce resource that is essential in the production process, then other producers may be barred from entering the market. In the Caribbean, this happens with land on which bauxite is found, which is usually under the control of one corporation.

- **Existing-firm barriers**: firms that are already established in the industry may prevent new firms from entering through excessive advertising that new firms may not be able to match or by charging low prices that firms just entering may not be able to charge.

- **Start-up costs**: some industries require high investments that the firm may not be able to recover for a long time. If this is the case, then firms that enter the industry must be prepared to spend a long time making and absorbing losses until their investments start generating revenues. The telecommunications industry tends to be like that – firms must invest huge sums of money in the infrastructure needed to provide telecommunication services in the hope that they will attract enough customers to recover this investment eventually.

- **Economies of scale**: the advantage a firm gets from its size may make it impossible for any other firm to enter the market.

 Now it's your turn

Make a list of monopolies in your country – in both the public and private sectors. Which of the reasons listed above is responsible for creating and sustaining these monopolies?

Monopoly and pricing decisions

A monopoly is a price maker – it can raise its price without worrying that it will lose *all* its customers. The monopolist, however, does not have unlimited ability to raise the prices for its products. Each time the monopolist increases the price for its products, consumers will decrease the number of units that they demand. The monopolist, then, does not have complete control over price *and* quantity – it can control one *or* the other but not *both*. The monopolist's pricing decisions then affect the quantity sold; some price–quantity combinations are profitable and others are not. The monopolist adjusts its price until it finds the right combination that maximises profits.

Alternatively, the monopolist may adjust its quantity and then allow the market to work out the price at which each unit is sold. If the monopolist wants its price to increase, then it may decrease its supply on the market, creating a scarcity which then drives up price. If, instead, it floods the market with its products the result is a surplus which drives down the prices of the products.

Dangers of monopolies

As we have said before, a perfectly competitive market is the ideal against which all others are judged. The monopolist is one instance of an imperfect market, but as imperfect markets go, it is usually regarded as being the worst kind of market structure. The result is that many countries have laws that prevent the formation of monopolies. In 2008 in Jamaica, for example, the government prevented the largest and the second-largest cable-service providers from merging as it felt that a monopoly would have been created. Monopolies are dangerous for the following reasons:

- They may abuse their dominance of the market by raising prices or restricting output. This puts consumers at a disadvantage as they usually overpay for a monopolist's products.

- They are inefficient. Usually a monopolist's output could have been produced more cheaply and more efficiently under perfect competition. This is related to the fact that the absence of competition does not force monopolists to be as efficient as firms under perfect competition would have been.

- They do not allocate or use resources properly. The fundamental tenet of economics is that resources are scarce and, hence, they are to be used efficiently. Just the right quantity of resources is to be employed in the production of a good and, if businesses are efficient, then this is the inevitable result. Monopolists, however, are inefficient and, as a result, they may use too much of society's scarce resources (such as fuel) since they know they can recover the costs of these products in the prices that they charge.

 Now it's your turn

Competition is beneficial to a market – for both suppliers and consumers. What benefits do consumers give up when a market operates under a monopoly?

Monopolistic competition

As a keen student, you would have realised that neither of the two market structures that we have discussed so far is reflective of your own experiences. More than likely, as a consumer you buy non-identical products in markets that have many buyers and sellers. This, as you realise, is contrary to the assumptions of perfect competition. Additionally, monopolies are few and far between in the real world because of the presence of close substitutes for most products. As a result, the vast majority of businesses that you encounter are neither monopolies nor perfectly competitive. Most businesses operate under what is called

165

monopolistic competition. In this market structure, there are many sellers and buyers trading in non-identical or differentiated products. The differentiated nature of the goods being sold under monopolistic competition is the essential difference between perfect competition and monopolistic competition and this has implications for each firm's ability to make its own price.

 Now it's your turn

Explain how a producer of each of the following products may differentiate it from competitors' brands.

1. hairdressing services
2. bread
3. printers
4. dry-cleaning services
5. watches

Oligopoly

An **oligopolistic** market structure is one in which there are a few large suppliers of a product in a market. An oligopolistic market is not determined by the number of firms in the market but by the extent to which market share is concentrated in the hands of a few firms. As an example, a market may be considered oligopolistic even if it contains say 15 or even 50 suppliers; of this number, however, three or four of them may be very large and may be responsible for about 80 per cent of the products sold in the market, thus making it oligopolistic. Each firm in an oligopolistic market structure produces a branded product or has used extensive advertising and marketing to create an image of the firm. Advertising – usually the aggressive, comparative type – is, therefore, a major feature of oligopolistic market structures.

Given that oligopolistic markets usually contain just a few large firms, whose pricing and product policies are all known to each other, the degree of competition among the market leaders is very high. Firms usually have products and policies that are a direct response to their competitors' offers and use advertisements to promote them as being better than their competitors'. The competition in a oligopolistic market structure also manifests itself in a high degree of interdependence among

the firms – each firm's actions are based on the expected reaction of competitors. This interdependence often sees a price war starting among market leaders – one firm's price reduction results in a series of price reductions among other firms as each tries to undersell the other.

Pricing decisions under oligopolistic market structure

Given the competitive nature of oligopolistic markets, there are two broad approaches to pricing strategies in an oligopolistic market. In the first instance, firms may compete with each other, initiating a series of price wars that ultimately benefit consumers with low prices. Alternatively, firms may seek to avoid such expensive price wars by co-ordinating their pricing strategies. If this happens, then there are a number of options that a firm may have, each having a different degree of co-operation.

Price leadership

Even among the large firms in an industry, there may be one that is the undisputable market leader. Other firms may simply adopt the pricing strategy of this large firm, making changes to their prices whenever the market leader changes its own prices. This **price leadership** situation may exist even without firms communicating this as their intention. As a result, this is a very mild form of collusion.

Collusion

Firms may agree on some of the basic principles governing the pricing strategies of each firm. Broad areas of agreement may be identified and each firm is expected to implement these agreements in its own way. For example, the firms may agree on the basic range within which prices will move up or down and each firm will therefore select a price within this range. This **collusion** ensures that a firm's reduction in price may not lead to a price war once the reduction occurs within the given band.

Cartelisation

A cartel is formed when a group of suppliers of the same or related products agree to set prices and output in order to eliminate competition among members. **Cartelisation** creates a monopoly situation since competition among a few firms is replaced with intense collusion. The members of a cartel usually agree on the level of output that should be supplied to the market and each member is given a quota as to how many units of this output it can supply. Cartels seek to increase the price of the cartelised product by restricting output, thus creating scarcity. Cartels and related forms of intense collusion are usually forbidden by competition laws in many countries. The Organization of Petroleum Exporting Countries (OPEC) is one of the most powerful and enduring examples of a cartel. This cartel has created a virtual monopoly on the supply of petroleum and petroleum-related products to the world market.

Summary – Section B

- Market structure refers to the number of buyers and sellers in a market and the amount of power that each firm or consumer has in setting the prices at which they buy and sell.

- Perfect competition is a theoretical abstract that looks at competition under situations where there are many sellers and buyers, each being a price taker and not a price maker.

- A market structure is said to be a monopoly if it has one firm responsible for the supply of the good to a market. The monopolist is a price maker since it can reduce the quantity of good that it supplies and by doing this causes price to increase.

- Monopolies have tremendous power to set prices and, as a result, they are usually inefficient since they charge high prices in order to recover excessive cost.

- If a market has many sellers that supply a differentiated product then it is described as monopolistic competition. Each firm, on account of the fact that it sells a slightly different product, is able to charge a different price from its competitors.

- Oligopolistic markets contain a few large suppliers who are responsible for supplying most of the goods traded in the market. Under oligopolistic competition, firms are highly competitive and may form cartels in order to avoid competition.

End of section activities

Quick questions

With which market structure would you associate each of the following?

1 Buyers have many options although all the products are the same.

2 The market output is the output of a firm.

3 Even though there are many firms selling different products, there may only be one price.

4 Products may be slightly different and hence have different prices.

5 There is only one price in this market.

6 There are many suppliers but output may still be restricted in order to raise prices.

7 The most common market structure in reality.

8 The market structure that is most unfair to consumers.

9 The market structure under which barbers and hairdressers are likely to operate.

10 Many barriers to entry exist in this market.

Applying what you have learnt

1 If monopolies are dangerous to consumers, why do most public-sector agencies operate as monopolists? Make a list of the public-sector agencies in your country that operate as monopolies. What do you think will happen if other businesses compete with them?

2 'Monopolies are always a bad idea.' Organise a debate among your classmates on this statement. Choose the members for two teams and determine the time allotted for each speaker.

3 Cartels are formed in oligopolistic market structures, but what factors impact the formation of cartels? Explain how each of the following factors

167

determines whether or not cartels will be formed and how successful they would be:

a many firms exist in the market

b products are homogeneous

c products have many substitutes

d the cost of manufacturing products is similar for all firms.

Model exam questions

Question 1

a Explain what is meant by the term 'market structure'. (3 marks)

b Discuss two factors that determine suppliers' ability to be price makers. (6 marks)

c In light of your discussion in (b), explain why cartels may be illegal in some countries. (3 marks)

Question 2

a List two differences between a monopoly and a perfectly competitive firm. (2 marks)

b Explain why monopolies are likely to be inefficient. (3 marks)

c Discuss two reasons for the formation of barriers to entry. (6 marks)

Question 3

a What is the main difference between perfectly competitive firms and firms under monopolistic competition? (3 marks)

b Outline two reasons why perfect competition is impractical. (6 marks)

c Why is perfect competition considered the ideal market structure? (3 marks)

Question 4

Carl Potter owns a marble and stonework company that manufactures tiles and marble products. It is one of only three such producers in the area.

a Give the name of the market structure in which Carl operates his business. (1 mark)

b Outline two characteristics of this market structure. (4 marks)

c Carl is unwilling to enter into a price war with his competitors. Explain two alternative pricing strategies that he can pursue. (6 marks)

d Carl has made an offer to buy two of his competitors. Explain why the government may look upon this move with concern. (5 marks)

e Discuss the extent to which consumers will be sensitive to changes in the price of tiles made by Carl. (4 marks)

9 Financing the business venture

> A bank is a place where they lend you an umbrella in fair weather
> and ask for it back when it begins to rain. – *Robert Frost*

Investors can use their knowledge of the stock exchange to maximise their returns.

How to make $7 million from $180

Grace Groner lived a life that, to many, was one of poverty. She wore old clothes that she bought in garage sales or in closing down sales; she walked everywhere she went rather than buy a car, and her small house was sparsely furnished with cheap, mismatched pieces. The one television in the house was a huge hulking set that looked like it had been bought on the eve of the Second World War. Even though she lived in one of the richest towns in America, one filled with luxury cars and homes, she spent her money wisely and indeed would not have bought a house had her friend not left one to her in a will. When she died, however, at 100 years old, she surprised everyone by leaving US$7 million dollars in charity to the Lake Forest College, which she had attended as a teenager. In short, she was a millionaire who hid her wealth well. But how did Grace come to be a millionaire? It certainly was not on account of her job – she was a secretary for 43 years in a laboratory – nor was it on account of any inheritance, since she grew up in a small farming community and was orphaned by the age of 12. Rather, in 1935 she spent $180 and bought three shares at $60 each and never sold them. Each year she simply reinvested what she earned from them until the sum accumulated to US$7 million. Having no children and no immediate family (she never married), she left this sum in its entirety in a will for her alma mater. Her wealth accumulation was a result of two important factors – savvy use of the system and shrewd money-management skills, two of the important ideas in this chapter.

In this chapter you will:

- discuss the role played by the financial sector in your country
- say why commercial banks are necessary
- discuss the function of a country's central bank
- discuss how and why commercial banks and central banks are related
- discuss personal budgeting and other approaches used to manage income

- differentiate between short- and long-term financing
- discuss the differences between savings and investments
- discuss the role of the stock market
- discuss the obligations that government has to society and the economy
- identify steps that businesses could take to protect the environment

- outline what the government can do to protect consumers
- outline the regulatory environment within which businesses operate
- discuss systems of taxation
- discuss the support offered to businesses to foster their development
- assess the social services offered by government.

SECTION A   Banking

The financial sector

Perhaps on the news last night you heard of 'interest rates on commercial papers increasing' or about 'the stock market being bullish over the past month'. You may have ignored these pieces of news as they seem very far removed from your reality. But are they? You will soon come to appreciate that what takes place in the financial sector has grave implications for the rest of the country, including you, as it affects the prices you will have to pay for the new cellphone that you have been admiring or the returns you can gain on the money your parents may be forcing you to save in the bank. The financial sector is made up of all firms that protect and invest customers' money or who make money available to members of the public as loans. The financial sector is important because it plays the vital role of financial intermediation.

 Now it's your turn

Some societies, such as the Aboriginal tribes of Australia, have no financial sector – there are no banks in which to save money or from which to access loans. How do you think these societies function? Discuss three problems that they would face as a result of having no banks.

 Think about it

How much do houses cost in your country? Do you think you will be able to save enough money to buy a house in the next ten years? How old do you think you will be before you have saved enough to be able to buy a house? How can you use the financial sector to help you get a house before you are too old to enjoy it?

Banks and banking

When you think of the financial sector, perhaps your first thought is of banks. This is understandable as they are the most popular and perhaps the most easily understood entity in the sector. Banks operate on a simple premise – they take money from customers in the form of deposits, which they secure and invest until the customers return and ask for their money. Banks can do this because they do not expect that *all* customers will return for their money at the same time. So, for every $1 they get in deposits, they may choose to invest $0.80 and keep $0.20 for those who turn up suddenly to ask for their money. If, however, everyone turns up suddenly, requesting their deposits and whatever interest they have earned, then the bank may be in trouble as it would have only 20 per cent of each customer's money.

What we have not said so far, of course, is that there must be a reason for individuals to put their money in banks. This reason is tied up in the fact that banks offer interest payments to individuals who deposit their money with them. This means that the bank will give each customer a few cents on every dollar that they deposit with the bank. Obviously then, given this offer, individuals are willing to take their money to the bank instead of keeping it under their mattresses. Similarly, banks must have an incentive to be willing to pay individuals for the opportunity to hold on to their money. This incentive is found in the fact that banks use customers' money to make more money. For example, as we said before, banks play the role of **financial intermediation** – they match people with excess funds to those who need funds. They take money from one person with the promise of **interest** payments; they then use this money to lend to others who, in turn, pay interest to the bank.

Think about it

When we talk about interest rates, there are two rates to consider – the one the bank charges to those to whom it lends money and the one the bank has to pay to its depositors. These two rates are related as, if the bank wants to make any profit, it must charge its borrowers more in interest than it pays its depositors. The difference between these two interest rates is called the spread and if a bank pays out 10 per cent in interest and receives 13 per cent in interest payments, then the spread is 3 percentage points. Visit the websites of some commercial banks and work out their spreads on some loans. Do you think the spreads you are seeing are fair? What do you think is a fair spread for banks to accept?

Types of banks

By popular reckoning, banks are underused. The average person deposits a sum of money in a bank account and then withdraws it when it is needed. More frequently, a bank account is used merely to deposit a monthly salary, with regular and small withdrawals being made over the month. It may surprise you to discover that banks offer a wide range of services and that there are actually many different types of banks categorised according to the services that they offer and the clientele that they hope to serve. While your idea of banking may closely

resemble the situation we described above, you will soon come to see that this is not representative of the full role and function of the banking sector. There are basically two types of banks that members of the public can access – **commercial banks** and merchant banks. We will spend a great deal of time in this section talking about commercial banks; before we do, however, something else has to be said.

Retail versus wholesale banks

Wholesale banking refers to banks that focus on a few large clients (usually other businesses) with whom they engage in large transactions, usually at discounted rates. **Retail banking**, on the other hand, is an approach to banking that offers standard, day-to-day services to customers who may want to do anything from, say, opening an account to making a standing-order arrangement. Retail banking is based on getting a large number of customers, each of whom contributes a small amount to the bank's bottom line. Most banks will offer a mix of retail banking and wholesale banking services so as to target both groups of clientele.

Commercial banks

A commercial bank is a deposit-taking institution that raises funds by issuing various deposits, which they use to make loans and investments. Commercial banks are the most popular form of bank and usually when one uses the term 'bank', it is a commercial bank that is

The Republic Bank of Trinidad and Tobago (RBTT) has subsidiary operations in Guyana, Jamaica, Cayman, Grenada and Barbados, making it one of the largest and most successful commercial banks in the Caribbean.

being referred to. Commercial banks offer three types of account:

- **Checking accounts**: customers who have checking accounts are able to access the funds in their accounts, by writing cheques or, more popularly, by using debit cards to make purchases or withdrawals.

- **Savings accounts**: holders of savings accounts are unable to write cheques but are able to access their funds by making an over-the-counter transaction or by swiping a bank card.

- **Timed accounts**: funds in timed accounts are frozen for a fixed period. This means that holders of timed accounts are restricted from accessing the funds (or do so with great penalties) before a specified time has elapsed.

Role of commercial banks

In a country, commercial banks will play the following roles:

- **Facilitation of the clearing system**: commercial banks ensure that payments by cheques can be made. A bank will honour cheques drawn by its members or may even perform inter-bank clearing – it may process cheques that its members have even if they have been drawn on another bank. Commercial banks usually have a quick turnaround time on clearing cheques that are drawn on accounts that they hold – usually customers are able to present such cheques at the counter and walk away with cash within a few minutes. Cheques drawn on other accounts, however, may take a few days (usually from three to five working days).

- **Encouraging the storing of wealth**: individuals store wealth when they put funds aside for the future. Banks are usually thought of as being secure – it is unlikely that deposits will be lost, or that a bank will go out of business with customers' deposits – and, as a result, individuals have an incentive to store their wealth in a bank. Banks further encourage the storing of wealth by offering a return in the form of interest payments on the deposits that they hold.

- **Provision of loans**: commercial banks bring together the holders of excess funds and those who need such funds. This process is called financial intermediation and we have already described this. Commercial banks offer various types of loans.
  - **Secured loans**: secured loans are loans which are backed by collateral.
  - **Unsecured loans**: unsecured loans are issued to customers who do not pledge an asset to secure and cover the loans. From the bank's perspective, unsecured loans are more risky than secured loans and, hence, it will charge a higher rate of interest on these loans.
  - **Mortgage loans**: mortgage loans are given to buy or refurbish houses. They have a very long maturity period – sometimes up to 30 years – and are usually issued only to well qualified customers. The house that the loan is used to purchase usually secures the loan.
  - **Student loans**: loans made to students (usually at the tertiary level) to finance tuition, boarding or other school-related expenses. They are usually unsecured and are seen as being very risky. The high risk associated with student loans develops from the fact that the loans are usually made out to students (not to their parents); students' earning potential is uncertain – they may not be able to secure jobs when they leave college or may not be disciplined enough in making the payments.
  - **Bank overdrafts**: a bank overdraft allows pre-approved account holders to withdraw more money than they have in their accounts. Usually, the overdraft limit is specified and the repayment time is limited to a few months.
  - **Motor-vehicle loans**: these loans are given to people who are able to prove that they have found a motor vehicle that they would like to buy. Most commercial banks will not finance 100 per cent of the cost of the motor vehicle unless it is a new car.
  - **Personal loans**: these loans may be taken in order to pay for a vacation, insure a car, take care of a family emergency (such as medical expenses) or to buy a new computer.

- **Transforming the risk characteristics of loans**: the bank accepts the risk of lending customers' deposits. Some of the bank's depositors would never lend their funds *directly* to individuals to buy cars or houses. However, because the bank accepts the risk of making such loans, these customers are happy giving their money to the bank, which in turn makes it available to these customers. This is a highly sophisticated function that banks are in a unique position to play – they are able to investigate potential borrowers thoroughly and they are also able to invest in sophisticated systems of collecting from delinquent customers. Without commercial banks, therefore, it is unlikely that as many loans would be given.

- **Encourage trade**: banks guarantee payment for goods by issuing and honouring cheques, bank drafts and documentary credit. These services reduce the risk inherent in a transaction – especially those between partners in different countries – and encourage each partner to trade.

 Now it's your turn

Banks must consider three different and potentially conflicting aims when they make decisions. These are outlined below.

1 **Profitability**: like all other businesses, the main aim of a bank is to make a profit. They do this by lending at high interest rates – the more risky a borrower is, the higher the interest rate that the bank can charge that customer.

2 **Liquidity**: a bank must have some cash in the vault or in the cashiers' drawers in order to satisfy depositors' demand for cash. The more cash it has lying around, the lower the level of profit that it stands to make from lending at high interest rates.

3 **Security**: banks must be stable and secure with no risk of immediate closure. Stability comes from being conservative in lending and moderate in risk taking.

Having read the above, answer the following questions:

1 Explain how each aim conflicts with the others.

2 Discuss which aim or aims the bank is satisfying and which one(s) it is not in each of the following situations:

  a A bank lends only if consumers have collateral to stand as security.

  b A bank offers loans of ten times' customers' monthly salaries at high rates of interest.

  c A bank only invests in government papers that are sure to be repaid but have a low level of return.

Services offered by commercial banks

Commercial banks also offer a wide range of services to their customers:

- offering advice and financial-management tips to customers
- creating opportunities and facilities for payments through the electronic transfer of funds in the form of standing orders or credit transfers
- processing money transfers through telegraphic money orders
- providing opportunities to accept late deposits through night safes
- providing customers with chequebooks and debit cards in order to provide easy access to funds on deposit
- providing credit cards to qualified customers to make short-term loans readily available
- supplying customers with periodic (usually monthly) summaries of transactions and the status of their funds on deposit
- acting on behalf of their customers by receiving or arranging to make payments, providing proof of wealth or handling customers' wealth.

 For you to research

Go to the websites of some of the commercial banks in your country. Make a list of the services that each offers. Are they fairly similar or different?

Central bank

A country's **central bank** is an institution that acts as the official bank of the government and other banks (commercial and otherwise) in the country. A country's central bank is different from its commercial banks in one important way – members of the public cannot open accounts at or access the services of the bank; rather, the bank acts on behalf of the government, carrying out banking transactions that are necessary for the operation of the government and management of the country.

A country's central bank is usually owned and operated by the government and as such is a nationalised institution. Many central banks of other countries (such as the United States), however, are independently managed. Central banks usually perform the following functions:

- **The government bank**: in the same way as you or your parents have an account at a commercial bank, through which payments are passed and from which loans are issued, the government also has an account which contains the money that it collects and the loans that it receives. This account is kept at the central bank. More importantly, it is the central bank that is responsible for managing the country's debt. In playing this role, it issues financial instruments, such as bonds, when the government wants to raise funds by borrowing and then it ensures that payments are made in a timely fashion to service these debts.

- **The banks' bank**: each commercial bank in the country is mandated by law to keep an account at the central bank. Each bank's account will have what is called a **cash reserve** that is usually set by law. A cash reserve is a mechanism used by the government to prevent banks overextending themselves and therefore putting their customers at risk. Banks are required to keep a percentage of the deposits that they receive. They are not allowed to lend this money; instead it is kept at the central bank.

- **The central note-issuing authority in the country**: the central bank is the only note-printing and note-issuing authority in the country. It can print and introduce new money to the economy, but this usually happens only after intense consideration of the implications.

☞ Now it's your turn

The central bank is responsible for printing money. Why doesn't it simply print more money since 'times are so hard' and the 'cost of living is so high'?

- **Advisor to the central government**: the government has two sets of policy tools – fiscal policy, which deals with taxation and how such revenues are spent; and monetary policy, which deals with the amount of money in the economy and the interest rates at which money can be borrowed. Monetary policy is usually the area in which the central bank has tremendous expertise and it dispenses advice and suggestions to the central government on this subject.

- **Lender of last resort**: if a commercial bank in the country has an emergency need for funds as a result of an unprecedented number of people calling for their deposits, then it may turn to the central bank for funds. When the central bank lends to commercial banks it usually charges a rate of interest that is designed to discourage the bank from getting into that position again.

The central bank and the commercial bank

It is now clear that the central bank is very different from the commercial bank in a number of ways. Primarily, these differences surround the central bank's role in managing the economy, printing money and serving the government – roles that are not played by the commercial banks of the country. It is also clear that a relationship exists between the commercial banks of a country and its central bank. This relationship stems from three facts:

- The central bank is the banker to the commercial banks since each commercial bank keeps its cash reserves in an account at the central bank.

- The central bank is a lender of last resort. This means that when a commercial bank faces a shortfall in its cash needs, it turns to the central bank for a loan through what is called an open-market system.

- The central bank is one of the entities in the country that regulate the operations of commercial banks. As a regulatory entity, the bank licenses and administers the relevant laws and acts that guide the operations of commercial banks. It does this through on-site visits and by off-site monitoring, effected through the analysis of the bank's return and statements. Areas in which the central bank is likely to regulate the commercial banks in a country are:
  - **Entry and exit of banks**: banks usually have to apply for a licence to operate, which is granted only if certain criteria are met. In Jamaica, for example, a bank will not be granted a licence to operate if the country's central bank (the Bank of Jamaica) does not think that its directors, managers or shareholders (holding 20 per cent or more of total share capital) are 'fit and proper'.

- **Reporting on its performance**: banks are usually asked to inform the government and members of the public about their performance. In Trinidad and Tobago, for example, the law requires that commercial banks submit to the Central Bank of Trinidad and Tobago, at specified times or when it is requested, detailed statements outlining:
  - assets and liabilities
  - loans and advances
  - earnings and expenses
  - any other financial data that the Central Bank may require.
- **Deposits and other financial instruments traded**: laws are often passed that govern what banks can do and how much they are allowed to accept in deposits. Recall that, to a bank, deposits are liabilities (money that the bank owes to its customers); if it accepts too much in deposits then it is exposing itself to immense risk. In Jamaica, for example, the law states that 'a bank shall not incur deposit liabilities and other indebtedness for borrowed money which, together with all interest accrued thereon, exceed in the aggregate, twenty-five times the amount of its capital base'. It is the central bank's role to ensure that this limit is not passed.
- **Quality of capital and assets**: banks must maintain a stated portion of their assets as liquid assets – this is in addition to reserves they may have at the central bank.
- **Restrictions on services**: there are some activities in which banks are not allowed to engage. The Banking Act in Jamaica, for example, prevents banks from buying land for the purpose of resale or from lending to connected parties.
- **Cash reserves**: banks must keep a percentage of their deposits in the form of reserves at the Central Bank. The Banking Act in Jamaica, for example, instructs banks that 'the amount of its deposit with the Bank of Jamaica shall be the average amount of such deposit as at the close of business on each business day in the week'.

Managing personal income

We now turn our attention to what individuals can do to better manage their incomes. Personal finance has become very important in recent times, especially since a person's ability to access loans is directly related to how well he or she has displayed a mastery of some of the key principles of personal finance. Managing one's income is done against the background that wants are insatiable and resources are limited. There are various strategies that can be used to manage personal income. Some of these are:

- **Budgeting**: this is the process of allocating one's income in a planned way before it is actually spent. When people make budgets, they normally decide on the items that they would like to purchase, consider their incomes and then decide how much to allocate to each item. Budgeting may result in some items that are desired not being bought at all.

Now it's your turn

Imagine that you are the mother or father of a family of five. The family's combined income is US$1800 per month (you can convert this to your home currency) and you must make a budget. The family has three children, who are attending secondary school. Your expenses are as follows (the amounts needed for some expenses are fixed, while you must decide how much you put towards the others):

- rent – 25 per cent of your income
- utilities (water, electricity and so on) – 10 per cent of your income
- food and groceries
- entertainment
- transportation
- school-related expenses – 10 per cent of your income
- savings
- incidentals/emergency.

Which items are compulsory? Which ones can you give up if money is 'tight'? Based on the expenses above and the income that you are working with, create a *believable* budget for the family of five of which you are a part – remember the family consists of two parents and three children. You may have to sacrifice some items if the money is not enough. Be prepared to share your budget with your classmates and discuss which budgets are most realistic.

- **Prioritising**: prioritising means identifying the most important items that must be bought and ensuring that you have put money aside for these items. Other inessential items are usually bought if and only if you have sufficient funds after the priority ones have been paid for.

- **Track spending and income**: keeping old pay stubs is a useful way of following how your salary has changed over a period of time. Additionally, recording how much money is spent on various items over time gives you a chance to see the area in which your expenses are increasing most rapidly.

- **Establish a saving plan**: establishing a saving plan is a useful way of managing your money. A saving plan ties you down to a set target within a certain time frame and ensures that you are consistent with your savings.

- **Manage your debt**: debt is a burden on future income. When you borrow money, you are committing money that you have not received as yet to a good that you are now enjoying. Living debt-free is difficult for most people and, indeed, there is nothing wrong with deciding that you will take up some debt. The important thing to remember, though, is that too much debt is bad for a number of reasons.

Short-term and long-term financing

Individuals and businesses often find that they need more money than they currently have. When this occurs, the financial intermediation role of the financial sector comes into play. Individuals experiencing a shortfall of funds can approach an entity in the financial sector in order to seek financing. There are many entities that they could approach for such a loan and usually the one they choose will depend on whether their needs are long-term or short-term.

Short-term sources of financing

These are usually available through the money market – which is a market for loans that must be repaid within a short time (usually within five years). Commercial banks operate in the money market because individuals can access short-term loans from them. Other banks (such as merchant banks) that offer short-term loans are also described as being in the money market. The money market usually consists of the following instruments and facilities:

- **Credit arrangements**: such an arrangement exists under many circumstances, but usually one

enters a credit agreement in order to be able to buy goods immediately and to pay for them over an extended period. A credit-card agreement, a hire-purchase contract, a trade credit and even a bank overdraft are all examples of credit arrangements (we will discuss each of these in a more detailed manner further on in the chapter).

- **Bank overdrafts**: the essential point to remember about a bank overdraft facility is that it allows individuals to spend more money than they have in their bank account. This means that the bank may allow the customers to write cheques and/or make withdrawals up to a certain limit beyond what they have in the account. Essentially, in a bank-overdraft agreement the bank pre-approves a loan that an individual can access in the event that it is needed. A bank overdraft carries with it an interest rate charge and usually must be paid off within a month or two.

- **Bills of exchange**: bills of exchange allow one business to lend money to another business. A bill of exchange is simply a document that outlines how much money is being loaned and at what interest rate. The borrower accepts the bill by signing it and then the money is transferred to him. When the bill matures (usually within three months), then the borrower repays the lender along with whatever interest was negotiated.

- **Commercial papers**: a commercial paper is an unsecured promissory note that banks and other businesses with good credit ratings issue to raise short-term loans. A promissory note is simply a promise to repay the sum at a future date. This instrument is usually unsecured (not backed by any collateral), since the business that issues it is usually one with a good track record.

Long-term sources of finance

Some businesses and individuals may want to secure financing for a longer period of time than the money market allows. In this case, such individuals would turn to the capital market for financing. The capital market disburses loans that are repayable over a period of up to 30 years and that, as a result, usually have lower rates of interest. Some facilities available through the capital market for long-term financing are:

- **Share capital**: by now you will have a good idea of what share capital is; however, it may be worth recapping some of the important points. Share capital is obtained by selling a part ownership of a company to members of the public, who share in the risk of running the company and are also entitled to a share of its profits.

- **Borrowing**: long-term loans may also be obtained from banks. These loans are repayable over a long period – sometimes up to 30 years.
- **Debentures and other loan stock**: **debentures** are really loans, except that they are different from other long-term loans in one important respect. Debentures that a company issues are usually traded on the stock market (a market for second-hand shares), while loans from a commercial bank are not.
- **Bonds**: these are financial securities issued by companies (and governments) to raise long-term loans. **Bonds** have a fixed rate of interest called the coupon rate and holders of bonds are entitled to this until the bond matures – at which time they get back the original amount that they had spent on the bond.

Savings

Two words that are often confused in how they are used are 'savings' and 'investments'. The difference between the two is very subtle and yet it is very important. **Savings** refer to the part of income that is unused, usually as a result of consumption (or expenditure) being less than income. This money is unused because it may be needed for an emergency and, as a result, it is easily accessible. Such money may be kept in a savings or checking account or even (but hopefully not!) in a jar buried under a tree at the back of your house. In short, money that is saved is simply any portion of income that is set aside but remains fairly easily accessible for the future. As a result of these characteristics, savings do not usually carry a high level of risk – the saver is almost certain that she will be able to recover *all* of her savings at some point in the future. The absence of risk means that money saved usually accumulates a very small amount of interest; this is usually not a major concern to savers, however, as the aim of savings is usually not to accumulate wealth but to secure future spending power. Popular forms of savings are discussed below.

Sou-sou or partner

This is an informal saving scheme among friends and acquaintances. In this scheme, each person contributes a specified amount of money at stated intervals (e.g. weekly, monthly) to a pool. The sum of monies received each period (called a 'hand') is then paid over to one member until all members have received a 'hand' from the pool. The paying over of hands is called a 'draw'. If there are five members in a weekly partner scheme, then at the end of each week, the value of the pool is usually equal to five times each person's contribution – this is not so if any person has more than one 'hand' and hence receives more than one 'draw'. The person who gets the first draw gets his contribution along with the contribution of the other four members in the scheme. In essence, he gets a loan to the tune of the other members' contributions and will spend the next four weeks repaying them. Similarly, the person who receives the last draw would have provided loans to the other four members over the first four weeks of the scheme and is then repaid in the last week.

Think about it

Would you join a partner or sou-sou? If you did, would you prefer an early or a late draw? Why?

Credit unions

A **credit union** is a kind of financial co-operative in that it is owned by its members. Members save with the credit union and come to own 'shares' in the organisation. As members, savers also qualify for loans at reduced rates and with little or no security. Credit unions are usually formed to promote the development of their members who usually have a common interest – for example, an association of a nation's teachers may start a credit union for its members. This union may have special savings plans and loans to cater to the needs of teachers. A credit union is different from a bank in a number of ways. Primarily, credit unions are owned by members while banks are not. Only members of credit unions are allowed to save in and access the services that they offer; indeed, given the fact that members usually have a common interest, many credit unions have restrictions on who can join. Banks, on the other hand, do not usually restrict 'membership' to any special group of people and, as a result, they have a wide and varied customer base. The final difference between banks and credit unions lies in the loan process. Members of credit unions must satisfy fewer requirements to access loans and, hence, are more likely to obtain loans than members of bank. Additionally, loans offered by banks are usually at a higher rate of interest and this also prevents many from accessing these loans.

Investment

Investment is different from savings since it is used to achieve long-term goals such as home ownership, wealth accumulation, insurance or entrepreneurship. Like savings, investment is the portion of income that is used to secure future spending power. Unlike savings, investment is usually risky and, indeed, an investor may come to the end of an investment only to realise that he has less money than he had originally invested or, in a worst-case scenario, may find that he has no money at all. Investment is usually not easily accessible as money invested must wait until a pre-stated maturity date or is not held in a liquid form – assets must be sold (or liquidated) in order to access the invested sum. Examples of investment are:

- **Assets bought to generate income**: a motor car, for example, may be bought to transport passengers or to deliver goods.
- **Investing in stocks**: buying companies' shares with the hope that they can be resold at a higher price.
- **'Fixing' money**: depositing money in a high-interest account for a fixed period of time.
- **Entrepreneurship**: using personal funds (or loans) to start a business with the hope of making a profit.
- **Unit trust**: investment may take the form of a unit trust or a mutual fund. A group of investors may come together and buy a number of diverse securities to create a portfolio. Each person owns a portion of the portfolio, which may be managed by a trust manager. As a member of the unit trust, each individual is entitled to a share of the dividends or returns and these are passed on to members periodically.

The stock market

As we have said before, the stock market is a market for trading second-hand shares. When a company goes public (starts offering shares to members of the public) it makes an **initial public offering** (IPO) and these shares are issued directly by the company, usually through a broker. After this IPO, however, the owners of these shares usually try to sell them on the stock market in an effort to make a profit. If the owners of shares

A stock market has many traders who buy and sell shares for customers.

can find someone willing to buy them at a price greater than they paid for them, then they would make a profit. This trade takes place on the stock market or stock exchange, where thousands or even millions of units of shares are traded daily. Generally speaking, share prices respond to market forces of demand and supply in much the same way as the prices of other products do. When a company commands the confidence of the public, then demand for its shares increases and, as a result, this drives up the price. On the other hand, a loss of consumer confidence in a company results in share prices being driven down by falling demand for the company's shares. Confidence in a company may increase if it has just announced high levels of profit, recently developed a unique product that would revolutionise the market or has employed an executive who is respected as a brilliant manager. Companies listed on the stock exchange (those who, having gone public, are allowed to sell shares to members of the public) may find that when the economy in general improves, then demand for their shares – and as a result their prices – also increases.

Online trading

The stock market has become more popular as an investment option with the advent of online trading. To fully appreciate online trading, it is perhaps useful to appreciate how the bulk of trading occurs. Most investors in the stock market usually use an agent or a broker to buy shares to create a portfolio. A broker is an experienced professional who is able to offer advice on the best stocks to buy or when it may be appropriate to buy or sell a stock. Having created a portfolio, an investor depends on the broker to provide information on the portfolio, to keep track of market variables and to make important decisions about the portfolio. The investor makes frequent calls to the broker to instruct her about the number of units of a particular stock that she is to buy or sell. The broker would then approach the market to fulfil her client's wishes. With online trading, many of the services of the broker are eliminated and the investor interacts with the market directly using an internet-based interface. This internet-based interface is provided by an online broker who may do little to actually guide or trade on behalf of the investor.

Using the internet platform provided by the broker, an investor enters an order for a stock directly into the system or even trades directly with other people using a similar platform. The platform also allows traders to track changes in market conditions (measured by what is called an index), receive real-time changes in the share prices, research information such as the performance of a particular stock over the past few weeks and follow news about and affecting the companies whose shares are being traded on the stock exchange. Some platforms allow investors to simulate portfolio creation – in this process, investors see how their portfolios would have performed had they bought or sold a particular stock a few weeks or months ago. Given that online trading frequently reduces or eliminates the need for a broker, this type of trading is frequently called 'self-directed trading'.

Bull and bear markets

A stock market in which investors show a high level of interest and have a high demand for stock, resulting in many units being traded each day, is described as a **bull market**. Given the high demand for stock, a bull market usually has high and rising share prices

as consumers compete for available units. Under other circumstances a market may be described as being a **bear market**. Such a market has low and falling prices since investors show little or no interest in available shares. Bear markets are characterised by a large number of people selling or attempting to sell their stock as they may have lost confidence in the economy or in the companies on the stock market. Since, in a bear market, many investors want to sell their shares at the same time, they are forced to engage in a price war leading to price reductions and ultimately in suppressed prices.

These words – bear and bull – are also associated with traders in a stock market and not just with the condition of the stock market. A bull is a person who is optimistic about the market conditions; bulls have the feeling that share prices will increase and that if they buy stock today, they will be able to sell at a higher price in the future. Bears, on the other hand, take a negative view of the market and believe that share prices will fall over the foreseeable future. As a result, they are more likely to sell their shares today, hoping to buy them back at a lower price in the future. A final type of trader is a stag. A stag is an investor who buys and sells shares quickly, in order to take advantage of changes in the market or to make a profit.

Think about it

A bull market is usually called a sellers' market and a bear market is called a buyers' market. What do you think these terms mean? Why is each market described as such?

Role of the stock market

- The stock market provides a profitable source of liquid investments to individuals who stand to make a quick profit through shrewd investment.

- The stock market is an indication of the confidence that investors have in an economy. Investors are likely to invest in the companies in an economy that is growing and developing – when stock market activities are positive and upbeat, this is a sign that the investing public approves of the direction of the economy. This is sometimes all that is needed to get economic activity running at full speed.

Summary – Section A

- The financial sector operates on the premise that people in need of funds are to be matched with those with excess funds. It does this by paying interest to savers and charging interest to those who borrow.

- Wholesale banking targets a few large customers who access services at a reduced rate; retail banking on the other hand offers services to customers who use the banks to perform standard day-to-day transactions such as cashing a cheque or making deposits.

- Merchant banks offer services to corporate customers – in other words, other businesses. Commercial banks, however, are deposit-taking institutions that offer loans and other services to the average person.

- Commercial banks play an important role in the economy – they ensure that cheques clear, that individuals can create wealth and that loans are available to qualified members of the public.

- A central bank is the official bank of the state; it is responsible for printing the country's money and keeping the government's account.

- The central bank regulates the commercial banks in a country by ensuring that they follow rules laid out in the country's laws.

- Individuals can use many strategies to manage their personal finances. The most popular strategy is to use a budget to allocate scarce resources over competing needs.

- When faced with inadequate funds, individuals and businesses may turn to the money market or the capital market for loans or funding arrangements. The money market is used to access short-term loans while the capital market is used to access long-term loans.

- Investments and savings are related but are different in some important ways – savings are usually kept idle and, as a result, are accessible with little effort and earn little or no interest. Investments on the other hand are usually tied up over a long period of time and stand to provide the investor with a high rate of return.

- The stock market is used to trade shares issued by companies. Shares are traded based on investors' confidence in the economy in general and in the company's fortunes specifically.

End of section activities

Quick questions

Provide short answers to the following questions.

1 Explain what is meant by 'financial intermediation'.

2 Why do banks keep a cash reserve?

3 How are retail banks different from commercial banks?

4 Why would a person choose to open a timed deposit account?

5 List three ways in which banks encourage international trade.

6 How are fiscal policies different from monetary policies?

7 List three areas in which the central bank usually regulates commercial banks.

8 Explain why budgeting makes no sense without also prioritising.

9 Explain why promissory notes are usually unsecured.

10 Why are savings usually easily accessible but investments are not?

11 Why is confidence in a company important in determining its share price?

12 Why are brokers not as important when investors trade online?

Applying what you have learnt

1 A partner or sou-sou usually has many members and therefore may run a for a long time – if there are 12 members, for example, each contributing and getting a draw every month, then the plan will be finished in a year.

  a Explain why this long period may be a drawback for some people.

  b What are some of the other problems that plans such as sou-sou have?

  c Why do you think people still use partners and sou-sou even though these plans have drawbacks?

2 Commercial banks offer very low rates of interest on deposits. Many people think that money should never be kept in a bank when options such as the stock market, business investments and unit trusts exist. Do you agree with this view? List some of the pros and cons of keeping money in a bank.

3 The inflation rate affects the interest on money that you save because inflation causes prices to increase and erodes the value of money.

  a With an inflation rate of 10 per cent, how much more would you have to pay for each of the following items after a year?

    • cellphone – $3500

    • digital camera – $10 300

    • orange juice – $120

  b What is the minimum interest rate that you should expect your bank to pay on the deposits that you have in your account there, if the inflation rate in your country is 10 per cent? Why?

  c Investigate the inflation rate in your country and compare it with the interest that banks offer on deposits. Which is more – the inflation rate or the rate of interest? What does this mean for savers who have their money in banks?

Model exam questions
Question 1

  a Explain the difference between:

    i a commercial bank and a merchant bank

    ii a checking account and a savings account.

                  (6 marks)

  b Outline how the services that commercial banks offer and the role that they play may benefit each of the following people:

    i a farmer wanting to expand his operations

    ii an importer of Japanese used cars

    iii a compulsive spender wishing to save up for something important.   (6 marks)

  c Discuss two reasons why someone would save in a credit union and not in a bank.   (6 marks)

  d List two ways in which the financial sector of your country contributes to the economy.   (2 marks)

Question 2

  a The central bank is the government's bank. List three functions that it performs in this capacity.

                  (3 marks)

  b Why are banks required to keep cash reserves at the central bank?   (3 marks)

  c Outline the conditions under which a central bank would lend money to a commercial bank.

                  (4 marks)

Question 3

Karen left high school seven months ago and has been working as a sales agent in a bookshop. She has realised, however, that she does not have enough money to finance her lifestyle as her bills are often unpaid and she usually runs out of money halfway through the month. She is thinking of applying for a credit card to supplement her income.

a Discuss two ways in which the commercial banking system in Karen's country can help her manage her money better. (4 marks)

b Outline two strategies that Karen can use to manage her money better. (6 marks)

c Advise Karen as to whether or not she should take out a credit card. (3 marks)

Question 4

When compared with investment, savings usually earn little interest. Saving, however, is more popular than investment.

a List two differences between savings and investments. (2 marks)

b Why do savings earn less interest than investments? (3 marks)

c Why are people more likely to save than invest? (4 marks)

d Jamal received a lump sum of money. He is trying to decide if he should invest it or save it. Explain how each of the following factors affects his decision:

i commercial banks offer low interest rates

ii profit that can be made on stocks is very high

iii he and his wife are about to start a family. (6 marks)

The role of government

What does the government in your country do? In an age of cynicism about government, it is tempting to answer that question by saying 'Absolutely nothing!' The truth, though, is that many of the services that you take for granted are provided through and by the government – the roads on which you drive, schools that you attend, hospitals that offer medical services and police that protect you from crime. The government in your country performs many roles for a large number of people, all with different needs. Some of these roles are discussed below.

Security of the state

The UN is one forum through which a government can use diplomacy and communication to secure its state.

In a general sense, this role is wrapped up in ensuring that the country remains safe from attacks from other countries. Securing the state, however, is a much more complicated process than having an army that is prepared to fight in the event of war. Diplomacy has replaced brute force in state security and the role of the government in relation to securing the state is really ensuring that the country maintains a good relationship with its neighbours and trading partners, and plays its part in the community of nations. The government, therefore, makes an effort to keep the country at peace by having open communication with countries with which it may have disagreements. Diplomats and ambassadors are usually appointed to ensure that the country engages others in communication and iron out any misunderstandings that exist. Securing the state has also evolved in recent times as new threats present new challenges.

In the Caribbean, for example, while terrorist activities are fairly rare, organised crime is a problem in countries such as Jamaica and Haiti. The drug trade is also a major challenge to state security as many countries have seen their ports used as shipment points. Food security – the ability to feed ourselves as a region or even as individual countries – along with the dependence on imported fuel is also of concern as this may undermine the government's ability to secure the state.

Protection and the general welfare of citizens

It is the government's role as well to ensure that the rights of each citizen are protected. Laws must be passed, therefore, to ensure that large companies, private individuals or even the government itself do not infringe on the rights of any minority group or individual. For example, in Jamaica, the Noise Abatement Act was passed recently to ensure that parties and street dances cannot continue to play loud music after 2 a.m. as the noise would be infringing on the rights of other individuals to peace and quiet. The general welfare of citizens is also secured by ensuring that infrastructure and social services are provided for the benefit of the population. Infrastructure, such as roads, bridges, airports and bus parks, along with social services such as healthcare, policing and education, are all responsibilities of the government.

> **Now it's your turn**
>
> Who are minority groups? Make a list of three examples of minority groups in your country and give an example of a law that has been passed or that you think should be passed to protect each minority group.

Working conditions of employees

The government is responsible for setting the minimum standards that employers are to meet in relation to their treatment of workers. The maximum number of working days per week and the maximum number of working hours per day are set by the government and employers are expected to abide by these. Employers are expected to provide job security for workers and the government has passed laws that ensure this. Job security is created when employers ensure that workers feel that they are in a job that they are not likely to lose at a moment's notice or for no apparent reason. The law requires, therefore, that there is due cause before a worker is fired and that if a worker is employed in a clear vacancy, he or she be made a permanent worker eventually.

 Now it's your turn

Governments usually implement a minimum wage as one way of protecting workers. Based on what we have said about the equilibrium price in Chapter 8, why might the minimum wage cause unemployment?

Protection of the environment

One of the sad truths about most capitalist societies is that businesses may find that it is actually more profitable to destroy the environment in carrying out their production process than to protect it. Dumping toxic waste in water is far easier and cheaper than designing a recycling system for ensuring that clean water is extracted from waste and reused by the business. The government has the responsibility to ensure that companies who would want to maximise profits at the expense of the environment are regulated. It does this by employing the following strategies:

- **Zoning**: zoning refers to creating defined geographical areas for business activities and restricting the use of other areas for production. This ensures that areas that are environmentally fragile or important are protected from intense human activity.

- **Quotas**: when too much of a scarce natural resource is being used, the government may pass laws that forbid businesses from using more than a certain number of units, their quota, within a given time.

- **Licensing and permits**: the government may require that a licence be sought and granted before production can take place – the licence may restrict the use of a certain good or restrict access to a certain area. Generally, the government would set up a board or agency that assesses each application for a permit and may refuse based on the impact that the proposed activity may have on the environment. The agency with

licence-granting power may also have a quota system that ensures that too many businesses are not in a certain area or that too many units of a particular product are not being used.

- **Environmental impact statements**: the government may require that a business about to engage in production produces, or pays for the cost of producing, what is called an environmental impact statement. This statement outlines the impact that the business activity is expected or likely to have on the environment. The government may insist that an independent third party completes the statement as a mean of ensuring that the assessment is accurate. Based on the assessment, the government may then require the firm to adjust its operations or to implement some kind of corrective measure.

- **Banning**: some products are so dangerous to the environment that their use has been completely banned by the government. CFCs (chlorofluorocarbons), for example, which were once used in refrigerators and aerosol containers, have been completely banned in most countries because of their effect on the ozone layer.

Creating a business-friendly environment

The government ought to ensure that investors feel comfortable doing business in their country. Investors need to know that they have the protection of the government from unfair competition from foreign firms and from exploitation by powerful trade unions. Investors are also often concerned about the extent to which they have to deal with the demands of bureaucracy as they interact with the public sector.

Consumer protection

Businesses are large and are in a position to abuse the power they have over consumers. While consumers can 'vote with their feet' by going elsewhere to do business, this does not always act as an effective check and balance on the actions of business. The government will, therefore, pass laws that protect consumers from being mistreated by large businesses. Generally, government's protection of consumers is anchored in four rights that consumers have:

1 **The right to safety**: suppliers cannot knowingly sell a product that will cause harm to consumers. This also means that consumers have the right to a safe place to shop.

2 The right to be informed: consumers have a right to review full information about a product – its risk, instructions for use, ingredients and manufacturer information – before buying or using it. This means that producers are obligated to warn consumers of any danger associated with using the product. It is for this reason that pharmaceutical companies must inform consumers of the potential side-effects of using their products and cigarette manufacturers must warn consumers that smoking is bad for their health.

3 The right to be heard: this assures consumers that they will receive full and sympathetic consideration when their rights have been abused. When governments formulate policies, consumers will also be duly considered so that they are not marginalised.

4 The right to choose: consumers have a right to a variety of products and competitive prices.

☞ **Now it's your turn**

Explain why the mere existence of a monopoly may actually be a violation of the rights of consumers.

It falls primarily to the government to protect consumers and it cannot assume that producers and distributors will, of their own choice, respect the rights of consumers. To this end, governments usually implement the following:

- **Inspection and health standards**: food-producing businesses (such as restaurants) must make themselves available for periodic inspection by officials who ensure that their facilities meet minimum standards.

- **Food handler's licence**: people involved in the preparation of food for others usually have to successfully complete short classes on handling food, at the end of which they receive permits.

- **Labels**: products must be properly labelled so that consumers can make informed decisions about the products they consume.

- **Honesty in advertising**: advertisements should not misrepresent a product, its features, its capabilities or its price.

- **State agencies**: the government usually establishes an organisation or bureau that is responsible for investigating customers' complaints.

- **Prevention of monopolies**: monopolies restrict a consumer's right to choose and hence the government is likely to take steps to prevent the development of monopolies. Such steps may include forbidding mergers or even breaking up a business.

- **Legislation**: the government may pass regulations in the following areas:

  - **Creation of price controls**: a price control is the establishment of a maximum (or, in rare cases, minimum) price at which an item can be sold. Price control may be set when the government feels that suppliers are practising price gouging – charging high prices because an item is scarce or essential. Price control is often set below the equilibrium price and as a result it suppresses supply while stimulating demand leading to scarcity.

  - **Food and drug standards**: minimum standards are usually established for the production of certain goods and services. For example, many countries have seen purified and spring-water supply increasing exponentially over the last few years as consumers have become more health conscious and water has become fashionable. Standards bodies have adopted various standards for defining purified water – regular drinking water has an acceptable amount of bacteria (500 colony-forming units per millilitre – 500 cfu/ml); water that has been purified, however, should have no more than 100 cfu/ml according to the standards adopted by most countries.

  - **Hire-purchase legislation**: such laws protect the hirer (person making a purchase of an asset on hire purchase) and the vendor (person selling the asset). Hire-purchase acts cover various situations – including delivery, installation, discounts, interest, insurance, rebates and non-payment of fees. For example, the Hire Purchase Act in Jamaica provides that if an item under a hire-purchase agreement is to be insured and the hirer fails to do so, then the vendor may insure the item and add the cost of insuring it to the original hire-purchase price for the hirer to pay.

Now it's your turn

We have just looked at seven roles of the government in society. Can you think of any other role that the government ought to be playing?

Taxation

Taxation is the process through which the government raises the bulk of its revenue to finance its spending. A tax is a mandatory payment that individuals and businesses pay to the government. A tax is usually quoted as a rate per unit of income or per unit of expenditure – a tax rate of 10 per cent, for example, means either that individuals must pay 10 per cent of their income over to the government or that they must pay 10 per cent more than the stated cost of an item. There are generally three types of taxation system:

- **Progressive taxation**: in a progressive taxation system, the proportion of taxes collected (the tax rate) rises as income increases. For example, individuals who earn between $1000 and $2500 per month may be asked to pay only 12 per cent over as taxes, while other individuals who earn above $2500 may be asked to pay taxes at a slightly higher rate of 15 per cent. In this system, then, high-income earners are asked to finance a greater share of the country's payments than low-income earners are required to do.

- **Regressive taxation**: a regressive taxation system is one in which the tax rate falls as income rises. At high levels of income, individuals are asked to pay less tax from each dollar they earn; whereas at low levels of income, more money is paid over to the government from each dollar earned. This is the opposite of a progressive system and it puts pressure on the poor to pay the taxes needed to finance a budget.

- **Proportional taxation**: in a proportional taxation system, the tax rate remains fixed regardless of the amount of income earned. So, whether an individual earns one thousand dollars or one million dollars, he may be asked to pay only 12 per cent as taxes.

Now it's your turn

Look at the three countries below and say which type of taxation system exists in each country.

	Tax rate on high income	Tax rate on low income
Country A	12%	12%
Country B	15%	18%
Country C	18%	12%

Which taxation system is best?

The answer to this question, as you would imagine, depends on a number of variables. The pros and cons of regressive and progressive taxation systems are discussed below.

Advantages of progressive systems

- A progressive system seems fair since people pay taxes based on their ability – the rich pay more than the poor, which appears to be ideal since they have more money.

- In addition, progressive taxation makes the redistribution of wealth from the rich to the poor possible. Wealth redistribution occurs when the government employs various strategies to share the income and wealth of the rich with the poor. Progressive taxation systems ask the rich to pay more money, which is then used to supply services to the poor, and, in this way the government redistributes income.

Disadvantages of progressive system

- When those who use their resources wisely to become wealthy are asked to pay higher taxes, it appears that they are being punished for being successful. Progressive taxation systems, therefore, may actually deter entrepreneurs from investing in a country.

- Progressive taxation systems may encourage tax evasion and avoidance.

Advantages of a regressive taxation system

- It encourages large investments in the country since investors would want to take advantage of the low level of taxation at high levels of profit.

- In a low-income society, a regressive tax system maximises the tax revenues that the government is able to collect. Since most people would have low income in such a society, using a progressive system would be futile.

Disadvantages of a regressive taxation system

- It seems unfair to the poor to further marginalise them by asking them to pay more of their low income in taxes than the rich are paying.

- It redistributes wealth in the wrong direction – from the poor to the rich.

The role of taxation

- **To raise revenue for government spending**: the money collected from taxation is used to finance important public-sector spending such as repairing roads, providing healthcare, security and education. Taxation is normally the major source of financing the budget.

Now it's your turn

Think critically about elasticity of demand – a concept we met in an earlier chapter. If the government wants to raise revenue to finance its budget, what type of products should it tax – elastic or inelastic ones? Justify your answer. For each pair of products in the list below, identify which one would yield the most revenue if it was taxed. Give reasons for your answers.

1. ice cream or cow's milk

2. cooking salt or hair products

3. cigarettes or blank CDs

4. car batteries or printers

- **To redistribute income**: governments often use taxation to redistribute income from the rich to the poor. In a progressive taxation system, the rich are charged a higher rate of tax than the poor. Luxury items that the wealthy are able to afford also generally attract a higher rate of taxation than basic, necessary items that the poor need to buy.

- **To redistribute wealth**: inheritance, lottery winnings and other windfalls which create wealth are normally taxed.

- **To meet the high costs of certain public goods and services**: the users of certain goods/ products may be asked to pay a tax unique to that good to help defray the cost of producing these goods. For example, in Jamaica, the high cost of building Highway 2000 is being defrayed by the toll that users of the highway have to pay.

- **To curtail demand for certain items**: the government may determine that the consumption of some goods is unwise, unsafe, unhealthy or uneconomical and as a result apply a tax to these items in an effort to discourage their consumption. Examples of such items include cigarettes, rum and, in some cases, gambling.

- **To curb imports**: governments have used taxation such as tariffs and custom duties to reduce the amount of a good being imported. Tariffs make imported goods relatively more expensive vis-à-vis local goods and are normally used to address balance-of-payment deficits.

- **To prevent dumping of low-quality goods**: when foreign goods are refused in their home markets for quality reasons, these goods are normally sold to small islands in the Caribbean at a low price. This is referred to as **dumping**. To prevent this, the government normally imposes a tax on goods suspected of being dumped to make them unattractive to local consumers.

Types of taxes

There are two broad types of taxes – direct taxes and indirect taxes.

Direct taxes

Direct taxes are paid directly to the government by the person or entity on which it is imposed. The payer does not pay it over to another party who then pays it to the government. Usually the government takes direct taxes out of a person's income before he or she receives it. Businesses, however, must pay these taxes to the government as soon as they have calculated their profits for the period. These taxes are levied (charged) directly upon the gross income of individuals and on the profits of companies and are normally expressed as a percentage of income/profit. A direct tax taken out of income before the worker receives it is called a pay-as-you-earn (PAYE) tax. Owners of companies, on the other hand, must pay corporation taxes on the profits that the company makes. In addition to income and corporation taxes, some other examples of direct taxation are:

- **capital-transfer tax**: paid on receipt of assets and legacies
- **capital-gains taxes**: paid on the profit gained from the sales of assets
- **death or estate duties**
- **interest taxes**: paid on savings and investments.

Indirect taxes

Indirect taxes are taxes paid on goods and services and are due only when people buy these goods and services. Some common examples of indirect taxes are value-added taxes (VAT), purchase and sales taxes (GCT), customs and excise taxes. Value-added taxes are charged on the goods each time value is added to the product at each stage of the production process. Indirect taxes on various consumer goods with inelastic demand tend to rise more quickly than they do on other goods. The main drawback of indirect taxes is that they are regressive – since everyone (rich and poor) has to pay the same level of taxes. Additionally, the demand for some goods will fall if taxes cause their prices to rise. The final problem with indirect taxes is that the amount collected will depend on the amount of the good bought; as a result, government is never sure how much revenue these taxes will bring in.

Government's assistance to businesses

The government has a vested interest in the growth and development of small and micro businesses as these businesses represent the potential of the economy. As a result, the government will create facilities, programmes and revolving funds that small businesses can access for financial support and assistance. Governmental support can take the form of:

- **Loans**: money can be made available at reduced rates of interest to qualified people interested in starting a business. These loans are usually disbursed after an application and approval process that is less rigorous than that of the regular banking system. Usually, the government creates organisations or agencies to offer loans

for specific purposes such as agriculture, export and import or marketing. Alternatively, the government may choose to use the regular banking system to disburse loans to small and micro businesses by subsidising the loans that they offer to specific sectors or people. For example, the government may decide to pay 60 per cent of the interest charges in loans that are made to qualified farmers for the purpose of investing in their farms.

 Now it's your turn

Investigate the different sources of government loans and financial assistance that small and micro businesses can access in your country. Do you think they are sufficient? Why or why not?

- **Technical assistance**: the government may choose to offer technical assistance in functions that small and micro businesses are often poor at. Such areas may include accounting and record keeping, marketing and distribution, and satisfying legal requirements. The assistance may take the form of training and development of managers of small and micro businesses or the provision of these services at reduced cost.

- **Research and information centres**: the ministry responsible for the growth and development of small businesses (usually the ministry of industry or commerce) may develop a database of case studies that model best practices in starting up and operating a business; it may also provide general information on running and operating a business, on various types of feasible business ideas and about primary research that is of relevance to entrepreneurs. This information is usually in a research and information centre.

- **Subsidies and grants**: a subsidy arrangement is an agreement that the government will cover part of a producer's production cost if the producer promises to reduce his selling price by this amount. So, for example, the government may decide to pay 30 per cent of the production cost of each good produced so that the producer can sell the product at a reduced price. By doing this, the government makes the product more competitive on the market as its price is lower when compared with other products that have not been subsidised. A grant is money that is given to a recipient who can demonstrate that they need it. It is not a loan that is to be repaid; rather, it is a gift with conditions – such as how or for what purpose it is to be used.

- **Incubators**: these are a recent development that the government can use to support small businesses. An incubator is a centre that offers new businesses low-cost offices with basic business services such as accounting, legal advice and administrative assistance. It is modelled on the system used in hospitals when premature babies are placed in incubators for a few days after birth to receive support until they gain strength. In the same way, businesses are most likely to fail shortly after they have started and usually because the overhead costs associated with important services, such as accounting, are too high. The incubators are designed to support businesses in the critical stage of early development and thus increase their chance of growing into large businesses.

Social services provided by government

It is perhaps in this area that the government is most visible. Indeed, it is taken as a given that social services such as healthcare and education, and infrastructure such as road networks will be provided by the government. The provision of these services has a positive effect on the quality of life that citizens of a country can enjoy. Some of the social services provided by the government are discussed below.

Healthcare

Healthcare services are provided to ensure that the population remains healthy. Usually they are offered through hospitals and clinics that are staffed by doctors and healthcare professionals, and paid for by the government. Healthcare is usually offered at a discounted or subsidised rate – although in some territories in the Caribbean, healthcare is free. Healthcare is one of the most important social services that the government can offer, as a healthy population is linked to increased productivity. Inadequate healthcare is often cited as one of the push factors that cause people to leave territories in the Caribbean.

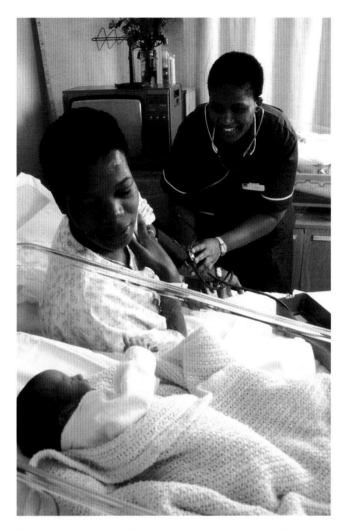

The government provides social services such as healthcare for all its citizens.

National Insurance Scheme (NIS)

Workers usually contribute a portion of their salary each month to a pension scheme that they can access at retirement or in the event that they are injured on the job. Usually, the family of the worker will also receive a lump-sum payment in the event that the worker dies.

Education

Like healthcare, education is geared towards developing and securing the human resources of a country. Investing in education will create a literate, numerate and informed population that has the capacity to become a productive workforce. Education is provided at a subsidised rate or free of cost by the government and is usually compulsory for all children up to the age at which they would qualify for secondary school.

Roads and transportation

The creation of a road network that links cities, towns and communities to each other and to other important points within the country such as hospitals, the country's capital and airports is one of the government's most important tasks. Without this network, it would be challenging for businesses to remain competitive or to satisfy their customers. An effective, properly designed and well-maintained road network is important if the cost of production – and ultimately the price of goods – is to be kept low as transportation costs are one of the expenses that businesses would have to absorb or pass on to their customers in the form of higher prices. Transportation is also another service that the government may have to provide as, if it is left in private hands, it may be unaffordable for those on low incomes.

Summary – Section B

- The government is responsible for securing the state and its population, providing social services and infrastructure and creating laws for the welfare and comfort of the citizens.

- The government also has an important role to play in protecting the environment, which may suffer as a result of businesses' attempts to maximise profit.

- Individuals in a society are usually asked to pay taxes in order to provide revenues to finance government expenditure. Taxes are progressive, regressive or proportional.

- If people are asked to pay taxes based on their ability, then this system is either progressive (where the rich pay taxes at a higher rate) or regressive (where the poor contribute more taxes per dollar of income than the rich do). Proportional taxes are those that everyone pays at the same rate regardless of their income.

- Taxes can also be direct or indirect. Direct taxes are taken out at source and paid directly over to the government, while indirect taxes are incurred when certain items are bought or services are accessed.

- Aside from raising revenues for the government, taxes are used to curb spending, redistribute income and wealth and reduce demand for imported goods.

- Government can support the growth and development of businesses by offering loans, technical assistance and support in the form of training, incubators and sourcing markets.

End of section activities

Quick questions

Provide short answers to the following questions:

1 Government must secure the state and protect its citizens. How are these two roles different? How are they similar?

2 How can zoning be used to protect the environment?

3 What are the four rights of consumers that governments usually try to protect?

4 What is a progressive taxation system?

5 What are direct taxes?

6 Why are indirect taxes considered regressive?

7 How can taxation redistribute income from the poor to the wealthy?

8 What is an incubator?

Applying what you have learnt

1 What kind of taxation system exists in your country – is it regressive, progressive or proportional? How do you know?

2 Many people have argued that they pay too much tax. These people have suggested that governments should get rid of income taxes and increase indirect taxes such as value-added taxes (VAT) or general-consumption taxes (GCT). Do you think this is a

good idea? Why or why not? How will this affect such things as:

a the revenues that governments collect?

b the extent to which it disadvantages the poor or the rich?

c how easy it would be to collect such taxes?

d the level of tax evasion possible?

3 Imagine that your class is a country and that you are a part of the government and that your classmates are its citizens. Make a list of at least five functions that your government would have to perform for the members of your class. For each function say how you will perform it. Now think of the money that you would need for the services that you will offer. How will you finance these services? How much tax would you have to collect from each individual in the class? How would you tax them – progressively, regressively or proportionally? Why?

Model exam questions

Question 1

a List any three functions of the government of your country. (3 marks)

b Explain how the government fulfils its role and obligation for **each** function listed above in (a). (9 marks)

c Explain why taxation is important for the operation of the government of your country. (3 marks)

Question 2

a Why is it usually the government's responsibility to ensure that the natural environment is protected? (3 marks)

b Explain how **each** of the following can be used to protect the natural environment:

i zoning

ii quotas

iii banning. (9 marks)

c Outline one step that a business can take to ensure that it protects the environment. (3 marks)

Question 3

a The government is usually involved in offering social services to the citizens of a country.

i List any three social services that the government offers to the citizens of your country. (3 marks)

ii Explain how each of the three social services you listed contributes to the development of your country. (6 marks)

b Discuss two reasons why the government usually offers these social services, even though they may also be offered by private businesses. (6 marks)

10 Social accounting and economic institutions

"
Economic advance is not the same thing as human

progress. – *John Clapham*

Haiti, no stranger to national disasters, was severely damaged by an earthquake in 2010.

Tragedy in Haiti – a region's response

On 12 January 2010, an earthquake of magnitude 7.0 struck the capital of Haiti. It was the strongest recorded earthquake to have hit any country in this part of the world and it damaged 80 per cent of all buildings (commercial and residential) in the capital, Port-au-Prince, dislocating, injuring or killing at least three million people (one-third of the country's population). Indeed, as of 23 February 2010, the government of Haiti reported that 222 517 people had died as a result of the earthquake. What made the earthquake even worse was that it caused

serious disruption to the communication and transportation infrastructure and to the regular functioning of the government. Haiti, already burdened by a number of problems prior to the earthquake, was in no position to respond appropriately. Fortunately, as a part of CARICOM and a number of other organisations, Haiti benefited from the generosity of other countries. CARICOM's response to the crisis was initiated primarily through the Caribbean Disaster Emergency Management Agency (CDEMA), a CARICOM institution. Within a day of the disaster, Jamaica (which is the designated Sub-Regional Focal Point – SRFP – for Haiti) had dispatched a Jamaica Defence Force vessel with emergency relief supplies and technical, medical and military personnel. This support continued in critical areas such as monetary donations to the government of Haiti, provision of temporary shelter material, pre-packaged food, and search and rescue personnel and technical support at the highest level in emergency and disaster management. For example, within a few days, over 15 500 cases of drinking water, tinned products and food items, 565 kg of rice and sugar and 132 temporary shelter kits and generators were distributed to Haitians by the CDEMA. In addition, 32 40-foot containers of food and 3000 boxes of water, over-the-counter medical supplies and other miscellaneous items were shipped to Haiti through the SRFP from other governments across the region. This outpouring of support is one of the benefits of being part of a regional organisation, which is one of the key ideas in this chapter.

In this chapter you will:

- explain the difference between a country's standard of living and its quality of life

- outline the factors that affect a country's standard of living and the quality of life of its citizens

- calculate and interpret various measures of national income

- explain the differences between economic growth and development

- discuss the importance of human resource development for growth and development

- discuss the importance of international trade in modern economies

- explain the concepts of 'balance of trade' and 'balance of payments'

- offer solutions to balance-of-payment problems

- outline the functions of economic institutions in the Caribbean

- discuss economic problems that affect Caribbean countries

- offer solutions to economic problems that affect Caribbean countries.

SECTION A   Social accounting

Standard of living

Imagine two hypothetical countries. In one country, citizens live in relative comfort – they are able to access modern, sophisticated technology as soon as it becomes available, they have a high level of disposable income which they are able to spend on things such as vacations, eating out and private schools for their children, and they are expected to live a full life, relatively free from the threat of violence and basic diseases. In the other country, however, citizens have to contend with an overburdened healthcare system and an inefficient education system; infants have a high chance of dying at birth and citizens wrestle with the constant threat of violence and other social problems. In this country, citizens have few luxuries that they can enjoy and do not have a high level of disposable income.

Each of these countries has a different **quality of life** and, quite likely, this is due to the **standard of living** in each country. A country's standard of living is a measure of the wealth and material comfort to which its citizens have access. As a measure of comfort, a country's standard of living makes the assumption that a country with a high rate of material comfort should

have citizens who have a relatively high quality of life. By material comfort, we mean the extent to which citizens have access to modern goods and services and how advanced and sophisticated the country's economy is. Standard of living is indicated by the following factors:

- **Level of consumption of goods and services**: countries with a high standard of living have high levels of consumption of goods and services. This is related to the fact that citizens in such countries are likely to possess a relatively high level of income, which causes demand to be very high. This high demand results in a high level of production and employment, causing the overall economy to boom.

- **Average disposable income of the population**: a country with a high standard of living usually has citizens whose average disposable income is also very high. Disposable income refers to income after taxes have been paid and this is usually high in highly developed countries as most citizens are usually well educated and, as a result, are employed in rewarding jobs.

- **Level of national ownership of capital equipment**: countries with a high standard of living are usually involved in capital-intensive production. This requires a high level of investment in large machinery and equipment. Countries with a low standard of living, on the other hand, are likely to be engaged in primary production, which given its labour-intensive nature, requires fewer machines and pieces of equipment.

- **Access to modern technology**: countries with a high standard of living are usually at the very centre of cutting-edge developments in technology. The result is that these citizens have greater access to technology. Additionally, the higher level of disposable income that such citizens have means that they are likely to be early adopters of new products and hence are likely targets for price skimming. Furthermore, technology is usually diffused to other countries only after these markets have been fully exploited and saturated. Usually, citizens in countries with high standards of living have the first chance to access modern technology.

- **Investment in research and technology**: a high standard of living is usually linked to high levels of investment in technology and in new cutting-edge research for a number of reasons. The main reason, however, is that most industries are built around capital-intensive production, and therefore it is only natural that the government (through the education system) and private-sector interests (through research grants and so on) will invest much of its resources in research and technology.

☞ **Now it's your turn**

Think about your country and assess it based on the five indicators of standard of living outlined above. Rate each indicator on a scale of 1–5, with 1 being the lowest and 5 the highest. How do you rate your country's standard of living? Discuss your rating with some of your classmates.

Quality of life

While it is generally true that citizens in countries with high standards of living have a better quality of life, this is not always the case. Some countries have a high

Countries differ in their standard of living and their quality of life as these photos from Haiti and Curaçao show.

standard of living yet a relatively low quality of life. Quality of life is related to standard of living but is different in one important respect. While standard of living measures the wealth of a country, quality of life measures the extent to which this wealth translates into a better life for its citizens. This distinction is important because it is possible for a country to be very wealthy while at the same time its citizens are very uncomfortable and unhappy with their way of life. Take, for example, a highly industrialised country with a high level of access to technology but whose citizens must endure a high crime rate and live in highly polluted cities. Such citizens certainly live in a wealthy country, but their quality of life is significantly low. Standard of living, then, measures the *potential* a country has to provide a comfortable life for its citizens – countries with high standards of living are more likely to have citizens with high quality of life. Ultimately, however, quality of life is measured by how well its citizens are able to access and enjoy the country's wealth. Factors such as crime, pollution, life expectancy and **infant mortality rate** all affect quality of life – if these are high, regardless of how wealthy a country is, citizens' quality of life is low. Quality of life is indicated by the following variables:

- **Crime rate**: citizens in countries with a high level of crime are likely to feel unsafe and may not be able to enjoy living in the country. They may, for example, have to give up some activities such as staying out late at night, investing in expensive cars and taking trips to isolated areas. Furthermore, a high crime rate creates a hostile and volatile society where the security forces and thugs engage in escalatory and retaliatory actions that make all citizens feel uneasy.

- **Social services**: the government is responsible for providing social services such as healthcare and public education. Private-sector interests can also offer these services, at a higher price than the government would but usually more effectively and at a higher quality. Regardless of how high a country's standard of living is, if these services are not efficiently and effectively provided for all to access and enjoy, then the quality of life of its citizens will be very poor. In addition, either through public–private partnership or on its own, the government is expected to provide recreational facilities such as parks and theatres. The provision of these services ensures that citizens' lives are enhanced and improved as they live in the country. For example, one of the problems experienced by countries with high standards of living is a lack of green areas in cities and main towns. The creation of these 'concrete jungles' is a major problem affecting the quality of life enjoyed by citizens.

- **Diet and nutrition**: this is a relatively recent issue that has become more significant as obesity becomes associated with countries with high standards of living. Diet and nutrition refer to the access to basic nutrients that citizens – especially children – have. Traditionally, this point has been discussed in relation to the lack of access to fruits, vegetables and dairy products for children in poor countries. While this problem still exists and continues to be of grave concern, attention has also been turned to the problem of overindulgence in fatty foods, which is usually a problem in wealthy countries. Fast food and other unhealthy meals have taken over in many countries where individuals are too busy to prepare home-cooked meals and where they have the income to satisfy their demand for fast food. This has the potential to lead to obesity and to an increase in lifestyle-related diseases in such countries.

- **Life expectancy**: life expectancy is defined as the number of years that an individual is expected to live. Life expectancy is a measure of how good a country is at keeping its citizens healthy – in some countries, diseases, poor healthcare, violence, pollution and poor nutrition reduce the average life expectancy, while other countries have fewer incidences of these problems and, as a result, individuals have a much longer life expectancy.

- **Infant mortality rate**: this is the number of infants who die before they pass one year of age. This rate is determined by calculating the number of deaths per 1000 live births. A rate of 4 per cent, for example, means that 40 children out of every 1000 live births die before they reach the age of one. This measure is an assessment of a country's ability to offer essential services (such as sterile facilities for delivery and healthcare for the immunisation and treatment of children) to infants and mothers. In some countries, children who are stillborn are not included in the number of deaths per 1000 as the healthcare system may have had little to do with these deaths.

- **Access to public utilities**: in some countries access to electricity, running water and telecommunication facilities (such as internet and cellular services) is limited to people living in the main cities. Citizens living far inland or even on the outskirts of these cities may find that these services are not available to them as it may not be considered economically feasible for the services to be provided for them.

Think about it

Would you rather live in a rich country that is highly polluted or in a poor country that has a low level of pollution?

National income (NI) – gross domestic and national products

One of the most important elements of the economic environment is the **national income**, which seeks to measure the sum of all incomes that arise as a result of economic activities involved in the production of goods and services. In the same way as an individual, a family or even an organisation has an annual income, a country also has an annual income, which is referred to as its national income (NI). NI can be thought of in two different ways – as **gross domestic product** (GDP) or as **gross national product** (GNP). GDP refers to the value of goods and services produced by an economy in a given period (usually a year). More precisely, GDP refers to the value of goods produced within the physical space defined as a country – regardless of who produced these goods, whether citizens or foreigners. GDP therefore provides some indication of total output produced within a country and the total income that such output generates. However, the total income received by citizens of that country will differ from GDP for two reasons:

- Some domestic factors of production (land, labour, capital and enterprise) create goods and income that are not for residents of that country. In other words, foreigners within the country will take out of GDP the income that they earn.

- In the same way, some of the country's residents may live or produce abroad and the money they earn from this production must be added to the country's GDP.

When these two adjustments to GDP have been made, the result is GNP. GNP, then, is the income earned by the citizens of a country from all production in which they are involved, whether at home or abroad. GDP, therefore, measures income *produced in* a country, while GNP measures the income produced in and *received by* a country. To convert GDP to GNP, it is necessary to:

- add income received by domestic residents from assets owned in other countries (inflow of income)

- then subtract income paid out to non-residents who own assets in the country (outflow of income).

A numerical example may help to make the point clear. A country has GDP of $10 000 million; of this amount, however, foreign citizens earned $150 million from their investments in the country. The country also has citizens who earned $225 million from investments abroad. The country's GNP is therefore calculated as shown in Table 10.1.

Alternatively, one could simply subtract the outflow of income from the inflow of income and use this to adjust GDP. The difference between the inflow and the outflow of income is called net factor income from abroad and it is:

- negative if outflow is greater than inflow

- positive if inflow is greater than outflow.

Using this approach of finding net factor income from abroad, GNP can be calculated as shown in Table 10.2.

	$(millions)	$(millions)
GDP	10 000	
Add inflow of income	225	
	10 225	
Less outflow of income	150	
GNP		**10 075**

Table 10.1 From GDP to GNP.

	$(millions)	$(millions)
GDP		10 000
Inflow of income	225	
Less outflow of income	150	
Net factor income from abroad		75
GNP		**10 075**

Table 10.2 From GDP to GNP.

Think about it

Some people think that income earned by citizens living abroad is not to be considered as national income as most of this income never comes back into the country. What do you think?

Measuring NI

NI is measured through a process of national-income accounting, which is based on the idea that national income can be measured in three different but related ways:

- NI is the total amount of output produced in the country. This is called the **output method** of calculating NI and sees national income as the sum of the monetary value of all final goods that a country (its firms and government) produces.

- NI is the income received by those who produce and ultimately sell the goods. From this **income** perspective, NI is equal to the sum of the income that the producers of goods receive from sales that they make during a year. More generally, to account for profit (which would make the income approach and the output approach result in different figures), NI is seen as the factor income received from employing the factors of production.

- The amount of expenditure incurred by those purchasing the output. This **expenditure** approach to calculating NI argues that the sum of money spent by the government, consumers, firms and buyers abroad must be equal to the dollar value of goods produced by the country.

An example – the economy of Nonesuch

An example showing the different approaches at work may help to make their differences and similarities clear. It should be emphasised that each approach measures the same thing and hence should be equal – regardless of the approach taken, GDP should be the same. For our example, let us imagine a country called Nonesuch, which has an economy that has only six individuals and a private sector that produces only two goods (bread and raisins). Economic agents in the country are as follows:

- Randolph, the fearless leader who is responsible for running the country
- Lester, who produces raisins
- Angela, who produces bread
- Clive and Peter who work for Lester and Angela respectively
- Sophie, a skilled 'multi-tasker' who works for the government providing all public services to the citizens of Nonesuch.

GDP by the output method

By the output approach, GDP is the monetary value of final goods produced in the economy of Nonesuch. If, for example, $5000 worth of raisins and $8500 worth of bread are produced and $11 500 worth of services

are supplied by the government, then the GDP for the country is $25 000 – which is the sum of all the goods produced. Note that we have made an assumption that none of the raisins produced by Lester were bought by Angela and used to make bread. If, however, some of the raisins Lester produced were bought by Angela and used to make bread, then we have counted these raisins twice – once when Lester produced them and again when Angela added value to them. This is called double counting and must be avoided. To ensure that we do not double count, we distinguish between intermediate and final goods and introduce the idea of value added.

Intermediate goods are outputs of one firm that become the input for another firm. **Final goods**, on the other hand, are not used by other firms as raw materials for their production process – at least not during the period under consideration. When goods are used as input for another process, then we say that value has been added to these goods. Adding value results in a good being more expensive at the end of its production process than it was at the start; this means that each time a good is used in a new production process, it becomes more refined, useable, valuable and hence more expensive. For example, if Angela buys all the raisins that Lester produces for $5000 and uses them to make bread, which she then sells for $8500, then she has added value of $3500. In this case, then, the final value of GDP is actually $20 000, which is calculated as shown in Table 10.3.

In short, by the output method, GDP is the sum of the monetary value of all final goods and value added at earlier stages of production.

GDP by the income method

The production of a nation's output creates income as the factors of production must be used up and must be paid for. Labour must be employed, land must be

	$	$
Government		11 500
Raisins produced by Lester		5 000
Value added (by Angela):		
Output (raisin bread)	8 500	
Input (raisin)	5 000	3 500
National income		**20 000**

Table 10.3 National income by output method.

rented and capital must be used (usually borrowed). The payment for these factors of production is called a factor payment and the sum of these factor payments is also GDP. There are four basic factor payments that economists use in calculating GDP:

- **Income from employment**: this is the factor payment to labour and is primarily made up of wages and salaries. Taxes paid must also be accounted for and these are usually added back to wages and salaries to arrive at a true figure.

- **Income from self-employment**: this is fairly similar in principle to income from employment.

- **Rent**: this is the payment for the use of land and other factors that are rented. Of course, many businesses and individuals own and do not rent their own housing; this is accounted for, however, by introducing the concept of imputed rent – home owners are viewed as renting accommodation from themselves. The figure for rent thus contains payments for rented houses plus a figure for imputed rent for the use of housing that is owner-occupied.

- **Profits**: the payment for using entrepreneurial ability and capital is profit and this is also included in calculating GDP.

When these four factor payments are added together, then GDP at factor price is found. Using the example of the economy of Nonesuch, we can show how GDP would be calculated using the income approach:

- Clive, Peter and Sophie earn a total of $7500 after taxes for working for their respective employers. They pay $350 in taxes to the government.

- Lester earns a profit of $3150 selling raisins while Angela's profit is $3500.

- Both Lester and Angela had to rent land and other factors at a total cost of $5500.

Table 10.4 shows GDP using the income method.

GDP by the expenditure approach

If we add up all the expenditure made to purchase the final goods produced, then we would have calculated GDP using the expenditure method. This is the sum of four broad categories of purchases:

- **Consumption expenditure (C)**: the dollar value of all goods sold to end users.

	$	$
Income from employment	7 500	
Add direct taxes	350	7 850
Profit:		
Lester	3 150	
Angela	3 500	6 650
Rent		5 500
GDP		**20 000**

Table 10.4 GDP using the income approach.

- **Investment expenditure (I)**: expenditure on the production of goods to be used in the future or in producing other goods. Investment expenditure includes stock building (building up inventory), fixed capital formation (purchasing fixed assets) and residential investments (construction of new housing). Some of the investment that takes place is simply used to replace what has been depleted as a result of wear and tear (depreciation). This is called replacement investment and is not to be included in investment expenditure. Investment expenditure included in GDP, then, is net of depreciation.

- **Government expenditure (G)**: money spent by the government to provide goods and services (whether it is providing healthcare or attending a conference in Washington) is considered a part of GDP.

- **Net exports (X – M)**: a part of consumption expenditure is on goods produced abroad and, since the purchase of these imported goods overstates GDP, it should be subtracted from GDP. Similarly, goods produced locally but sold abroad in the form of exports should be added back to GDP. The difference between exports (X) and imports (M) is called net export and this figure is used to adjust GDP. If exports are less than imports, then net exports are negative and must be subtracted from GDP; however, net exports are positive if exports are more than GDP and, in this case, are added to GDP.

	$	$
Consumption		6 500
Investment		
Stock building (Lester)	2 500	
Fixed capital formation (Angela)	1 500	
Residential investment (Sophie)	2 700	6 700
Government		3 500
Net exports		
Exports	5 900	
Less imports	2 600	3 300
GDP		**20 000**

Table 10.5 GDP using the expenditure approach.

Using the economy of Nonesuch, we can model how GDP is calculated using the expenditure approach:

- Peter, Clive, Lester and Angela together spent $6500 on bread and raisins.
- Lester invested $2500 in new stock.
- Angela invested $1500 in new equipment.
- Sophie bought a house valued at $2700.
- Randolph spends $3500 providing services such as healthcare to citizens of Nonesuch.
- residents of Nonesuch imported $2600 worth of goods and exported goods valued at $5900.

GDP is therefore the sum of these four categories of expenditure: GDP = C + I + G + (X – M). This is shown in Table 10.5.

Net national income

The word gross is in GDP and GNP because we have not taken depreciation into account. Depreciation is also called capital consumption and occurs because fixed assets are used up in the process of producing other goods. Depreciation is therefore not income earned by any of the factors of production and hence should not be included in GDP or in GNP. Having found GNP by adding net factor income from abroad to GDP, we must now subtract capital consumption from GNP to obtain net national income. When we use the term national income, unless otherwise stated, then we are referring to net national income.

Per capita income

If we were to divide up a country's NI equally among its population, then each person's share is called his **per capita income**. Per capita income is a measure of a country's wealth since it measures how much each person in the country earns over a year. Since NI will vary with the size of an economy – as the economy's size increases, so does its NI – then it is impossible to compare two figures for NI and make any reasonable conclusions about the countries involved. Using an analogy of a family and its earning power may help to show why. In a large family of 9 people where 5 of them are working, total income is likely to be very high, say $63000. A small family of three, on the other hand, with only two people working, is likely to have a considerably smaller total income of say only $27000. However, the small family is not necessarily poorer than the large family simply because its income is less. Since there are more people in the large family, it is expected that they would need more money to sustain them. If the $63000 were shared among the nine members of this large family, then each person earns $7000; whereas in the small family, dividing the $27000 among the three people in the family results in each person getting $9000. Each person in the smaller family is actually better off than their counterpart in the larger family.

For a country, the approach is the same. A country's NI is divided among those who make a claim on it – its population. A few things are to be taken into consideration, however, when looking at per capita income. The per capita income is an average and, as such, it is affected by extreme values. The result is that it may not be the best measure of the typical income earned by citizens of a country. In countries where most people are unemployed, or underemployed, then the per capita income will be very small, reflecting the fact that those who earn must take care of those who do not through the funding of various social programmes.

⟳ Making connections: mathematics

The per capita income is really a measure of the average income earned by each person in a country. What are some of the advantages and disadvantages of averages that must be considered when we are interpreting the per capita income?

Some drawbacks of NI and per capita income

NI is not the best measure of a country's wealth for a number of reasons:

- **Illegal activities**: GDP does not measure illegal activities, which are a source of income (though undesirable) for many individuals. It means that a country's GDP and per capita income may be very low but in reality some citizens are wealthier than this suggests because they earn income from illegal activities such as gambling, the drug trade or prostitution.

- **Informal economy**: the informal economy is the sector of the economy which the government cannot measure. A mechanic, for example, may repair a car and be paid in cash without the government ever knowing about this activity since no taxes are paid on the transaction. Other people are gainfully employed in the formal economy, but also 'hustle' by engaging in part-time activities such as making and selling cushions, designing posters and fliers on their computers or offering private lessons from home. This is a valid source of income that cannot be measured by the

The underground or informal economy has many transactions that are never recorded by the government.

Business in your world

The informal economy in the Caribbean

It has always been a struggle for a government to measure the size of its informal economy; most economists in the Caribbean agree, however, that the informal economies of the countries in the region are quite large. Recent research by Professor G. Vuletin reported that the informal economy is quite low in some Caribbean countries but, in others, it is worryingly high. The table below shows the estimates made by Professor Vuletin using data from 2002 and 2003.

With the possible exception of the Bahamas, these figures represent large informal economies. The larger an informal economy is, the greater the level of tax evasion and avoidance that can take place and, as a consequence, the lower the level of revenues that the government is receiving. An informal economy that is 50.6 per cent of GDP means that for every $100 dollars of income earned by people in the

Countries	Informal economy as a percentage of GDP
The Bahamas	15.9
Grenada	22.5
St. Kitts and Nevis	24.2
Trinidad and Tobago	24.4
Barbados	24.5
Antigua and Barbuda	31.2
Dominica	34.2
Jamaica	35.0
Guyana	36.7
St. Lucia	41.5
Dominican Republic	44.8
Belize	46.8
St. Vincent and the Grenadines	50.6

formal economy, almost $51 are earned by people in the informal economy, on which little or no tax is paid. It means, then, that in a country like St. Vincent and Grenadines, the GDP is not a true reflection of the level of wealth of citizens.

How Professor Vuletin estimated the size of the informal economy is interesting and novel. He used a method that combines many factors, including electricity consumption, to determine how large the informal economy of each country is. He argued that if GDP grows by 12 per cent but electricity consumption increases by 18 per cent, then the difference between the two is a good measure of the size of the informal economy. This argument is based on the notion that increases in GDP are fuelled by increases in electricity at a fairly constant rate – any excess in electricity use

not reflected in GDP resulted from it being used in the informal economy. He also considered other things, such as the size of the labour force compared with the size of the labour supply. If there are 20 people of working age in the population yet only eight of them are working, then Professor Vuletin concludes that the majority of the others are in the informal economy.

Discussion

1 Can you think of any problems with Professor Vuletin's approach to measuring the informal economy?

2 Discuss some of the benefits and problems of the informal economy.

government and, as a result, GDP and per capita income are likely to be underestimated.

- **Non-marketed activities**: if a homeowner hires a contractor to repaint his house, then this service gets counted as GDP. If, instead, he paints it himself, then the value of this service and the income it would have generated are omitted from GDP. Do-it-yourself repairs and voluntary work are all valuable contributions to the development of a society, yet these have no impact on the GDP of a nation or may even reduce it.

- **GDP places no value on leisure**: as a country gets richer, then its citizens are likely to take more time off from work in the form of leisure time. This may actually be counted as a reduction in GDP, even though the country's quality of life is actually improving. For example, in less-developed countries doctors work as many as 15 hours per day for six days per week. This 90-hour working week results in 4500 hours of work for such doctors over a year; this is significantly more than the 40-hour working weeks (2000 hours for the year) that are standard in other countries. If the diet and nutrition of citizens in less-developed countries improve and the crime rate is lowered thus reducing the need for doctors to work long hours, then this results in less wages and salaries being paid out to them. This reduction in the amount paid in wages and

salaries is actually counted as a decrease in GDP even though the country is improving.

- **Economic 'bads' as well as 'goods' are counted**: when a disaster occurs, lives are lost, property is destroyed and the country's development is threatened. Yet this usually improves GDP as more is spent on rebuilding and repairing, infrastructure and expanding social programmes such as the healthcare system. This kind of spending is considered an economic bad and the citizens of the country are certainly not better off, yet the country's GDP is likely to have increased.

- **GDP does take into account the destruction of the environment**: some countries have very high GDP and per capita income but only at the expense of the environment. As a result, they are highly polluted and life in these countries is very uncomfortable.

Think about it

What is your country's national income or per capita income? Do you think that it is an accurate reflection of how much money each person has? Do people earn far more or less than they have on paper as indicated by the per capita income? What do you think accounts for this?

Economic growth and development

Growth is certainly one of the most elusive economic imperatives of most governments in the Caribbean. **Economic growth** takes place when a country produces more in one year than it did in the previous year. If a country's NI increases over a year, then the country has recorded positive growth. Negative growth occurs when the economy's output in one year is less than it was in a previous year. While economic growth is desirable, many experts regard economic development as being more important than growth. Economic growth is a quantitative measure of changes in the physical size of the economy. This increase in size and capacity of the economy does not necessarily mean that society has improved. Growth can take place without noticeable improvements in the quality of life of individuals in the society. Alternatively, even when an economy grows, this increase in income may not be equally shared among the citizens of a country; rather, the increase may be centralised in the hands of a few individuals.

Economic development does not focus on quantitative changes in the size of an economy; rather, development is focused on improvements in the quality of life that citizens of a country enjoy. Development leads to citizens enjoying a better quality of life and not necessarily in the economy growing. With development, citizens have more time for leisure, feel a greater sense of safety and security, have better access to quality government services and live longer and fuller lives. Based on the discussion we have had so far, it is clear that although GDP (meaning NI) can increase, the positive outcomes of development are not necessarily achieved. In short, growth can be occurring in a country but development is not taking place. There are a number of reasons for this, but primarily this is related to the distribution of income. Income distribution refers to how a country's NI is shared among its citizens – some countries have a high level of NI but it is not shared equitably and, as a result, it is controlled by a small number of people. If this is the case, a country's wealth is centralised in the hands of a few privileged people and economic growth is likely to simply make these few people better off without improving the quality of life for everyone.

Say, for example, in a country with only three people – A, B and C – the NI is $12 000. Of this amount A earns $9000, B earns $500 and C earns $2500. The per capita income is $4000 ($12 000 ÷ 3) but in reality each person's income is far different from this. In another country with three people (X, Y and Z), NI may only be $6000, with X earning $2200, Y earning $1800 and Z earning $2000. The per capita income is $2000 ($6000 ÷ 3), which is very close to what is actually earned by the citizens of the country. Obviously then, quality of life is not entirely dependent on the size of the 'pie', but also on how the pie is shared.

Measuring development

Statisticians have devised measures of development based on quality-of-life indicators. One of the most popular measures is the Human Development Index (HDI), which analyses development based on the benefits it brings to a country's citizens. The HDI is calculated by considering three variables:

- life expectancy at birth, which is a measure of a population's health and longevity and is an assessment of a country's healthcare system
- knowledge and education, measured by the adult literacy rate and enrolment rates at the primary, secondary and tertiary levels
- standard of living as measured by the per capita income of the country

Using a complex formula, each country's HDI is calculated based on these variables and the index is used to separate countries into three categories – developed (high development), developing (middle development) and underdeveloped (low development). The index is scored out of a maximum possible score of one and a minimum possible score of zero – the closer a country is to one, the more developed it is, and the closer a country is to zero, the less developed it is. In 2007, Barbados was the only Caribbean country that was rated as being a developed country.

Human resources and economic growth and development

Economists have long accepted that it is primarily the innovativeness of the human resources available in a country that will create growth and enable development. Innovativeness may manifest itself in new technology that greatly improves the capacity of businesses and their workers to produce more, or in new processes and systems that create efficiency and productivity at work. The creation of innovation requires that human resources be trained and be exposed to development on the job. Human resources create growth and enable development in the following ways:

- Increased productivity results in increased output and an increase in national income. If distributed evenly, this increase is likely to lead to economic development.
- The creation of ideas and innovations has a multiplier effect on the economy as it results in new products and techniques that are likely to impact all industries.
- Human resources create synergy by harnessing and co-ordinating technology to do more than it would otherwise be able to do.
- Human resources are responsible for creating the systems and procedures within which production takes place. These systems and procedures create efficiency and productivity and lead to economic growth.

International trade

International trade describes the exchange of goods and services for commercial gain between nations. International trade is vital to the health of an economy for a number of reasons:

- **Specialisation**: in the same way as firms and individuals within a country specialise in the production of a good or a service, which they produce in abundance, countries also specialise. This international specialisation means that trade must take place in order for countries to access the goods that they do not produce. Similarly, countries need markets that will take their excess production. International trade ensures that this is possible.
- **Mutual gains from trade**: some countries have an advantage over other countries in producing some goods. If countries focus on the production of goods in which they have an advantage, then they, their trading partners and the rest of the world benefit by being able to access these goods produced at high quality and sold at relatively low prices. There are two types of advantage that a country may have – an absolute advantage (which occurs when the country is able to use fewer units of resources to produce a unit of the product) and a comparative advantage, which is more complicated to explain

and understand. Country A has a comparative advantage over Country B in producing a good if:

- Country B can produce the good more efficiently than Country A can, but
- Country B has other goods that it can produce more cheaply and
- Country A has no other goods that it can produce as efficiently.

An example may illustrate the point. Some lawyers type better than their secretaries and hence have an absolute advantage in practising law and in typing. However, lawyers stand to gain more money practising law for a hour than they would gain typing for a hour. It is perhaps best, therefore, that they allow their secretaries to type while they practise law. Secretaries, therefore, have a comparative advantage over lawyers in typing. In the same way, even if a country is better at producing *all* goods, it may find that it is better at producing one or two. It should, therefore, specialise in the production of these goods and trade with the rest of world to obtain the others.

- **Foreign currency**: international trade is one of the major sources of foreign currency that a nation has. When it sells its goods to its trading partners, a country receives payments in their currency (or in some other common and popular currency) that it can then use to buy other goods.
- **Geographical and climate factors**: some countries are not able to produce some products as a result of the terrain or weather that they may have. Other countries are, however, ideal for the production of these items. Given the year-round, warm tropical weather that exists in the Caribbean, for example, it is ideally suited for the production of tourism services for European countries.
- **Enhancing the quality of life**: trading allows countries with a low standard of living and a low quality of life to access high-quality goods produced in other countries.
- **Increased choice for consumers**: international trade gives consumers greater options in terms of the goods they are able to buy.
- **To break the power of monopoly**: sometimes the only challenges to a local monopoly come from the options that are provided by goods imported into the country.

Balance of payments

The government keeps track of its trade with the rest of the world in a **balance-of-payments** account. Transactions in the balance-of-payments accounts generate either inflows or outflows of foreign currency and these payments are classified as such in the accounts. A transaction that leads to a payment from foreigners (such as exporting a nation's output) is recorded on the credit side of the account as a positive item. On the other hand, if the country has to pay foreigners in another currency, then this transaction is recorded as a debit item with a negative sign. At the end of a period, the account must balance and equal to zero. The reason for this is quite simple and we will explore it in more detail soon. First, let us look at the different ways in which transactions are categorised.

Current and capital accounts

The balance-of-payments account is divided into two sections. The first section is called the **current account** and records transactions in four main activities:

- Trade in goods such as the sale of potatoes to a foreign market or the purchase of used cars from a foreign supplier.

- Trade in services such as the flow of currency generated by tourism in the Caribbean.

- Income, which is divided into two parts:

  - income, received by a country's citizens who may be employed by firms in other countries

  - income, received from investments made overseas.

- Transfers, which are also divided into two parts:

  - Payments received or made by the government from or to foreign bodies such as the Caribbean Development Bank (CDB). Usually such payments are in relation to interest payments on loans.

  - Payments to and receipts from bodies such as the CDB which do not involve the government.

While the overall balance-of-payments account must balance, it is possible, indeed likely, that the current account will have a deficit – the total amount of outflow of foreign currency is greater than the inflow of such funds. This is made likely by the fact that most countries have a huge import bill, owing to the number of goods and the amount of services that they demand from overseas.

The other part of the balance-of-payments account is called the **capital account** and it is used to record transactions related to the international movements of ownership of financial assets such as investments in banks in other countries. It is important to point out and for you to note that the capital account does not record the trade in capital goods such as machines and equipment – these are actually recorded in the current account under trade in goods. Instead, the capital account is used to record international trade in financial instruments such as ownership of the shares of foreign companies, bank loans or government money-market instruments. Just like the current account, the capital account is used to record the inflow and outflow of currency – when residents of a country buy investments abroad, this results in a capital outflow of currency, even though residents now own more foreign investments. If foreigners buy investments in a country, then this is recorded in that country's balance-of-payments accounts as a capital inflow of currency. It is also possible (but not as likely) that the balance on the capital account will be a deficit.

The balance on the balance-of-payments account

Let us return to the idea of the balance-of-payments account balancing and being equal to zero. The current account records trade in goods and services, while the capital account records trade in financial assets. Each of these accounts will have different balances, even though the overall balance on the balance-of-payments account must be equal to zero. This means that if the current account has a deficit then there must be a surplus on the capital account that is sufficient to wipe out this deficit. This leads us to the conclusion that the balances on the current and capital accounts are opposite but of equal size, so that when they are added together they wipe out each other. Think about the question: 'How may countries develop deficits on their current accounts?' The answer lies in the observation that the inflows on their capital accounts must be such that they can finance the deficits on their current accounts. Table 10.6 illustrates this point. Note that the current account shows a deficit that is close to but not exactly equal to the surplus on the capital account. This is due to the fact that statisticians who capture the information sometimes miss some of the data and, as a result, a balancing figure is inserted to make the balance equal to zero.

	$ (millions)	$ (millions)
Current account		
Trade in goods	−45 000	
Trade in services	18 650	
Income	18 350	
Transfers	−12 500	
Current account balance		−20 500
Capital account		
Financial instruments		19 600
Balancing item		900
		0

Table 10.6 Balance-of-payments account.

When economists speak of the balance-of-payments deficit, therefore, they are referring to the balance on the current account (or, less frequently, on the capital account); never the balance on the overall account.

Balance of trade

A related concept is that of the **balance of trade**. The balance of trade describes the difference between imports and exports of goods and services. Like a current-account balance, it can either be a deficit or a surplus. A balance-of-trade deficit exists when the value of a country's imports is more than the value of its exports. This means that it has to spend more foreign currency paying for imports than it receives from its exports. If the reverse occurs, however, then a balance-of-trade surplus exists. You will recall that the trade in goods and services is just a portion of the current account, which also includes trade in income and transfers. The balance of trade is a major indicator of whether the current-account balance will be a deficit or surplus.

Addressing the balance-of-payments deficits

Before we look at *how* to address the deficit on the balance-of-payments account, let us first look at *why* we need to. Balance-of-payments deficits (particularly on the current account) may result in inflation being imported from a country's trading partners – when most of a country's goods and services are imported, then price increases on the world market are imported into the country. A high level of imports also puts pressure on the country's exchange rate, driving up the price of foreign currency which consumers demand in order to buy imported products. The balance of trade is also an indication of the health of the economy – it shows whether or not local producers are able to create products that are able to win the battle being fought on the shelves of foreign markets.

Correcting a balance-of-payments deficit requires that the country discourages imports and encourages exports. This is done through one or a combination of the following:

- **Tariffs**: a **tariff** is a tax on imported goods. When these are imposed, the government hopes that they will make imported goods more expensive and less desirable compared with local goods. A tariff is one of the many protectionist measures that the government may choose to initiate in the event of a current-account deficit. **Protectionism** is the philosophy that a country should protect local producers from imported products. Other protectionist measures, which are also likely to fix the balance-of-payments deficit, include:

  - **Licences**: an importer may need to apply for special licences in order to import goods. If the government sees fit, then it can choose to reject the application.

  - **Quotas**: the government may impose an upper limit on the quantity of goods that can be imported into the country.

Think about it

Protectionist policies such as those described above are often seen by some people as being bad for trade and for an economy. Others believe that free trade (trade that has no protectionism) is harmful for an economy. What arguments does each side use to support its opinion? Which view do you take?

- **Exchange control**: in order to purchase imported goods, the buyer requires the currency of the nation from which the goods originated or some other currency that both buyer and seller agree to use. If the government wants to discourage the importation of goods, then it may place restrictions on the sale or purchase of foreign currency, known as **exchange control** – these restrictions may range from limiting the amount that any one person may buy to completely banning the sale of a specific currency.

- **Devaluation**: it is well established by now that countries need foreign exchange to trade in goods and services. Individuals can buy foreign currencies from the foreign-currency market. Here they will have to pay a certain amount of their local currency to buy another country's currency. Usually, the amount individuals pay for a unit of another country's currency is set by the market (demand and supply of these currencies determine their prices); this is called a floating exchange-rate regime. In other instances, however, the government may choose to legislate the price at which a currency is sold. If this happens, then a fixed exchange-rate regime exists and the government may change the price of a currency to make it more or less attractive. If the government devalues its currency, then it takes more units of local currency to buy one unit of foreign currency. Conversely, foreigners now find that the country's currency is cheaper. This **devaluation**, therefore, results in imports being expensive and exports being cheap. This drives demand for imported goods down but drives up demand for exported goods, resulting in a reversal of the balance-of-payments situation.

- **Borrowing from other countries**: this measure creates an inflow (which results in a surplus) in the capital account which is used to finance the deficit in the current account. Borrowing is not sustainable as it will create an outflow in later years in the form of interest payments.

- **Accepting gifts from other countries**: this is an unlikely and unsustainable approach to fixing a deficit as it depends on the largesse of others. However, it does result in a smaller outflow of funds and helps to address the deficit problem.

- **Importing on credit**: the country may choose to import on credit so as to create temporary relief for its deficit problems. Importing on credit shifts the outflow of funds associated with imports to a later date and maintains the deficit at its current level.

- **External assistance**: a country may receive balance-of-payment support from international agencies such as the International Monetary Fund (IMF) or the World Bank. We will talk about these organisations and such assistance in more detail in the next section.

 Now it's your turn

Outline the chain of events that would occur if a nation's currency were to appreciate in value.

 Now it's your turn

What is the main difference between the current account and the capital account?

Summary – Section A

- The standard of living that a country enjoys is a measure of the wealth that the country possesses and is indicated by such variables as average level of disposable income of the population, the extent to which the country has invested in capital equipment and the access to modern technology that citizens have.

- A country's quality of life describes the extent to which a country's potential to provide a suitable and adequate life for each of its citizens is realised. Quality of life is affected by variables such as the crime rate in the country, diet and nutrition and healthcare.

- National income is a measure of the output of a country over a given period, usually a year. National income is measured as gross domestic product (GDP) or as gross national product (GNP), with the former being a measure of how much income is produced in a country and the latter a measure of how much income is received by a country.

- GDP is measured as the sum of output of final goods (the output method) or as the sum of income received by those who produce and sell the goods (the income method) or as of the sum of money spent on purchasing all the goods produced in a country (the expenditure method).

- Net national income is an adjustment to calculate GNP to take into account the value of depreciation of assets over the period in consideration. Net national income is what is loosely referred to as national income (NI).

- A measure of how well a country's income can be shared among citizens in a nation is the per capita income, which is simply the country's national income divided by all those who make a claim on it – its population.

- National income and per capita income are ineffective measures of a country's quality of life because they do not measure sources of income such as the informal economy, and they ignore the value of leisure time and include economic 'bads' such as expenditure on hurricane repairs.

- While growth describes an increase in the size of the economy, development examines the nature and quality of the increase and describes an improvement in the quality of the economy. Growth can take place without development, as the benefits of growth may not be equally shared amongst the population.

- Human resources play an important part in the growth and development process. They lead the innovation process and contribute to the knowledge economy through the development of ideas.

- International trade takes place when countries practise international specialisation as a result of absolute and comparative advantage, geographic factors and a need to access modern goods that they may not be able to produce.

- The balance of payments is an account in which all transactions between a country and the rest of the world are recorded. It has two broad sections – a current account and a capital account, either one of which may record a greater outflow of funds than inflow and experience a deficit.

- The overall balance-of-payments account must have a balance of zero and this means that the deficit on one section of the account must be completely wiped out by the surplus on the other section.

- A country can address its balance-of-payments deficit by practising protectionism; monitoring, fixing or devaluing its exchange rate; or by borrowing from another country.

End of section activities

Quick questions

Are each of the following statements true or false? If the statement is false, explain why.

1 The higher a country's standard of living, the higher its quality of life will be.

2 Since GNP includes income from abroad and GDP does not, GNP is always more than GDP.

3 Adding up the value of all final goods describes what is done in order to find GDP using the output method.

4 When using the income method of calculating GDP, taxes must be added back to income received by workers.

5 When calculating GDP using the expenditure approach, exports are subtracted and imports added.

6 When finding a country's per capita income, we divide its national income by the number of its citizens who are working.

7 If two countries have equal per capita income, then they are at the same stage of development.

8 The term 'non-market activities' describes part-time work that is paid for, without the knowledge of the government.

9 When growth takes place, the economy may not develop because only a few people benefit from the increased income.

10 Economic development focuses on increases in the size of the economy and how the increase is used to benefit all citizens.

11 Human resources are not as important in driving development as technology because computers can do more work than people.

12 A country should not trade if it can produce all goods better than its trading partners.

13 Trade in capital assets such as machines and equipment should be included under the capital account section of the balance-of-payments account.

14 A balance-of-payments deficit means that either the capital account or the current account or both accounts are in deficit.

15 If the balance of trade is a surplus, then this means that the current account will also have a surplus.

16 A devaluation of a country's currency makes imports cheap and exports expensive.

Applying what you have learnt

1 Some people think that population size affects the standard of living. Do you think this is so? Should large populations have lower or higher standards of living? Some people argue that each individual has two hands but one mouth and hence can produce twice as much as he can eat. Do you think arguments like this are valid?

2 Many governments face challenges in trying to estimate the size of the informal economy.

   a Why is it so hard to estimate the size of the informal economy?

   b Make a list of some the activities that take place in the informal economy in your country.

   c Estimate how much money you think is made each year by someone who works in any aspect of the informal economy.

   d About how much money in taxes does the government lose from this one person's activities in the informal economy?

   e Why may indirect taxes solve this problem of collecting taxes from people in the informal economy?

   f How can the government try to capture information about the informal economy?

3 If the balance-of-payments account is always equal to zero and balances, how can a country have a balance-of-payments deficit or surplus?

Model exam questions
Question 1

   a Explain the main difference between a country's standard of living and its quality of life.   (3 marks)

   b Give two possible reasons why a country's standard of living may be high but its quality of life very low.
   (6 marks)

   c Discuss two steps that the government can take to improve the quality of life for all citizens in a country.
   (6 marks)

Question 2

   a Explain how a country's gross domestic product (GDP) is different from its gross national product (GNP).   (3 marks)

   b Outline the main elements of calculating GDP by either **one** of the following methods:

   i income method

   ii expenditure method.   (6 marks)

   c Discuss two steps the government may take to increase the country's GDP.   (6 marks)

Question 3

   a Explain how economic growth and economic development are different.   (3 marks)

   b Economic growth can occur without economic development. Give two reasons why this is so.
   (6 marks)

   c Outline two steps that the government can take to ensure that economic growth results in economic development.   (6 marks)

Question 4

   a How is a country's balance of trade different from its balance of payments?   (4 marks)

   b Outline one consequence of having a current-account deficit.   (3 marks)

   c Discuss how each of the following may actually make a country's current-account deficit worse:

   i its goods become less competitive on the world market

   ii a hurricane destroys all crops and ground provisions.   (6 marks)

As a region, the Caribbean has a number of institutions that offer support services of one kind or another. The Caribbean is made up primarily of small developing countries, which have had to depend on the strength that lies in number and in unity. As a result, Caribbean islands have become members of various organisations such as the World Bank, or have formed organisations of their own (such as CARICOM). As globalisation deepens, countries have had to integrate their economies to a greater extent and this has led to the creation of new institutions, such as the Caribbean Single Market and Economy (CSME) and the Free Trade Areas Americas (FTAA). Some of the major economic institutions operating in the Caribbean are described below.

Caribbean Community (CARICOM)

CARICOM has a regional forum each year at which the head of state for each member is present.

CARICOM is a Caribbean-based institution, formed in 1973, that is best known for promoting integration and trade among its 15 members. The organisation also has the following goals:

- To foster the development of less-developed countries in the Caribbean by ensuring that the benefits of integration are shared equitably.
- To harmonise the foreign policy of Caribbean territories by presenting a united front to the rest of the world.
- To negotiate with the rest of the world in matters of trade and commerce.

As a Caribbean-based organisation, CARICOM has institutions that cater to the needs of its member states. Perhaps the most popular of these institutions is the Caribbean Examination Council (CXC®), which is responsible for designing and administering assessment instruments that are used as certification of competence at the secondary level and as matriculation for tertiary education. There are 20 institutions in total that are operated by CARICOM, the Caribbean Agriculture Research and Development Institute (CARDI) and Caribbean Food and Nutrition Institute (CFNI) being two that are also easily recognised. Institutions such as the University of the West Indies (UWI) and the Caribbean Development Bank (CDB) are called associate institutions since they were not created by CARICOM.

A major part of the operation of CARICOM is the creation and use of a common external tariff (CET). A CET is a tariff that is applied by all members at the same rate to all goods being imported into the markets of the member countries. Since the tariff is the same rate in all countries, an importer will find that no one economy is more attractive than another on the basis of tariffs and, by doing this, CARICOM levels the playing field. If one member country decides to charge a tariff that is less than that being charged by other members, then it stands to gain and this would violate the treaty agreement. In situations where a country finds that an imported good is not being produced within CARICOM (whether by that country or any other member country), it may apply to have the CET waived. Indeed, in 2008, the Heads of Government meeting in The Bahamas agreed to suspend the CET for a certain category of goods for two years in order to reduce the cost of living for citizens in member countries.

Caribbean Single Market and Economy (CSME)

The CSME is a deepening of the integration process that was started by CARICOM. The essential difference between the CSME and CARICOM is the full integration of the economies of the member countries of CARICOM. Under the CSME, citizens, goods and services of member countries of CARICOM are able to move freely throughout CARICOM countries without barriers such as tariffs. The CSME is a vision of the Caribbean (at least those countries that are members of CARICOM) as one single economic space – in the same way as you are free to set up a business, seek employment, travel or sell goods in any part of your country, under the CSME, citizens of member countries will be able to travel to, work and study in and trade with other member countries without restrictions.

The CSME has two important elements – a single market and a single economy. A single market is a unification of the markets of many countries, which allows the free movement of goods and services within that merged market. A single economy, like a single market, is also a unification but on a greater scale. In a single economy, many independent territories or countries unify their economies, thus creating a single economic space spread out over many countries. The CSME, therefore, is both a single market as well as a single economy and hence is a relationship among member countries that is much more integrated than CARICOM is. For example, under the CSME, citizens of member countries will be able to transfer money to another country through cash (notes and coins), cheques and electronic transfers without first seeking permission and without any restrictions. Additionally, they will be able to buy shares in any company in any country and will benefit from a common interest rate across all member countries.

The essential element of the CSME is the free movement of productive resources and final goods throughout member countries. 'Free movement' applies to:

- **Capital**: citizens of member countries may move money and investments across member countries without restrictions.

- **Services**: service providers may offer their services, without restriction, to all citizens of member countries of the CSME.

- **Goods**: goods originating in CARICOM attract no import duties, tariffs or other trade restrictions as they are traded across member countries of the CSME.

- **People**: citizens of CSME countries are able to travel from one member country to another with the ease that one can travel within one's own country. University graduates, media workers, sports people, musicians, artists, managers, supervisors and other service providers will no longer need work permits before they can work in another member country, and they will enjoy the same rights, conditions and benefits of work as the citizens of that country.

Of the 15 members of CARICOM, all except The Bahamas have joined the CSME. These 14 countries are expected to benefit from the CSME through:

- the greater opportunity that citizens have to travel

- increased employment arising from the fact that citizens of each member state have a larger job market to which they can apply

- improved standards of living as member countries find a wider market for their products

- greater variety of competitive high-quality goods from which consumers can choose

- increased opportunities for nationals of member states to study and work in CARICOM countries.

Caribbean Development Bank (CDB)

The CDB is a financial institution for Caribbean countries. As a development bank, the CDB makes loans to its member countries for financing social and economic programmes with development as its underlying goal. The CDB was established in 1970 and currently has 27 members – 18 of which are from the Caribbean, with the remainder being from South America, Europe and Asia. Members are able to access loans at reduced interest rates and grants for the development of infrastructure and the provision of social services. The functions of the CDB are:

- to facilitate the development of less-developed countries in the Caribbean

- to create opportunities for countries to access financial resources needed for their economic growth and development

- to stabilise economies by providing financial support when needed

- to offer help and assistance in the event of emergencies such as earthquakes or hurricanes.

World Bank

In 1944, delegates from many countries in the world attended a conference at Bretton Woods to negotiate financial and trade matters. The conference led to the creation of five institutions – one of which was the World Bank. The World Bank is actually a group of two institutions – the International Bank for Reconstruction and Development (IBRD) and the International Development Association (IDA). These institutions are mandated to fight poverty by making low-cost loans to developing countries that may not otherwise be able to access funds. The IBRD makes loans to middle-income countries while the IDA offers loans to the world's poorest countries. IDA loans are interest-free and are for a long period of time. Bank loans are often accompanied by Structural Adjustment Policies (SAPs), which are strict conditions that the bank thinks will address inflation and excessive government spending. Borrowing countries must comply with these conditions before a loan can be granted and must maintain them in order to remain on the bank's borrowing list. SAPs usually include measures to stimulate home-based production, alter (in most cases lower) the exchange rate and reduce government spending. The bank has come under tremendous criticism as a result of the effects of these policies on the poor in borrowing countries.

Inter-American Development Bank (IADB)

The IADB, like the CDB, is a bank that has the economic and social development of its member countries as its main objective. Its borrowing members are drawn from Latin America and the Caribbean and it also has non-borrowing countries, which are usually highly developed European or other developed countries. The IADB makes loans to borrowing countries at commercial rates of interest – meaning that the interest charged on these loans is comparable to what would have been charged by regular commercial banks. The IADB has preferred creditor status, which means that its borrowers must repay the bank first, before their other creditors. The bank is financed in much the same way as the IBRD – from contributions made by its members and from its borrowing on the international capital market.

Organisation of Eastern Caribbean States (OECS)

The Eastern Caribbean is a group of islands that form an archipelago-like outline in the Lesser Antilles. Nine of these islands have come together to form the OECS, although two of these nine islands (Anguilla and British Virgin Islands) are only associate members. The OECS promotes the deep integration of the economies of its member countries and their smooth economic development and growth. As a part of this integration, except for the British Virgin Islands (which still use the British currency), the members of the OECS all use the Eastern Caribbean dollar and most are members of the Eastern Caribbean Central Bank (ECCB). As a part of the Caribbean, all members of the OECS are also members of CARICOM and it is expected that the OECS will be seamlessly merged into the CSME eventually.

 Now it's your turn

Why would a country that is already a part of CARICOM join the OECS? What benefits does one offer that the other does not?

Organization of American States (OAS)

The OAS is a hemispheric association of independent states in the Americas – made up of countries from North America (Alaska and Canada) down to South America and including the Caribbean. The focus of the OAS at its conception was to protect its member countries from aggression by external parties and to maintain peace among these member countries. While these have remained important goals, the economic and social development of its members is also an important goal of the OAS. Other goals of the OAS include:

- strengthening democracy
- promoting and defending human rights
- fostering free trade by the removal of tariffs
- implementing measures to prevent the trade in illegal drugs
- promoting sustainable development
- reducing poverty.

Economic Commission for Latin America and the Caribbean (ECLAC)

ECLAC is one of five regional organisations established in 1948 by the United Nations (UN). These five organisations are responsible for promoting the economic development of various regions – ECLAC being the one that has responsibility for Latin America and the Caribbean. Currently there are 44 member countries of ECLAC along with nine associate member countries. Members are all from Latin America and the Caribbean along with a few European and Asian countries and the United States who all have historical or economic interests in Latin America and the Caribbean. ECLAC is not a donor agency nor is it a bank that lends money. Rather, its focus is on co-ordinating the development of its member nations by collaborating with its member states and a variety of local, national and international institutions in evaluating best practices and policies. ECLAC, in many of these instances, also offers technical assistance and support, training and information services to its member countries. ECLAC also engages ministers and technical support officers of member countries in sessions that discuss important issues related to their economic and social development. These sessions are held every two years in even years (2010, 2012, 2014 and so on) and result in publications that are usually available free of cost.

Association of Caribbean States (ACS)

The ACS was formed to promote communication and co-operation among Caribbean countries. The ACS is concerned with two major goals – promoting the common interests of Caribbean nations and working to eliminate barriers from its colonial past. Most Caribbean countries are members and many European and Asian countries are observer states. The ACS is different from CARICOM in a few important ways – the ACS does not have any agreement on tariffs and it does not integrate economies of member countries as deeply as CARICOM does. The operations of the ACS are anchored in four major areas:

- **Trade**: the organisation makes an effort to promote trade through forums and economic co-operation. These actions are co-ordinated by the Special Committee on Trade Development and External Economic Relations.

- **Transport**: the Special Committee on Transport works to secure airborne passengers and minimise airborne crimes such as drug trafficking and kidnapping.

- **Tourism**: the Special Committee on Sustainable Tourism encourages tourism that is environmentally friendly and also profitable to the region.

- **Natural disasters**: the ACS has a Special Committee on Natural Disasters that helps countries cope with and respond to natural disasters.

European Union (EU)

In a sense, the EU is to Europe what CARICOM is to the Caribbean. The European Union is an economic and political union of 27 European countries. As an economic union, the EU has a single economy which allows for the free movement of goods, services, capital and people among member countries. Member countries also have common policies on trade and the use of natural resources, regulating such activities as fishing, forestry and agricultural output. In addition, 16 of the 27 member countries have embraced the monetary union by adopting a common currency called the euro.

The EU is important to the Caribbean because it is one of the major institutions responsible for making a large portion of the donations that the region receives. The EU makes donations to developing countries through the European Commission's Humanitarian Aid Office (ECHO). African, Caribbean and Pacific countries (ACP) are major recipients of this aid, receiving as much as 48 per cent of all aid in 2006 and the Caribbean has received a total of approximately US$169 billion since 1995. In 2003, for example, the EU assisted the population of Dominican Republic when the country was affected by floods; in 2004, it assisted Jamaica and Grenada who were both affected by Hurricane Ivan. Recently, in 2010, following the earthquake, the EU pledged US$1.73 billion in aid to Haiti over a three-year period.

World Trade Organization

The World Trade Organization (WTO) is an organisation that is responsible for supervising and liberalising international trade. It has a system of rules that provides a framework for members when they negotiate or have disputes. These rules are developed through a set of meetings among member countries that create proposals that these countries ratify. These meetings are called 'rounds' – the Uruguay Round took place between 1986 and 1994 and the Doha Round is currently being negotiated. The WTO has rules that govern trade in goods, intellectual property and services. It also has general principles that govern such concerns as trade and the environment, trade and development, regional trade agreements (such as CARICOM), balance-of-trade restrictions and trade and technology transfer.

The primary concern of the WTO is to ensure that no one country benefits from trade at the expense of the others. Against this background, preferential trade agreements – those that give some countries increased or privileged access to an overseas market – are seen as discriminatory and are not allowed by the WTO. It is in this area that the WTO's operations have most often affected the Caribbean, which had preferential trade agreements with the United Kingdom in the trade of agricultural products such as bananas and historically significant products such as sugar. These agreements were born out of the heritage of slavery in the Caribbean but have all been overturned or significantly reduced by the WTO.

Caribbean Basin Initiative (CBI)

The CBI is a set of trade initiatives initiated by the United States in 1983 and expanded in 2000 that provide Caribbean Basin economies with duty-free and preferential access to US markets. The CBI is expected to be taken over by the proposed Free Trade Area of the Americas (FTAA), a proposed hemispheric free-trade agreement among all the countries in North, Central and South America along with the Caribbean.

North American Free Trade Agreement (NAFTA)

NAFTA is an agreement that exists between the United States, Canada and Mexico that led to the creation of a trade bloc in North America and the elimination of trade barriers among these countries. Citizens in NAFTA countries are allowed to temporarily live and work in any of the three countries that make up NAFTA once permission is sought and granted. Given that the United States and Canada are highly developed countries, it is usually Mexicans that take up this opportunity to work in Canada or the United States. The result is that the United States and, to a lesser extent, Canada have a constant supply of cheap labour from Mexico. This has caused a reduction in the demand for such workers from the Caribbean.

Caribbean Canadian Agreement (CARIBCAN)

CARIBCAN is a programme initiated by the Canadian government to provide countries in the Commonwealth Caribbean with preferential access to Canadian markets. The agreement is aimed at promoting trade, investment and co-operation between the Caribbean and Canada. Like many other regional agreements or initiatives, CARIBCAN will become a part of the FTAA when it starts up.

Organization of Petroleum Exporting Countries (OPEC)

OPEC is a cartel formed by the countries that are responsible for supplying the world with petroleum. As a cartel, it determines the quantity of oil that is available on the world market and thus exerts great influence over the price at which oil is sold. Although no Caribbean country is a member of OPEC, it remains an important organisation in the Caribbean as its decisions have grave implications for the region's balance of trade.

 Now it's your turn

Copy the table below into your exercise book. Carry out some research on the internet to determine which organisations each country is a member of. Which organisation has the greatest number of members? Which one has the least?

Country	CARICOM	CSME	CDB	IADB	OECS	OAS	CBI
Trinidad and Tobago							
Barbados							
Guyana							
Jamaica							
St. Lucia							
St. Vincent and the Grenadines							
Grenada							
Antigua and Barbuda							
St. Kitts and Nevis							
The Bahamas							
Belize							
Cuba							
Haiti							
Dominica							
Montserrat							

Eastern Caribbean Common Market (ECCM)

The ECCM is a common-market agreement that exists among the countries of the Eastern Caribbean. Its members include Dominica, Grenada, Montserrat, St. Lucia, St. Kitts and Nevis and Antigua and Barbuda. As a common market, there is free trade among members as well as free markets in each of the factors of production in each member country.

Free Trade Area of the Americas (FTAA)

The FTAA is an extension of NAFTA and is a proposal to remove barriers to trade among all countries in the Americas. Given Cuba's ideological differences with the United States and the resultant embargo, it is not expected that it will be included. This proposal would create a hemispheric free-trade area, which has implications for the Caribbean. In the first instance, it is expected that countries in the Caribbean will have access to a larger market in which to sell their products. It also means, however, that Caribbean producers will find that both their local and foreign markets will become more competitive as trade restrictions are lifted.

Economic problems in the Caribbean

The Caribbean is made up of a group of middle- and low-income countries, beset by a number of social and economic problems. From the high rates of crime in many countries to the low level of economic development, each country in the Caribbean has challenges that it must overcome. Some of these challenges are outlined below.

Unemployment

People who are out of work but are interested in working or are looking for a job are said to be unemployed. Not all people who are not working, therefore, are said to be unemployed – a person must be actively seeking a job (by checking the classifieds, searching for jobs or making applications) before they are considered unemployed. In some countries, economists and statisticians who measure the **unemployment** rate may even specify that the person must have actively sought a job in the last four weeks before they are considered unemployed. Over time, as people are unable to find a job and remain unemployed, their spirits are broken and they become disenchanted and stop actively searching for a job. The official rate of unemployment in a country is, therefore, a bit misleading as it does not include these people.

Unemployment, though tricky to define, is a major problem in the Caribbean.

 Now it's your turn

Consider the following cases and say whether the person described is unemployed or not (using the economists' definition). In each case, give a reason for your answer.

1 John, who is in his third year of university, is on summer holiday and is now looking for a summer job.

2 Timz, who used to work as a teacher, was made redundant seven months ago. He has decided to take a little time to 'cool off' before he starts hunting again.

3 Kerrina has been offered a position as a secretary in a company that will open six months from today. She is waiting for that to start but for now is just relaxing at home.

4 Una is a dressmaker who has not received an order for a job in the past five months. She has used that time to make adjustments to the design of her house.

5 Jacko is 19 and graduated from high school two years ago. He spends most of his time hanging out with friends and every now and then he may stumble across a quick way to make a few dollars.

6 Grace dreams of starting her own business making and selling furniture. She is now writing a business plan to take to the bank in order to get a loan to start the business.

Some Caribbean countries have high rates of unemployment and there are many possible reasons for this:

- **Real-wage unemployment**: real-wage unemployment occurs when wages are too high and, as a result, the supply of workers outstrips the demand for such workers.

- **Frictional unemployment**: frictional unemployment results from the job market not matching job seekers with available jobs quickly enough. This type of unemployment occurs when the labour market is inefficient at advertising available jobs and sourcing workers to fill them.

- **Seasonal unemployment**: some industries may find that demand for their products decreases at certain times of the year, leading to seasonal unemployment. Tourism and farming are good examples of seasonal industries.

- **Structural unemployment**: structural unemployment occurs when there are long-term changes in the fundamental structure of an economy, creating dislocation of workers. For example, as many Caribbean islands move from simple, agrarian economies to more service-based economies, workers in the agricultural industries have been left without jobs.

- **Technological unemployment**: technological unemployment is really a form of structural unemployment that occurs when new technologies are used to replace or reduce the need for workers.

- **Cyclical (or demand deficient) unemployment**: the economy will go through periods of boom (growth and high levels of production) and bust (a decline in output or a contraction in the economy). During periods of bust, it is expected that unemployment will be high, and this is known as cyclical unemployment.

☞ Now it's your turn

Outline which type of unemployment has occurred in each of the following situations:

1 Clem used to work in a factory that made portable CD and cassette players. He lost his job as a technician when the popularity of MP3 music resulted in the closure of the factory.

2 Susan is currently at home because the dressmaker that she assists has no orders for new jobs. She expects that when parents start needing uniforms for their children going back to school she will have some work again.

3 The trade union of which Keith was a member negotiated high wages that Keith's employer could not afford. They then had to make Keith redundant.

4 Kevin graduated from university three months ago and has been applying for jobs since then.

5 Shieka is a chemist who used to work at a paint factory but lost her job when the factory was converted to a villa. The government has encouraged the development of the tourism industry and some factories have simply done some remodelling and converted their buildings to villas.

Unemployment has the following effects on Caribbean countries:

- **Loss of output**: a reduction in employment directly leads to a reduction in the level of output that the economy can produce. Additionally, people who are unemployed are not able to demand as many goods and services as before and this creates a further reduction in the economy's level of output and perhaps even more unemployment.

- **Loss of human capital**: prolonged periods of unemployment may result in the unemployed losing their skills or their desire to work.

- **Inequalities in the distribution of income**: unemployment creates a lower class consisting mostly of the poor. The income of the unemployed is far less than that of the employed and hence as one groups becomes richer, the other becomes poorer.

- **Social costs**: unemployment is likely to lead to social problems such as crime.

- **Greater pressure on the state**: when the unemployment rate is very high, the state must help to support the unemployed through welfare payments such as unemployment insurance.

Population density

Population density is a measure of the extent of over- or under-population of a country or area. It is measured as the number of people living in a square mile or square kilometre. If this number is very large, then it means that the area is overpopulated, while a small number represents an equally challenging situation of under-population.

In the Caribbean, population density is slightly higher than in many other more developed countries, suggesting that Caribbean countries have a less than optimal population density. It is difficult to prescribe an ideal population density as a number of factors must be considered. In particular, how many people live in each square kilometre is perhaps as important as how accessible and hospitable the land space in a country is. Guyana, for example, has a population density of four people per square kilometre, primarily because most of its land space is inaccessible and inhospitable. It is likely that even though its population density is very low, overpopulation takes place in areas where citizens are able to settle.

Overpopulation results in pressure being placed on the nation's natural and financial resources as citizens struggle to find and make a place in an economy or a society that cannot absorb them. Additionally, overpopulation is more of a problem for urban centres and, indeed, it is likely that even in countries that are not overpopulated, urban centres and towns are bursting at the seams as rural–urban drift takes hold. Underpopulation, on the other hand, brings its own set of challenges. Under-population stifles the growth of local industries as demand is likely to be low; in addition, it may affect the labour supply and the competitiveness of businesses.

Think about it

Which one do you think population density affects more – economic growth or development? China is perhaps the most populated country and by all standards is overpopulated, yet its economy has grown rapidly over the past few years. Would you rather live in a rich country that is overpopulated (like China) or a less developed one that has just the right number of citizens (like Guyana)?

Debt burden

The Caribbean's debt burden arises from the fact that Caribbean governments have had to borrow extensively in order to balance their budgets. A country's budget is said to be balanced when government spending is exactly equal to the revenue that it gets through taxation. A fiscal deficit exists when the government spends more than it collects, while a fiscal surplus is the opposite (the government collects more than it spends). When a deficit occurs, the government must borrow to make up the shortfall. This debt is usually to be repaid over a long period and every year some of the nation's revenues must go towards servicing this debt. This yearly amount that is taken out of the nation's revenue is called the debt burden and, in many countries, as much as 60 cents of every dollar collected as taxes must be used to address the debt burden. Guyana, for example, is considered the most indebted Caribbean country and, in 2006, its debt was 183 per cent of GDP, which was reduced to 120 per cent of GDP in 2007 after the IADB cancelled US$470 million of its outstanding debt.

A high debt burden has the following effects on a country:

- **Fiscal austerity**: if the debt burden is high, then the country must dedicate a huge chunk of its yearly budget to servicing this debt. This results in less money being available for social services such as health and education, for paying public-sector workers and investing in infrastructure. This is likely to harm a country's development.

- **Lack of flexibility**: a high debt burden removes the ability the government has to address emergencies such as damage and destruction caused by natural disasters. The country's debt is usually serviced before all other items; once this has happened, it is unlikely that much money will be left over.

- **High interest rates**: when the government has a huge appetite for debt, then its demand for funds drives up interest rates and pushes investors out of the market for loans.

Economic dualism

Economic dualism is a situation where two distinct economies exist in a country, at different levels of development and sophistication. One economy is usually characterised by modern technology, capital-intensive modes of production and highly trained workers. The other economy, however, is usually simple, is based on primary production and involves very little capital investment and technology. The average level of income in each economy is very different and this usually leads to inequities in the income distribution within the country. Economic dualism is created or sustained by how the government of a country chooses to develop industries – some industries are seen as important for national development and are likely to receive more assistance from the government than others which are not perceived in the same way. Tourism in the Caribbean, for example, has usually been one of the key industries that the government supports and develops and this usually comes at the expense of other industries such as agriculture or manufacturing.

 Now it's your turn

Make a list of the industries in your country (some common examples are listed below, to help you get started). Sort the industries into two lists – 'advanced' and 'less advanced'.

- baking
- new and used cars
- clothing and textiles
- retailing
- agricultural
- food processing
- car repairs and servicing
- hotels and tourism

Solutions to economic problems

Foreign Direct Investment (FDI): this describes investment in a country of a long-term nature made by businesses located in another country. FDI is usually more than foreigners simply owning businesses in a country; in other words, not all instances of multinational investments are really FDI. FDI usually involves a greater level of commitment on the part of the investor – transfer of technology, skills and knowledge is usually a major part of the FDI. In addition, the extent to which profits will be ploughed back into the country is very high as the foreigner makes an attempt to secure the country's goodwill. FDI is useful to Caribbean governments since:

- it generates employment within the region
- it modernises an economy by introducing developed quality goods and services
- it usually provides workers with higher than average incomes
- as cash-rich companies, the businesses involved participate in the development of the region by investing in sports and the arts.

Human resources development: perhaps the most effective way of solving the region's unemployment problems is by developing its human resources. This makes workers more employable and more likely to create employment opportunities for themselves. This has implications for economic problems such as unemployment, economic dualism and migration. Governments can develop their country's human resources by expanding the opportunities that citizens have to access tertiary education. Providing student loans or increasing spaces available are effective ways in which this could be done. In addition, taking steps to improve the quality of the secondary system ensures that more students graduate and are able to attend university.

Development of the manufacturing sector: the manufacturing sector forms a necessary link between the primary and the tertiary sector. In many Caribbean countries, there is an over-reliance on primary products and industries, which have experienced reduced demand on the world market. The result is that industries involved in primary production have recorded high levels of unemployment and low levels of income. This problem can be solved by ensuring that a vibrant manufacturing industry exists in the country, which will be able to take primary products and produce secondary products. This would require a greater degree of linkages within the economy and would result in increased employment and investments. There are a number of initiatives that a government may implement in order to improve a country's manufacturing industry:

- Promote linkage industries by offering special incentives (such as low-interest loans) to businesses interested in key strategic areas.
- Encourage a climate of low interest rates so that entrepreneurs may be more inclined to access loans for investments. The government may do this by reducing its borrowing on the local market. When

the government borrows on the local market, it competes with investors for the loans that the local financial sector provides and drives up interest rates. This is called the crowding-out effect.

- Provide tax breaks or tax holidays for investors wishing to enter certain industries.

- Offer special and technical support (in the form of training, incubators, chambers of commerce and centres of excellence) to young entrepreneurs.

- Subsidise the output of locally produced manufactured products.

Summary – Section B

- Countries in the Caribbean are small and do not wield much power relative to other large, rich developed countries such as the United States. Joining international and regional institutions is one way these countries have of bolstering their position in world affairs.

- There are a number of regional organisations and agreements which Caribbean countries are a part of. These organisations and agreements, which include CARICOM, ACS, OECS and OAS, are designed to foster closer economic and political relationships among Caribbean countries.

- There are also a number of international organisations that Caribbean countries are involved with. These organisations, which include the World Bank, the WTO and the EU, offer loans and technical support to Caribbean nations and create the legal framework in which nations operate.

- As globalisation deepens, countries in the Caribbean are venturing into relationships that involve more economic and political integration than before. The CSME and the FTAA are two examples of such close unions that are likely to come on stream soon.

- The Caribbean faces a number of economic problems, including unemployment, migration and economic dualism. These problems affect the region's efforts at development.

- These problems can be solved by encouraging FDI, developing the region's human resources and diversifying into and strengthening the region's manufacturing sector.

End of section activities

Quick questions

Identify which economic institution is described by each of the following clues. If the clue describes more than one institution, then include both.

1 A bank that offers loans to countries who cannot get such loans elsewhere.

2 An agency that does not offer loans or grants but offers technical assistance in order to develop member countries.

3 A Caribbean institution with a common external tariff.

4 A proposal to increase the level of free trade in the Western hemisphere.

5 An organisation that sets and enforces the rules regarding how countries trade with each other.

6 An organisation that tries to promote the common interests that Caribbean nations have.

7 An agreement that allows Caribbean countries to access American markets under preferential arrangements.

8 A bank that offers loans to countries at the market rate of interest.

9 An economic union in the Caribbean with a common currency.

10 One of the few examples of economic and political union in the world.

11 Member countries are able to buy company shares in any member country.

12 A Caribbean-based institution that offers low-cost loans.

Applying what you have learnt

1 Go online and research what is meant by 'globalisation'. Do you think that it is a threat to Caribbean countries? Why or why not? How can being a member of various regional and international economic institutions help a country realise the benefits or minimise the threats of globalisation?

2 John Donne, an English clergyman and poet, once said 'No man is an island.' Others have now modified that to: 'No island is an island.' What does this mean? When the FTAA becomes effective, Cuba will be the only country in all of the Americas that will not be a part of it. How do you think this will affect Cuba?

3 The CSME proposes that citizens of any member country can live and work in any other member country. Do you think you would want to move to another CARICOM country to work? If so, which one? Which CARICOM countries do you think will attract many residents from other countries? Which one do you think will not attract as many? Do you think that the CSME may result in uneven development among member countries?

4 Imagine that you are the prime minister of a country that has **one** of the following problems:
- unemployment
- migration
- economic dualism
- debt burden.

As prime minister, explain how you would use each of the following elements to address any one of the problems above.
- interest rate
- taxation
- exchange rate
- government spending
- laws

Model exam questions
Question 1
a List any three international or regional organisations of which your country is a member. (3 marks)
b List two roles played by one of the organisations listed in (a). (4 marks)
c Explain two ways in which any one of the organisations listed above aids in the development of your country. (6 marks)

Question 2
a List any three economic problems that your country experiences. (3 marks)
b Outline one cause of any problem listed in (a). (3 marks)
c Discuss one negative effect that the problem focused on in (b) has had on your country's economy. (3 marks)
d Outline two measures the government may take to address the problem focused on in (b) and (c). (6 marks)

11 School-based assessment and optional paper

School-based assessment (SBA)

Overview and guidelines

The SBA is a project that is done before CXC®-administered CSEC® exams and which contributes a maximum of 40 per cent of the overall marks that a student scores in the subject. The project is research based and requires that you submit a business plan on one of the three important areas in profile dimension 2:

- production
- marketing
- finance.

In other words, you will have to think of a business idea and create a business plan for one aspect of the business – either how its production and operations will be organised, or how its marketing function will be controlled and structured or, finally, how it will be financed.

The activity around which the business plan is designed must be a legal activity and must lend itself to research and application of the principles encountered in the course (the detailed mark schemes, below, in Tables 11.1–11.3 give an idea of exactly which principles are needed for each aspect of the plan). The report should be between 1000 and 1200 words in length (excluding appendices) and should be submitted in a soft folder or file jacket. Teachers are able to deduct marks from your work if you do not comply with the project length, so make sure you plan and manage your project carefully.

You are allowed to work in a group or as an individual, so discuss with your teacher the approach you think you would be more comfortable with.

Grading of the SBA

While the entire project is marked out of 40, the criteria used for assigning marks will be different and depend on which area of the business plan you pursue – a detailed mark scheme for each aspect of the plan is shown below in Tables 11.1–11.3. Regardless of the aspect of the plan on which you choose to focus, the 40 marks are distributed across the three profile dimensions (PI–P3) of the syllabus as follows:

- organisational principles (P1)   (10 marks)
- production, marketing and finance (P2)   (20 marks)
- the business environment (P3)   (10 marks)

In this book, Chapters 1–5 contain the topics that make up profile 1; these topics include contracts, insurance, economic system, forms of business, communication, functions of management and organisational charts. Profile 2 is covered by Chapters 6–9 and includes topics such as production, marketing, finance and demand and supply. Finally, Chapter 10 addresses profile 3, which considers concepts such as international trade, regulations and ethics.

If you choose to focus on the **production aspect** of the business plan, then your work will be marked as follows (Table 11.1):

Criteria	P1	P2	P3	Total
Description of the business	2			2
Justification of location		4		4
Selection of appropriate labour		4		4
Sources of fixed and working capital		4		4
Role of the entrepreneur	4			4
Type of production		2		2
Levels of production		2		2
Quality-control measures		2		2
Use of technology	2			2
Linkages		2		2
Potential for growth	2		2	4
Government regulations			2	2
Ethical issues			2	2
Communication of information in a logical way, using correct grammar			4	4
Total	**10**	**20**	**10**	**40**

Table 11.1 Mark scheme for Establishing a Business: Production.

If instead you decide to explore the **marketing aspect** of a business plan, then your work will be assessed as follows (Table 11.2):

Criteria	P1	P2	P3	Total
Description of the business	2			2
Organisation of the marketing department	4			4
Market research:				
Target population (qualitative and quantitative)				
Price				
Competitors				
Substitutes				
Sales forecast		6		6
Product (branding and packaging)		4		4
Pricing		2		2
Place (distribution channels)		4		4
Promotion mix		4		4
Government regulations			2	2
Use of technology	4			4
Consumer complaints			2	2
Ethical issues			2	2
Communication of information in a logical way, using correct grammar			4	4
Total	**10**	**20**	**10**	**40**

Table 11.2 Mark scheme for Establishing a Business: Marketing.

Finally, if you choose to research the **finance aspect** of the business plan, then the following mark scheme will be applied (Table 11.3):

Criteria	P1	P2	P3	Total
Description of the business	2			2
Purposes for which finance is needed (operating expenses)		4		4
Organisational chart (selection of appropriate labour)	4			4
Cost of producing goods (prime and overhead expenses)		3		3
Capital goods		3		3
Sources of finance (including government subsidies and grant)			2	2
Collateral (guarantor, cosignatory)	2			2
Capital instruments (equity: shares; debt: loans)		4		4
Implication of capital mix selected		2		2
Projected performance* (revenue, costs)		4		4
Use of technology (for payments, receipts, payroll and so on)	2			2
Government regulations			2	2
Ethical issues			2	2
Communication of information in a logical way, using correct grammar			4	4
Total	**10**	**20**	**10**	**40**

* Students should include simple balance sheets comprising assets, liabilities and capital.

Table 11.3 Mark scheme for Establishing a Business: Finance.

Draft model SBA

What follows is a point-by-point suggested outline of the SBA for each aspect of the business plan. Feel free to deviate from it in areas that are specific to the business that you are thinking of proposing. However, make every attempt to cover the essential areas. For the sake of the presentation here, we will assume that we are proposing to start a bakery, called Sweet Tooth Pastry. We will use this proposed business to show you how to construct the business plan for each aspect of the business (production, marketing and finance).

Option 1 – establishing a business: production

You will have to gather information using both primary and secondary sources. Secondary sources include:

The internet

- use a search engine to research the baking process, technology and labour required
- visit government websites to research regulations that affect the baking industry

- visit the websites to gather information about the conditions governing loan acquisition
- use search engines to identify assistance that the government offers to the baking industry.

Brochures and catalogues:

- Established bakeries may have catalogues and brochures about their operation and their available products; these can act as inspiration for how to design your own bakery
- Banks and other sources of finance will have brochures that outline the various financing options that they offer.

Primary sources of information include:

Site visits:

- visit bakeries to observe their operations
- actually purchase products or access other services offered by a bakery to get a 'feel' of how the service is delivered
- visit schools, restaurants and so on to see whether they have a need for products that you are likely to supply.

Surveys and interviews:

- Conduct questionnaire-based research to determine the answers to the following questions:

  - What products do people want from a bakery?

  - Are people interested in dining in or taking out their purchases?

  - What other services could you offer to enhance your competitiveness?

  - What time of the day, day of the week or month of the year do people usually buy their pastries? (This affects your opening hours and how you structure your operations.)

Conduct interviews of managers or workers in bakeries to determine:

- how supply of raw material is organised
- ideal locations for bakeries
- how quality is controlled.

The project could contain the following distinct sections, which you may choose to organise into chapters:

Chapter 1 – introduction and overview

- **Rationale for choice of business**: why was this business type chosen? Are other bakeries doing well in the area? Is there a business opportunity as a result of the absence of a good bakery in the area? Is there a recognised baker whose products could be used to draw customers to the shop or who could join the staff? From research that you have done, what are the views of prospective customers on the establishment of a bakery in the area?

- **Description of the business**: what is the name of the business? What products and services would it offer? How will it be operated – will there be seating areas for customers to sit and enjoy pastries? Will it be take-out only? Will people be able to host birthday parties for children at the bakery? What are its opening hours?

Chapter 2 – factors of production

- **Raw material required**: what raw material will be needed to produce the bakery's products? How will you procure the raw material – locally or through imports? Are raw materials scarce? Are they controlled by a single monopoly? Are they seasonal?

- **Labour required**: how many certified trained bakers do you need to run the kitchen? How many people would you need for support staff in the kitchen? What about administrative workers?

- **Capital investment**: how would you obtain fixed and working capital? Do you have any of your own?

- **Role of the entrepreneur**: what role would they play in running the business? What functions would they perform in the business? Would they be a part of the staff complement in any aspect of the business? Would they become a owner/manager and, if so, how would they effect this role? Would they merely provide the investment and take ownership of the idea?

Chapter 3 – organisation of the factors of production

- **Type and level of production**: what area of production does the business fall in – primary, secondary, tertiary? What about the level of production? Is it subsistence, domestic or export?

- **Location analysis**: where will the business be located? Will it be close to suppliers or close to customers/consumers? Why was the location chosen? Are there advantages that the business enjoys as a result of its location?

- **Use of technology**: what technology will be needed in the production process? Will labour be used instead of technology? Will mass production take place and how will this be facilitated? Will pastries be made to order (custom made) or mass produced? How does this affect the type of technology that is used?

- **Quality control**: how will quality be ensured in the supply of raw materials? Will raw materials be supplied on a daily basis? How will you ensure that the pastry remains fresh? How will you ensure quality during the production process? Will random sampling be carried out? Will products be standardised through the use of technology?

Chapter 4 – operating environment

- **Growth of the business**: what opportunities exist for the growth of the business? Is the market large enough to support the expansion of the business? With what businesses does the bakery have backward or forward linkages? Is there room for growth by exploiting these linkages or creating new ones?

- **Government regulations**: what laws exist that govern the operation of bakeries? Do you need a licence, a food handler's permit or a health inspector's certificate in order to operate? What rules govern packaging information to which consumers must have access?

- **Ethical issues**: how do you ensure that whatever claims you make through advertising are consistent with the production process or with the product?

Appendices

- Use this section to include such details and samples of any primary research you had to do to gather data to construct your business plan.

- Any piece of supporting important information gathered from the primary or secondary information may also be included here, provided you had referred to it in the body of the work in Chapters 1–4.

- Graphs, charts and tables used to support claims made may also be included here.

Option 2 – establishing a business: marketing

For this business plan, you will need primary and secondary sources of information as well.

Secondary sources
The internet

- Visit government websites to research regulations that affect the baking industry and advertising and promotion.

- Visit the websites of competitors to see what products and services they offer and at what price.

Brochures or catalogues

- Use brochures or catalogues of established bakeries to determine the prices at which they sell their products.

Primary sources of information include:
Site visits

- Visit competing bakeries to determine the products that they offer and the prices at which they sell these products.

- Visit schools, restaurants and so on to see whether they have a need for products that you are likely to supply.

Surveys

- Conduct questionnaire-based research to determine the answers to the following questions:
- Who normally makes decisions regarding purchases at bakery – parents or children?
- What products do people want from a bakery?
- What time of the day, day of the week or month of the year do people usually buy pastries?
- What other products do people who buy pastries buy?
- What do people who do not buy pastries consume as a snack?
- How many slices of cake, pastries or loaves do people consume on a daily/weekly basis?
- How many hours of TV do consumers usually watch? Do they listen to the radio? Read the newspaper? If yes, which radio stations and which newspapers? How will they access advertising messages?
- How much are consumers prepared to spend on pastries?
- Are they sensitive to price increases?
- Are they sensitive to changes in income?

The information you collect can be used to organise your plan into the following sections or chapters:

Chapter 1 – introduction and overview

- **Rationale for choice of business**: why was this business type chosen? Are other bakeries doing well in the area? Is there a business opportunity as a result of the absence of a good bakery in the area? Is there a recognised baker whose products could be used to draw customers to the shop or who could join the staff? From research that you have done, what are the views of prospective customers on the establishment of a bakery in the area?

- **Description of the business**: what is the name of the business? What products and services would it offer? How will it be operated – will there be seating areas for customers to sit and enjoy pastries? Will it be take-out only? Will people be able to host birthday parties for children at the bakery? What are its opening hours?

- **Organisation of the marketing department**: will there be a marketing manager or will the entrepreneur play this role? How many workers will be in the department? What functions will they play?

Chapter 2 – market research

- **Target group**: who will the business target? How many people are in this target group? What age group are they? What are their buying patterns? What is their average income? What factors influence their behaviour?

- **Price**: what is the average price at which pastry items can be sold? Are customers price sensitive?

- **Competitors**: are other bakeries servicing the market? What strengths and weaknesses do these competitors have?

- **Substitutes**: what products can consumers buy as light snacks instead of pastries, bread, cakes and so on? What are the prices of these substitutes? What unique selling point do the bakery's products have over other substitutes?

- **Sales forecast**: how many units do you expect will be sold per day? Per month? Per year? How does this translate into sales revenue on a monthly/yearly basis?

Chapter 3 – the marketing mix

- **Product**: how will the product be branded? How will its brand image be created and maintained? What decisions regarding packaging will be made?

- **Pricing**: what pricing approach will be used? How will pricing be used to complement the brand image of the product?

- **Place**: how will the product be distributed? Will the bakery have other outlets? Will it distribute its products directly to consumers or through a network of distributors?

- **Promotion mix**: will the products be advertised through mainstream electronic or print media?

Will the bakery be involved in public relations such as charity work (whether at the national or local level) or scholarship? Will the bakery be involved in promotions such as giveaways and sweepstakes?

Chapter 4 – operating environment

- **Government regulations**: what laws exist that govern marketing and advertising of baked products? Are there regulations that govern the administration of sweepstakes and promotions? What about other regulations that may affect the business's operations, such as its pricing strategy or packaging and labelling decisions?

- **Ethical issues**: how do you ensure that whatever claims you make through advertising are consistent with the production process or with the product?

Appendices

- Use this section to include such details and samples of any primary research you had to do to gather data to construct your business plan.

- Any piece of supporting important information gathered from the primary or secondary information may also be included here, provided you had referred to it in the body of the work in Chapters 1–4.

- Graphs, charts and tables used to support claims made may also be included here.

Option 3 – establishing a business: finance

Having collected information, you can write up your proposal using the following format:

Chapter 1 – introduction and overview

- **Rationale for choice of business**: why was this business type chosen? Are other bakeries doing well in the area? Is there a business opportunity as a result of the absence of a good bakery in the area? Is there a recognised baker whose products could be used to draw customers to the shop or who could join the staff? From research that you have done, what are the views of prospective customers on the establishment of a bakery in the area?

- **Description of the business**: what is the name of the business? What products and services would it offer? How will it be operated – how many workers will be needed? How will they be distributed within the organisation? (Provide an organisational chart.)

- **Use of technology**: what technology will be used in the running and operation of the bakery? Will the payroll system be computerised? Will computerised cashing or point-of-sale systems exist? How will customers be queued for serving – will manual or electronic systems be used?

Chapter 2 – revenues and costs

- **Purposes for which financing is needed**: what day-to-day recurring expenses will the business have? How much will it have to use to satisfy these expenses on a monthly/yearly basis?

- **Production cost**: what costs are associated with producing the product? What costs are specific and limited to the production of the product (prime costs)? What costs are considered overhead costs? Express these costs over units of time (month, quarters, years and so on).

- **Capital goods**: what capital goods will be needed for operations? How much will these cost?

- **Projected performance**: how well do you expect the business to do over the first two or three years? How much will it receive in total revenues? How much will it have to consider paying out in associated costs? Will the business make a profit, a loss or will it break even?

- **Financial statements**: prepare projected balance sheets showing assets, capital and liabilities at each year end; if possible, prepare other statements such as trading and profit and loss accounts based on estimated figures.

Chapter 3 – capital mix

- **Capital**: how much capital will the business need? How will the business be capitalised – through loans or through shares? How will the share capital be made up?

- **Sourcing finance**: how will the money needed to establish the business be found? Are

government loans, grants or other forms of assistance available? What are the prerequisites needed to access these?

- **Collateral**: how much security will have to be put up in order to access loans? Will the lender accept guarantors or co-signers in lieu of collateral?

- **Implications**: what are the implications of share capital versus loan capital? How much loan servicing will the business have to do each year? How much dividend will the business have to pay out each year? How much of the business's ownership has been sold?

Chapter 4 – operating environment

- **Government regulations**: what laws exist that govern how taxes are to be filed or returned? The employment and payment of workers? The recording and reporting of accounting information?

- **Ethical issues**: how do you ensure that a true and fair representation of the business is provided through the reporting of accounting information?

Appendices

- Use this section to include such details and samples of any primary research you had to do to gather data to construct your business plan.

- Any piece of supporting important information gathered from the primary or secondary information may also be included here, provided you had referred to it in the body of the work in Chapters 1–4.

- Graphs, charts and tables used to support claims made may also be included here.

Optional paper

The optional paper (Paper 03/2) is an alternative to the SBA that private candidates are asked to sit. The paper is designed to be similar to the SBA and, as such, is based on the same area of the syllabus as the SBA and weighted in the same way – as is shown opposite in Table 11.4.

Proficiency	Profile I (organisational principles)	Profile 2 (production, marketing and finance)	Profile 3 (the business environment)	Total
General	10	20	10	40

Table 11.4 Weighting of Paper 03/2.

The optional paper is based on a case study. A case study is usually a contrived situation that allows the candidate to apply the principles of business to a real-world context. Information about a business, a business activity or a business situation is shared with the student and she must bring to bear her knowledge of business to answer questions using the case study as a base. The exam is one hour long and students' understanding is assessed through 14 compulsory questions, although each question may have sub-parts. Below is a sample of a case study of the sort that you will see in the exam.

'Irie Mon T-Shirt'

Timz owns a T-shirt store, called Irie Mon T-Shirt, on the busy tourism strip of Montego Bay. He buys plain T-shirts of various colours and then uses a special printing process to print messages and pictures on the front of the T-shirts. The printing on the T-shirt is done manually and, as a result, each batch of T-shirts has the same message. Once a message or picture template has been cut, it is used to run a batch of between 25 and 35 T-shirts before another template is cut and a new batch begins. Timz has been thinking that he needs to start mass producing but is afraid that this may be too expensive for him to afford. He has also been toying with the idea of expanding the business and employing a few more people to man the production process as his skills are being stretched too thinly. At the moment, he has only two workers as well as himself.

One of the ideas that he knows he can implement in order to improve his sales is to create custom-made T-shirts with personalised messages or pictures. This

would, however, require a greater level of organisation on his part and a more efficient system to communicate with external parties such as customers and suppliers of T-shirts. In addition, while he thinks it is a great idea, he must also do some market research to see how feasible it really is. He also thinks that more could be done to target tourists, with whom he currently does very little business.

Questions
Organisational principles

1 What kind of business does Timz now have?
(1 mark)

2 From the case study above, outline one disadvantage of this kind of business. (2 marks)

3 Discuss one method of communication that Timz can use to establish effective working relationships with his customers **or** his suppliers. (3 marks)

4 What is likely to happen to Timz's span of control if he decides to increase the size of the business?
(2 marks)

5 What effect is this change in the span of control likely to have on the business? (2 marks)

Production, marketing and finance

6 Identify how the following factors of production are used in Irie Mon T-Shirt:
a labour
b entrepreneurial ability. (2 marks)

7 Discuss one advantage that Timz is likely to experience if he starts mass producing. (2 marks)

8 Explain why custom making T-shirts may be unprofitable if he starts mass producing. (3 marks)

9 By citing an example from the case study above, how would an investment in technology benefit Irie Mon T-Shirt? (3 marks)

10 Discuss two promotional strategies that Timz can use to target tourists. (4 marks)

11 By giving a reason for your answer, say what aspect of the marketing mix already gives the business an advantage if it manages to target tourists? (3 marks)

12 List three sources from which Timz may be able to access financial support to expand his business. (3 marks)

The business environment

13a Discuss what the government can do to assist Irie Mon T-Shirt. (3 marks)

13b How does the country benefit from the government assisting businesses like Irie Mon T-Shirt? (3 marks)

14a How does Irie Mon T-Shirt contribute to the quality of life of people in the country? (2 marks)

14b How is it possible that even if the size of the business increases, the quality of life of its workers may not improve? (2 marks)

Glossary

acceptance a clear, visible and unambiguous act of agreement to an offer.

advertising the use of print or electronic media to deliver a persuasive and/or informative message.

agglomeration the practice of bulking together small individual items for the purpose of handling.

airway bill a document given to the shipper as a receipt of the good being received by the carrier and as evidence of the contract between them.

arbitration the use of an impartial third party to listen to and make a judgement on the grievance between workers and management.

articles of association a document that is created before a business is incorporated. It lays down the rules that govern the internal running of the business and contains information such as the rights and obligations of directors.

assurance a special type of insurance taken out on a person's life, which promises a monetary payment to the family of the insured in the event of his disablement or death.

autocratic leader a leader who allows little or no discussion with or participation of subordinates before a decision is made.

backward linkage a firm has a backward linkage with another if it has to depend on the other one for its input.

balance of payments an account in which the government of a country keeps track of its trade with the rest of the world.

balance of trade the difference between a country's imports and exports of goods and services.

bank draft a type of cheque in which the bank guarantees that the funds to clear the cheque are available in the account.

bank overdraft a short-term loan facility that allows pre-approved account holders to withdraw more money than they have in their accounts.

bankrupt a state in which an economic entity is legally declared to be unable to pay its debts, resulting in its creditors having the opportunity to organise the sale or takeover of its assets in an effort to settle outstanding amounts.

barter the exchange of goods and services for other goods and services without the use of money.

bear market a market characterised by a large number of people selling or attempting to sell their stock as they may have lost confidence in the economy or in the companies on the stock market.

beneficiary the person indicated on an insurance policy to receive payment in the event of the loss of or damage to the insured item or person.

bill of lading evidence that one business (called the shipper) has given another business (called the carrier) cargo to transport to a specified place and usually to a specified individual (called the consignee).

bill of exchange a document that outlines how much money is being loaned and at what interest rate.

bonds financial securities issued by companies (and governments) to raise long-term finance at a fixed rate of interest.

brain drain brain drain occurs when a country's trained and qualified citizens migrate to another country.

brand a name, sign, symbol or combination of all three that is used to identify a particular product.

brand equity the (positive) effect that knowing the brand name has on consumers; usually manifested in a willingness to pay more for products sold under the brand.

brand franchise a franchise arrangement where a new outlet is established to sell the franchisor's brand exclusively.

branding the set of activities that a business performs that ensure that consumers associate its products with high quality and solid performance.

breach in a contract, breach occurs when one party fails to honour the terms of the contract.

budgeting the process of allocating one's income in a planned way before it is actually spent.

bull market a stock market in which investors show a high level of interest and have a high demand for stock, resulting in many units being traded each day.

bureau of standards an agency of the state that is responsible for ensuring that consumers are aware of the minimum standards that they should accept and that producers comply with these standards when producing a product.

business plan a comprehensive written description of the nature and elements of a proposed business.

capital money, technology, machines and equipment used to start, operate and expand a business.

capital account the section of the balance-of-payments account that is used to record transactions related to the international movements of ownership of financial assets such as investments in banks in other countries.

capital-intensive production a model of production where a greater part of the production cost is associated with investment in equipment and machines.

cartelisation a practice by firms in an oligopolistic industry to come together and form a cartel that sets prices and output in order to eliminate competition among members of the industry.

cash discount a discount a customer enjoys as a result of paying for an item bought on credit within or before a specified time.

cash reserve a mechanism used by the government to ensure that banks do not lend all the funds that they receive as deposits and by doing so overextend themselves.

central bank an institution that acts as the official bank of the government and other banks (commercial or otherwise) in the country.

certificate of incorporation a document that shows that a business has satisfied all the legal requirements to receive its own identity and has been duly incorporated.

chain of command the chain of command is the unbroken line of reporting relationships from the bottom to the top of the organisation. It defines the formal decision-making structure and provides for the orderly progression of information up and down the hierarchy.

checking accounts deposits in these accounts can be accessed by writing cheques or using a debit card.

cheque a written instruction in which an individual permits a bank, in which he or she has money, to make a payment of a specified amount to a specified person.

clustering this occurs when firms operating in the same line of business are located close to each other.

cold calling soliciting sales from persons (whether over the telephone or face to face) who did not set an appointment or who did not request a visit.

collateral collateral is an asset owned by the borrower, which is offered as security for a loan, with the understanding that the collateral may be seized if the loan is not properly serviced.

collusion a model of price determination used by oligopolistic firms, which involves an absence of competition and broad areas of agreement on pricing.

commercial bank a deposit-taking institution that raises funds by issuing various deposits, which it uses to make loans and investments.

commercial paper an unsecured promissory note that banks and other businesses with good credit ratings issue to raise short-term loans.

commodity money the use of objects with high innate, functional or practical value as money.

communication the sharing of information and understanding between or among agents.

company a company is an incorporated entity that is owned by persons and entities who invested in the company by buying its shares.

complements complements are products that are usually consumed together.

comprehensive insurance auto insurance that covers all damage sustained by all parties in an accident as well as fire and theft.

conflict an inevitable but potentially beneficial disagreement between two or more organisational members or teams.

conglomerates organisations that have invested in other businesses called subsidiaries, which are involved in the production or marketing of unrelated products or products in unrelated industries.

consideration what each party in a contract must give up in order for the contract to be valid.

consumers people or economic entities who use up goods and services.

contract a legally binding agreement in which one or more parties promise to undertake some obligation for another party or parties.

contribution the principle of insurance that holds that an individual cannot collect the full amount from all insurance policies if an item insured under many policies has been destroyed; rather, each insurer should make a contribution to the payment the individual would receive.

controlling the process of ensuring that the human and financial resources of the business are harnessed to achieve the objectives of the business.

convenience products products that are bought frequently and, hence, do not need much consideration and shopping around before they are bought.

co-operative a non-profit business operated for the benefit of members who pool their resources to cater to a common need.

co-ordinating the function of management that is concerned with creating a single cohesive unit out of the many departments and work units in the business.

copyright an exclusive right given to the owners of intellectual property to use, distribute and modify their property for a specified number of years.

corporate citizens firms that act unselfishly and play a part in the social development of the country by donating to charity, assisting special-interest groups and granting scholarships.

corporation a business which has been incorporated and given a separate and distinct identity from that of its owners; as a result, its owners enjoy limited liability.

cottage industry production that takes place in settings (such as the home, at church or even at school) that were not meant to support business activities.

counter-offer a revised response to an offer in which the original offer is rejected and a new offer is made.

credit arrangements an agreement that allows one to buy goods immediately and to pay for them over an extended period.

credit card a card issued by a financial institution that allows holders to borrow up to a predetermined sum for short periods of time.

credit union a financial cooperative in which members who are also owners save and come to own shares and the right to access loans at reduced rates.

creditor any person or economic entity to whom money is owed. The creditors of a business are traders from whom it bought on credit.

current account the section of the balance-of-payments account in which a country's trade in goods and services and its income are recorded.

cyclical (or demand deficient) unemployment unemployment caused by the periodic contraction of the size of the economy.

dealer franchise a franchise arrangement where the franchisee has been given the right to sell the franchisor's product and is allowed to sell other products.

debenture long-term loans that are secured by the reputation of the businesses that issue them.

debit card a card that allows holders to access funds that they have in their accounts at a bank.

delegating this is the process of authorising subordinates to make decisions through the downward transfer of authority.

demand the willingness and ability to buy a product at particular prices.

democratic leader a leader who allows subordinates to participate in the decision-making process and who allows contending views to exist until a consensus is reached.

devaluation a reduction in the value of a country's currency that results in its imports being more expensive and its exports being cheaper.

diagonal relationship relationships that exist among workers at different levels in different departments.

direct production direct production occurs in a society when no trading takes place; rather, individuals attempt to produce all the goods and services that they consume.

direct selling a distribution channel in which the producer sells directly to the end users, rather than using intermediaries.

direct taxes taxes paid directly to the government at source before the taxpayer receives his or her income.

directing the function of management that ensures that a structure exists that supports workers and provides guidance as they perform their tasks.

discharge of contract a contract is said to have been discharged when the obligations outlined in the contract have been executed or terminated prematurely.

discount an offer by the seller of an item that results in a reduction in the price that buyers of the item are expected to pay.

diseconomies of scale a situation where a business is operating at a more than optimal size, resulting in costs increasing at a faster rate than outputs.

distribution chain the series of intermediaries responsible for moving a good from the producers to the end users.

diversification the process of becoming involved in many business ventures usually in different or unrelated industries and usually with the intention of spreading risk.

dividend the share of profit to which shareholders are entitled on a yearly basis.

documentary credit an arrangement in which an importer pays funds over to a bank which then promises to make the payment to the exporter when the goods have been delivered. This process removes much of the uncertainty surrounding the creditworthiness of the importer.

domestic production at this level of production, producers employ all the available resources available to them to produce more than they will consume, with the excess being traded to satisfy the needs of the nation.

double coincidence of wants a situation that occurs when two traders have goods that each other wants.

dumping the selling of substandard goods at low prices in secondary markets.

e-commerce the purchase of a product or service using the internet as the medium for placing the order.

economic development improvements in the quality of life that citizens of a country enjoy.

economic dualism a situation where a country has two distinct economies at different levels of development and sophistication.

economic growth an increase in the size of an economy, measured by an increase in its national income over a year.

economic system a mechanism that deals with the manner in which countries organise their means of production and which sees to the production, distribution and consumption of goods and services.

economies of scale the benefits a large business enjoys when it finds that it is possible to increase its output with a less than equivalent increase in costs.

economy a system responsible for regulating and organising the production, distribution and consumption of goods and services among a group of people.

elasticity the responsiveness of demand to changes in any of the underlying variables that affect demand.

entrepreneur the person who accepts the risk involved in starting and operating a business.

equilibrium equilibrium exists when both suppliers and consumers are in agreement on the number of units of a good to be sold and the price at which they are to be sold. This occurs when the quantity supplied is equal to the quantity demanded.

exchange a system associated with the introduction and existence of indirect production in which individuals acquire those goods that they do not produce.

exchange control restrictions on the sale of foreign exchange such that limits are placed on the amount that any one person may buy, or a complete ban on the sale of a specific currency.

executive agency a public-sector entity that is attached to a ministry or department of the government but has a separate and distinct management and funding mechanism.

experimental research a method of collecting primary data in which two groups of subjects are chosen, with one group being exposed to a controlled situation to see how their behaviour and reactions differ from those of the other group.

export production at this level of production, more than enough goods are produced to satisfy domestic consumption and, hence, the excess is exported.

external economies of scale economies of scale that a firm experiences as a result of changes in the industry or the activities of other firms in the industry.

factors of production the elements that are brought together in the production process to make production possible.

fiat money money whose value lies in the amount stated on its face given the government's promise to honour it up to that amount.

final goods goods that are used or involved in the production of other goods and services.

financial intermediation the process by which banks and other financial institutions match people who have excess money with those who need loans.

fixed capital capital held in the form of machinery and equipment, which has a long life and is used to drive production.

focus-group interview a focus group is a small group of people who meet under the direction of a discussion leader to communicate their opinions about an organisation, its products or other issues.

forward linkage a firm has a forward linkage with another if its output becomes the input for the other firm.

franchise a form of business in which an established firm (the franchisor) licenses another firm (the franchisee) to sell its products or use its production process and/or its name and image.

franchise agreement an agreement between two firms that permits one to use the other's name, ideas and products in exchange for a fee.

franchisee the party in a franchise agreement whose right to use a product, idea or name is made possible by the payment of fees to its original owner.

franchisor the party in a franchise agreement who has exclusive ownership of the product, idea or name that another firm must pay to use.

free market a market structure in which the forces of demand and supply determine what goods are produced and the price at which they are sold.

frictional unemployment unemployment that occurs when the job market does not match job-seekers with jobs at a fast enough rate.

frustration in a contract, frustration occurs when performance becomes impossible or even illegal given radical changes in events subsequent to the creation of the contract.

go public the process of changing a company's status from being privately owned to being publicly owned. This process involves getting the company listed on the stock exchange.

go-slow a protest action that workers engage in by slowing down the rate of production or deliberately under-producing.

going-rate pricing a pricing strategy in which businesses offering similar products charge the same price, which is close to a perceived going rate.

goods products that are tangible and, as a result, can be seen, touched and stored.

grievance procedure this is an outline of the ideal and expected series of steps and courses of action that are to be taken in the event that a conflict arises between management and workers and owners.

gross domestic product (GDP) the value of goods produced within the physical space of a country – regardless of who produced these goods, whether citizens or foreigners.

gross national product (GNP) the income earned by the citizens of a country from all production in which they are involved, whether at home or abroad.

hierarchical structure a structure that creates horizontal, diagonal and vertical relationships among the workers in a business.

hierarchy the hierarchy in a business is the order or levels of management in a firm, from the highest to the lowest, and shows who is in charge of each task, each speciality area and the organisation as a whole.

hire purchase a payment plan in which the buyer rakes possession of the item before final payment is made with the understanding that regular payments will be made to cover the cost of the item as well as whatever interest is charged.

horizontal relationship relationship among workers at the same level across different departments.

import licence permission granted (or sold) by the government to an importer to bring in a specified quantity of a good within a given period.

incorporated status bestowed on a business after it has acquired its own identity and is able to trade in its own name without its owners being responsible and liable for any actions.

indemnity the principle of insurance that ensures that the insured does not end up in a more advantageous position after an accident as a result of insurance payment.

indirect production indirect production takes place in a society when individuals specialise in the production of a few goods that they produce in excess of their needs. They trade the excess so as to obtain those that they do not produce.

indirect taxes taxes paid on goods and services that are due only when people buy these goods and services.

infant mortality rate this is the number of infants who die before they reach one year of age.

inferior goods goods whose demand decreases when income increases.

informal economy the portion of the economy that undertakes business activities that the government cannot measure.

initial public offering (IPO) an IPO is an issue of shares made directly by the company through a broker and usually immediately after going public.

insurable interest the principle of insurance that argues that people who benefit from insurance in the event of a loss (of life or of property) are somehow connected to the loss – in short, they must have an interest in the insured item or property.

insurance the pooling of risk made possible by the frequent and periodic payment of premiums to a company that promises to restore an asset to its original condition in the event of an accident or loss.

interest the price of borrowing money since it is the fee (in the form of money) paid by those who borrow money.

intermediate goods outputs of one firm that become the inputs for another firm.

internal economies of scale economies of scale that a firm experiences as a result of its own increase in size or scale of operations.

international trade the exchange of goods and services for commercial gain between nations.

investment the portion of income that is used to secure future spending by taking risks in long-term illiquid speculation or venture.

labour the effort made by the worker in order to ensure that production takes place.

labour-intensive production a model of production where a greater part of the production cost is associated with paying workers.

laissez-faire leadership a leadership style in which subordinates are expected to use their own initiative to work with broad guidance and supervision within stated parameters.

layaway plan a payment plan in which the buyer is given an extended but specified period to pay for an item, during which time the seller holds on to the item.

legality the principle of insurance that states that an individual cannot insure against an illegal act in order to avoid responsibility for it afterwards.

life expectancy the number of years that an individual is expected to live from a particular point, usually birth.

limited liability status enjoyed by the owners of incorporated businesses. It gives them the assurance that their personal assets are protected against the mistakes and losses of the business. As a result, such owners stand to lose only what they have invested in the business.

linkage industries industries are linked if the output of one industry becomes the input for another industry.

liquidity the extent to which a business has cash and cash equivalents to cover its debts and immediate liabilities.

local government the area of government that offers services that cater to the needs of citizens in a specific community or area.

lockout an action taken by employers to prevent workers from accessing the production facilities or the work site by locking the gate or doors.

long-term planning the creation of the major goals of the organisation that provide the overall structure within which the organisation operates on a day-to-day basis.

loss-leader pricing a pricing model in which one product is sold at a low price while a component or complementary product is sold at a high price.

management information system (MIS) a system for capturing and sorting data and providing information for the efficient organisation and operation of the business.

market a situation or context that allows transactions to occur and in which a sale is possible. Alternatively, a market is the total number of buyers and sellers and potential buyers and sellers of a product.

market research a systematic study of the market carried out by a business to gather information about its customers and the market in which its products are sold.

market structure the number of buyers and sellers that exist in a market.

marketing a management process that involves profitably satisfying consumers' wants and needs by anticipating and addressing their concerns.

marketing co-operative a co-operative that sources markets for its members, usually by amalgamating the small portions that each member is able to produce so as to attract buyers who are interested in large bulks.

marketing mix the decision that a firm makes about the four basic elements of marketing – the products, their prices, how they are promoted and distributed.

mark-up pricing a method of pricing that involves simply adding an amount to cost in order to obtain a profit.

matrix structure an organisational structure in which workers come together to form temporary teams.

mediation the use of an impartial third party to facilitate communication and negotiation between the parties in conflict.

medium of exchange any item that is widely demanded and accepted by the members of society and hence can be used as an intermediary object in exchange for goods and services. Money is the most popular medium of exchange.

medium-term planning specific and detailed plans that have time spans of a few years.

memorandum of association a document that is created before a business is incorporated. It gives information about the company and governs its relationship with the outside world. It contains the name and address of the company as well as the share capital of the company.

merchandising strategies employed by sellers to ensure that products are displayed optimally and store layout is ideal so that consumers are most likely to make a purchase.

migration migration occurs when citizens of a country or any geographically defined area permanently relocate to another country or area.

mixed economic system an economic system that has both a private sector and a public sector and in which both the government and private citizens own the productive resources in the country.

money any item that is widely accepted as a medium of exchange and carries with it the legal support and recognition of the government.

money order an arrangement in which one individual or organisation pays a sum of money to an institution – usually the post office or a bank – and asks this institution to make the payment to another individual or organisation.

monopolistic competition a market structure in which there are many sellers, each selling a differentiated product to many buyers.

monopoly a market structure in which there is only one supplier of a product for which there are no close substitutes.

mortgage loans loans with a long maturity period that are given to buy or refurbish houses.

motivating this is the process of creating a work environment that encourages workers to increase their productivity and their overall commitment to the business.

multinational corporation a business that owns or controls production facilities in more than one country.

national income the sum of all incomes that arise as a result of economic activities involved in the production of goods and services in a country over a specified period, usually a year.

nationalisation the process that the government engages in when it buys a private-sector business and essentially makes it a public-sector operation.

nationalised industry a public-sector business that offers goods or services for sale to members of the general public.

observational research a type of research in which trained people observe and record the actions of potential buyers.

offer a clear, unequivocal and direct approach or expression of interest of one party to another.

oligopolistic a market structure in which there are a few large suppliers of a product.

ombudsman a person appointed by the government to regulate its activities and to investigate cases of abuse of power by state agencies.

ordinary shareholders shareholders whose dividends fluctuate with the profit of the business and who receive dividends after preference shareholders have already been paid.

organising a process that is concerned with ensuring that the business is structured so as to achieve its objectives.

packaging the term describes not just the act of putting goods in packages, but also to the act of taking goods produced by another firm and creating a system of labelling, warehousing and distribution for these goods

partnership a partnership is a business owned by between two and 20 people, who have a common aim of making a profit.

partnership deed a document which outlines the terms, conditions and agreement that govern the establishment and operation of a partnership.

patent an exclusive right given to the owners of inventions and new products to use, distribute and modify their property for a specified number of years.

penetration pricing a pricing approach in which a new product is introduced at a low price, which is then increased as the product gains a foothold in the market.

per capita income the average portion of national income earned by each citizen in the country.

perfect competition a market structure in which there are many sellers, each selling a perfectly homogeneous product (at prices set by the market) to many buyers who have perfect information.

performance in a contract, this happens when the agreement has run its course and all parties in the contract have performed their obligations.

personal selling the use of a sales force to make personal presentations via face-to-face meetings, telephone or the internet in order to push sales and build relationships.

planned economic system an economic system in which the government or some central authority owns the productive resources in a society and hence determines price, output and production.

planning the process of establishing objectives and setting operations in motion to achieve these objectives.

population density an index of the extent of the over- or under-population of an area, measured as the average number of people living in a square mile or square kilometre.

preference shareholders shareholders whose dividends are stated at a fixed percentage of how much they have invested and who are entitled to receive their dividends first. Given their relatively risk-free status as owners, preference shareholders are not allowed to make decisions in the running of the company.

premium this is a regular (for example, monthly, quarterly, annually) payment that the insured party or beneficiary pays to the insurance company.

pressure groups organisations that are formed to represent the welfare of special-interest groups and to put pressure on businesses to act in line with the objectives of these groups.

price the sum of values that consumers are prepared to give up for the consumption of a product.

price-adjustment policy a promise by a store that if an item is offered at a reduced price within a certain time after it was bought by a customer, then the customer is able to return with the receipt and get a refund equivalent to the saving he missed out on.

price control the establishment by the government of a maximum (or, in rare cases, minimum) price at which an item can be sold.

price-elastic demand demand that is very responsive to a change in price – small changes in price bring about disproportionately larger changes in quantity demanded.

price elasticity of demand the extent to which a change in price causes quantity demanded to change.

price-inelastic demand demand that is unresponsive to a change in price – large changes in price result in disproportionately smaller changes in quantity demanded.

price leadership a price-determination model used by oligopolistic firms in which one firm sets the price that all other firms follow.

price skimming a pricing strategy in which a seller charges an initially high price to target early adopters and then lowers it as demand from early adopters falls.

primary production the stage of production that involves the extraction of raw materials from their natural environment for their use in production or for consumption.

primary sources sources from which information that no one has collected before can be obtained.

primary stakeholders people or entities to whom the business has a legal obligation and whose fortunes are directly linked to the organisation and, as a result, they take a keen interest in its activities.

private limited company a company that cannot advertise shares for sales to the general public and whose ownership is limited to 20 people.

private sector the part of the economic system in a mixed economy where businesses and organisations are owned by private individuals and offer services and goods to the public in an effort to maximise profit.

producer a person or economic entity responsible for adding value to a set of resources by combining or modifying them to create a new good or offer a service.

producer co-operative a co-operative that tries to source or assist members in buying or accessing machinery and equipment.

production the process of using various resources to create a finished product.

productivity the relationship that exists between inputs and outputs such that an increase in inputs causes output to increase at a faster rate.

pro forma invoice a document that indicates that one party is willing to sell goods to another party at a specified price or under certain conditions.

progressive taxation a taxation system in which the proportion of taxes collected rises as income increases.

proportional taxation a taxation system in which the tax rate remains fixed regardless of the amount of income earned.

protectionism the practice of using laws, taxes and bureaucratic measures to restrict the level of imports entering a country.

proximate cause the principle of insurance that holds that the cause of the loss must be established, as only those risks insured against can be compensated.

public limited company a company with no restrictions on how its membership can be constituted or how its shares may be traded.

public relations a promotion technique in which a marketing department makes a sustained effort to create a positive image of the firm and its product by controlling its communications with the public.

public sector the part of the economic system in a mixed economy where businesses and organisations are owned by the government and offer services and goods to the public, usually at a reduced price.

purchase requisition this document indicates the quantity and type of goods or services that a business will need within a given period.

quality of life a measure of the extent to which the wealth that a country has translates into a better life for its citizens.

quantity demanded the number of units of a product that consumers are willing to buy at a certain price.

quantity supplied the number of units of a good that suppliers are willing to produce at a specified price.

quota restricting the number of units of a product that can be produced, imported or used in order to protect the environment or the local economy.

real-wage unemployment unemployment that occurs when high wages reduce demand for labour and cause unemployment.

regressive taxation a taxation system in which the tax rate falls as income rises.

retail bank a bank that has many small customers, usually made up of ordinary citizens, with whom it engages in small transactions.

retail co-operative a co-operative that offers savings to its members by buying in bulk at wholesale prices and selling back to the members at reduced prices.

retailer a retailer is a business that buys products in large quantities, either from wholesalers or directly from the manufacturer, with the intention to resell these products to consumers.

royalties payments made by one party to another for permission to use a product or idea to generate income.

sales promotion a sales promotion occurs when a temporary promotional measure, such as a giveaway, is put in place to increase market demand or sales.

savings the part of income that is kept idle, usually as a result of consumption (or expenditure) being less than income.

savings accounts deposits in these accounts can be accessed by making withdrawals by visiting the bank and making an over-the-counter transaction or using a bank machine.

scab labour a scab worker is one who is employed to temporarily replace a worker who is on strike.

scarce a situation that occurs when limited resources restrict the supply of a good relative to its demand.

seasonal unemployment unemployment caused by the fluctuations in demand as a result of changes in the season or time of the year.

secondary production production in which a primary product is further processed to change its form and increase its utility to the consumer. Alternatively, it involves combining different primary products or even primary and secondary products to create one finished good.

secondary sources sources from which information that others have already collected for their own purposes can be obtained.

secondary stakeholders people or entities to whom the business has no legal obligation but who are able to exert influence over the business activities.

secured loans loans that are backed by collateral.

services products that are intangible and can only be experienced or enjoyed. They cannot be touched, felt or stored.

share capital the portion of a company's capital that was raised by selling shares.

shareholders these are people and entities who become owners of a company by buying its shares.

shopping products products that are bought only after buyers have given extensive thought and consideration to all options.

short-term planning plans that are concerned with the day-to-day operations of the business.

sick-out a form of industrial action in which workers refuse to work, under the pretext of being ill.

simple contract a contract that involves matters that one is likely to encounter in one's daily routine activities and which does not have to be written, witnessed or signed to take effect.

sleeping partner a partner who contributed capital to the establishment of the business but who is not involved in the management and operation of the partnership and, as a result, enjoys limited liability.

sole proprietorship a business that has one owner who keeps all the profits.

sole trader a person who owns a business operated by himself.

span of control this refers to the number of subordinates who are under the direction of a manager.

specialisation specialisation occurs when a person or a business or even a society focuses resources and skills in the production of a single good or service or a particular aspect of a good or service.

speciality contract this type of contract requires signing and special processes and procedures before it becomes valid; it is usually drawn up by lawyers and involves extensive legal and complicated jargon.

speciality products products with special and unique characteristics or brand identification and appeal for which consumers are willing to make a special effort.

stakeholders individuals or entities who have an interest in the affairs of a business, usually because they are affected by it.

standard of living a measure of the wealth and material comfort to which citizens of a country have access.

statement of account a document that gives details on the credit transactions in which the business engages with other firms.

stock card a document that outlines how many units of stock a business received, used and sold over a period and how many units are still available.

stock exchange a market for the buying and selling of companies' shares.

strike a simultaneous action by a majority of workers to call attention to their complaints and to put pressure on management by refusing to work.

structural unemployment unemployment that is caused by long-term changes in the fundamental structure of an economy, creating dislocation of workers.

subrogation this is the principle of insurance that gives the insurer the right to pursue a claim from the party legally responsible for an accident.

subsidiaries firms that are owned by a parent company.

subsistence production production that takes place when an individual produces enough of a product for her (or her family's) own consumption.

substitute a substitute for a good is one that satisfies the same demand.

supply the willingness and ability of producers to produce and/or sell a good.

surplus the word 'surplus' is used in a number of ways. It always refers, however, to the excess of receipts, income, revenues or inflow of funds over payments or outflow of funds. When used in relation to co-operatives, for example, the term describes the excess of the co-operative's income over its expenditure.

survey research an approach to gathering data that involves interviewing a large number of people so as to find out the opinions of the majority.

tariff a tax that importers of a product must pay in order to import a good into a country.

taxation the process through which the government raises the bulk of its revenue to finance its spending by collecting compulsory payments from citizens of the country.

technical economies of scale economies of scale that arise from investment in and the efficient and intensive use of machines and equipment.

technological unemployment unemployment that occurs when technology and capital-intensive methods of production replace or reduce the demand for workers.

telegraphic money transfer a method of payment in which money is transferred from an account at one bank to another account at a different bank.

tele-marketing a traditional method of retailing products in which the sales force uses telephone conversations to meet new customers and make sales.

terms of sale the arrangements that a business has with its customers as to how payment for a good will be made.

tertiary production the production of services by combining primary and secondary products with labour.

third-party insurance auto insurance that does not cover the damage sustained by the insured vehicle in the event of an accident; rather, it covers only the damage to the other vehicle or property involved in the accident.

timed accounts deposits in these accounts either cannot be accessed before a specified time has passed or can be accessed only by paying a penalty.

trade a mutual exchange of goods or services for other goods, services or money.

trade discount a discount a customer enjoys because he buys in bulk.

trademark a unique and distinctive logo, name, symbol or word that identifies and distinguishes a product or a business from others.

trade union an organisation responsible for protecting the interest of workers who are its members.

traditional economic system an economic system in which direct production dominates and few or no organised systems for trading exist.

unemployment this occurs when people are out of work but are actively seeking employment.

unlimited liability a situation in which the owners of a business stand to lose all the money they invested in the business as well as their personal assets.

unsought products products that consumers do not know about and have no interest in without producers engaging in extensive advertisements.

utmost good faith the principle of insurance that requires that people seeking insurance tell the insurer all the details that would affect the insurer's assessment of the risk that is being undertaken.

venture capital capital obtained from an investor who buys a part ownership of the business.

vertical relationship a relationship shared among workers at different levels of the organisation.

wholesale bank a bank with a large clientele, usually made up of businesses and commercial entities, with whom it engages in large transactions.

wholesalers businesses that buy products in bulk from the manufacturer and then sell them back in smaller quantities to retailers.

work to rule a protest action by workers that involves doing the minimum level of work required of them.

workers' co-operative a co-operative where workers own and operate the business and pay themselves from the revenues it generates.

working capital capital held in the form of cash or cash equivalents (such as stock and debtors) that is used to keep the business going from one day to the next.

zoning creating defined geographical areas for business activities and restricting the use of other areas to residential or historical purposes.

Index

Acknowledgements

The authors and publishers are grateful for the permissions granted to reproduce copyright photographs and materials in either the original or adapted form. While every effort has been made, it has not always been possible to identify the sources of all the materials used, or to trace all copyright holders. If any omissions are brought to our notice, we will be happy to include the appropriate acknowledgements on reprinting.

Cover image Glyn Thomas / Alamy; p. 1 AFP/ Getty Images; p. 5 D Alderman / Alamy; p. 8 Imagebroker / Alamy; p. 14 Angelo Cavalli / Corbis; p. 18 Neal & Massy; p. 20 Simon Belcher / Alamy; p. 25 TCL Group; p. 26*t* The Barbados Shipping and Trading Company Ltd; p. 26*b* CJG Caribbean / Alamy; p. 35 DDL; p. 38 STR / Reuters / Corbis; p. 53 Ian Townsley / Alamy; p. 56; p. 58 Radius Images / Corbis; p. 63 Image provided by Claudia Pegus; p. 66 Charlie Schuck; p. 72 Leo Mason / actionplus; p. 74 Jeff Greenberg / Alamy; p. 88 Brian Stablyk; p. 93 Karin Duthie / Alamy; p. 96 Mike Abrahams / Alamy; p. 105 Michael Runkel Barabados / Alamy; p. 107 Danita Delimont / Alamy; p. 111 Paolo Patrizi / Alamy; p. 116 A. J. D. Foto Ltd / Alamy; p. 122 Mar Photographics / Alamy; p. 129 Paul Hebditch / Alamy; p. 130 Sparky; p. 135 Steve Hamblin / Alamy; p. 139 Paul Thompson Images / Alamy; p. 140 Roger Overall; p. 144 Alejandro Ernesto / epa / Corbis; p. 148 Tim Hill / Alamy; p. 156 jonathan tennant / Alamy; p. 157 AFP/ Getty Images; p. 163 Neil Emmerson; p. 169 Bubbles Photolibrary / Alamy; p. 172 Art Directors & TRIP / Alamy; p. 178 Imagebroker / Alamy; p. 183 UN Photo / Devra Berkowitz; p. 189 Angela Hampton Picture Library / Alamy; p. 192 dpa / Corbis; 194*t* Jan Sochor / Alamy; p. 194*b* Robert Harding Picture Library Ltd / Alamy; p. 200 Rod McLean / Alamy; p. 209 UN Photo / Eskinder Debebe; p. 214 Jake Lyell / Alamy

t = top of page, *b* = bottom of page